REAL-WORLD SOLUTIONS FOR DEVELOPING HIGH-QUALITY PHP FRAMEWORKS AND APPLICATIONS

Real-World Solutions for Developing High-Quality PHP Frameworks and Applications

Real-World Solutions for Developing High-Quality PHP Frameworks and Applications

Sebastian Bergmann
Stefan Priebsch

Wiley Publishing, Inc.

Real-World Solutions for Developing High-Quality PHP Frameworks and Applications

Published by
Wiley Publishing, Inc.
10475 Crosspoint Boulevard
Indianapolis, IN 46256
www.wiley.com

Published by Wiley Publishing, Inc., Indianapolis, Indiana

Published simultaneously in Canada

ISBN: 978-0-470-87249-9
ISBN: 978-1-118-09822-6
ISBN: 978-1-118-09824-0
ISBN: 978-1-118-09823-3

Manufactured in the United States of America

10 9 8 7 6 5 4 3 2 1

For general information on our other products and services please contact our Customer Care Department within the United States at (877) 762-2974, outside the United States at (317) 572-3993 or fax (317) 572-4002.

Wiley also publishes its books in a variety of electronic formats. Some content that appears in print may not be available in electronic books.

Library of Congress Control Number: 2010939958

ABOUT THE AUTHORS

SEBASTIAN BERGMANN (thePHP.cc) holds a degree in computer science and is a pioneer in the field of quality assurance in PHP projects. His test framework, PHPUnit, is a de facto standard. He is actively involved in the development of PHP and is the creator of various development tools. Sebastian Bergmann is an internationally sought-after expert. As an author, he shares his long-standing experience in books and articles. He is a frequent speaker at conferences around the world.

STEFAN PRIEBSCH (thePHP.cc) is a co-founder and Principal Consultant with thePHP.cc. He holds a degree in computer science and is the author of various books and technical articles. As a consultant, he helps customers to improve development processes and make better use of PHP, with a focus on software architecture, OOP, design patterns, and tools and methods. Stefan is a frequent speaker at IT conferences around the world.

CREDITS

EXECUTIVE EDITOR
Carol Long

PROJECT EDITOR
Tom Dinse

CONSULTING AND TECHNICAL EDITOR
Elizabeth Naramore

PRODUCTION EDITOR
Daniel Scribner

COPY EDITOR
Gwenette Gaddis

EDITORIAL DIRECTOR
Robyn B. Siesky

EDITORIAL MANAGER
Mary Beth Wakefield

FREELANCER EDITORIAL MANAGER
Rosemarie Graham

ASSOCIATE DIRECTOR OF MARKETING
Ashley Zurcher

PRODUCTION MANAGER
Tim Tate

VICE PRESIDENT AND EXECUTIVE GROUP PUBLISHER
Richard Swadley

VICE PRESIDENT AND EXECUTIVE PUBLISHER
Barry Pruett

ASSOCIATE PUBLISHER
Jim Minatel

PROJECT COORDINATOR, COVER
Katherine Crocker

PROOFREADER
Louise Watson, Paul Sagan,
Word One New York

INDEXER
Ron Strauss

COVER DESIGN
Michael E. Trent

COVER IMAGE
© istockphoto.com/Dmitry Mordvintsev

CONTENTS

FOREWORD

Building and assuring quality software is not a new concept, and few will argue it is not important. I have had the privilege of building truly mission-critical operational software for many years—the kind where people's lives can be at stake. During that time, I learned lots about how to implement and drive a quality process from project inception to mission-critical use. Creating a high-quality process is not trivial, requires the support and commitment of the organization's leadership, and can impact choice of people, systems, processes, communications, and even organizational structures.

In my opinion, the challenges of the Internet's broad reach and pace dwarf the challenges of the mission-critical systems I was building. While many of these new systems are "only" business-critical, the truth is that they are no less critical and are dealing with additional layers of complexity such as more distributed development teams, well-known and evolving security attacks on web standards and software, internationalization challenges, shorter release cycles in SaaS settings, and more. In addition, in e-commerce applications, where downtime directly equates to money, the requirement for a strong quality-assurance program is even more critical and requires a special emphasis on compliance, quick time to fix (and time to verify and deploy that fix), and ability to run real-time end-to-end transactions to ensure not only that the application is up, but also that transactions can actually occur. In addition, the increasing emphasis on user experience also means that perceived quality has become increasingly critical and a functioning system that is not delivering the desired user experience has to be enhanced within a very short time frame without compromising on quality. The quality process and systems have to support such rapid turnaround of changes at high quality.

Suffice to say that these challenges have led to significant innovation and changes in approach when it comes to quality assurance compared with the well-established past practices of building mission-critical software. Software development has made huge strides over the past years in establishing strong best practices and awareness around quality assurance. Some key advances include a recognition that the developers must be a huge part of the quality process and cannot defer sole responsibility to the quality team. Continuous integration methodology mitigates one of the biggest challenges and bottlenecks in pushing out quality software—the integration stage. A more strategic focus on automated testing enables pushing out fixes faster, and not only meeting agreed-upon SLAs but exceeding SLAs to deliver end-user satisfaction.

This book puts a strong focus on many of the required quality-assurance disciplines with a very practical focus on PHP and covers people, systems, processes, and tools. The authors of this book have a great mix of both practical and theoretical knowledge of the subject, and I cannot think of better authors to write such a book. Not only do they have practical experience from a diverse set of real-life projects, but they also have created and contributed to quality tools within the PHP eco-system. In addition, the focus on case studies is invaluable as a way to learn from others and understand how everyone tailors his best practices to his situation.

I am sure this book will serve you well in taking the quality of your projects to the next level and help you instill an even stronger sense of pride in the software you are creating within your teams and your management.

—ANDI GUTMANS
MENLO PARK, CA
February 2010

INTRODUCTION

Experience: that most brutal of teachers. But you learn, my God do you learn.

— C.S. LEWIS

ABOUT THIS BOOK

According to the TIOBE Programming Community Index, PHP is the most popular programming language after C/C++ and Java.[1] Gartner predicts that dynamic programming languages will be critical to the success of many next-generation application development efforts and sees PHP as one of the strongest representatives of this type of programming language.[2] Since the beginning, PHP was designed for web application development and was likely one of the driving forces behind the dot-com boom at the turn of the millennium. Since then, PHP has matured to a general-purpose programming language that supports both procedural and object-oriented programming. In the past, subjects such as performance, scalability, and security were hot in the PHP community. In recent years, however, architecture and quality are getting more attention. In our consulting practice, we see more enterprises that want to modernize their PHP-based software and to base their development processes on agile values. The modernization of a code base is usually driven by a migration from PHP4 to PHP5 or by the introduction of a framework to standardize development.

Against this backdrop, it is hardly surprising that a plethora of PHP frameworks exists. All these frameworks want to help with solving recurring use cases and the standardization of application development. Dynamic and static testing techniques as well as automated builds and continuous integration are no longer alien concepts to PHP developers. Especially in enterprise-critical applications, simple PHP programming has evolved into software engineering with PHP.

Is This a PHP Book?

Based on examples from the PHP world, this book teaches the planning, execution, and automation of tests for the different software layers, the measuring of software quality using software metrics, and the application of appropriate practices such as continuous integration. We assume the reader is either an experienced PHP developer and interested in quality assurance for PHP projects or a developer who is proficient enough with another programming language to follow the examples.

---

[1]TIOBE Software BV, "TIOBE Programming Community Index for December 2010," accessed December, 2010, http://www.tiobe.com/index.php/content/paperinfo/tpci/index.html.

[2]Gartner Inc., "Dynamic Programming Languages Will Be Critical to the Success of Many Next-Generation AD Efforts," 2008, accessed April 10, 2010, http://www.gartner.com/DisplayDocument?ref=g_search&id=832417.

This book cannot and does not want to be an introduction to (object-oriented) programming with PHP5. And although many companies think about quality-assurance measures for the first time while migrating from PHP4 to PHP5, topics related to migration of PHP applications and environments are not covered in this book. For those topics, refer to *Professionelle Softwareentwicklung mit PHP 5: Objektorientierung Entwurfsmuster, Modellierung und fortgeschrittene Datenbankprogrammierung* by Sebastian Bergmann (dpunkt.verlag, 2005, ISBN 978-3-89864-229-3) and *PHP migrieren: Konzepte und Lösungen zur Migration von PHPAnwendungen und -Umgebungen* by Stefan Priebsch (Carl Hanser Verlag, 2008, ISBN 978-3-446-41394-8).

In addition to developers, project leaders and quality-assurance engineers should be concerned with the topic of quality assurance. We hope this book fosters mutual trust among all stakeholders of a software project and motivates all readers to improve the internal quality of their software (see the "Internal Quality" section in Chapter 1).

Structure of the Book

Following the idea that we learn best through experience—and especially from the experience of others—this book brings together case studies that allow a look behind the scenes of well-known enterprises and projects and imparts valuable practical experience.

The first part, "Foundations," explains how we define and understand software quality and how you can test the different layers of software. Part II, "Best Practices," shows tried and true approaches and strategies (for instance, with regard to the writing of unit tests) and how the developers of Digg Inc. and the TYPO3 project implement them. The "Unit Testing Bad Practices" chapter captures the same topic from a different angle and shows the pitfalls you should avoid while writing unit tests.

Part III, "Servers and Services," discusses testing service-oriented APIs and server components. Part IV, "Architecture," uses Symfony as an example to show how both a framework itself and applications built using it can be tested. Using the Graph component from eZComponents, we discuss how a good architecture of loosely coupled objects can enable even the testing of binary image data. Testing database interaction is a topic that affects multiple layers of an application's architecture and thus is worth its own chapter.

In Part V, "Q&A in the Large," the developers of studiVZ and swoodoo report on their experience with quality assurance in large projects and teams. Chapter 12, "Continuous Integration," brings together dynamic and static testing techniques and shows how the various quality-assurance tools can be effectively used together.

The last part, "Non-Functional Aspects," tops off the book with chapters covering usability, performance, and security.

ABOUT THE CASE STUDY AUTHORS

Robert Lemke, TYPO3 Association, and Karsten Dambekalns, TYPO3 Association

Robert Lemke is co-founder of the TYPO3 Association and leads the development of TYPO3 v5 (code name Phoenix) and FLOW3. He's passionate about agile development methods and clean code. Robert lives in Lübeck, with his wife Heike, his daughter Smilla, and Vibiemme, their espresso machine.

Karsten Dambekalns, learned the basics of web technology the hard way—by looking at other websites' HTML source code. After using OS/2, Windows, and Linux, he now uses a Mac. All this happened after he learned BASIC and Assembler on a good old Commodore C128. Using PHP since 1999, Karsten discovered TYPO3 in 2002 and got caught by its immense possibilities. Now he is part of the TYPO3 Phoenix and FLOW3 core development teams and is a Steering Committee member of the TYPO3 Association.

In their chapter, "TYPO3: The Agile Future of a Ponderous Project," Robert Lemke and Karsten Dambekalns show foundations and techniques that the TYPO3 project uses to improve the quality of their software in a sustainable way.

Benjamin Eberlei, direkt:effekt GmbH

Benjamin Eberlei is software developer at direkt:effekt GmbH. In his spare time, he is part of the Doctrine team, maintains some components for the Zend Framework, and contributes to a handful of other small open-source projects.

In his "Unit Testing Bad Practices" chapter, Benjamin Eberlei shows common mistakes you should avoid while writing unit tests in order to maximize the return on investment from automated testing of your software.

Matthew Weier O'Phinney, Zend Technologies Ltd.

Matthew Weier O'Phinney is Project Lead for Zend Framework and has been contributing to the project since before the initial preview release. He is an advocate for open-source software and regularly blogs and speaks on PHP best practice topics. You'll find him most often in Vermont, where he resides with his wife, daughter, son, and aging basset hound.

In his "Testing Service-Oriented APIs" chapter, Matthew Weier O'Phinney highlights the challenges of testing web services and presents solutions that proved successful in the Zend Framework project.

Tobias Schlitt

Tobias Schlitt has a degree in computer science and has worked for more than 10 years on professional web projects using PHP. As an open-source enthusiast, he contributes to various community projects. Tobias is a co-founder of Qafoo GmbH, which provides services for high-quality PHP development. This includes consulting and training for quality assurance and better programming, as well as technical support for several PHP QA tools.

In his "Testing a WebDAV Server" chapter, Tobias Schlitt shows that you sometimes have to resort to unusual methods to reach your goals when writing automated tests.

Fabien Potencier, Sensio Labs

Fabien Potencier[3] discovered the Web in 1994, at a time when connecting to the Internet was still associated with the harmful, strident sounds of a modem. Being a developer by passion, he immediately started to build websites with Perl. But with the release of PHP5, he decided to switch focus to PHP and created the Symfony framework[4] project in 2004 to help his company leverage the power of PHP for its customers. Fabien is a serial entrepreneur, and among other companies, he created Sensio, a services and consulting company specializing in web technologies and Internet marketing, in 1998. Fabien is also the creator of several other open-source projects, a writer, blogger, speaker at international conferences, and happy father of two wonderful kids.

In his "Testing Symfony and Symfony Projects" chapter, Fabien Potencier reports his experience from the Symfony project and shows how the testing of Symfony improved the framework's programming interfaces.

Kore Nordmann

Kore Nordmann has a degree in computer science. During his studies, he worked as a developer and software architect at eZ Systems, the manufacturer of the leading enterprise open-source CMS. In addition, he is developing and/or maintaining various open-source projects, such as eZComponents, Arbit, WCV, Image 3D, PHPUnit, and others. For several years, Kore has been a regular speaker at national and international conferences and has published several books and articles. He offers consulting as a partner in Qafoo GmbH.

In his "Testing the ezcGraph Component" chapter, Kore Nordmann describes how a well-designed architecture, together with the use of mock objects, enables even the testing of a component that produces binary output.

Michael Lively Jr., Selling Source LLC

Michael Lively has been working with PHP since 2001 and has been involved to some degree with the PHP testing community since 2005. He is the creator of the database testing extension for PHPUnit and makes other small contributions to PHPUnit. He is now an Application Architect for

---

[3]http://fabien.potencier.org

[4]http://www.symfony-project.org

Las Vegas-based Selling Source LLC. While working with Selling Source, he has worked on several projects, including enterprise-level loan management and processing platforms written in PHP that service millions of customers and hundreds of agents.

In his "Testing Database Interaction" chapter, Michael Lively Jr. documents the functionality of DbUnit, PHPUnit's extension for database testing, and shows how this powerful tool can be leveraged effectively.

Christiane Philipps, Rebate Networks GmbH, and Max Horváth, Vodafone GmbH

Christiane Philipps is CTO and Agile Enthusiast with Rebate Networks. She regularly writes about agile testing and agile leadership, topics that are dear to her heart, in her blog.[5]

Max Horváth is Lead Software Engineer with Vodafone Internet Services and has more than 10 years of experience with web development. At the time of this writing, he was the Team Lead Mobile Development at VZnet Netzwerke.

In their "Quality Assurance at studiVZ" chapter, Christiane Philipps and Max Horváth report how they successfully introduced PHPUnit and Selenium RC for one of Europe's largest social networking platforms.

Manuel Pichler, OnVista Media GmbH, and Sebastian Nohn, Ligatus GmbH

Manuel Pichler is the creator of PHP quality assurance tools such as PHP Depend,[6] PHPMD,[7] and phpUnderControl.[8] He is a co-founder of Qafoo GmbH, which provides services for high-quality PHP development.

Sebastian Nohn started developing dynamic websites in 1996 and has handled quality assurance in commercial and open-source projects since 2002. He was one of the first to use CruiseControl for the continuous integration of PHP projects.

In their chapter, "Continuous Integration with phpUnderControl," Manuel Pichler and Sebastian Nohn report how continuous integration, retroactively written unit tests, software metrics, and other static testing techniques helped improve the software quality of a legacy application.

Lars Jankowfsky, swoodoo AG

Lars Jankowfsky is the CTO of swoodoo AG and is responsible for the PHP-based flight and hotel price comparison service. He has been developing web applications for over 15 years and has used PHP since its early versions. Another passion of his is leading eXtreme Programming teams.

---

[5] http://agile-qa.de

[6] http://pdepend.org/

[7] http://phpmd.org/

[8] http://phpUnderControl.org/

In his chapter, "swoodoo: A True Agile Story," Lars Jankowfsky tells how swoodoo introduced agile methods and a service-oriented architecture to allow for the smooth and continuous evolution of their product.

Jens Grochtdreis

Jens Grochtdreis[9] is a self-employed web developer and consultant who specializes in front-end development and accessibility.

In his "Usability" chapter, Jens Grochtdreis shows how to develop websites that are comprehensible and easy to use, as well as how to test for usability.

Brian Shire

Brian Shire started programming around age eight on an Apple IIe. When he wasn't playing games, he was learning the Basic programming language. At the time of this writing, Brian was working for Facebook, Inc., where he focused on scaling their PHP infrastructure. In his four years with Facebook, the site grew from 5 million to over 175 million users. During this time, Brian became a primary contributor to APC, an opcode and user variable cache for PHP. He also made contributions to PHP itself and other PECL extensions. Brian has shared some of this knowledge and experience as a speaker at various conferences around the world. He currently resides in San Francisco, California, and maintains a personal and technical blog.[10]

In his "Performance Testing" chapter, Brian Shire provides motivation for performance testing of web applications and introduces the reader to the appropriate tools and processes for performance testing.

Arne Blankerts, thePHP.cc

Arne Blankerts has long-standing experience as Head of IT. His software fCMS makes innovative use of XML technologies and is vital to business-critical applications in international corporations. He is actively involved with the documentation of PHP. Arne Blankerts is an expert on IT security and writes about this in a magazine column. He is a sought-after speaker at international conferences and a book author, and he publishes articles in IT magazines.

In his "Security" chapter, Arne Blankerts shows how easy the development of fundamentally secure applications is if you know the common attack vectors and follow some important rules.

ERRATA

We make every effort to ensure that there are no errors in the text or in the code. However, no one is perfect, and mistakes do occur. If you find an error in one of our books, like a spelling mistake or faulty piece of code, we would be very grateful for your feedback. By sending in errata, you might save another reader hours of frustration, and at the same time, you will be helping us provide even higher-quality information.

---

[9]http://grochtdreis.de

[10]http://tekrat.com

To find the errata page for this book, go to http://www.wrox.com and locate the title using the Search box or one of the title lists. Then, on the book details page, click the Book Errata link. On this page, you can view all errata that has been submitted for this book and posted by Wrox editors. A complete book list, including links to each book's errata, is also available at www.wrox.com/misc-pages/booklist.shtml.

If you don't spot "your" error on the Book Errata page, go to www.wrox.com/contact/techsupport.shtml and complete the form there to send us the error you have found. We'll check the information and, if appropriate, post a message to the book's errata page and fix the problem in subsequent editions of the book.

P2P.WROX.COM

For author and peer discussion, join the P2P forums at p2p.wrox.com. The forums are a web-based system for you to post messages relating to Wrox books and related technologies and interact with other readers and technology users. The forums offer a subscription feature to e-mail you topics of interest of your choosing when new posts are made to the forums. Wrox authors, editors, other industry experts, and your fellow readers are present on these forums.

At http://p2p.wrox.com, you will find a number of different forums that will help you, not only as you read this book, but also as you develop your own applications. To join the forums, just follow these steps:

1. Go to p2p.wrox.com and click the Register link.

2. Read the terms of use and click Agree.

3. Complete the required information to join, as well as any optional information you wish to provide, and click Submit.

4. You will receive an e-mail with information describing how to verify your account and complete the joining process.

 You can read messages in the forums without joining P2P, but in order to post your own messages, you must join.

Once you join, you can post new messages and respond to messages other users post. You can read messages at any time on the Web. If you would like to have new messages from a particular forum e-mailed to you, click the Subscribe to this Forum icon by the forum name in the forum listing.

For more information about how to use the Wrox P2P, be sure to read the P2P FAQs for answers to questions about how the forum software works, as well as many common questions specific to P2P and Wrox books. To read the FAQs, click the FAQ link on any P2P page.

PART I
Foundations

1

Software Quality

WHAT'S IN THIS CHAPTER?

➤ An overview of external and internal quality

➤ Discussions of technical debt and constructive quality assurance

➤ A look at various software metrics

➤ A brief look at tools for measuring and improving software quality

This book deals with software quality in PHP projects. What, exactly, do we mean by the term "software quality"? One example of a software quality model is FURPS (Functionality, Usability, Reliability, Performance, Supportability), which was developed by Hewlett-Packard.[1]

Although the FURPS quality model applies to all kinds of software, there are even more quality attributes with respect to Web applications, namely findability, accessibility, and legal conformity.[2] Software quality is a multifaceted topic, as Peter Liggesmeyer states in the introduction to *Software-Qualität: Testen, Analysieren und Verifizieren von Software, 2. Auflage*.[3]

---

[1]Robert Grady and Deborah Caswell, *Software Metrics: Establishing a Company-wide Program* (Prentice Hall, 1987. ISBN 978-0138218447).

[2]Klaus Franz, *Handbuch zum Testen von Web-Applikationen* (Springer, 2007. ISBN 978-3-540-24539-1).

[3]Peter Liggesmeyer, *Software-Qualität: Testen, Analysieren und Verifizieren von Software, 2. Auflage* (Spektrum Akademischer Verlag, 2009. ISBN 978-3-8274-2056-5).

Every company developing software will attempt to deliver the best possible quality. But a goal can only be certifiably reached when it is clearly defined, which the term "best possible quality" is not. Software quality is multifaceted, thus software quality comprises many characteristics. Not all of these are equally important for the user and the manufacturer of the software.

A user's view on quality differs from a developer's view. We thus differentiate between *external* and *internal* quality, following Nigel Bevan's explanations of *ISO/IEC 9126-1: Software Engineering— Product quality—Part 1: Quality model* [4] in "Quality in use: Meeting user needs for quality."[5] In this chapter, we take a closer look at these two views.

EXTERNAL QUALITY

Customers, or the end users of an application, put their focus on quality aspects that are tangible for them. These quality aspects account for the *external quality* of the application.

➤ **Functionality** means that an application can actually fulfill the expected tasks.

➤ **Usability** means that a user can work efficiently, effectively, and satisfactorily with the application. Accessibility is a part of usability.

➤ **Reactivity** means short response times, which is crucial for an application in order to keep its users happy.

➤ **Security,** especially the security perceived by users, is another important factor for an application's success.

➤ **Availability** and **reliability** are especially important for Web applications with high user numbers. The applications must bear high loads and are required to work even in unusual situations.

All aspects of external quality can be verified by testing the application as a whole, using so-called *end-to-end tests*. The customer's requirements, for example, can be written down as acceptance tests. *Acceptance tests* not only improve the communication between the customer and the developers, but also make it possible to verify in an automated way that a software product fulfills all its functional requirements.

To improve an application's reactivity, we must measure the response time. We must use tools and techniques to find optimizations that promise the biggest win while keeping cost and effort low. To plan capacities, developers and administrators must identify potential future bottlenecks when an application is modified or traffic increases. All this information is required to assure the quality of an application with respect to availability and reliability in the long term.

---

[4]International Organization for Standardization, *ISO/IEC 9126-1: Software Engineering—Product quality—Part 1: Quality model*, 2008-07-29 (Geneva, Switzerland, 2008).

[5]Nigel Bevan, "Quality in use: Meeting user needs for quality," *Journal of Systems and Software* 49, Issue 1 (December 1999): 89–96, ISSN 0164-1212.

INTERNAL QUALITY

The needs of the developers and administrators of an application drive its *internal quality*. Developers put their focus on readable code that is easy to understand, adapt, and extend. If they do not do so, implementing the customer's future change requests becomes more difficult and thus more expensive over time. There is an increased danger that even small changes to the software will lead to unexpected side effects.

The internal quality of software is virtually imperceptible to customers and end users. End users expect software to satisfy all, or at least most, of their functional expectations and to be easy to use. If, upon acceptance, the product is "fast enough," most customers are satisfied.

Bad internal quality shows up in the longer term, though. It takes longer to fix even trivial bugs. Any changes or extensions to the software require a huge effort. Quite often, the developers sooner or later ask for a budget to clean up and refactor the code. Because customers or management often do not see the benefit of refactoring, these requests often are turned down.

 Refactoring *means modifying the internal structure of software, without changing its visible behavior.*

Automated developer tests of individual software modules (unit tests), discussed in Chapter 2, allow for immediate feedback about new bugs that have been introduced when changing the code. Without automated tests, refactoring the code is a tough job.

A main goal of quality assurance, or to be exact, quality management, is to make the costs and benefits of internal quality transparent to all parties that are involved. Bad internal quality causes additional costs in the long term. If these costs can be quantified, it is possible to make the case for achieving good internal quality, because that reduces costs. This seems to be the only way of making management or the customer consider allocating a budget for code refactoring.

TECHNICAL DEBT

Ward Cunningham coined the term "technical debt":

> Although immature code may work fine and be completely acceptable to the customer, excess quantities will make a program unmasterable, leading to extreme specialization of programmers and finally an inflexible product. Shipping first-time code is like going into debt. A little debt speeds development so long as it is paid back promptly with a rewrite. Objects make the cost of this transaction tolerable. The danger occurs when the debt is not repaid. Every minute spent on not-quite-right code counts as interest on that debt. Entire engineering

organizations can be brought to a standstill under the debt load of an uncon-solidated implementation, object-oriented or otherwise.[6]

Cunningham compares bad code with a financial loan that has an interest rate. A loan can be a good idea if it helps the project to ship a product more quickly. If the loan is not paid back, however, by refactoring the code base and thus improving the internal quality, a considerable amount of additional cost in the form of interest piles up over time. At some point, the interest payments reduce the financial scope, until finally someone must declare bankruptcy. With regard to software development, this means that an application has become unmaintainable. Every small change to the code has become so expensive that it is not economically feasible to maintain the code.

Lack of internal quality tends to be more of a problem when development is being outsourced to a third party. Performing quality assurance, and especially writing unit tests, raises the development cost in the short term without an immediately measurable benefit. Because the focus often lies on reducing the project costs and keeping the time to market short, the developers have no opportunity to deliver high-quality code. The dam-age is done, however, and the customer must bear considerably higher maintenance costs in the long term.

It is crucial for every software project, and especially outsourced projects, not only to define qual-ity criteria with regard to external quality, but also to ask for a sensible level of internal quality. Of course, this requires the customer to allocate a somewhat bigger budget, so the developers have some financial scope to account for internal quality.

Operating and maintenance costs of software are usually vastly underestimated. A medium-sized soft-ware project may last for one or two years, but the resulting application may be in operation for decades. The year 2000 problem proved that many applications are operational much longer than originally expected. Especially for applications that must be modified frequently, account for the biggest share of cost operation and maintenance. Web applications are known to require frequent changes, which is one of the reasons why many developers choose a dynamic language like PHP to implement them.

Other applications, for example, financial applications running on mainframes or telephone exchange software that needs to be highly available, are seldom modified. Although one new release per quarter may seem hectic for these kinds of applications, many Web applications require multiple releases each month.

Ron Jefferies reminds us that sacrificing internal quality to speed up development is a bad idea:

> If slacking on quality makes us go faster, it is clear evidence that there is room to improve our ability to deliver quality rapidly.[7]

It is obvious that the value of internal quality scales up with increasing change frequency of an application. Figure 1-1 shows that the relative cost of a bugfix in the coding phase of a project is 10 times, and in the operations phase is over 100 times, bigger than in the requirements phase. This proves that trying to postpone costs by delaying tasks in software development projects does not make sense from an economical point of view alone.

---

[6]Ward Cunningham, "The WyCash Portfolio Management System," March 26, 1992, accessed April 17, 2010, http://c2.com/doc/oopsla92.html.

[7]Ron Jefferies, "Quality vs Speed? I Don't Think So!" April 29, 2010, accessed May 1, 2010, http://xprogramming.com/articles/quality/.

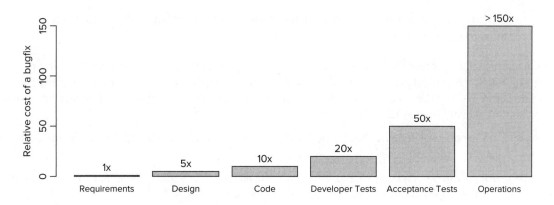

FIGURE 1-1: Relative cost of a bugfix[8]

CONSTRUCTIVE QUALITY ASSURANCE

Both *Capability Maturity Model Integration (CMMI)* and *Software Process Improvement and Capability Determination (SPICE)*[9] have a narrower view on quality assurance than many others, because they exclude testing.[10] All steps that CMMI and SPICE suggest with regard to organizational structure and process organization are prerequisites for the success of analytical activities like test and review of the finished software product and all measures of constructive quality assurance. Kurt Schneider defines constructive quality assurance as "measures that aim at improving selected software quality aspects on construction instead of afterward by verification and correction."[11]

The insight that avoiding bugs is better than finding and fixing them afterward is not new. Dijkstra wrote as early as 1972:

> Those who want really reliable software will discover that they must find means of avoiding the majority of bugs to start with, and as a result the programming process will become cheaper. If you want more effective programmers, you will discover

[8]Barry Boehm, Ricardo Valerdi, and Eric Honour, "The ROI of Systems Engineering: Some Quantitative Results for Software-Intensive Systems," *Systems Engineering* 11, Issue 3 (August 2008): 221–234, ISSN 1098-1241.

[9]CMMI is explained in detail at http://www.sei.cmu.edu/cmmi/, and in ISO/IEC 12207. SPICE is covered in ISO/IEC 15504.

[10]Malte Foegen, Mareike Solbach und Claudia Raak, *Der Weg zur professionellen IT: Eine praktische Anleitung für das Management von Veränderungen mit CMMI, ITIL oder SPICE* (Springer, 2007. ISBN 978-3-540-72471-1).

[11]Kurt Schneider, *Abenteuer Softwarequalität—Grundlagen und Verfahren für Qualitätssicherung und Qualitätsmanagement* (dpunkt.verlag, 2007. ISBN 978-3-89864-472-3).

that they should not waste their time debugging—they should not introduce bugs to start with.[12]

One approach to prevent the writing of defective software is *test-first programming*. Test-first programming is a technical practice that allows for constructive quality assurance by writing the test code before writing the production code. *Test-driven development*, which is based on test-first programming, ideally implies the following:

➤ All production code has been motivated by a test. This reduces the risk of writing unnecessary production code.

➤ All production code is covered by at least one test (code coverage). Modifications of the production code cannot lead to unexpected side effects.

➤ Production code is testable code and thus *clean code*.

➤ The pain that existing *bad code* causes is amplified, because that code cannot be tested or can be tested only with disproportional effort. This is a motivation to keep replacing existing bad code through refactoring.

Studies like that done by David S. Janzen[13] show that test-driven development can lead to significant improvements in developer productivity and better software quality.

Constructive quality assurance and normal software development cannot be clearly separated. Object-oriented programming and the use of design patterns improve the adaptability of software. Writing *clean code* (see next section) and concepts like a three-layer architecture or model-view-controller, when used properly, lead to significant improvements with regard to testability, maintainability, and reusability of the individual software components.

CLEAN CODE

In his book, *Clean Code*, Robert C. Martin lets Dave Thomas (among others) answer the question "what is clean code?":

> Clean code can be read, and enhanced by a developer other than its original author. It has unit and acceptance tests. It has meaningful names. It provides one way rather than many ways for doing one thing. It has minimal dependencies, which are explicitly defined, and provides a clear and minimal API. Code should be literate since depending on the language, not all necessary information can be expressed clearly in code alone.[14]

---

[12]Edsger W. Dijkstra, "The humble programmer," *Communications of the ACM 45*, Issue 10 (October 1972): 859–866. ISSN 0001-0782.

[13]David S. Janzen, *Software Architecture Improvement through Test-Driven Development* (University of Kansas, Electrical Engineering and Computer Science, Lawrence, Kansas, USA, 2006).

[14]Robert C. Martin, *Clean Code: A Handbook of Agile Software Craftsmanship* (Prentice Hall International, 2008. ISBN 978-0-132-35088-4).

Steve Freeman and Nat Pryce add to this thought by stating that code that is easy to test must be good:

> For a class to be easy to unit-test, the class must have explicit dependencies that can easily be substituted and clear responsibilities that can easily be invoked and verified. In software-engineering terms, that means that the code must be loosely coupled and highly cohesive—in other words, well-designed.[15]

Let's take a closer look at these terms.

Explicit and Minimal Dependencies

All dependencies of a method to test must be clearly and explicitly defined in the method's API. This implies that all required objects must be passed either to the constructor of the class or to the tested method itself (*dependency injection*). Required objects should never be created in the method's body, because this disallows swapping them out for mock objects. The fewer dependencies a method has, the easier it becomes to write tests.

Clear Responsibilities

The *single responsibility principle (SRP)*[16] states that a class should have one clearly defined responsibility and should contain only those methods that are directly involved with fulfilling that responsibility. There should never be more than one reason to change a class. If the responsibility of a class is clearly defined and its methods are easy to call and can be verified through their return values, then writing unit tests for a class is a rather trivial task.

No Duplication

A class that does too much and has no clear responsibility is "a splendid breeding place for duplicated code, chaos, and death."[17] Duplicated code makes software maintenance more difficult, because each code duplicate must be kept consistent, and a defect that has been found in duplicated code cannot be fixed in just one spot.

Short Methods with Few Execution Branches

The longer a method is, the harder it is to understand. A short method is not only easier to understand and reuse, but also easier to test. Fewer execution paths means that fewer tests are required.

---

[15]Steve Freeman and Nat Pryce, *Growing Object-Oriented Software, Guided by Tests* (Addison-Wesley, 2009. ISBN 978-0-321-50362-6).

[16]Robert C. Martin, *Agile Software Development. Principles, Patterns, and Practices* (Prentice Hall International, 2002. ISBN 978-0-135-97444-5).

[17]Martin Fowler, *Refactoring. Wie Sie das Design vorhandener Software verbessern* (Addison-Wesley, 2000. ISBN 3-8273-1630-8).

SOFTWARE METRICS

There are various software metrics for measuring internal quality. They are the basis for quantifying the costs that emerge from bad internal quality.

 A software metric is, in general, a function that maps a software unit onto a numeric value. This value says how well a software unit fulfills a quality goal.[18]

Testability is an important criterion for maintainability in the ISO/IEC 9126-1 software quality model. Examples for quantifying the testability based on object-oriented software metrics can be found in "Predicting Class Testability using Object-Oriented Metrics" by Magiel Bruntink and Arie van Deursen,[19] and in "Metric Based Testability Model for Object Oriented Design (MTMOOD)" by R. A. Khan and K. Mustafa.[20]

A good overview of object-oriented software metrics is *Object-Oriented Metrics in Practice: Using Software Metrics to Characterize, Evaluate, and Improve the Design of Object-Oriented Systems* by Michele Lanza and Radu Marinescu (Springer, 2006. ISBN 978-3-540-24429-5).

The following sections discuss some metrics that are especially relevant for testability.

Cyclomatic Complexity and npath Complexity

The *cyclomatic complexity* is the number of possible decision paths in a program or program unit, usually a method or class.[21] It is calculated by counting the control structures and Boolean operators in a program unit, and it represents the structural complexity of a program unit. McCabe claims that a sequence of commands is easier to understand than a branch in the control flow.

A large cyclomatic complexity indicates that a program unit is susceptible to defects and hard to test. The more execution paths a program unit has, the more tests are required. The npath complexity counts the number of acyclic execution paths.[22] To keep this number finite and eliminate redundant information, the npath complexity does not take every possible iteration of loops into account.

---

[18]Schneider, *Abenteuer.*

[19]Magiel Bruntink and Arie van Deursen, "Predicting Class Testability using Object-Oriented Metrics," *SCAM '04: Proceedings of the Source Code Analysis and Manipulation, Fourth IEEE International Workshop* (2004): 136–145. ISBN 0-7695-2144-4.

[20]R. A. Khan and K. Mustafa, "Metric Based Testability Model for Object Oriented Design (MTMOOD)," *SIGSOFT Software Engineering Notes* 34, Issue 2 (March 2009): 1–6. ISSN 0163-5948.

[21]Thomas J. McCabe, "A Complexity Measure," *IEEE Transactions on Software Engineering* 2, No. 4 (IEEE Computer Society Press, Los Alamitos, CA, USA, 1976).

[22]Brian A. Nejmeh, "NPATH: A Measure of Execution Path Complexity and its Applications," *Communications of the ACM* 31, Issue 2 (February 1988): 188–200. ISSN 0001-0782.

Change Risk Anti-Patterns (CRAP) Index

The *Change Risk Anti-Patterns (CRAP) Index*, formerly known as *Change Risk Analysis and Predictions Index*, does not directly refer to testability. We mention it here because it is calculated from the cyclomatic complexity and the *code coverage* that is achieved by the tests.

Code that is not too complex and has adequate test coverage has a low CRAP index. This means that the risk that changes to the code will lead to unexpected side effects is lower than for code that has a high CRAP index. Code with a high CRAP index is complex and has few or even no tests.

The CRAP index can be lowered by writing tests or by refactoring the code. The refactoring patterns *extract method* and *replace conditional by polymorphism*, for example, allow for shortening methods and reducing the number of decision paths, and thus the cyclomatic complexity.

Non-Mockable Total Recursive Cyclomatic Complexity

Miško Hevery, creator of the so-called Testability Explorer (`http://code.google.com/p/test-ability-explorer/`), a tool to measure testability of Java code, defined the *non-mockable total recursive cyclomatic complexity* software metric. The name is composed of the following parts:

> ➤ **Cyclomatic complexity:** This is the structural complexity of a method.

> ➤ **Recursive:** We look at the cyclomatic complexity of a method and take into account the cyclomatic complexity of the called code.

> ➤ **Total:** The structural complexity of object creation is also taken into account.

> ➤ **Non-mockable:** Any dependent code that can be replaced by a mock object is ignored. A mock object replaces the real object for testing purposes (see Chapter 2).

Basically, the *non-mockable total recursive cyclomatic complexity* measures the amount of complex code that cannot be replaced by mock objects for unit testing purposes. These kinds of complex dependencies that disallow isolating code for testing purposes lead to "pain" when testing. All these dependencies should be refactored, for example by introducing *dependency injection*, so that they can be replaced by mock objects.

Global Mutable State

The *global mutable state* is another metric that Miško Hevery has defined for his Testability Explorer. It counts all elements of the *global state* that a program unit writes to or could possibly write to. In PHP, these are all global and superglobal variables and static class attributes.

Changes to the global state are a side effect that not only makes each test more complex, but requires that every other test be isolated from it. PHPUnit, for example, supports saving and restoring the global and superglobal variables and static class attributes prior to running a test, and restoring them after the test, so that modifications of the global state do not make other tests fail. This isolation, which can be further enhanced by executing each test in its own PHP process, is resource-intensive and should be avoided by not relying on a global state.

Cohesion and Coupling

A system with strong cohesion is comprised of components responsible for exactly one clearly defined task. Loose coupling is achieved when classes are independent from each other and communicate only through well-defined interfaces.[23] The Law of Demeter[24] requires that each method of an object calls methods only in the same object and methods in objects that were passed to the method as parameters. Obeying the Law of Demeter leads to clear dependencies and loose coupling. This makes it possible to replace dependencies by mock objects, which makes writing tests much easier.

TOOLS

Software quality is multifaceted, and equally multifaceted are the tools that PHP developers can use to measure and improve the software quality of PHP projects.

PHPUnit

PHPUnit (`http://phpun.it/`) is the de-facto standard for unit testing in PHP. The framework supports writing, organizing, and executing tests. When writing tests, developers can make use of the following:

➤ Mock objects (see Chapters 2 and 9).

➤ Functionality for testing database interaction (see Chapter 10).

➤ An integration with Selenium (see Chapter 11) for browser-based end-to-end tests. Test results can be logged in JUnit and code coverage as Clover XML for continuous integration purposes (see Chapter 12).

phploc

phploc (`http://github/sebastianbergmann/phploc`) measures the scope of a PHP project by means of different forms of the *lines of code* (*LOC*) software metric. In addition, the number of namespaces, classes, methods, and functions of a project are counted, and some values, like the average complexity and length of classes and methods, are counted. Chapter 12 shows an example of how phploc can be used.

PHP Copy-Paste-Detector (phpcpd)

The PHP Copy-Paste-Detector (phpcpd) (`http://github/sebastianbergmann/phpcpd`) searches for duplicated code, the so-called *code clones* in a PHP project. Chapter 12 shows how phpcpd can be used for an automated and regular search for duplicated code in the context of continuous integration.

---

[23]Edward Yourdon and Larry Constantine, *Structured Design: Fundamentals of a Discipline of Computer Program and Systems Design* (Prentice Hall, 1979. ISBN 978-0138544713.)

[24]K. J. Lienberherr, "Formulations and Benefits of the Law of Demeter," *ACM SIGPLAN Notices* 24, Issue 3 (March 1989): 67–78. ISSN 0362-1340.

PHP Dead Code Detector (phpdcd)

The PHP Dead Code Detector (phpdcd) (`http://github.com/sebastianbergmann/phpdcd`) searches PHP projects for code that is not called anymore and thus potentially can be deleted.

PHP_Depend (pdepend)

PHP_Depend (pdepend) (`http://pdepend.org/`) is a tool for static code analysis of PHP code. It is inspired by JDepend and calculates various software metrics, for example the cyclomatic complexity and npath complexity that were previously mentioned. It also is possible to visualize various aspects of software quality. Chapter 12 shows how PHP_Depend can be used in the context of continuous integration, to keep an eye on relevant software metrics while developing.

PHP Mess Detector (phpmd)

The PHP Mess Detector (phpmd) (`http://phpmd.org/`) is based on PHP_Depend and allows the definition of rules that operate on the "raw data" software metrics that PHP_Depend has calculated. If a rule is violated, for example because the cyclomatic complexity exceeds a given limit, a warning or an error is triggered. Chapter 12 shows how the PHP Mess Detector can be used in the context of continuous integration.

PHP_CodeSniffer (phpcs)

The PHP_CodeSniffer (phpcs) (`http://pear.php.net/php_codesniffer/`) is the most commonly used tool for static analysis of PHP code. Its countless sniffs to detect *code smells*[25] range from formatting rules via software metrics to the detection of potential defects and performance problems. Chapter 12 shows how PHP_CodeSniffer can be used in continuous integration to enforce a certain coding standard.

bytekit-cli

bytekit-cli (`http://github.com/sebastianbergmann/bytekit-cli`) is a command line front-end for the Bytekit PHP extension (`http://bytekit.org/`). Bytekit allows for code introspection at bytecode level. With bytekit-cli it is possible to find code that generates output for a code review. Disassembling and visualizing of PHP bytecode is also possible.

PHP_CodeBrowser (phpcb)

The PHP_CodeBrowser (phpcb) (`http://github.com/mayflowergmbh/PHP_CodeBrowser`) is a report generator taking the XML output of other tools like the PHP Copy-Paste-Detector, PHP_CodeSniffer, and PHP Mess Detector as input. It generates a unified report, which is extremely useful in continuous integration (see Chapter 12).

CruiseControl and phpUnderControl

phpUnderControl (`http://phpUnderControl.org/`) is a modification and extension of CruiseControl (`http://cruisecontrol.sourceforge.net/`), the Java open-source solution that originally made continuous integration popular. Sebastian Nohn, in 2006, was one of the first to use

---

[25]Fowler, *Refactoring.*

CruiseControl in PHP projects.[26] In a meeting of the PHP Usergroup Dortmund in Germany, which was attended by Manuel Pichler, Kore Nordmann, and Tobias Schlitt, the idea was born to simplify the configuration of a continuous integration environment for PHP projects based on CruiseControl. The result was phpUnderControl, which—like CruiseControl in the Java world—has made continuous integration popular in the PHP world. Manuel Pichler and Sebastian Nohn describe how to install, configure, and operate phpUnderControl in Chapter 12.

Hudson

Like CruiseControl, Hudson (`http://hudson-ci.org/`) is an open-source solution for continuous integration. In the Java world, Hudson is superseding the outdated CruiseControl. This is not surprising, because Hudson is more robust and easier to handle, and it is being actively developed. The php-hudson-template project (`http://github.com/sebastianbergmann/php-hudson-template`) is a configuration template for PHP projects in Hudson.

Arbit

Arbit (`http://arbitracker.org/`) is a modular solution for project management. It features an issue tracker, a wiki, a code browser, and a continuous integration server. Arbit is currently still in alpha state and thus not really suited for production use. You should keep an eye on the project though.

CONCLUSION

A software quality goal can only be reached when it has been defined precisely. The software metrics that have been introduced in this chapter can help to define these goals. Instead of just gathering data because the continuous integration server makes it possible, the data should be used to answer dedicated questions about the quality of the inspected software product. The *Goal-Question-Metric* (*GQM*) approach by Victor R. Basili, Gianluigi Caldiera, and H. Dieter Rombach,[27] summarized by Kurt Schneider in just one sentence, can help:

> Do not measure what is easy to measure, but what you need to reach your improvement goals.[28]

This chapter outlined some goals for improving the internal quality of software, for example testability, maintainability, and reusability. We introduced some software metrics to measure these aspects. We hope the discussion of "technical debt" will improve mutual understanding between the various parties involved in a software project and made clear the importance of internal quality of software.

Most Web applications are changed and adapted quite frequently and quickly. Their environment, for example the size and behavior of the user base, is constantly changing. The internal and external quality are just snapshots. What was sufficient yesterday can be insufficient today. In a Web environment, it is especially important to monitor and continuously improve the internal quality, not only when developing, but also when maintaining the software.

[26]Sebastian Nohn, "Continuous Builds with CruiseControl, Ant and PHPUnit," March 7, 2006, accessed April 28, 2010, `http://nohn.net/blog/view/id/ cruisecontrol_ant_and_phpunit`.

[27]Victor R. Basili, Gianluigi Caldiera, and H. Dieter Rombach, "Goal Question Metric Paradigm," *Encyclopedia of Software Engineering,* 2 Volume Set (John Wiley & Sons, 1994. ISBN 1-54004-8.)

[28]Schneider, *Abenteuer.*

Software Testing

It's okay to never test code that never changes. For everything else, you need tests.

— Timothy Fitz

BLACK BOX AND WHITE BOX TESTS

In classical, non-iterative software development, programming and integration or system testing are two distinct project phases, and they often are executed by different teams. It makes lots of sense not to have developers test their own work. An independent tester approaches the product with a completely different view, because he does not know any implementation details. Thus, he is forced to focus on testing the API, and he uses the application in a different way than the original developer, who still thinks about the code intuitively and might tend to test the functionality that is already known to work. Independent testers usually develop enough destructive creativity to really put the developer's work to the test and try out really nonsensical input, interrupted actions, or even manipulated URLs. First-time users of an application, by the way, are also great testers.

Tests that are executed without knowledge about implementation details are called *black box* tests. Tests that are developed based on the source code of an application are called *white box* tests.

HOW MANY TESTS ARE NEEDED?

At first glance, testing a web application seems to be a rather trivial task. The program receives an input string (the HTTP request) from a browser and generates another string (usually HTML code), which is sent back to the browser where it is rendered. Other output formats like XML or JSON could be created as well, but they are also just strings. So any test must ensure the program generates a correct output string for a given input string.

Although it is, in fact, rather easy to make sure the output for one input string is correct, the vast number of possible input strings alone makes it impossible to determine whether the program generates a correct output for any input. Unfortunately, a program does not receive only "meaningful" input, so it does not suffice to test just a few input strings.

URLs can contain 37 different characters (these are the alphanumeric characters in uppercase and lowercase and a few special characters); every other character has to be URL-encoded. A list of all possible URLs with the maximum length of 20 characters has a few undecillion entries (that is a number with 37 digits). If we could list one million URLs per second, creating that list would take approximately 10^{23} years. However, because the sun is expected to turn into a supernova in about 10^9 years, destroying the earth, we most probably can't ever complete this task.

To reduce the number of input strings we have to test, we have to construct *equivalence classes*. An equivalence class contains a number of inputs that do not lead to a different program flow, even when calculations are performed with different input values. Let's assume you want to test a program that increments a given whole number. It doesn't matter whether this program uses an increment operation or an addition (or even a completely different approach) to accomplish its task. If we assume that PHP works correctly, testing a single representative input will suffice. If the program yields a correct output, we can assume that it works correctly without actually testing it for every single whole number.

Bounds and illegal input values require special attention. They form additional equivalence classes, in addition to the ones formed by normal, expected inputs. Every equivalence class requires a test. What happens, for example, when we try to increment the highest possible integer value? And what happens when we try to increment non-numeric values—for example, a string?

In practice, it is not always easy to identify equivalence classes—in other words, to test with representative inputs. As a general rule, you should always test the happy path first. (The happy path is the default scenario where no errors or exceptions should occur.) Then test bounds, like the highest possible input value as well as the highest allowed value plus one, and the lowest possible input value as well as that value minus one. If this is done, you can test nonsense input, like NULL values or illegal data types.

For black box tests, identifying equivalence classes is more difficult than for white box tests, where the case differentiations and execution paths usually give you a really good idea about the input values to test.

Because HTTP is a stateless protocol, there are, by definition, no dependencies between two subsequent HTTP requests. Again, testing an HTTP-based application seems to be easy, because every HTTP request must be tested only once.

As we all know, most web applications circumvent the statelessness of HTTP using cookies and server-side session management. Without a state, an application cannot distinguish between an anonymous user and a logged-in user, unless the credentials are retransmitted with every single HTTP request.

A stateful application can react differently to the same input, depending on its internal state. So it is not even sufficient to test all possible input values, even though we already know that there are more than we prefer. To fully test a stateful application, we would have to test the program with all possible input sequences.

A typical example for behavior that differs depending on the application state is trying to access a page with non-public content. An anonymous visitor is asked to log in, while a user who is already logged in gets to view the content, at least if he has the appropriate access rights.

It goes without saying that it is not possible to *fully* test a web application before the end of the world, when we cannot even list all possible inputs by then!

SYSTEM TESTS

The most intuitive way of testing an application is to test the system as a whole, by working with the software just as end-users would do.

Browser Testing

One of the big advantages of PHP applications is the possibility of immediately executing code that was just written, and looking at the result in the browser window. This instant feedback is probably one of the main reasons why so many developers prefer PHP over compiled languages like Java. It seems that testing an application in the browser is the way to go.

PHP applications do not just generate static HTML code. Using JavaScript, the DOM tree representing the HTML page in the browser can be manipulated at will. New page elements can be added, removed, or hidden. In conjunction with asynchronous HTTP requests that receive XML or JSON data structures, a full page reload can be avoided. Thanks to AJAX, web applications can provide a user experience that is quite similar to a classical GUI application.

The use of AJAX, however, makes the browser stateful, as opposed to the stateless HTTP protocol. The rendered HTML document becomes a client application that technically has a state that is completely independent from the server and communicates with the server with AJAX requests. Developers suddenly are facing new challenges when writing web applications—for example, locking deadlock and timeout problems.

In most cases, it is not sufficient to simply perform a static analysis of the HTML code generated by a PHP application. A static analysis could verify that the HTML code is syntactically correct or, when XHTML is used, well-formed, or it could make sure that a page contains (only) the desired information by a more or less complex parsing process. Because an increasing part of an application's functionality is implemented in JavaScript these days, any extensive test must also execute JavaScript code.

You could use a JavaScript engine like Rhino, V8, or SpiderMonkey, but because you would sooner or later also have to see an actual page rendering, testing in the browser becomes inevitable. As we all know, every browser family or even browser version has its own idiosyncrasies, not only with regard to page rendering, but also with regard to executing JavaScript code. Admittedly, the situation has improved over the last few years, but all these small differences between the browsers can still give web developers a hard time.

If the application to test does not behave as we expect it to in a browser test, it can be difficult to find out why. Does the same problem occur in other browsers? Will the behavior be the same with different security settings? Can invalid HTML or a bug in the JavaScript code be the reason, or even the database?

By nature, systems tests involve many different components, making it difficult to find the actual source of a problem. A failed test, regardless of whether it has been executed manually or automatically, shows that the software does not work as expected, but it doesn't tell you what the actual source of the problem might be.

In the "How Many Tests Are Needed?" section earlier in this chapter, we established that it is impossible to test an application with all possible input values. Even if we limit ourselves to testing all business cases or business rules with just one representative input, we quickly reach a complexity that is unmanageable. In a social network, for example, every friend must be able to comment on the latest blog entry of a user. If comments must be moderated, a new comment may initially not be visible to anybody except its author and the moderator. As soon as the comment has been approved, it must become visible. Now, is the author of this comment allowed to delete or modify it? Will modifications have to be moderated again?

To test business rules like these, you would have to log in to the application with two different accounts. Even if we bothered to do this, the next software release would raise the question of repeating all tests or otherwise risk that the application does not work as expected anymore due to unwanted side effects.

Writing a test plan describing which business cases and business rules have to be tested, which actions are required to do so, and what the expected results are is a tedious job. A test plan, however, documents all functional requirements of an application and thus is the basis for acceptance tests that the customer uses, to make sure that the application works as expected.

Automated Tests

Because manual testing of an application is time-intensive and nerve-stretching, tests should be automated as much as possible. Automation not only increases the speed of test execution, it also avoids human error. Besides the tiny amount of energy consumption, there is no additional cost for running the tests again and again. Test automation is a prerequisite for testing an application with different operating systems, databases, PHP versions, and configurations.

The initial approach to automating browser tests is the so-called "capture and replay" tools. Simple ones capture the mouse movements and all inputs, and replay them later. Because web applications are frequently used with different screen resolutions and window sizes, however, the tool should not capture actual screen positions, but the browser events at the JavaScript or DOM level.

Selenium is a free software tool that supports record and playback of browser tests though a Firefox extension. In conjunction with PHPUnit, a Java-based proxy server allows for remotely controlling a browser from a PHPUnit test. This makes it possible to run browser tests as part of continuous integration.

Selenium tests use assertions on the DOM tree to make sure the current HTML page fulfills certain criteria. Because the test is executed directly in the browser, JavaScript code is being executed, so AJAX applications can be tested with Selenium as well. Various assertions allow for checking for the presence of or the content of arbitrary HTML elements. The elements (or DOM nodes) are accessed by HTML IDs, CSS selectors, JavaScript code, or an XPath expression.

Because the remote control feature is realized as JavaScript that gets injected into the page to test, there are several limitations due to security restrictions. It is not possible to test a file upload, for example, because this would require JavaScript code to access the local file system to select the file to upload. Normally, you would not want any web page to have access to your file system. Some browsers allow circumventing of restrictions by using a special mode with fewer security restrictions.

System tests that test an application through its user interface are rather fragile, like all types of indirect tests. A seemingly harmless cosmetic change to the layout—for example, because an important advertisement must be displayed—can cause assertions to fail. It is important to plan the page structure well ahead and write conservative assertions to avoid frequently breaking tests. Chapter 11 describes various best practices for using Selenium. Fragile tests are also covered in Chapter 4.

In most cases, you don't want to run system tests against a live system. Your users probably will not be amused when their data is modified as if by an invisible hand. In some cases, setting up a test system can be harder than expected—for example, if the production system is extremely complex or potent and thus expensive.

In this case, it often is not possible to set up an identical test system for economic reasons alone. Often, the production database is just too large for the test system or there are legal reasons disallowing tests with real user data. This is often the case when credit card data is involved.

Test Isolation

One of the main functionalities of every web application is the creation of a user account and the user login. When users cannot log in to the system anymore, money is lost. Sign-up and login are thus usually among the most tested functionalities of web applications. To test the sign-up, usually a non-existing username and an unused e-mail address are required. If the test runs against a database already containing users, the first potential problem is a test failing with an error message because the username or e-mail address is already in use.

Let's assume that the first test, creating a user, has worked out. Before we can test whether the user can log in to the system, we usually have to confirm the e-mail address by visiting a URL containing a unique confirmation code. Having done this, we can test whether the user can log in. However, if creating the user fails, confirmation fails as well, probably because the test was unable to retrieve the confirmation code from the result page. Login fails as well, because there is no account with the given credentials.

If there are dependencies between tests, a single failing test can lead to a cascade of failing tests. This not only makes it difficult to isolate the original problem, but also undermines the trust in the tests and thus the code quality, because a minor problem can cause such a big impact and make a number of tests fail.

One important goal when testing software is to isolate the tests from each other. Ideally, every test has its own, minimal test environment. In practice, this means that every test requires a database with appropriate test data. This is the only way of testing workflows like sign up ⇨ confirm ⇨ login reliably. Every step must be independent from the previous tests.

Managing all these test environments, the so-called fixtures, is tedious. This effort may pay off for a few central functionalities, but the cost-benefit ratio of testing all application functionality in this way is definitely questionable.

Besides the effort required to manage and maintain all these test fixtures, the test environment must be set up for every test, which usually implies populating a test database. Depending on the application, it also can be necessary to create files in the file system or pre-populate caches with certain data to run a test. Test fixtures can become very complex at some point—for example, when you want to test how a social network deals with a user who has 50,000 friends. It is hardly possible to realistically test non-functional aspects like answering time with a reduced data set.

Acceptance Tests

System tests are usually black box tests, which means they are written and executed without any knowledge about the internals of the system being tested. Acceptance tests are system tests that are written by the customer. They make sure the software fulfills its specification and delivers the expected functionality.

Acceptance tests, at least with respect to the functional aspects, can be automated using a tool like Selenium. Even if you develop software for your own use, you should consider writing acceptance tests, because this forces you to think about the functionality from an end user's point of view, without worrying about implementation issues. This fits the test-driven development (TDD) paradigm, by the way.

The most important advantage of acceptance tests is that they can point out where the software does not fulfill its specification. White box tests are based on the existing code and focus on code coverage and path coverage to find missing test cases. Because no code exists for missing functionality, no white box test can point out the problem. Only a black box test that is based on the software specification can point at the missing code.

Limits of System Tests

Some non-functional aspects like layout defects or lack of usability cannot be tested automatically. It might be possible to create screenshots while testing and compare different versions, but no computer can replace the human eye when it comes to judging how perceptible a certain design element is or whether the whole design is harmonic.

Especially in projects that run over the course of several months or even years, testing that cannot start until the software is almost done can be problematic. When tests are automated and no manual testing is performed, it is no problem to repeat the tests as often as needed as the software grows. Still, it takes quite a while until the tests can be run. Starting testing earlier in the development process is desirable.

System tests are slow because they require a complex test environment, and all components of the application from database to browser are involved. It may not be a problem to run a test that runs for some hours when rolling a release.

After all, automated tests are still much faster than manual tests. But system tests are not well suited to providing developers with quick feedback by telling them whether a change has introduced an unwanted side effect. They cannot easily be executed concurrently, because they usually depend on databases, caches, and potentially files in the file system. If multiple tests come amiss, errors might occur that are almost impossible to reproduce. This is the exact opposite of what system tests are intended for.

UNIT TESTS

As opposed to end-to-end tests that test the whole application, unit tests only test a part of an application. Mostly a single class is tested, but often testing includes an aggregate object or even a whole architectural layer of the application. Unit tests are usually white box tests, because they are written based on the code to test.

Many developers want to reach the goal of writing unit tests with a high code coverage, which means that every line of the production code should be executed when running the tests. However, this code coverage is line-based, which does not take into account that code usually has multiple execution paths. The Npath Software Testing complexity metric that was introduced in Chapter 1 measures the number of execution paths of a code unit. This corresponds to the number of tests that are required to not only execute each line of code, but to achieve full path coverage. The PHP extension Xdebug can gather code coverage statistics that can be processed by PHPUnit and be rendered as HTML or saved as XML.

Code coverage alone does not mean that tests are extensive; it only shows parts of the code that are untested. There is currently no tool for PHP that can create path coverage statistics, but Xdebug and PHPUnit may support this in the future. For now, however, developers are forced to look at the code to test and figure out which execution paths are available and how to test them. The more complex the production code gets, the more difficult this is. By breaking down the code into smaller pieces, the number of required tests can be drastically reduced, as the following example shows:

```php
function a($a, $b, $c, $d)
{
    if ($a) {
      // ...
    }
    if ($b) {
        // ...
    }
    if ($c) {
        // ...
```

```
    }
    if ($d) {
        // ...
    }
}
```

The function `a()` has an NPath complexity of 16, because every `if` doubles the number of execution paths. Thus, 16 test cases are required to achieve full path coverage for the given function.

If we split the function into two smaller functions, we find that they both have an NPath complexity of just four:

```
function a($a, $b)
{
    if ($a) {
        // ...
    }
    if ($b) {
        // ...
    }
}
function b($c, $d)
{
    if ($c) {
        // ...
    }
    if ($d) {
        // ...
    }
}
```

Now, eight tests are sufficient. As we can see, it does definitely pay off to write short methods with few execution paths and to test them separately from each other.

Unit tests should execute quickly so every developer can rerun them after each change to the code and get immediate feedback on whether the code still works as expected. If test-driven development is practiced, the tests will be written before the production code. This forces developers to focus on the API instead of the implementation. Development starts with failing tests, because the functionality has not been implemented yet. By definition, a feature is completed when all its tests pass.

Test-driven development helps developers solve the concrete problem instead of trying to generalize. Thus, TDD can significantly increase productivity, because no speculative features and special cases that might be required in the future are implemented.

Even when no test-driven development is used, unit tests should always be written on the same day as the production code. As we will see later, code with architectural shortcomings is usually hard to test. Many developers make the mistake of not writing unit tests instead of modifying the architecture of the production code, so it becomes easier to write unit tests for it. Not writing unit tests should be avoided at any cost, because it does not become easier to write unit tests without changing the production code. If no unit tests are available to make sure that defects are not introduced while refactoring the code, nobody will dare to modify the production code in the future. A piece of unmaintainable legacy code is born.

Any problems that turn up while writing tests are usually signs of bad code. Conversely, good code is easy to test. Good unit tests are thus a strong indicator of high internal quality of the code.

Return Values

Basically, every automated test is just a comparison between a calculated value and a stored, known good result. Let's look at a simple function that adds two values:

```php
function add($a, $b)
{
    if (!is_numeric($a) || !is_numeric($b)) {
        throw new InvalidArgumentException('Not a number');
    }
    return $a + $b;
}
```

Writing a unit test for this function is trivial, at least as long as the code has no further dependencies.

```php
class CalculatorTest extends PHPUnit_Framework_TestCase
{
    public function testAddReturnsSumOfTwoIntegers()
    {
        $this->assertEquals(7, add(3, 4));
    }

    /**
     * @expectedException InvalidArgumentException
     */
    public function testAddThrowsExceptionWhenFirstParameterIsNotNumeric()
    {
        add('nonsense', 4);
    }
    /**
     * @expectedException InvalidArgumentException
     */
    public function testAddThrowsExceptionWhenSecondParameterIsNotNumeric()
    {
        add(3, 'nonsense');
    }
}
```

This example shows how a unit test for PHPUnit should be written:

➤ All tests for the `Calculator` are embraced in the class `CalculatorTest`.

➤ `CalculatorTest` inherits from `PHPUnit_Framework_TestCase`.

➤ The tests are public methods with a name starting with `test`.

➤ Inside the test methods, assertions like `assertEquals()` are used to compare calculated values with expected values.

The `CalculatorTest` example also shows that it is quite possible to write unit tests for procedural code. If `add()` were a method of a class `Calculator`, the test would look almost the same.

At first glance, it may seem over the top to write unit tests for a simple function like add(). However, the unit test makes sure not only that the function returns a sensible value, but that it can be repeated at any time to make sure the code still works as expected after refactoring. This makes it possible to avoid regressions. The true value of a unit test shows over time, when the tests suddenly tell the developer that a seemingly harmless change has altered the behavior of the code.

Another advantage of writing unit tests for simple functions like add() is that you can find out—in a safe environment, so to speak—how the code behaves for unexpected input. If non-numeric values are passed as parameters, for example, an exception should be thrown.

It is also worth thinking about bounds. What happens when the first parameter is the highest value that can be represented with a 32- or 64-bit integer? You might expect an overflow, but in fact PHP uses a float instead, which means that the range is bigger, but precision is lost. It is certainly better to write a unit test to find out how code behaves rather than debug a consequential error in the application.

Exceptions are not real return values, but for the purpose of testing, we can treat them like return values. The annotation @expectedException makes PHPUnit generate an implicit assertion that resembles the following code:

```
public function testAddThrowsExceptionWhenFirstParameterIsNotNumeric()
{
try {
add('nonsense', 4);
$this->fail(/* ... */);
}
catch (Exception $e) {
$this->assertType('InvalidArgumentException', $e);
}
}
```

If no exception is thrown when add() is called, the test fails.

Dependencies

Unfortunately, we do not live (or write code) in a perfect world, where all unit tests are as simple as the one shown in the previous section. In real life, code has dependencies, usually even more than we want it to. These include:

- ➤ Constants (global constants or class constants)
- ➤ Global variables (accessed by global or $GLOBALS)
- ➤ Superglobal variables
- ➤ Functions (user-defined or built-in)
- ➤ Classes (user-defined or built-in)
- ➤ Static methods
- ➤ Static attributes
- ➤ Objects

We can test code only when all its dependencies are fulfilled. Implicit dependencies are problematic, because they can be determined only by reading the source code. It is preferable to make dependencies explicit in the form of constructor and method parameters that have type hints. This technique is called *dependency injection.*

If interfaces are used as type hints instead of class names, the class is not coupled to a specific implementation, but only the promise that the passed object will have certain public methods that can be called for sure.

While it is rather trivial to deal with implicit, global dependencies for a single, isolated class, these dependencies quickly turn into a nightmare as the code gets more complex. Cascading global dependencies can make seemingly harmless code changes cause problems that show up in a different program area, which makes these kinds of problems extremely hard to debug.

Using explicit dependencies not only makes the code easier to test, but also helps to write objects with a single, clearly defined responsibility. The code is easier to use and to reuse, because the API's method signatures clearly tell which dependencies a class has. Using interfaces increases loose coupling of code.

Side Effects

Procedural and object-oriented programming both rely on side effects. A typical side effect would be to change a variable in the global or in some outer scope. This implies changing the system state, which in imperative programs is represented by all global and local variables.

In the previous section, we showed an example of a function that just returns a return value, but causes no side effects whatsoever. In reality, however, this is a rare case. In most cases, code invokes methods in other objects, causing side effects that usually do not directly influence the return value. With regard to testability, side effects are therefore quite an issue.

If the side effects of a function or method can be limited to interaction with other objects that have been passed as parameters (Law of Demeter), side effects are not really troublesome anymore in unit tests, as we will soon see.

All global and implicit dependencies like static method calls not only make testing harder, but also make it very hard to predict the application's behavior as the code gets more complex.

REAL-LIFE EXAMPLE

We are going to write unit tests for a controller of a fictitious MVC framework and demonstrate how decoupling of code and reducing dependencies increase the testability. Some refactorings will almost magically make the code much easier to test.

We want to test a method of an MVC controller that is responsible for the first step to resetting a user's password. An e-mail containing a URL to visit is sent to the user. The URL contains a random code. In the second step, which we don't show, a new password is generated and transmitted after the given URL has been visited.

We will not show you the full code of the controller, but only the method we are going to test. To keep the listings simple, we will also leave out irrelevant code from all the other classes that we show.

Please keep in mind that the following examples are not production code. For didactic reasons, we have deliberately made some architectural mistakes that we are going to fix now, step by step:

```
class UserController
{
    public function resetPasswordAction()
    {
        if (!isset($_POST['email'])) {
            return new ErrorView(
                'resetPassword', 'No email specified'
            );
        }
        $db = new PDO(Configuration::get('DSN'));
        $statement = $db->prepare(
            'SELECT * FROM Users WHERE email=:email;'
        );
        $statement->bindValue(
            ':email', $_POST['email'], PDO::PARAM_STR
        );
        $statement->execute();
        $record = $statement->fetch(PDO::FETCH_ASSOC);
        if ($record === FALSE) {
            return new ErrorView(
                'resetPassword',
                'No user with email ' . $_POST['email']
            );
        }
        $code = CryptHelper::getConfirmationCode();
        $statement = $db->prepare(
            'UPDATE Users SET code=:code WHERE email=:email;'
        );
        $statement->bindValue(
            ':code', $code, PDO::PARAM_STR
        );
        $statement->bindValue(
            ':email', $_POST['email'], PDO::PARAM_STR
        );
        $statement->execute();
        mail(
            $_POST['email'],
            'Password Reset',
            'Confirmation code: ' . $code
        );
        return new View('passwordResetRequested');
    }
}
```

First, we check whether a POST variable e-mail exists. If it does not, we return an instance of ErrorView with an appropriate error message. This is a simplification, of course, because error messages are not always presented by a special view, and when we process forms, more than one error at a time can occur.

If an e-mail address has been specified via POST, we try to find the user with that e-mail address in the database. If no user is found, we return an instance of ErrorView with an appropriate error message. Otherwise, a random confirmation code is calculated and stored in the database. This makes it possible to find the user later, using the confirmation code as search criterion.

Now we send a confirmation e-mail to the user. To keep things simple, this e-mail contains only the confirmation code. In reality, the e-mail would contain some explanatory text and a clickable link with the confirmation code as URL parameter.

Finally, an instance of View is returned that has been parameterized with the name of the view script that we want to display. This view script would normally render text asking the user to check his e-mail.

As mentioned before, this example is incomplete. We currently do not know whether saving the data to the database was successful. We also do not check whether a confirmation code has already been stored with the user record. We assume that the confirmation code will be deleted from the database after a new password is generated.

The global configuration contains a static method that provides access to all configuration settings. These settings are stored in an associative array:

```
class Configuration
{
    protected static $values = array();
    public static function init(array $values)
    {
      self::$values = $values;
    }
    public static function get($key)
    {
        if (!isset(self::$values[$key])) {
            throw new Exception('No such key');
        }
        return self::$values[$key];
    }
}
```

As in common MVC frameworks, we use a generic class View that requires the name of a view script as a parameter:

```
class View
{
    protected $viewScript;
    public function __construct($viewScript)
    {
        $this->viewScript = $viewScript;
    }
}
```

The derived class ErrorView has an additional constructor parameter, namely the error message:

```
class ErrorView extends View
{
    protected $errorMessage;
    public function __construct($viewScript, $errorMessage)
    {
        $this->errorMessage = $errorMessage;
```

```
            parent::__construct($viewScript);
        }
    }
```

To keep the example simple, we ignore the actual implementation of View and the view script.

A helper class CryptHelper exists with a method to generate a random confirmation code:

```
class CryptHelper
{
    protected static $salt = '...';
    public static function getConfirmationCode()
    {
        return sha1(uniqid(self::$salt, TRUE));
    }
}
```

The generated confirmation codes may not be sequential or predictable. They must be unique at least as long as a password reset is unconfirmed.

Analyzing the Code to Test

The controller that we want to test has quite a few dependencies, besides some built-in PHP functions that we just rely on:

➤   The POST variable email

➤   The DSN key in Configuration

➤   The class PDO (and thus the PDO [PHP Data Objects] extension)

➤   Depending on the content of the POST variable email, the classes CryptHelper and View, or the class ErrorView

➤   Sending e-mail

All dependencies are implicit, so we can take them into account only in a white box test. Strictly speaking, there are even more implicit dependencies: The code requires a database with a table Users, containing at least the columns code and email. Depending on the situation, a record for the given e-mail address must exist in this table.

The controller returns an instance of View, but also causes side effects by writing to the database and sending e-mail.

When running the method resetPasswordAction(), the following errors can occur:

➤   The POST request does not contain an e-mail address.

➤   The configuration does not contain a DSN.

➤   The database is not available.

➤   The database does not contain a table Users, or this table is missing one of the columns email or code.

➤   The database does not contain a user with the given e-mail address.

➤ Writing to the database with the UPDATE statement fails.

➤ The e-mail cannot be sent.

The current controller code ignores some of these errors. We do not check whether the UPDATE statement was successful or whether the mail has been sent successfully.

The enumeration also does not take into account that one of the classes Configuration, CryptHelper, View, or ErrorView might not exist. Because this would lead to an unconditional fatal error, we do not really have to write a unit test. It is more of an integration problem anyway. The same holds true for problems with the database schema. The resulting SQL errors would quickly point us to the source of the problem, at least as long as we actually look at the database error messages, which we do not do right now.

The controller has an NPath complexity of 4. Because both if statements contain a return statement, the following three execution paths are relevant for us:

➤ No e-mail address is given

➤ No user found for given e-mail address

➤ The happy path, where everything works fine

Setting Up a Test Environment

Every unit test requires a test environment, also called a *fixture*. Unit test fixtures tests should be as simple as possible. Complex fixtures are a strong indicator for bad internal quality of the tested code.

To test the controller—or the resetPasswordAction() method, to be specific—we need a database with a Users table containing at least the columns email and code. We use a SQLite database, because SQLite is available in PHP by default and requires no external database server. The simplified database schema stored in the file schema.sql looks like this:

```
CREATE TABLE "Users" (
    "id" INTEGER PRIMARY KEY AUTO_INCREMENT NOT NULL,
    "username" VARCHAR UNIQUE NOT NULL,
    "email" VARCHAR UNIQUE NOT NULL,
    "code" VARCHAR
);
```

Now we need a SQLite database. Ideally, we use an in-memory database, because this makes the test run faster and does not add any dependency to a file system. In addition, we do not have to worry about deleting the database when the test ends. A further advantage, which should not be underestimated, is that we can run an arbitrary number of unit tests in parallel, without having to worry about tests accessing the same database:

```
$db = new PDO('sqlite::memory:');
$db->exec(file_get_contents(__DIR__ . '/schema.sql'));
```

Now we create a test user in the database:

```
$db->exec(
    "INSERT INTO Users (username, email)
```

```
    VALUES ('John Doe', 'user@example.com');"
);
```

Because the controller reads the Data Source Name (DSN) from the configuration, we have to initialize it accordingly:

```
Configuration::init(array('DSN' => 'sqlite::memory:'));
```

To simulate a form with an e-mail address field submitted by a POST request, we set $ POST['email'] to a suitable e-mail address:

```
$_POST['email'] = 'user@example.com';
```

Now we can execute the controller:

```
$controller = new UserController;
$view = $controller->resetPasswordAction();
```

Most of these initializations would be the front controller's responsibility. Because we want to test the controller in isolation, however, we do not utilize a front controller. Good frameworks help the developer to test objects independently in isolation.

The return value is easy to check, because resetPasswordAction() returns an instance of View on success and an instance of ErrorView on error.

So we write two tests:

```
class UserControllerTest extends PHPUnit_Framework_TestCase
{
    protected function setUp()
    {
        $this->db = new PDO('sqlite::memory:');
        $this->db->exec(
            file_get_contents(__DIR__ . '/schema.sql')
        );
        $this->db->exec(
            "INSERT INTO Users (username, email)
            VALUES ('John Doe', 'user@example.com');"
        );
        Configuration::init(array('DSN' => 'sqlite::memory:'));
            $this->controller = new UserController;
    }
    protected function tearDown()
    {
        unset($this->db);
        unset($this->controller);
        Configuration::init(array());
        $_POST = array();
    }
    public function testDisplaysErrorViewWhenNoEmailAddressGiven()
    {
        $_POST['email'] = '';
        $view = $this->controller->resetPasswordAction();
        $this->assertType('ErrorView', $view);
    }
    public function testDisplaysViewWhenEmailAddressGiven()
```

```
    {
        $_POST['email'] = 'user@example.com';
        $view = $this->controller->resetPasswordAction();
        $this->assertType('View', $view);
    }
}
```

Right now, we cannot distinguish between a missing e-mail address and a non-existing user, because in both cases, an instance of ErrorView is returned. We could analyze the text of the error message, but in reality we would probably use subclasses of ErrorView or introduce a class representing an error message, and create two subclasses of this class. Because we know it's easy to distinguish between both errors, we just ignore this problem for now and deal with it when we have to.

All test methods are executed independently from each other. PHPUnit executes the setUp() method before each test method. setUp() is responsible for setting up the fixture. After executing the test method, tearDown() is executed to destroy the test fixture. Because we have to populate $_POST differently for each test case, we have not put this into the setUp() method.

We do not supply an e-mail address to the first test case, to force the first if statement to return from the method. In the second test case, we supply an e-mail address, so the method is completed successfully. We store "John Doe" to the database in setUp(), after all.

It is important to make sure that tearDown() destroys the test fixture properly, especially when the tested code has dependencies on $_POST or Configuration.

Neglecting to clean up after each test case can quickly lead to spurious test results, because the test isolation is violated.

Avoid Global Dependencies

Our controller requires a central configuration to retrieve the DSN from. This forces us to initialize Configuration with sensible defaults for each test case. This is not as easy as it may seem, because we have to read the controller code to figure out which values are read from Configuration.

The question is this: Does the controller really have to know that a configuration object exists? Because only one value is being read, the dependency on a central class like Configuration does not really seem justified. It is better to make the DSN a constructor parameter of the controller:

```
class UserController
{
    protected $dsn;
    public function __construct($dsn)
    {
        $this->dsn = $dsn;
    }
    // ...
}
```

Now the controller does not need to know about Configuration, so we can remove its initialization from setUp() and the resetting from tearDown(), respectively:

```
class UserControllerTest extends PHPUnit_Framework_TestCase
{
```

```
    protected function setUp()
    {
        $this->db = new PDO('sqlite::memory:');
        $this->db->exec(
            file_get_contents(__DIR__ . '/schema.sql')
        );
        $this->db->exec(
            "INSERT INTO Users (username, email)
            VALUES ('John Doe', 'user@example.com');"
        );
        $this->controller = new UserController('sqlite::memory:');
    }
    protected function tearDown()
    {
        unset($this->db);
        unset($this->controller);
        $_POST = array();
    }
}
```

We have improved the application design by removing a dependency of the controller. The responsi-bility to provide the controller with a sensible DSN has been shifted to the code that instantiates the controller.

Test Independently from Data Sources

The controller's dependency on a database is a big problem, because we mix different concerns that should be separated into two distinct layers of the application, namely data access and logic.

As of now, we cannot test the controller without a database. Because we use SQLite, the unit tests do not require an external database server, but as soon as we have to use database-specific features, we will run into trouble.

It is desirable to keep the unit tests independent from the database, which means separating the different concerns of data access and logic. To achieve this, we simply move the code that is access-ing the database to a new class. Because we deal with only one database table, using a Table Data Gateway design pattern is a good idea.

> **TABLE DATA GATEWAY**
>
> An object acting as a gateway to one database table. One instance manages all records in the table. (Martin Fowler, *Patterns of Enterprise Application Architecture* [Addison-Wesley Professional, 2002 ISBN 978-0321127426].)

The new class extends `TableDataGateway`, and we will call it `UsersTableDataGateway`. The base class, which is not really relevant in this example, could contain helper methods like parameter replacement or construction of WHERE clauses:

```
class UsersTableDataGateway extends TableDataGateway
{
    protected $db;
```

```php
    public function __construct(PDO $db)
    {
        $this->db = $db;
    }
    public function findUserByEmail($email)
    {
        $statement = $this->db->prepare(
            'SELECT * FROM Users WHERE email=:email;'
        );
        $statement->bindValue(':email', $email, PDO::PARAM_STR);
        $statement->execute();
            return $statement->fetch(PDO::FETCH_ASSOC);
    }
    public function updateUserWithConfirmationCode($email, $code)
    {
        $statement = $this->db->prepare(
            'UPDATE Users SET code=:code WHERE email=:email;'
        );
        $statement->bindValue(':code', $code, PDO::PARAM_STR);
        $statement->bindValue(':email', $email, PDO::PARAM_STR);
        $statement->execute();
    }
}
```

The second method is still lacking a check whether the UPDATE statement was successful. To achieve this, we can either analyze the SQL error code or configure PHP to throw exceptions when a database error occurs. For PDO, this is easy to achieve:

```php
$this->db->setAttribute(PDO::ATTR_ERRMODE, PDO::ERRMODE_EXCEPTION);
```

A failing UPDATE statement now causes a PDOException that must be caught and handled elsewhere in the code.

The controller does not communicate with the database anymore; instead, it has a dependency on TableDataGateway:

```php
class UserController
{
    protected $gateway;
    public function __construct(TableDataGateway $gateway)
    {
        $this->gateway = $gateway;
    }
    public function resetPasswordAction()
    {
        // ...
        $record = $this->gateway->findUserByEmail(
            $_POST['email']
        );
        // ...
        $this->gateway->updateUserWithConfirmationCode(
            $_POST['email'], $code
        );
        // ...
    }
}
```

Because all methods that interact with the database are now encapsulated in one class, we can replace this class with one that does not talk to a database for test purposes:

```
class MockUsersTableDataGateway extends TableDataGateway
{
    public function findUserByEmail($email)
    {
        return FALSE;
    }
}
```

We create another subclass of `TableDataGateway`, overwriting the method `findUserByEmail()` with an implementation that unconditionally always returns FALSE. Mock objects like this one are simple throwaway objects that do not contain real logic and do not make any decisions, but just offer a certain API so type hints work, because the mock object is a subclass of the object it replaces.

Mock objects return hard-coded data instead of communicating with external resources. Mock objects are used instead of the "real" objects in unit tests to save time and execute less code that is not tested directly. Ideally, only one object is tested, with all dependencies replaced by mock objects. This reduces the number of potential error sources.

Our unit tests no longer require a database. It does not matter which e-mail address we specify, because the mock object pretends not to find the record in the database anyway. Now we'll test the execution path that does not find the given e-mail address:

```
class UserControllerTest extends PHPUnit_Framework_TestCase
{
    protected function setUp()
    {
        $this->gateway = new MockUsersTableDataGateway;
        $this->controller = new UserController($this->gateway);
    }
    protected function tearDown()
    {
        unset($this->controller);
        unset($this->gateway);
        $_POST = array();
    }
    public function testDisplaysErrorViewWhenNoUserFound()
    {
        $_POST['email'] = 'nonsense';
        $result = $this->controller->resetPasswordAction();
        $this->assertType('ErrorView', $result);
    }
}
```

If we had implemented the gateway with a static method like `UsersTableDataGateway::findUserByEmail()`, a class name would have been hard-coded in the controller, which makes it impossible for us to use a mock object. Thanks to a new feature in PHP 5.3, namely Late Static Binding, we can replace the hard-coded class name with a variable, which in turn allows for calling the static methods in a different class for testing purposes:

```
class UserController
{
```

```
    protected $gatewayClass = 'UsersTableDataGateway';
    public function setGatewayClass($className)
    {
        $this->gatewayClass = $className;
    }
    public function resetPasswordAction()
    {
        $gatewayClass = $this->gatewayClass;
        // ...
        $record = $gatewayClass::findUserByEmail($_POST['email']);
        // ...
        $gatewayClass::updateUserWithConfirmationCode(
            $_POST['email'], $code
        );
        // ...
    }
}
class UserControllerTest extends PHPUnit_Framework_TestCase
{
    protected function setUp()
    {
        $this->controller = new UserController;
        $this->controller->setGatewayClass(
            'MockUsersTableDataGateway'
        );
    }
    // ...
}
```

There are a few issues with this, however. First, you do not know whether the value passed to setGatewayClass() is a valid class name. Even if it is, there is no guarantee that this class has findUserByEmail() and updateUserWithConfirmationCode() methods with appropriate signatures. When replacing an object by a mock for testing purposes, these two problems are not an issue, because the type hints in the constructor of UserController ensure that the passed (mock) object has a correct type. Also, a static gateway might have a state that violates test isolation.

PHPUnit executes each test case independently, but within one PHP process. A class that has been initialized once would have to be explicitly reset in tearDown() using a reset() method, or we would have to deal with global state.

As you can see, using static classes has no real advantages, and it bears some risks and has disadvantages. So you should write code as if static methods did not exist.

To create another test case that tests the controller's behavior when the UPDATE statement goes wrong and an exception is thrown, we can use the following mock object, which unconditionally throws an appropriate exception:

```
class MockUsersTableDataGateway extends TableDataGateway
{
    public function findUserByEmail($email)
    {
        return array(
            'id'       => 42,
            'username' => 'John Doe',
            'email'    => 'user@example.com',
```

```
        'code'      => NULL
    );
}
public function updateUserWithConfirmationCode($email, $code)
{
    throw new PDOException(/* ... */);
}
}
```

A mock object is usually used only for one test case. This leads to a large number of mock objects that we have to write and maintain. Any change to the API of the mocked object requires us to adapt all derived mock objects.

STUBS AND MOCK OBJECTS

A stub is an object that replaces the real object for testing purposes. Methods can be configured to return certain values. A mock object also allows the definition of expectations.

Stubs and mocks are two ways of replacing an object for testing purposes. *xUnit Test Patterns: Refactoring Test Code* defines not only test stubs and mock objects, but also the variants fake object, dummy object, and test spy. (Gerard Meszaros, *xUnit Test Patterns: Refactoring Test Code* [Addison-Wesley, 2007. ISBN 978-0-131-49505-0].)

To make the maintenance of mock objects easier, PHPUnit can create mock objects programmatically on the fly. This is more robust, because changes to the mocked class influence the mock object less. It also makes test code more readable:

```
class UserControllerTest extends PHPUnit_Framework_TestCase
{
    protected $usersGateway;
    protected function setUp()
    {
        $this->usersGateway = $this->getMock(
            'UsersTableDataGateway', array(), array(), '', FALSE
        );
        // ...
    }
    // ...
    public function testDisplaysErrorViewWhenNoUserFound()
    {
        $this->usersGateway
            ->expects($this->once())
            ->method('findUserByEmail')
            ->will($this->returnValue(FALSE));
        // ...
    }
}
```

In `setUp()`, we have PHPUnit create a mock object for the `TableDataGateway` class. The method `getMock()` expects up to seven parameters, but all except the first one are optional. The first parameter is the name of the class to mock. By default, all methods are mocked, which means they are replaced by empty methods that do nothing. The second parameter lists methods that should be mocked. If it is given, only the listed methods are mocked. The third parameter contains an array of values that are passed as constructor parameters to the mocked object. The fourth parameter is a string that represents the mock object's class name. If this string is empty, a random name is used for the mocked class. The fifth parameter is a Boolean value that controls whether the constructor of the mocked class is called. In our case, it is important to pass FALSE; otherwise, we would have to pass a PDO instance as constructor parameter. The full documentation of all parameters can be found in the *PHPUnit Manual* by Sebastian Bergmann, which is available at `http://www.phpunit .de/manual/current/en/index.html`.

Of course, we can (and have to) add at least some functionality to a mock object. PHPUnit offers a so-called fluent interface that allows for nested method calls to define expectations in a way that they almost make up a readable sentence. In the above example, the mock object expects the method `findUserByEmail()`, which returns the value FALSE, to be called exactly once. PHPUnit automatically generates the source code for the mock object, which probably looks similar to the code we have written by hand. Because the mock object is a subclass of the mocked class, all type hints are fulfilled and the mock can be used instead of the real thing at any time.

PHPUnit creates implicit assertions from the expectations. If the method `findUserByEmail()` is not called, or is called more than once when executing `testDisplaysErrorViewWhenNoUserFound()`, the test fails.

We have now "simplified" the problem of reading a user for a given e-mail address from a database, to asking another object whether a user exists for the given e-mail address. We do not really care whether this object talks to a database or any other external data source.

A simple refactoring, namely moving a few lines of code to a new class, has greatly improved the application architecture. The two different concerns—data access and logic—are now cleanly separated from each other. This increases the testability. We can now test the logic independently from a data source and do not have to deal with database fixtures anymore.

Testing Asynchronous Events

Let's look at the next problem, namely the sending of e-mails by the controller. This is an asynchronous communication with an external system; the `mail()` function passes the e-mail to send to a mail transfer agent (MTA). On Unix systems, this is normally done by calling `sendmail`.

Within the PHP program, we cannot detect when and if the MTA actually sends this e-mail. The Boolean return value of `mail()` only tells whether the e-mail to send was successfully handed off to the MTA. A FALSE is thus a sure sign that sending the mail failed, but a TRUE does not mean that the mail was actually sent; it may have been only handed off to the MTA.

Sending e-mail asynchronously has an advantage: The PHP program does not have to wait until the e-mail is sent. A busy mail server could make the PHP program wait longer than the end user is willing to wait for the next HTML page to render in his browser. A thorough test of the mail sending process thus requires integration tests. One could create a special e-mail account that is checked automatically or even manually. Sending of e-mail is asynchronous, so an automated check is not trivial to implement, because you can never tell whether the mail has already been received or how long you still need to wait.

Because sending e-mail is a critical functionality for most web applications, you could consider monitoring the live system to make sure e-mails are actually sent. A production system could send an e-mail to a special account every five minutes, and another program could poll this account and raise an alarm when no e-mail was received for, say, 10 minutes. This alarm still does not guarantee that no e-mails are sent. Network failures or a problem with the receiving MTA could also be the reason.

For many larger applications, critical functionality like registration or login are continuously monitored in the live system. Besides the lost revenue and lost reputation, few things are more annoying for an Internet company than end users calling to inform the company that their site does not work.

If we test sending e-mails indirectly by asking a server to send an e-mail and use a client to ask another server whether it has received that mail, many different components are involved in the test. A failing test can thus not tell us where an error occurred. The only way to increase the reliability and also the significance of a test is to reduce the number of components that are involved and avoid indirect testing.

When running unit tests, it would be possible to configure PHP in such a way that, instead of using a real MTA to actually send mail, the mail is only logged.

This would allow us to test without time delay whether e-mails were actually sent. The unit test now has a dependency on the file system, though, because the e-mails must be logged somewhere. If multiple tests that send e-mail run concurrently, it is difficult to tell who sent which e-mail. Thus the dependency on the file system violates the test isolation.

A much better idea is to move the `mail()` function call to a new method or function. Many developers use a global constant that puts the program in test mode:

```
function send_mail()
{
    if (TEST_MODE) {
        log(/* ... */);
    } else {
    mail(/* ... */);
    }
}
```

Such a solution does work, but misconfiguring the constant TEST_MODE is an additional source of errors, which is a disadvantage. If other parts of the application contain similar case differentiations, the system might not work as expected as soon as the test mode is activated. In the above example, no more e-mails would be sent. So it is much better to perform additional logging in the test mode:

```
function send_mail()
{
    if (TEST_MODE) {
        log(/* ... */);
```

```
        }
        mail(/* ... */);
    }
```

This, however, means that real e-mails will be sent when running a unit test. In most cases, customers should not be bothered with test e-mails, so the code that sends e-mails should be replaced by a mock object for unit testing purposes. The mock object, of course, does not send e-mail. Similar to what we did in the last section, the test only makes sure that we ask to send e-mail. We do not care whether e-mail is actually being sent.

The class `Mailer` is particularly simple:

```
class Mailer
{
    public function send($recipient, $subject, $content)
    {
        return mail($recipient, $subject, $content);
    }
}
```

The controller now has a new dependency, namely a dependency on `Mailer`. We have to change the constructor accordingly:

```
class UserController
{
    protected $gateway;
    protected $mailer;
    public function __construct(TableDataGateway $gateway, Mailer $mailer)
    {
        $this->gateway = $gateway;
        $this->mailer = $mailer;
    }
    // ...
}
```

In the `resetPasswordAction()` method, we replace the `mail()` call by a call of the `send()` method in `Mailer`:

```
class UserController
{
    public function resetPasswordAction()
    {
        // ...
        $this->mailer->send(
            $_POST['email'],
            'Password Reset',
            'Confirmation code: ' . $code
        );
        // ...
    }
}
```

The class `Mailer` can be tested with separate unit tests, to make sure it can really send e-mails. The advantage is that e-mails need only be sent to a single test account, rather than the e-mail addresses of the real users. If `Mailer` uses SMTP instead of the `mail()` function, we could record the communication between `Mailer` and a real mail server, just to replace it by a mock object for the unit test. Chapters 7 and 9 describe this process in greater detail.

Again, we have improved the application's architecture just by a simple refactoring. We can change the implementation of `Mailer` at any time—for example, to send e-mail by SMTP. Any additional parameters that might be required become constructor parameters of the alternative implementation, so `UserController` does not have to deal with them. This works well, as long as object creation is strictly separated from object usage. If we were to instantiate `Mailer` directly in the controller, then either the controller would have to know all dependencies of `Mailer`, or we would have to read the parameters from a central configuration.

We can now write a unit test that checks whether the controller sends an e-mail to the user:

```php
class UserControllerTest extends PHPUnit_Framework_TestCase
{
    protected function setUp()
    {
        // ...
        $this->mailer = $this->getMock(
            'Mailer', array(), array(), '', FALSE
        );
        $this->controller = new UserController(
            $this->usersGateway, $this->mailer
        );
        // ...
    }
    protected function tearDown()
    {
        // ...
        unset($this->mailer);
        // ...
    }
    public function testSendsEmailToTheUser()
    {
        $_POST['email'] = 'user@example.com';
        $usersGateway
            ->expects($this->once())
            ->method('findUserByEmail')
            ->with('user@example.com')
            ->will($this->returnValue(
                array('id' => 42,
                'username' => 'John Doe',
                'email' => 'user@example.com',
                'code' => NULL)));
        $mailer
            ->expects($this->once())
            ->method('send')
            ->with('user@example.com');
        $this->controller->resetPasswordAction();
    }
}
```

This test requires a mock gateway that returns a record for the given e-mail address. The with('user@example.com') clause makes sure the controller passes the correct e-mail address to the gateway. The mock gateway acts as if it found a matching record in the database and returns it. Just like the real mailer, the mock mailer's send() method expects user@example.com as the first parameter. We ignore the additional parameters for now.

We still do not check whether sending of the mail went wrong. To do this, we have to modify the tested controller method slightly. The mock mailer can be configured to return a Boolean value by calling will($this->returnValue(FALSE).

This allows us to simulate that the actual mail sending goes wrong, without even attempting to actually send an e-mail message.

Storing Changes in the Database

If our controller finds a user matching the e-mail address given by POST, a random confirmation code is sent out by e-mail. The resetPasswordAction() method must store the confirmation code in the database, so we can match it with user accounts later.

We have already moved the whole database interaction to its own class. Now we have to make sure the controller calls the updateUserWithConfirmationCode() method with the correct parameters. To achieve this, we define another expectation for our mock object:

```
class UserControllerTest extends PHPUnit_Framework_TestCase {
    public function testStoresConfirmationCode()
    {
        $_POST['email'] = 'user@example.com';

        $this->usersGateway
          ->expects($this->once())
          ->method('findUserByEmail')
          ->with('user@example.com')
          ->will($this->returnValue(
              array('id' => 42,
                    'username' => 'John Doe',
                    'email' => 'user@example.com',
                    'code' => NULL)));

        $this->usersGateway
          ->expects($this->once())
          ->method('updateUserWithConfirmationCode')
          ->with('user@example.com');

        // ...
    }
}
```

Because we want to test the controller's side effects, but not its implementation, we do not care about the order in which methods are called in the mock gateway.

Note that we have created a new test case testStoresConfirmationCode() instead of adding another expectation to testSendsEmailToUser().Writing an individual test case for every single functional aspect is a good idea. This not only allows a failing unit test to clearly communicate what went wrong, but also makes the unit tests the documentation of all features of the tested code. A clear naming scheme for the tests helps to achieve this. When calling PHPUnit with the `--testdox` switch, test documentation is automatically generated from the test method names.

The unit test makes sure that `updateUserWithConfirmationCode()` is called for the user that was specified by POST. Until now, we have ignored the second parameter, namely the confirmation code.

Unpredictable Results

How can we make sure that a sensible confirmation code is passed when calling the method `updateUserWithConfirmationCode()`? The obvious solution is to modify the mock gateway's expectations to expect a sensible second parameter. Because `CryptHelper` returns a random value, however, defining another expectation is not possible. We cannot even make an assertion on the confirmation code, because it is only a local variable in the controller.

The solution is not making the confirmation code a public attribute of the controller or adding an accessor method, but replacing the random value by a predictable value for testing purposes. This value can then be used in the expectation.

Until now, `CryptHelper` looked like this:

```
class CryptHelper
{
    protected static $salt = '...';
    public static function getConfirmationCode()
    {
        return sha1(uniqid(self::$salt, TRUE));
    }
}
```

The `getConfirmationCode()` method is static, so we had to hard-code the class name `CryptHelper` in the controller:

```
class UserController
{
    public function resetPasswordAction()
    {
        $code = CryptHelper::getConfirmationCode();
        // ...
    }
}
```

Static methods cannot be mocked without the negative effects we mentioned earlier, so we modify `CryptHelper` to use instance methods instead of static methods:

```
class CryptHelper
{
    protected static $salt = '...';
    public function getConfirmationCode()
    {
        return sha1(uniqid(self::$salt, TRUE));
    }
}
```

CryptHelper now becomes another dependency of UserController, which can easily be replaced by a mock object:

```php
class UserControllerTest extends PHPUnit_Framework_TestCase
{
    protected function setUp()
    {
        // ...
        $this->cryptHelper = $this->getMock(
            'CryptHelper', array(), array(), '', FALSE
        );
        $this->controller = new UserController(
            $this->usersGateway, $this->mailer, $this->cryptHelper
        );
        // ...
    }
    protected function tearDown()
    {
        // ...
        unset($this->cryptHelper);
        // ...
    }
    public function testStoresConfirmationCode()
    {
        // ...
        $cryptHelper
            ->expects($this->once())
            ->method('getConfirmationCode')
            ->will($this->returnValue('123456789'));
        $this->usersGateway
            ->expects($this->once())
            ->method('updateUserWithConfirmationCode')
            ->with('user@example.com', '123456789');
        // ...
    }
}
```

We have to adapt UserController, of course:

```php
class UserController
{
    protected $gateway;
    protected $mailer;
    protected $cryptHelper;
    public function __construct(TableDataGateway $gateway,
        Mailer $mailer,
        CryptHelper $cryptHelper)
    {
        $this->gateway = $gateway;
        $this->mailer = $mailer;
        $this->cryptHelper = $cryptHelper;
    }
    public function resetPasswordAction()
    {
        // ...
        $code = $this->cryptHelper->getConfirmationCode();
```

```
        // ...
    }
}
```

The unit test does not depend on random values anymore. We use a hard-coded confirmation code instead that can easily be used as an expected value. If we needed multiple confirmation codes for one unit test, we could write a mock object that returns one value from a sequence of confirmation codes:

```
class MockCryptHelper
{
    protected $index = -1;
    protected $codes = array('...', '...', '...', ...);
    public function getConfirmationCode()
    {
        $this->index++;
        return $this->codes[$this->index];
    }
}
```

To keep the example simple, we just ignore the fact that a test might ask for more confirmation codes than the mock object holds. The mock object is freshly generated for each test, however, so this case will probably never occur.

Encapsulating Input Data

The UserController is now fully tested. Still, there is additional potential for improvements. The controller does not have any implicit dependencies on other classes anymore, but it reads input from the superglobal array $_POST.

To get rid of this last global dependency, we introduce a Request object that contains all input data:

```
class Request
{
    protected $post = array();
    public function __construct(array $post)
    {
        $this->post = $post;
    }
    public function getPost($key)
    {
        return $this->post[$key];
    }
    public function hasPost($key)
    {
        return empty($this->post[$key]);
    }
}
```

The example is again simplified. We just show the methods for POST data. A real Request object would also contain accessors for GET data, cookies, and probably all the other superglobal variables

$_SERVER, $_ENV, and $_FILES.[1] By using the Request object, the controllers and hopefully the rest of the application become independent from the superglobal variables. We have created another explicit dependency in the form of a parameter, but there are no more implicit, global dependencies in the controller:

```
class UserController
{
    public function resetPasswordAction(Request $request)
    {
        // ...
    }
}
```

Instead of passing Request to the action method, we also could make it a constructor parameter of the controller. Because we create the Request object in the test method and not in setUp(), it is better to make Request a parameter of the action method. Otherwise, we would have to modify Request to now require the input data as constructor parameters.

It is now particularly easy to fake input data:

```
class UserControllerTest extends PHPUnit_Framework_TestCase
{
    public function testDisplaysErrorViewWhenNoUserFound()
    {
        $request = new Request(
            array('email' => 'user@example.com')
        );
        $result = $controller->resetPasswordAction($request);
        // ...
    }
}
```

Encapsulating the input also makes it much easier to test complex input like file uploads in isolation. What's more, input data cannot be modified, unless we add setter methods, of course. After Request has been initialized in the application's bootstrap file, we can delete the superglobal variables to force all developers to read input from the Request object.

Further Reflections

Just as we encapsulate input data in a Request object, we can encapsulate all output in a Response object. This allows us to fully decouple the controllers from the views. Instead of setting output in the view, we can store it in the Response object. Depending on the success of the controller method, we can instantiate a suitable view object that fetches data from the Response object. This makes Response a mediator between controller and view. It is much easier to deal with cookies and headers, because they are stored instead of being output directly.

---

[1]We deliberately ignore $_REQUEST, because one can never tell where data in $_REQUEST comes from, which can quickly lead to security problems.

The actual output is generated from the information in `Response`:

```
class Response
{
    public function addError(/* ... */)
    {
    }
    // ...
}
```

All error messages are also collected in the `Response`. This way, the controller does not have to return an instance of `ErrorView` to display an error; it just has to set an appropriate error message. For testing purposes, we can either use the real `Response` object or a mock when we define the error messages as expectations. The error messages can be objects containing information about the form fields to which they refer.

CONCLUSION

Most of the value of unit tests and system tests lies in combining both. By testing small units of code, we can make sure they work as expected. When integrating tested units of code, we can focus on the interface. Because the individual code units behave very predictably, there are fewer potential sources of errors. Depending on the size of the code unit, we can distinguish between the following types of tests:

➤ Acceptance tests in the shape of end-to-end tests make sure that the software works as expected.

➤ Edge-to-edge tests—for example, when using Model-View-Controller—make sure that the Front Controller selects the correct Controller for a given request, triggers the right action, and so on.

➤ Integration tests make sure that code units that are already unit-tested work together as expected.

➤ Unit tests make sure that a code unit works in isolation, without its dependencies.

The goal of all tests is to discover problems as early as possible. A Tweet from Jason Huggins on August 22, 2009, gives a good explanation of the main difference between end-to-end tests (he calls them functional tests) and unit tests (`http://twitter.com/hugs/status/3462632802`):

"Functional tests can tell you something broke. Unit tests can tell you what broke."

The relationship between end-to-end tests, unit tests, and the internal and external quality of the tested software is elaborated on in *Growing Object-Oriented Software, Guided by Tests* (Steve Freeman and Nat Pryce, Addison-Wesley, 2009, ISBN 978-0-321-50362-6):

> *Running end-to-end tests tells us about the external quality of our system, and writing them tells us something about how well we [...] understand the domain, but end-to-end tests don't tell us how well we've written the code. Writing unit tests gives us a lot of feedback about the quality of our code, and running them tells us that we haven't broken any classes [...].*

PART II
Best Practices

3

TYPO3: The Agile Future of a Ponderous Project

Robert Lemke and Karsten Dambekalns

WHAT'S IN THIS CHAPTER?

➤ The history of TYPO3

➤ Principles and methods for the TYPO3 project

➤ Practical application of principles and methods

➤ Test scenario problems and solutions

INTRODUCTION

When we started the development of TYPO3 v5, quite a few people were astonished by the courage or—depending on the point of view—foolishness behind the project. After all, we were about to start over new after more than 10 years.

The History of TYPO3: Thirteen Years in Thirteen Paragraphs

In fall 1997, Kasper Skårhøj started to gather requirements for a system to allow his customers to update the content of their websites without influencing the design; the term *content management* was basically unknown at the time.

In spring 1998, Kasper wrote three prototypes that were more and more powerful and built up know-how. In summer of that year, the development was being commercialized under the hood of the Superfish.com brand. Strategic goals were defined and by the end of the year, Superfish.com teamed up with Saatchi & Saatchi.

In early 1999, another version of the TYPO3 kernel was written from scratch. Nobody suspected that this kernel would last for the next 10 years. During the course of the year, it became evident that Superfish.com headed in another direction, so Kasper Skårhøj left the company. By mutual agreement, he was allowed to keep all rights to TYPO3 to further develop the project on his own. To bring the work to an end, Kasper Skårhøj decided in August to work on TYPO3 for the next six months. Without the pressure of commercialization, he managed to meet his own high quality goals.

Six months turned into 12, and in August 2000 Kasper Skårhøj finally published a beta version of TYPO3 under GPL on the Internet.[1] The one-man project entered the stage of the open-source world and awaited community feedback. A few months later, a growing community existed and the development was driven by new ideas and feature requests of the users.

In summer 2001, Kasper Skårhøj cleaned up and optimized the TYPO3 kernel again. First steps were taken to ensure extensibility at a later stage. At this time, nobody paid much attention to backward compatibility.

In May 2002, following an endless beta test, the first stable version of TYPO3 was released. An extensive test in the German *PHP Magazin* followed, where TYPO3 scored well—just like in a test in the German *iX* magazine that had been published six months before. In November, another milestone followed: Version 3.5.0 had an extension manager that allowed for easy installation of extensions in TYPO3. The extension manager was also bound to survive the following years.

In 2003, the TYPO3 users wrote countless extensions for the system that were made available to other users through the TYPO3 Extension Repository—a part of the TYPO3 website that was relaunched in 2002. The Extension Manager directly interacted with this website. The TYPO3 Extension Repository grew wildly over the following years. In October 2003, the first developers got direct access to the CVS repository of the TYPO3 kernel.

Despite the success and the growing community, the development of the TYPO3 kernel was still almost exclusively done by Kasper Skårhøj. Feature requests and bug reports showed up in his mailbox and ended up in a growing text file. In 2004, another step toward more transparency was performed and a public bug tracker was introduced.

The year of the future turned out to be 2005. Toward the end of the year, a new project logo was launched, the first TYPO3 print magazine was launched, and the first TYPO3 conference took place in Karlsruhe, Germany. To pave the path technically, the leading developers of the system met in the north of Denmark for a workshop and agreed on a roadmap toward TYPO3 5.0.

In April 2006, TYPO3 4.0 was released, the most ambitious release in the history of the project. The number of developers grew, and in August, the first TYPO3 Developer Days took place in Switzerland. During this event, the TYPO3 5.0 development was officially started, and two brainstorming sessions produced a long list of ideas and necessary features.

During 2007, the work on TYPO3 4.x was kept up, and in April TYPO3 4.1 was released, while work on version 5.0 seemed to stall. In February 2008, the new framework FLOW3 was introduced.[2] It was the result of the work on TYPO3 5.0 to this date. At the same time, a subversion server and

---

[1] http://typo3.org

[2] http://flow3.typo3.org

the new project platform TYPO3 Forge[3] went online. In April, TYPO3 4.2 was released. During the TYPO3 Transition Days, a common roadmap for approximating TYPO3 4.x and 5.0 was published.

For the release of TYPO3 4.3 in spring 2009, some FLOW3 concepts were backported to make caching, MVC, templating, and object persistence available to the developers as early as possible and made the future migration to TYPO3 5.0 easier. In summer 2009, the first alpha version of FLOW3 was released, and the feedback on TYPO3 4.3 multiplied the feedback on the new concepts.

Daring to Start Over!

Why did we decide to start over from scratch? In May 2005, a group of TYPO3 developers met for a week in Denmark to discuss the future of the system, keeping far away from civilization and the Internet. A mix of brainstorming, presentations, and discussions brought the insight that radically starting over was inevitable. We had looked back on the previous years and, despite our pride in our accomplishments, could not deny the fact that the growth had led to quite a few problems:

➤   Many obsolete parameters, old code, and strange behaviors, that ensured backward compatibility

➤   Diverging architectural and programming styles

➤   Code that was based on PHP4 and did not make use of new language features

➤   Big changes that were risky, because nobody could assess possible side effects

We wanted the code base of version 5 to be fundamentally cleaned, and we planned to achieve that goal by *radical refactoring*. Highly motivated, we went back home and started to do our homework: We looked at other systems, experimented with new techniques, and analyzed our own mistakes. As a result of this, we gained the following insight: Refactoring requires a good unit test coverage, which is something that TYPO3 did not have. We briefly considered writing tests for existing code but quickly realized this would be too much effort and too risky.

So we abandoned the idea of radical refactoring by the end of 2006 and started to go down the easier path of rewriting. This was easier because we had to deal with much less code to start with. We could develop, test, and extend everything very cleanly. Compatibility with old code was by definition no longer a problem. We could use all the new techniques and paradigms that we had gotten to know in 18 months of research without any obstructions.

Now we faced a new problem: TYPO3 v4 has an extensive infrastructure that programmers can use. Suddenly, we were alone in the dark and had to deal with all the small problems like templating, working with files, storing data, and the like. This is the reason why the framework FLOW3 came into existence, initially as a basis for TYPO3 v5 and without a name of its own. After some time, we realized that this framework could also be of interest for other PHP developers. So the first spinoff of the TYPO3 project was born.

Our Experience with Testing

For the TYPO3 5.0 development, we knew from day one that we could not do without automated unit tests. This realization stems from the positive experiences that we have gained in various projects before.

---

[3]http://forge.typo3.org

The increasing number of TYPO3 extensions in the Extension Repository made us realize the importance of quality assurance. A project for reviewing extensions was started. The quality of an extension's code should be assessed based on fixed criteria like code quality, documentation, and usability. We did the first reviews with lots of vigor, but we quickly realized we would have to revisit every new version of each extension, and new extensions were created more quickly than we were able to review the existing ones. After a while, we ditched the project and chalked it up to experience.

Despite this failure, we took another shot at manual extension reviews; we thought security reviews would be much faster to perform, because you can stop after you have found the first security problem. The authors then looked for further security problems by themselves and asked us to re-review the extension after they had fixed the problems. Again, the problem was that we could not handle the amount of work within the available time.

Both attempts showed us that manually performing extensive, repetitive, and boring tasks is bound to fail.

Automated testing is possible only when suitable tests, namely unit tests, exist. The T3Unit extension was a first attempt to get the TYPO3 developers to write unit tests. The extension provides a test runner in the TYPO3 GUI and thus makes PHPUnit usable in TYPO3.

Running the tests in the context of the user interface has some big disadvantages though: Various functionality and variables are available that might not exist without a valid login. This can lead to spurious test results. What's more, some common programming practices in TYPO3 4.x caused problems. The database access is done via an object that is stored in a global variable. Parts of the system configuration are stored in a similar way. Manipulating this data as part of a test is difficult or even impossible.

In part, we made these mistakes in the early days of FLOW3. We also developed our own test runner, providing an instance of the framework to the tests. To prevent changes to this instance from affecting other tests, we have to clean up before each test, which makes the tests very slow. In addition, the FLOW3 under test and the outer FLOW3 instance running the tests mutually influence each other in some respects.

Thus, in recent years, we have become more familiar with and appreciate the value of real unit tests.

POLICIES AND TECHNIQUES

Open-source projects are quite different from commercial projects. For one thing, the development leaders of free software projects usually have a large number of highly motivated individuals at hand. On the other hand, the tasks, schedules, and quality standards cannot be enforced with traditional project management measures, because everybody involved enjoys free will. Principles and techniques thus play a much bigger role than strict guidelines and control.[4]

Based on our experience from the last 10 years in the TYPO3 project and commercial projects that we have implemented based on TYPO3 and other platforms, we have selected a few important principles and methods for the TYPO3 v5 project on which we want to elaborate.

---

[4]The most important guidelines for collaboration in the TYPO3 community are summarized in a code of conduct at `http://typo3.org/community/code-of-conduct/`.

Bittersweet Elephant Pieces

Developing complex software like TYPO3 from scratch imposes not only technical but also psychological challenges on the developers: The pressure to get everything right this time is particularly high, and thus the first brushstroke on the white canvas is really difficult. For this reason, we did not even try to specify the project as a whole and in every detail. You do not eat an elephant whole, but piece by piece.

Based on our experience, projects—especially in the open-source world—have the biggest chance for success when they are split into smaller, self-contained sub-projects. Bigger projects have the disadvantage that developers push less attractive tasks like documentation and testing to the end, which usually means that they are never completed. Thus, the bitter tasks must be intermingled with the sweet ones to form bittersweet elephant pieces.

The goals of the TYPO3 v5 development had been established in various workshops and countless discussions. Our attempt to develop objectives followed a simple backward calculation: Let's assume I want to create a new page in my CMS; what technical requirements does that imply? A lot, of course: a "page" concept, a user interface, a model-view-controller framework, object persistence, and much more. These requirements are divided into distinct projects, each with the goal of developing the simplest solution that could possibly work.

With regard to quality, this goal has prevented us from developing functionality that later turns out to be unnecessary. This is an important aspect, when one considers that unused code usually is not maintained and causes strange error messages at a completely inappropriate time.

These development goals for the TYPO3 distribution, the FLOW3 distribution, and its packages and sub-packages are maintained on our TYPO3 Forge website.

Ideally, the implementation of a new function detailed in a task does not take longer than one day; that way, we make sure that the task is not too big and can be fulfilled by a voluntary developer.

Test-Driven Development

Luckily, the PHP ecosystem has now realized that writing tests is not a waste of time; it allows for some relaxation on the due date of a project. Even when change requests or bugs occur at the last minute, the developer can still rely on the safety net of the tests and integrate his changes without any bad surprises.

We have already mentioned that one of the main reasons to redevelop TYPO3 from scratch was the fact that virtually no meaningful unit tests existed. Extensively using automated unit tests from day one was thus a pre-arranged matter for the new version. Even more important than the fact that a new functionality of a bugfix is being developed is how this is being done, namely by utilizing test-driven development (TDD).

Test-driven development is proactive quality assurance. This does not only mean that parts of the code are tested from the start; it also means that a strong focus remains on the main goals. The two ground rules state:[5]

➤ Write new code only when an automated test fails.

➤ Eliminate redundant code.

---

[5]Kent Beck. *Test-Driven Development: By Example*. Addison-Wesley, 2003. ISBN 978-0321146533.

These rules have important implications:

➤   The design must be organic, with runnable code that provides feedback between the decisions.

➤   Developers write their own tests, while they develop.

➤   The design must comprise many components with strong cohesion and loose coupling, to allow for easy testing.[6]

We talk about the positive effects later; for now the question remains: What is so special about writing tests before writing the tested code? Is there a difference, after all?

Quite a few projects are being developed following the scattershot principle: When there is still time left after developing the desired functionality, tests are being written. If the tests do not cover enough code, you have another shot at them. The problem with this approach is that one gives away all the advantages that test-driven development offers, and the tests lull the developers into a false sense of security, because the TDD mantra is ignored.[7]

The TDD Mantra

➤   **Red:** Write a test that does not work.

➤   **Green:** Make the test work as quickly as possible, regardless of which sins you have to commit.

➤   **Refactor:** Remove all redundant code that was written only to make the test work.

By repeating these three steps, we can make sure that only required functionality is being developed. In addition, we can make sure that the test actually works. Quite often, a test is developed and executed in the test runner. After it passes, the developer continues with the next test. However, the test never actually failed, so we cannot be sure whether it is going to fail when the code under test is incorrect.[8] All members of our core team are compelled to develop using test-driven methodologies whenever it is possible. Even when it may be tempting to depart from this mantra because of time constraints, this approach paid off long ago with higher quality tests and code.

Tests as Documentation

A common recurring task for all the core team members is reviewing the work of other developers in the form of patches or commits. We assess whether the code contains security or other technical problems and whether the code does what the feature promises. An experienced developer usually can do a first review without even knowing much about the actual subject matter. But to

---

[6]A system with strong cohesion is composed of components that each have exactly one clearly specified task. Loose coupling is reached when components are as independent as possible from each other and only communicate through well-defined interfaces. (Edward Yourdon and Larry Constantine. *Structured Design: Fundamentals of a Discipline of Computer Program and Systems Design.* Prentice Hall, 1979. ISBN 978-0138544713.)

[7]Kent Beck. *Test-Driven Development: By Example.* Addison-Wesley, 2003. ISBN 0-3211-4653-0.

[8]It is not our intention to bash a certain project, but you should look at the tests of well-known PHP projects. We are quite sure you can tell (probably even in our own project) which tests were written in retrospect and possibly even do not make sense anymore.

judge whether a feature is implemented correctly, he needs additional knowledge about the scope and application of the functionality. Tests are an important source of information in these kinds of code reviews, because they document the assumptions that a developer makes in his implementation. If no tests exist for a certain aspect, this functionality has probably not been implemented yet. Conversely, one can assume that all assumptions that have been made in the form of test methods apply to the code, at least as long as the tests do not fail.

The following listing shows an example for a method name of a test class that clearly tells what happens when you ask `getObject()` for an unknown object:

```
/
@test
@expectedException \F3\FLOW3\Object\Exception\UnknownObject
@author Robert Lemke <robert@typo3.org>
/
public function getObjectThrowsAnExceptionIfTheSpecifiedObjectIsNotRegistered ( ) {
// . . .
}
```

If you consistently stick to this kind of naming scheme, PHPUnit can create an agile documentation listing all assumptions that the tests make.

Continuous Integration

Manual reviews are always necessary, but they are quite an effort, so code should be reviewed manually when all other possibilities have been explored. Many problems that show up while running a test stem from the fact that some new code does not match up with the current code base, because other developers have added new code to the repository in the meantime.

Because we also faced these kinds of integration problems, we introduced the rule that new code must be committed at the end of each day, and we installed Hudson, a continuous integration server,[9] as seen in Figure 3-1.

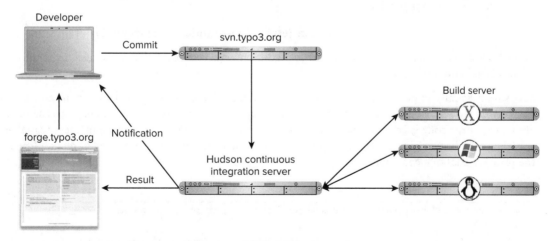

FIGURE 3-1: The CI server topology of the TYPO3 Forge

[9]Information about Hudson is available from `http://hudson-ci.org/`. You can also download Hudson from that site.

Every time a developer checks in code to the repository, Hudson starts a new build that is run separately on Windows, Linux, and MacOS servers to detect any platform-dependent problems. The results are aggregated on the central CI server and are processed for presentation on `forge.typo3.org`. At the same time, the developer and the package maintainers are informed about the success or failure of the build via Jabber.

All packages hosted on the TYPO3 Forge can use this infrastructure. In the future, all packages developed for TYPO3 v5 or FLOW3 will be published only in the official package repository when they have been thoroughly checked before. This means not only running unit tests or checking for existing documentation, but also performing further analysis that allows us to make a statement about the quality of the code. A rule set for PHP CodeSniffer[10] that monitors adherence to the coding standard is already available.[11] By all this, we hope to greatly improve the quality of extensions that will be developed for TYPO3.

Most scripts and configuration files for our Hudson implementation are available for download at the TYPO3 Forge.[12]

The communication between the developers, beyond integrating the code, plays an important role in trying to reach a good quality. Only when all involved parties are well informed about the plans of everybody else can frictional losses and integration problems be avoided (although they cannot be eradicated). To achieve this, we have created our own microblogging platform, using the open-source Twitter clone Laconica, found at `http://beat.typo3.org/`.

This enables developers to tell others what they are currently doing and where they have run into problems. This service—to a certain extent—replaces the standup meetings that the SCRUM methodology suggests and that are not possible in distributed teams.

Clean Code

> Clean code that works.
>
> **— Ron Jeffries, co-founder of eXtreme Programming**

To be honest, we all have produced code that made us wonder after a few days, weeks, or months what it is actually doing, or we've wondered what the variable name means.

Software is usually in production for many years, is adapted and extended, is being maintained by a varying team of developers, and is being read far more often than it is being written. Thus the readability of source code is crucial. Even though source code can work if it is written in a less readable way (because the computer does not really care about the readability of source code), readability is the primary goal of clean code.

---

[10]Information about PHP_CodeSniffer is available from `http://pear.php.net/package/PHP_CodeSniffer`.

[11]See `http://forge.typo3.org/projects/show/package-flow3cgl` for more information.

[12]See the Continuous Integration page at `http://forge.typo3.org/wiki/team-forge/Continuous_Integration` for more information.

To make source code readable like plain text, it is important to put lots of attention toward the naming of variables and methods. It takes hard work, but if you succeed, even the customer should be able to tell by looking at the source code whether it implements the desired business process.

If the code is readable, extending it is much easier. It is important to use a consistent naming scheme, so it is possible to "guess" the right spelling. These basic rules can help achieve this:

➤ Method and variable names are always in `lowerStudlyCaps`.

➤ Class names are always in `UpperStudlyCaps`.

➤ Setter and getter always have the form `setPropertyName()` and `getPropertyName()`.

➤ Getters for Boolean values are always named `isAttributeName()` or `hasThingName()`.

It is also important to communicate the purpose of a method through its name.

We have spent quite some time with pertinent discussions and have not refrained from widespread renaming, if it was necessary. Fear of a change (or laziness) should never prevent a sensible activity! Some examples:

➤ If `getValidator()` returns a new object, `createValidator()` is a better name.

➤ `setFactory()` seems to expect a factory instance, but a class name is expected instead. `setFactoryClassName()` would be better.

➤ `getSpecialConfiguration()` and `loadSpecialConfiguration()` do not make clear what is special about them. In this case, this is legacy, and the special can be removed; what used to be the "normal" configuration had been renamed "Setting."

In domain-driven projects (as discussed later in this chapter), the ubiquitous language is especially important. This language should be reflected in the source code and determine the choice of method and variable names.

Beginners in object-oriented programming often get the feeling that the code is an endless chain of delegations, where most methods do not really do any work. After you get used to this, it becomes obvious that this distribution of responsibilities has many advantages with respect to the maintainability of the system. One advantage is readability: A method that calls five other methods with clear and meaningful names should be easier to understand than a long method containing the source code in one piece.

Next to naming, the placement of source code is also important. We have decided on a strict rule of one class per file, and we reflect namespaces in the file system; files are always named like the class they contain. This makes it very easy to find the source code of a class, not only for developers, but also for the autoloader.

Refactoring

Code without care decays like the garden behind your house. To keep the carved out code and the elaborate system design, the code must be cherished and maintained; otherwise, programming quickly turns into tinkering and quick solutions and workarounds make structure and style vanish.

Refactoring, or modifying code without changing its behavior, is the best tool for this job. It reverses the previously described process and leads to code that has more clarity and simplicity. This works out, however, only when a few rules are kept in mind:

➤ Either we develop or refactor; we never do both at the same time.

➤ Refactoring requires unit tests as a safeguard.

➤ Work with little steps and with discipline.

The last item is simplified when commonly known refactoring patterns like the ones described by Martin Fowler are used.[13] That way, the modifications to eradicate the *code smells* (imperfections) are dismantled in small, almost trivial tasks.

Examples of code smells include:

➤ **Duplicated code:** Identical code in more than one spot in the program always bears risks and means more work when code must be changed.

➤ **Long methods:** The more code a method has, the more difficult it becomes to understand and maintain.

➤ **Big classes:** Classes containing too much code often do too much and duplicated code is often found.

If we work in little steps and use unit tests to make sure the behavior of the refactored code is not modified, the design of the software can be improved continuously while it is being developed.

By using refactoring and unit tests, we could remove almost half the code when developing FLOW3, introduce PHP namespaces, and replace existing method names with better ones, without running into any major problems.

Programming Guidelines

Clean code requires the developer to stick to certain basic rules. If individual developers stick to their personal preferences, these rules must be written down for larger projects. Only then will it become possible to quickly adapt to the rules and avoid ambiguities. Many projects have coding guidelines, usually more or less in the form of text, plus additional examples.

These guidelines usually focus on two areas: the code's look and the programming style. The former mainly deals with indentation and the position of braces, while the latter deals with the choice of method and variable names and preferred program constructs.

We have created new guidelines[14] for TYPO3 v5. To achieve this, we used the guidelines of TYPO3 v4 as a basis, adapted them to the new programming style, and added a few things that were missing or unclear in the existing rules.

---

[13]Martin Fowler. *Refactoring. Improving the Design of Existing Code*. Addison-Wesley Professional, 1999. ISBN 978-0201485677.

[14]These new guidelines are available at `http://flow3.typo3.org/documentation/coding-guidelines`.

Quite often, guidelines become rather long. Inspired by a document we found on the Internet,[15] we have summarized the most important facts of the coding guidelines in our "Coding guidelines on one page," shown in Figure 3-2. This one page gives information not only about the most important rules on where to put braces and how to indent the code, but also about type hinting and source code documentation.

If this information is not sufficient, you can still look at the original coding guidelines.

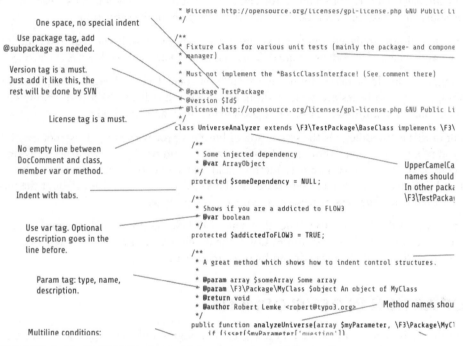

FIGURE 3-2: The FLOW3 "Coding guidelines on one page" (excerpt)

Such guidelines must be maintained. The requirements can change, new technologies come up, and ambiguities turn up. In fact, we had to revise our guidelines a few times, and we did the same for the TYPO3 v4 guidelines.

If you stick to conventions that are not fashionable anymore, there is a danger that developers will be scared off. If the developers do not stick to the guidelines, the result is a stylistic hodgepodge that makes things even more complicated. If the guidelines are changed, existing code must be adapted. Nobody expects this to happen in one task, but you should not avoid the adaptation or be afraid of anything; after all, that is why we have unit tests, right?

Domain-Driven Design

The planning of a software project directly influences the quality of the finished product. The product's quality is directly related to the question of how well it performs. This does not mean

---

[15]See "Java Coding Conventions on One Page" by William C. Wake at http://www.xp123.com/xplor/xp0002f/codingstd.gif.

the product is easy to install or bug-free (customers have the right to expect that anyway), but whether the product does what the customer needs. (This is not necessarily what the customer wants—a problem we will solve as well.)

Domain-driven design (DDD) lets you approach this goal. With the customer's help, the problem domain is analyzed to allow the developers to really understand what is going on. During this process, the customer usually develops a much clearer vision of what he or she needs, and the developers learn the customer's language. This leads to a ubiquitous language that is written down in a project glossary. This way, developers and customers can be sure they are talking about the same thing.

If the customer's needs are analyzed and the developers are disciplined, only the required functionality is developed and generalized code is avoided. This makes software lean and less error-prone.

While modeling, care should be taken not to induce an "it is done" feeling. Diagrams are drawn by hand, for example. This motivates everyone to think creatively and reduces the fear of changes to existing results. Thus, domain-driven design is a good match with agile methods.

Another result of this methodology is the separation of business processes and infrastructure in the software. If you talk to a customer about suppliers, containers, and trucks, he will (rightfully) tell you that his containers do not have a `save()` method, and that suppliers do have a number, but they do not create it by themselves. The clear separation will make decisions or revisions about the infrastructure easier even when business processes are already in existence.

In our case, this way of thinking led to the development of FLOW3 as an individual project; it is the infrastructure we need for the CMS. Within FLOW3, the development of the persistence layer that is almost invisible to the client code was driven by these requirements.

COURSE OF ACTION IN DEVELOPMENT

Talking about theory is great, but how do all these great paradigms and techniques work in practice? Does test-driven development work? Does continuous integration really help?

Developing New Code

One of the most fundamental principles of test-driven development is that code is written only when a test fails. So how should you develop new functionality? By writing the required tests first. This principle does indeed work very well in practice.

The biggest advantage—in addition to the excellent test coverage you naturally get—is that developers are forced to view new parts of the program from the user's perspective. This is because to write the test code, developers must get a feel for the new part of the program—what it does, and how it does it. Subsequently, only the code needs to be developed to finish the task, which means making the test pass.

We use PHPUnit[16] as a test framework and have added some useful features to our test base class (as discussed later in this chapter). As we previously mentioned, we initially made our tests depend on our own test runner, which was a mistake. This makes it more difficult to use standard tools like

---

[16]Find PHPUnit at `http://www.phpunit.de/`.

Phing that assume that the default test runner of PHPUnit can be used. We would strongly suggest that you fully encapsulate your tests, so it is possible to run them with a stock PHPUnit.

It is important to ask how far you should take testing. Test coverage plays an important role, so we use the code coverage analysis that PHPUnit offers in conjunction with Xdebug. You should not try to force reaching 100% code coverage with your tests, though. It is more important to test critical parts. Complex code needs more tests, because each test should test only one aspect. A simple *getter* method can do without a test.

Extending and Modifying Code

Software is never finished. Even a simple program can be extended almost arbitrarily.[17] In real-world applications, it is quite common that new requirements turn up every day. If the existing functionality has been developed with the test-driven methodology, such changes are easy to do; the existing tests make sure that nothing breaks accidentally.

As soon as we extend code, changes to existing code are required, either to allow for new functionality or just to make new parts available. Developers should be well aware of the hat they are wearing. A programmer at work either wears the development hat or the refactoring hat:

➤ **Development hat:** While wearing this hat, new functionality is being developed. Existing code is not modified.

➤ **Refactoring hat:** With this hat, existing code is being restructured, without changing its functionality.

Before refactoring code to add new functionality, we must make sure there are enough tests for the existing code. If that is not the case, new tests must be written first. A positive side effect is that nothing helps to understand (foreign) code better than writing tests for it. If tests already exist, reading them can also help to better understand the code.

Sometimes it is difficult to work with a test-driven methodology. Potentially, changes to the code are necessary in so many different places that it would be irresponsible to modify the tests up front or to write new tests. In this case, it is crucial to make sure that after the modifications to the code, there is enough test coverage. Again, a code coverage analysis with Xdebug and PHPUnit can be helpful.

When the necessary changes are done, and all tests still run (or run again), the code is checked into Subversion and the continuous integration server is friendly enough to tell us that all tests run.

Optimizing Code

Speed

When developing FLOW3, we tried to keep away from optimizations. If you try to write fast code to start with, you usually run into trouble. The gut feeling does not always tell the truth, so clean code with a strong focus on the task should have priority. After a while, you reach the point where you must write better code from the start. In that case, we throw in a profiling day. In our project, we tend to say "Performance is a feature that we can build in afterward." It is, of course, reckless to say so.

---

[17]See http://99-bottles-of-beer.net/; the PHP examples show an astonishing complexity.

Realistically speaking, performance optimizations can require big changes. They are a problem only rarely, though, because in very modular code, only a few lines of code must be changed even when big changes are due. These changes can be made rather safely, guarded by unit tests and refactoring techniques. Luckily, these modifications usually do not require us to modify public interfaces. The handling of a car is not different for the driver if a stronger motor was built in; the driver will simply notice the higher speed.

To optimize effectively, you need to know which code parts are slow; guesswork or belief does not help. We like to use the profiling features of Xdebug[18] in that case. The resulting cachegrind file is being interpreted using KCachegrind[19] and Webgrind;[20] the latter is usually sufficient and much easier to install. The output for Webgrind can be seen in Figure 3-3.

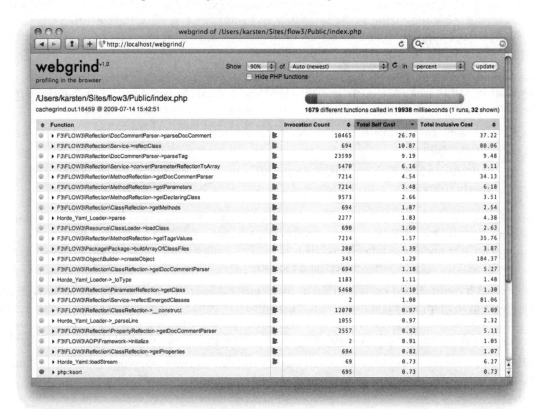

FIGURE 3-3: Webgrind output for a FLOW3 run

Another profiling tool is XHProf.[21] Its advantage over Xdebug is that it is much faster and has its own web frontend to analyze the gathered data.

---

[18]The Xdebug home page is `http://xdebug.org/`.

[19]For more information and to download KCachegrind, see `http://kcachegrind.sourceforge.net/`.

[20]Webgrind is available at `http://code.google.com/p/webgrind/`.

[21]XHProf is available from the PECL website at `http://pecl.php.net/package/xhprof`.

Readability

Readability is crucial for the maintainability of code. If a new programmer can read the code like a book, he can work on the code much faster than if he must figure out cryptic variable names and lengths methods.

To optimize the code readability, we use refactoring. Unfortunately, in the PHP world, refactoring is much less comfortable than, for example, in the Java world, where efficient refactoring tools exist. So, in most cases, we use the search and replace functionality of our IDE. Next to a solid knowledge of regular expressions, good naming schemes for variables, methods, and classes have proven successful. It is much easier to find every occurrence of a customer's ID when the variable name is `$customerID` instead of `$c`.

Finding and Fixing Bugs

Test-driven development leads to bug-free code—in theory, at least. In practice, of course, bugs occur. To fix a bug, a test is written that reproduces this bug and expects correct behavior, and thus it fails. This way, you can make sure the bug never shows up again, because the test would immediately show this. You also know when the bug was fixed—as soon as the test does not fail anymore.

Only after the test has been written can you try to fix the bug. Never before that. Never ever.

Disposing of Old Code

When building software, we write new code. If we write working, clean code, we can be proud of ourselves for a good reason. Still, disposing of old code is one of the most important jobs of a developer.

When fixing bugs, when developing new functionality, and when extending existing code, at some point, you wear your refactoring hat. If you wear this hat, you encounter code that nobody needs anymore. There are several reasons for this:

➤ Old code has become obsolete because of new code.

➤ Requirements have been dropped, so the code is not needed anymore.

➤ Code was developed that was not required yet.

Code that becomes waste due to the first two reasons should be disposed of on creation—when new code is being developed or when requirements change. Most often, however, the third reason determines the emergence of dead code, namely writing more code than is required. In our project, we successfully deal with such needless code by quickly analyzing the code and then deleting it right away. If some function is removed, we run a global search to check if other parts of the code use this function. If that is the case, the existing code must be refactored first, so it works without the function we want to delete. If the dependencies are resolved, the code (and the now failing unit tests covering it) can safely be deleted. For every test, we make sure the failure was expected. This is the case for all tests that directly test the deleted code; it is safe to remove these tests.

If a test fails unexpectedly, we must take a closer look. If we are lucky, the test was poorly written and just needs to be cleaned up to remove the wrong dependency on the removed parts of the code.

It is quite possible, though, that we find code that depends on the removed functionality. In that case, we have to rectify until the test passes again.

TEST RECIPES

After some practice, writing tests becomes rather easy and is lots of fun, but time and again, trouble is ahead that might end up in rotten compromises. Quite often, we hear sentences like "this method cannot be tested in isolation" or "it is not possible to write a test for this class." Both of these are possible. When working on FLOW3, we found some solutions that might be of interest for other developers.

Inadvertently Functional Unit Test

Problem: Some unit tests are in fact functional tests, because they test more than one isolated method. Occurring errors are hard to attribute to a certain function.

Solution: Use mocks and stubs for all parts that you do not want to test. Use dependency injection, to pass mock objects to the target class.

PHPUnit offers some great functionality to ease the work with mock objects. If the tested function contains database queries, for example, you do not want to test whether a certain result ends up in the database (you know that the database works, after all), but you want to make sure your code generates the correct SQL code and calls the appropriate functions, so the result ends up in the database.

For example:

```
/**
 * @test
 */
public function logPassesItsArgumentsToTheBackendsAppendMethod() {
    $mockBackend = $this->getMock(
        'F3\FLOW3\Log\Backend\BackendInterface',
        array('open', 'append', 'close')
    );
    $mockBackend->expects($this->once())
        ->method('append')
        ->with('theMessage', 2, array('foo'), 'Foo', 'Bar', 'Baz');
    $logger = new \F3\FLOW3\Log\Logger();
    $logger->addBackend($mockBackend);
    $logger->log('theMessage', 2, array('foo'), 'Foo', 'Bar', 'Baz');
}
```

Access to the File System

Problem: The code to test is directly accessing the file system.

Solution: vfsStream[22] is a very usable tool to emulate a file system. vfsStream registers a stream handler that can be used with the commonly used PHP functions like `fopen()` or `file_put_contents()`.

---

[22]Information about vfsStream is available at `http://code.google.com/p/bovigo/`.

For example:

```
/**
 * @test
 * @author Robert Lemke <robert@typo3.org>
 */
public function theLogFileIsOpenedWithOpen() {
    $logFileURL = \vfsStream::url('testDirectory') . '/test.log';
    $backend = new \F3\FLOW3\Log\Backend\FileBackend(
        array('logFileURL' => $logFileURL)
    );
    $backend->open();
    $this->assertTrue(
        \vfsStreamWrapper::getRoot()->hasChild('test.log')
    );
}
```

Here is the method to test:

```
/**
 * Carries out all actions necessary to prepare the logging backend,
 * such as opening the log file or opening a database connection.
 *
 * @return void
 * @author Robert Lemke <robert@typo3.org>
 */
public function open() {
    $this->fileHandle = fopen($this->logFileURL, 'at');
    if ($this->fileHandle === FALSE) {
        throw new \F3\FLOW3\Log\Exception\CouldNotOpenResource(
            'Could not open log file "' . $this->logFileURL .
            '" for write access.',
            1229448440);
    }
}
```

Constructors in Interfaces

Problem: It is generally a good idea to code against interfaces instead of classes. This effectively decouples client code from the concrete implementation and makes dependency injection easier. It gets difficult, though, when interfaces specify a constructor method because testing frameworks like PHPUnit requires their own constructor to make mock objects work.[23] Thus, aspects in FLOW3 can be imposed only on classes that do not implement an interface requiring a constructor. Otherwise, the contract with the original interface cannot be kept (except if the method signature incidentally matches the PHPUnit constructors), which leads to a fatal error in PHP.

Solution: Avoid constructors in interfaces. If you cannot avoid specifying a constructor in an interface, you can still extend the class to test in a custom mock class and combine this with other techniques like an accessible proxy class.

---

[23]The FLOW3 mechanism for aspect-oriented programming, just like PHPUnit, creates proxy classes that require additional constructor arguments.

Testing Abstract Classes

Problem: Abstract classes or classes with abstract methods cannot be instantiated and thus cannot be tested.

Solution: Create a proxy class using the PHPUnit method `getMockForAbstractClass()` and test it. All abstract methods are automatically being mocked.

For example, first, the test:

```
public function someAbstractTest() {
    $concrete = $this->getMockForAbstractClass('AbstractClass');
    $this->assertTrue($concrete->concreteMethod());
}
```

This is the class to test:

```
abstract class AbstractClass {
    abstract public function abstractMethod();
    public function concreteMethod() {
    return TRUE;
  }
}
```

Testing Protected Methods

Problem: Methods that are declared as protected or private cannot be tested in isolation.

Solution: At least protected methods can be tested through an accessible proxy class. We have added a method `buildAccessibleProxy()` to the test base class that is used in FLOW3 projects; it looks like this:

```
/**
 * Creates a proxy class of the specified class which allows
 * for calling private/protected methods and access of protected
 * properties.
 *
 * @param protected $className Fully qualified name of the original class
 * @return string Fully qualified name of the built class
 * @author Robert Lemke <robert@typo3.org>
 */
protected function buildAccessibleProxy($className) {
    $accessibleClassName = uniqid('AccessibleTestProxy');
    $class = new \ReflectionClass($className);
    $abstractModifier = $class->isAbstract() ? 'abstract ' : '';
    eval($abstractModifier . 'class ' . $accessibleClassName .
        ' extends ' . $className . ' {
            public function _call($methodName) {
                $methodReflection = new ReflectionMethod(
                    $this, $methodName
                );
                if ($methodReflection->isPrivate()) {
                    $methodReflection->setAccessible(TRUE);
```

```
                    $methodReflection->invokeArgs(
                        $this, array_slice(func_get_args(), 1)
                    );
                } else {
                    return call_user_func_array(
                        array($this, $methodName),
                        array_slice(func_get_args(), 1)
                    );
                }
            }
            public function _callRef($methodName,
                &$arg1 = NULL,
                &$arg2 = NULL,
                &$arg3 = NULL,
                &$arg4 = NULL) {
                    switch (func_num_args()) {
                        case 0 : return $this->$methodName();
                        case 1 : return $this->$methodName($arg1);
                        case 2 : return $this->$methodName(
                            $arg1, $arg2
                        );
                        case 3 : return $this->$methodName(
                            $arg1, $arg2, $arg3
                        );
                        case 4 : return $this->$methodName(
                            $arg1, $arg2, $arg3, $arg4
                        );
                    }
            }
            public function _set($propertyName, $value) {
                $this->$propertyName = $value;
            }
            public function _setRef($propertyName, &$value) {
                $this->$propertyName = $value;
            }
            public function _get($propertyName) {
                return $this->$propertyName;
            }
        }
    ');
    return $accessibleClassName;
}
```

This method generates a class that supports accessing each method or property declared as protected. It is even possible to access methods declared as private; the required mechanism from call() can just be converted to callRef(). This is the class and a test that demonstrates the feature's usage:

```
class Foo {
    protected $bar;
    protected function bar() {
        return $this->bar;
    }
}
```

```
/**
 * @test
 * @author Robert Lemke <robert@typo3.org>
 */
public function fooDoesWhatIExpect() {
   $foo = $this->getMock(
      $this->buildAccessibleProxy('\Foo'),
      array(),
      array(),
      '',
      FALSE
   );
   $foo->_set('bar', 'baz');
   $result = $foo->_call('getBar');
   $this->assertSame('baz', $result);
}
```

CALLING NON-PUBLIC METHODS VIA THE REFLECTION API

Since PHP 5.3.2, we can call non-public methods using the reflection API. Sebastian Bergmann describes in his blog article "Testing Your Privates" (`http://sebastian-bergmann.de/archives/881-Testing-Your-Privates.html`) how this functionality can be used.

Use of Callbacks

Problem: If you want to mock a method that returns values depending on the input parameters, it is often helpful to use PHPUnit's method `returnCallBack()`. Sometimes, though, it seems awkward to actually write the callback method in the test class.

Solution: This dilemma can be elegantly solved by using anonymous functions. With PHP 5.3, the power of anonymous functions has been greatly expanded, so powerful callbacks are possible.

If you want to allow certain method calls, but perform specific actions when certain parameters are passed, you can do the following:

```
$request = $this->getMock('F3\FLOW3\MVC\Web\Request');
$getMethodArgumentCallback = function() use (&$request) {
   $args = func_get_args();
   if ($args[0] === 'request') return $request;
};
$mockJoinPoint = $this->getMock('F3\FLOW3\AOP\JoinPointInterface');
$mockJoinPoint->expects($this->any())
              ->method('getMethodArgument')
              ->will($this->returnCallback($getMethodArgumentCallback));
```

This example shows how exceptions can be thrown in a controlled way while running a test:

```
$throwStopException = function() {
   throw new \F3\FLOW3\MVC\Exception\StopAction();
};
```

```
$controller = $this->getMock(
    'F3\FLOW3\MVC\Controller\RESTController',
    array('throwStatus')
);
$controller->expects($this->once())
            ->method('throwStatus')
            ->with(400)
            ->will(
              $this->returnCallBack(array($throwStopException, '__invoke'))
              );
$controller->resolveActionMethodName();
```

This is the simulation of an endless loop with a break condition:

```
$requestCallCounter = 0;
$requestCallBack = function() use (&$requestCallCounter) {
    return ($requestCallCounter++ < 101) ? FALSE : TRUE;
};
$mockRequest = $this->getMock('F3\FLOW3\MVC\Request');
$mockRequest->expects($this->any())
            ->method('isDispatched')
            ->will($this->returnCallBack($requestCallBack, '__invoke'));
$mockResponse = $this->getMock('F3\FLOW3\MVC\Response');
$dispatcher = $this->getMock(
    'F3\FLOW3\MVC\Dispatcher', array('dummy')
);
$dispatcher->dispatch($mockRequest, $mockResponse);
```

INTO THE FUTURE

So far, we are successful using the policies and techniques that we have introduced in this chapter. FLOW3 has very clean code and almost no superfluous code, and all developers stick to the programming guidelines. In the future, the team will grow and we will face the problem of controlling, integrating, and motivating an increasing number of developers.

For a long time, it has been possible to inspect each change to the source code. This is not viable in the long run. We will have to rely on the automatisms to make sure that coding guidelines are met and that the system is still executable.

Integration and motivation of developers needs time, and it means work for all parties involved. We buy this time by using automated tests. The continuous integration provides the developers with permanent positive feedback and encourages a way of working that puts quality above quantity. The management of all involved parties and the communication remain the biggest issues, but thanks to the techniques and processes we have introduced, we should still have enough time, without sacrificing quality.

Unit Testing Bad Practices

Benjamin Eberlei

The increasing importance of software quality in PHP projects in recent years has led to an increasing adoption of unit testing in software projects based on the PHP language. Writing unit tests is as complex as writing production code, but requires a completely different focus, different programming skills, and different patterns to yield a successful testing experience. This case study shows some of the common mistakes that are made when writing unit tests and shows examples of those mistakes in test suites of popular PHP frameworks.

WHY TEST QUALITY MATTERS

You might ask yourself why the quality of tests matters. Since test code is never going to production, it might seem like "second class code" that can be ugly. After all, as long as it tests that the production code is first class and working correctly, then it is acceptable, right? Wrong!

This perspective may be valid for the first few weeks or months of a project, but it comes at the cost of maintenance problems at a later time, whenever the requirements for production code change. An elaborately tested application should have at least the same number of lines in test code as in production code, if not many more. For any change in production code, the unit tests that rely explicitly and implicitly on the changed behavior need to be adjusted, because they would indicate failure otherwise. Therefore, production code changes can potentially affect much more test code than you might imagine.

Requirements change quickly and unexpectedly in most software projects, so a developer often must rethink how the production code works. If the tests affected by changes to production code are hard to maintain, the release cycle of the software product increases. Nevertheless, programmers have experienced that, on average, unit tests significantly enhance the quality of software, reduce developers' stress levels, reduce debugging overtime hours, and increase confidence in application deployment.

To benefit from unit tests, a development team is forced to maintain a high-quality test code, because only then can they work productively. Only when the use of tests decreases long-run costs, maintenance time, and release cycles can you justify the use of tests to management and customers.

Failure to maintain high-quality test code can lead to the exact opposite scenario and make the development experience very frustrating. Symptoms may include developers ignoring test failures or not writing new tests. The ultimate failure for a bad testing strategy is either management or developers stopping unit testing altogether, because of its negative impact on the business value.

BAD PRACTICES AND TEST SMELLS

This case study discusses unit testing bad practices and test smells and offers advice on how to avoid them. For each test smell, examples are shown from well-known PHP open-source projects.[1] Please be aware that this is in no way a criticism of these projects and their respective authors; it merely demonstrates that in many cases the quality of unit tests could be improved drastically, with resulting positive effects on the quality of production code. Furthermore, there are more code snippets from Zend Framework than from other open-source frameworks. This is because I am a contributor to this framework and have a much deeper insight into the test suite.

Some of the bad practices and avoidance strategies presented in this chapter may be obvious to the reader, but my experience shows that clean coding practices are often applied to production code only, and that all the best practices learned by years of experience are easily forgotten when writing test code.

The list of unit test bad practices and test smells covered in this chapter is neither complete nor very innovative. Gerard Meszaros collected a huge list of unit test smells in his book on xUnit test patterns (*xUnit Test Patterns: Refactoring Test Code*, Addison Wesley, 2007, ISBN 978-0-131-49505-0). If you are a developer or development team looking into introducing testing into your project, his book is a good starting point. Another list of bad practices and test smells with short descriptions is given in a blog post by James Carr on TDD Anti-Patterns (`http://blog.james-carr.org/2006/11/03/tdd-anti-patterns/`).

This case study is organized very simply in the pattern style and features a section on each bad practice with a description, a code sample, further notes, and advice to prevent the test smell from occurring.

---

[1]For developers of business applications written in PHP, examples from PHP open-source frameworks may appear insufficient to show unit testing bad practices. Frameworks have the extreme requirement that APIs are not allowed to change in minor versions, which ensures that test-code refactoring because of API changes is never necessary. Business applications, however, often have central domain-specific code that changes drastically between iterations. Therefore, test quality is a much more important factor for business applications than for frameworks.

Duplication in Test Code

A common rule for software development is to avoid code duplication at all costs. Yet programmers often do not apply this principle to test code. The negative impact of test code duplication is an increase in maintenance for any changes to the API of the duplicated parts. Suppose that the public interface of a class has to be changed due to new requirements. If tests for this class contain lots of duplicated code, a large set of test cases must be rewritten to incorporate this change. If this specific class is subject to rapid change, the constant changes to the test suite can be very time-consuming. Such a setup can easily lead the programmer to abandon the tests altogether.

A specific problem is the duplication code in the fixture setup of objects the code depends on. If some class is used throughout your code base, you might instantiate and configure it in lots of tests. This complicates changes to the constructor or other public methods of this class and may lead to compromises in the API and object model to avoid changes to the test code.

An example where the code for fixture setup is duplicated several times is the test case Zend_Controller_ActionTest (http://framework.zend.com/svn/framework/standard/trunk/tests/Zend/Controller/ActionTest.php, Revision 15295), where the setup for the Request, Response, and Test Controller fixture is duplicated several times and only very small parts are different for each test. The first occurrence of the fixture setup is given in the following listing:

```
class Zend_Controller_ActionTest extends PHPUnit_Framework_TestCase
{
    //[..]
    public function testRender()
    {
        $request = new Zend_Controller_Request_Http();
        $request->setControllerName('view')
                ->setActionName('index');
        $response = new Zend_Controller_Response_Cli();
        Zend_Controller_Front::getInstance()
                ->setControllerDirectory(
                dirname(__fiLE__) . DIRECTORY_SEPARATOR . '_files'
        );
        require_once(dirname(__fiLE__) . DIRECTORY_SEPARATOR .
                '_files' . DIRECTORY_SEPARATOR . 'ViewController.php'
        );
        $controller = new ViewController($request, $response);
        //[..]
    }
    //[..]
}
```

Originally, the setup for this test fixture[2] is seven lines long. This code is duplicated in 10 tests and is mostly used for assertions that are only two lines long. Duplication in test fixtures is a very common test smell and can easily be removed by extracting the relevant code into either the setUp() method called before every test, an extra creation method which takes parameters that control for differences between tests, or even a complete fixture utility class.

---

[2]A test fixture is the code that sets up objects into a predefined state for isolated testing purposes.

You can avoid duplication in test code in these ways:

➤ Extract test fixture code into its own creation utility methods in your `TestCase` classes. Consider creating a super or utility class that allows the creation of objects that are used in your application regularly. You can use parameters to model possible differences in setup of the objects in these utility methods.

➤ Create custom assertions for repetitive state or behavior verification tasks. Implementing custom assertions is a first step toward a domain-specific testing language that might even be relevant to the business or domain-specific requirements.

➤ Apply PHP Copy Paste Detector to your test suite regularly to detect larger copy-paste code blocks in the test code (PHP Copy Paste Detector is available at `http://github.com/sebastianbergmann/phpcpd`).

➤ For production code, you probably won't be able to prevent code duplication in test code completely, but you should decrease it as much as possible.

Assertion Roulette and Eager Test

It is often tempting to test several different aspects of a class in a single test as a way to minimize the time of developing tests. This temptation should be resisted for several reasons:

➤ The ability to clearly point to a piece of code that causes test failure, called Defect Localization, is not possible with tests that have many different assertions for different behaviors of the tested class.

➤ The test cannot clearly communicate the intended production code behavior, because of the multitude of aspects being tested.

➤ Testing all the different states in the lifetime of an object may violate the test-isolation principle, because different behaviors can affect each other. While these more complex tests are necessary to show that an object in a compile setup works as intended, they are fragile to changes to any point of the object lifetime. If possible, different features and behaviors should be tested in isolated test methods.

Eager test and assertion roulette are closely linked. An *eager test* is attempting to test several behaviors and states at once, such that a failure occurring in this test is of no real value to the developer in regard to locating the defect in the code. The developer must tear the test apart and find out what is tested. This might even lead to debugging sessions of the test code, although one benefit of unit testing is supposed to be the reduction of time consumed by debugging.

Assertion roulette describes a test where many different assertions are made about the state of a behavior such that a failure cannot be attributed to a specific assertion of the test.

A medium-sized example for an eager test is the test case for the `ezcUrl` (`http://svn.ezcomponents.org/viewvc.cgi/trunk/Url/tests/url_test.php?view=log`, Revision 10236) class in the eZ Components Url component, shown in the following code:

```
class ezcUrlTest extends ezcTestCase
{
    //[..]
    public function testRemoveOrderedParameter()
```

```
    {
        $urlCfg = new ezcUrlConfiguration();
        $urlCfg->addOrderedParameter( 'section' );
        $urlCfg->addOrderedParameter( 'module' );
        $urlCfg->addOrderedParameter( 'view' );
        $url = new ezcUrl(
            'http://www.example.com/doc/components',
            $urlCfg
        );
                $this->assertEquals(
                array(
                        'section' => 0, 'module' => 1, 'view' => 2
                ),
                $url->configuration->orderedParameters
            );
        $this->assertEquals('doc', $url->getParam( 'section' ) );
        $this->assertEquals('components', $url->getParam('module'));
        $url->configuration->removeOrderedParameter( 'view' );
        $this->assertEquals(
        array(
            'section' => 0, 'module' => 1
        ),
        $url->configuration->orderedParameters
    );
    try
    {
        $this->assertEquals( null, $url->getParam( 'view' ) );
        $this->fail( 'Expected exception was not thrown.' );
    }
    catch ( ezcUrlInvalidParameterException $e )
    {
        $expected = "The parameter 'view' could not be set/get".
            " because it is not defined in the configuration.";
        $this->assertEquals( $expected, $e->getMessage() );
    }
    // try removing again - nothing bad should happen
    $url->configuration->removeOrderedParameter( 'view' );
    try
    {
        $this->assertEquals( null, $url->getParam( 'view' ) );
        $this->fail( 'Expected exception was not thrown.' );
    }
    catch ( ezcUrlInvalidParameterException $e )
    {
    $expected = "The parameter 'view' could not be set/get".
        " because it is not defined in the configuration.";
    $this->assertEquals( $expected, $e->getMessage() );
    }
}
//[..]
    }
```

The given test verifies five different functionalities of the ordered parameter feature of ezcUrl. First, it asserts that of the given example URL, the first two ordered parameters are detected by their name. Second, it asserts that the parameter view can be removed from the ordered parameter list and that the configuration represents this change. You can tell by the test name `testRemoveOrderedParameter` that this assertion is the primary tested functionality. The third tested functionality is an exception thrown, when the test tries to retrieve the removed parameter. The fourth tested functionality tests that a second removal of the same parameter view does not throw an exception. The fifth functionality is again an expected exception thrown when the removed parameter is retrieved.

If any of these five different functionalities fails, the complete test fails. A developer confronted with test failure has more trouble finding the root cause than if the test were split into smaller tests.

You can avoid assertion roulette and eager tests in these ways:

➤ Resist the temptation to test several different functionalities of a class in one test.

➤ If you could not resist the temptation or inherited eager tests from another developer, use the feature to add concrete failure messages to assertions that help with defect localization. This is supported by all major testing frameworks.

➤ A unit testing purist would say a test may only have one assertion. This is not always a feasible solution, but using too many assertions in a single test is a good indicator for an eager test that should split up into several smaller tests.

Fragile Test

A fragile test fails even if the core functionality under test works correctly. This is often the case when business logic is tested through the user interface, for example through generated HTML code.

Both Zend Framework and Symfony support this kind of testing through their respective testing components `Zend_Test_PHPUnit_Controller` and Lime in combination with the `sfTestBrowser` class. They simulate a browser that goes through all stages of the application by starting a controller dispatching loop that accesses models and prints output to the view. Verification is done on the generated response (HTML, XML, or other formats) by asserting that certain content elements exist with CSS or XPath selectors. Selenium tests move a step further and run tests inside each configured browser, which is necessary to test JavaScript-related functionality of a Web site.

However, if the output generation of the Web site changes, the test might fail, although the core business logic that is tested still works correctly. This might happen if a designer removes an XHTML id or class element that is used for testing, or if the authentication method changes slightly and the testing browser sees an error page rather than the necessary page for a test success.

Testing through the UI also produces many false negatives. Maintenance of fragile tests can consume a considerable amount of time that is better invested in writing tests that directly verify results of the business logic, rather than going through several layers of an application to do so.

The example of fragile test that follows is from the Symfony Testing Browser documentation:

```
$b = new sfTestBrowser();
$b->get('/foobar/edit/id/1')
->checkResponseElement('form input[type="hidden"][value="1"]', true)
->checkResponseElement('form textarea[name="text1"]', 'foo')
->checkResponseElement('form input[type="submit"]', 1);
```

This example is very simple. The test browser requests a page of the Symfony application and checks for three different response elements. However, in practice, very complex business logic is often tested by asserting specific HTML responses of corresponding views. Testing business logic through the UI is a form of indirect testing and prone to error. High maintenance costs to constantly update the failing tests because of small changes in the application are a likely result.

A similar example from the Zend_Test_PHPUnit_Controller documentation has the same overall appearance:

```php
public function testAuthenticatedUserShouldHaveCustomizedProfilePage()
{
    $this->loginUser('foobar', 'foobar');
    $this->request->setMethod('GET');
    $this->dispatch('/user/view');
    $this->assertNotRedirect();
    $this->assertQueryContentContains('h2', 'foobar');
}
```

This test executes a test utility method to login a user foobar and then attempts to get the view user action. An assertion is made that no redirect is executed and that the page contains a <H2> HTML element with the username "foobar."

Both examples show testing of application states that are easily broken, although they might not even affect the tested behavior. You should be aware of the differences of unit testing and integration testing through the user interface. Testing business logic solely through the UI is considered bad practice.

Integration tests assert behavior of several components or the complete application in combination. These tests should test functionality only at a very rough level and focus on showing that parts of the application work in combination. Integration tests that verify fine-grained business logic elements of an application tend to turn into fragile tests.

Good *unit tests* check the behavior of a single component in isolation and replace all the dependencies with test doubles. Unit testing is like experimenting with all the side effects accounted for. The fundamental core of the business logic should always be tested with unit tests rather than integration tests. This ensures that they work independently of the application's current state and are flexible in use.

Both unit testing and integration testing have their respective strengths, and it is important to correctly differentiate between them to avoid high maintenance tests.

You can avoid fragile tests in these ways:

➤ In practice, fragile tests are hard to avoid. You need at least some tests to assure that the complete application is working with all its participating parts. However, try to minimize testing of complex business logic through the user interface and exclusively use unit tests for these tasks.

➤ Use integration tests to test that the glue of the application is working, but not to test results of the business logic.

➤ When retrofitting tests onto existing legacy code, you often cannot avoid testing business logic with integration tests. Make sure you start to refactor these pieces of code quickly, such that you can replace the integration tests with unit tests.

Obscure Test

The *obscure test* groups a set of different test smells together. In general, it means that a test is not obvious to understand and one of the following questions cannot be easily answered about its purpose:

➤ What is tested?

➤ Why does an assertion of X show that Y works?

➤ What dependencies are required to run this test and why?

Obscure tests should be avoided because they deprive your test suite of several beneficial properties. Tests cannot act as documentation to yourself and other developers if they are hard to understand. Additionally, obscure tests are hard to maintain because a developer has to understand the test before changing it. Both problems may lead to a dangerous ignorance of the obscure test.

Obscure tests also are a source of bugs in test code. If it's hard to understand what is happening, then clearly the code is not very simple and may contain bugs. Bugs in the test code are very nasty because they occur where they are least expected. If a test fails due to an error in the test code, you probably need to tear apart the production code before the true source of failure is found, which means you lose valuable time.

A test should be as easy and short as possible, empowering any developer to make a qualified statement about the inner workings and the validity of the test in a matter of seconds.

The different causes for obscure tests are listed in the following subsections.

Problems with Global State

Cases where global state affects the system under test are annoying for the developer, because tests may fail due to global variables not being configured correctly. For example, the singleton and registry patterns that ask for specific dependencies produce hard-to-test code, making it impossible to replace the dependencies in tests with mocks.[3] They also may be hidden deep inside the tested code, so you have to search for all the global dependencies when you set up a test. If global dependencies themselves have their own dependencies on other global objects, you can end up with a considerably complex setup to achieve test isolation or even being able to instantiate the object under test without triggering fatal errors, warnings, or exceptions.

Furthermore, complex static methods or global functions that execute considerable logic are hard to test. Each call to a static method or a function cannot be replaced by test doubles, because they cannot be exchanged at run time. Any test for a dynamic object that relies on static methods or functions can be problematic in setup because the code may execute statements that should never run on a testing system. This might be an expensive call to external systems, a Web service, or the database, which you should avoid.

---

[3]A *mock* is a replacement of an object with a dummy. It simulates behavior such that test isolation of objects with dependencies can be achieved by faking return values.

As you can see, a side effect of testing with global state is that you have to control all the global dependencies. Test setup methods have to reset singleton instances and registries and configure global objects before each test run. To an inexperienced developer, this may be an impossible task, because the configuration of the global dependencies looks random and no direct relationship to the system under test can be identified.

Another negative aspect of global state is that the global dependencies can be easily forgotten, causing test failures for seemingly random reasons. For example, there may be dependencies on the order of test execution. If global state is transferred between multiple tests, some very nasty bugs can occur that are hard to find.

An example of testing complexity because of global state is the front controller of Zend Framework, which implements the singleton anti-pattern.[4] The test setup for this class is not too complex yet, but any tests written by you that use parts of the Zend Framework MVC application as test fixtures require the same test setup in regard to the global variables.

As an example, the test `setUp()` for the `ViewRenderer` is shown in the following code. The `ViewRenderer` is a class inside the front controller that handles the specifics of selecting which view template should be rendered and how the view should be configured.

```
class Zend_Controller_Action_Helper_ViewRendererTest extends //[..]
{
    protected function setUp()
    {
        $this->basePath = realpath(dirname(__fiLE__) .
            str_repeat(DIRECTORY_SEPARATOR . '..', 2)
        );
        $this->request = new Zend_Controller_Request_Http;
        $this->response = new Zend_Controller_Response_Http;
        $this->front = Zend_Controller_Front::getInstance();
        $this->front->resetInstance();
        $this->front->addModuleDirectory(
            $this->basePath .
                DIRECTORY_SEPARATOR . '_files' .
                DIRECTORY_SEPARATOR . 'modules'
        )
            ->setRequest($this->request)
            ->setResponse($this->response);
        $this->helper =
            new Zend_Controller_Action_Helper_ViewRenderer;
            Zend_Controller_Action_HelperBroker::addHelper(
        $this->helper
        );
    }
}
```

---

[4]Because of the drawbacks of global state and other reasons, the front controller will be de-singletonized in the next major release of Zend Framework.

The front controller being a singleton requires that several dependencies and configuration properties be reset to a default state to ensure that the tests can run correctly. That includes non-global classes like the request and response objects that are dependencies of the global front controller. This example shows how global state also affects non-global dependencies and requires the use of them during testing. Furthermore, another global dependency is the `Zend_Controller_Action_HelperBroker`, which also must be configured correctly such that the `ViewRenderer` can be tested in a correct environment. This last statement in particular is very nonintuitive to a reader who is not familiar with how the Zend Controller works. Also, it shows how global state makes it hard to understand exactly how classes work in combination with each other. However, not calling this method results in some failing tests and a fatal error.

Another problem of global state is evident from this example: Objects dependent on global state can hardly be tested in isolation, but they also rely on the relevant code of their global dependencies. Using global state ties components together very strongly and prevents a developer's ability to unit-test the components. From my experience, applications that rely on global functions and static methods can be tested only via integration tests, because no hooks exist to replace parts of the application.

Because the `Zend_Controller_Front` is used in several other classes of the `Zend_Controller` component, tests for these have to reset the global state as well. Global state at central locations of your application opens Pandora's box and can seriously affect test quality.

You can avoid problems with global state in these ways:

➤ It is already a well-known practice to avoid global state in application development; however, there always seems to be a good reason to have central dependencies like database connection or validation in a global state, accessible only with static methods. Try to avoid global state at all costs and make use of the dependency injection pattern to inject dependencies deep into the application object graph.[5]

➤ PHPUnit introduced a feature that backs up global state that is nested inside static attributes of classes. Although this feature keeps the penalty for global state in your application low, you should avoid it nevertheless. Making dependencies explicit as opposed to using global state raises the quality of both production and test code.

Indirect Testing

Testing a class through the side effects it produces on its dependent classes is called *indirect testing*. This often happens when a developer feels his class cannot be really tested without the interaction with other classes. This is sometimes a different flavor of a fragile test through the user interface.

What makes indirect tests obscure are the asserted conditions that verify a state on a dependent class that has no direct relationship to the class that is tested.

---

[5]The Zend and Symfony Frameworks are replacing global state with dependency injection solutions in their next major releases, because of the negative experience developers and users had with global state.

One good example for indirect testing is the parts of the `ezcMvcDispatcherConfigurable` test:

```
class ezcMvcToolsConfigurableDispatcherTest extends ezcTestCase
{
    //[..]
    function testExternalRedirect()
    {
        $config = new simpleConfiguration();
        $config->route = 'IRController';
        $dispatcher = new ezcMvcConfigurableDispatcher( $config );
        $dispatcher->run();
        self::assertEquals(
            "BODY: Name: name, Vars: array ([CR] ".
            " 'nonRedirVar' => 4,[CR] 'ReqRedirVar' => 4,[CR])",
            $config->store
        );
    }
    function testRoutingException()
    {
        $config = new simpleConfiguration();
        $config->requestParser = 'FaultyRoutes';
        $dispatcher = new ezcMvcConfigurableDispatcher( $config );
        $dispatcher->run();
        self::assertEquals(
            "BODY: Name: name, Vars: array ([CR] ".
            " 'fatal' => 'Very fatal',[CR])",
            $config->store
        );
    }
    //[..]
}
```

The class `simpleConfiguration` in this case is used to configure the MVC dispatcher by specifying routes, view, controllers, and much more. Specific behavior of the dispatcher is tested by listening to specific responses that are called inside the `simpleConfiguration` class. During the whole dispatching process, content is written into the `$config->store` variable and matched by string comparison for verification of test success.

From the tests, it is not immediately obvious why the given assertions show that an external redirect or a routing exception occurred. Considerable logic depends on the inner workings of the configuration class, which itself is about 400 lines of untested code. Given the rather cryptic output, one cannot be sure if the test is really valid or the test success occurs because of a bug in the `simpleConfiguration` class.

You can avoid indirect testing in these ways:

➤   Indirect testing is often used to test objects that pass on their work to delegates, observers, or other types of subobjects. A better approach to test this kind of object setup is the use of mock object libraries, which allow for replacing dependent classes at run time.

➤   The two big PHP testing frameworks PHPUnit (http://phpunit.de) and SimpleTest (http://simpletest.org) both offer mock-object libraries that are easy to use.

Additionally, Mockery (`http://github.com/padraic/mockery`) is a relatively new independent mocking framework that has a very simple syntax and can be integrated into any testing framework.

Obscure Test Names

There are different cases where the names of tests account for obscurity in tests. In the best case, a test method name clearly communicates what is tested and what the expected outcome should look like. If this is not the case, the invested effort to understand the workings of the test increases automatically. Hints from the test method name can at least point the developer in the right direction.

One possible problem is the enumeration of test methods. A very general test method name is followed by a number. The message for a developer looking at these kinds of tests can be summarized as "There are many different behaviors for the functionality you are looking at, but please guess what these different behaviors are." This is especially annoying because PHPUnit reports the test method name of a failing test, which is great help for defect localization.

An example of enumerated test methods can be found inside `ezcWorkflowTest`:

```
class ezcWorkflowTest extends ezcWorkflowTestCase
{
    public function testProperties() { /** [..] */ }
    public function testProperties2() { /** [..] */ }
    public function testProperties3() { /** [..] */ }
    public function testProperties4() { /** [..] */ }
    public function testProperties5() { /** [..] */ }
    public function testProperties6() { /** [..] */ }
    public function testProperties7() { /** [..] */ }
    public function testProperties8() { /** [..] */ }
}
```

Looking at the full code, you can see that test one checks for a valid condition of the properties and the other tests check for exceptional behavior that can occur. While this piece of code is a really good example for testing all the possible edge cases, it would help to add some description of the expected exception to the method name, making it easier to understand.

Another case of obscure test-method names is extremely long camel-cased descriptions. This is the exact opposite of the previous test smell. This test smell can be observed in every test suite of all major PHP frameworks. Here are some of the test method names of the Model Test suite in CakePHP:

➤ `testHabtmDeleteLinksWhenNoPrimaryKeyInJoinTable()`

➤ `testHabtmSaveKeyResolution()`

➤ `testHabtmSavingWithNoPrimaryKeyUuidJoinTable()`

➤ `testHabtmSavingWithNoPrimaryKeyUuidJoinTableNoWith()`

The more camel-cased words there are in a method name, the harder it is to read. Often, test names do not differ at all except the last one or two words, making it difficult to see the difference between tests on the first glance. This test smell comes from the rigorous application of method name coding standards to test suites. Making an exception from the coding standard rule and using an underscore to separate distinct parts of the test method names can enhance the understanding of a test.

Symfony introduces a third case of test name smell, because its Lime framework does not support test methods at all. This leads to procedural style test suites, where no breaks between tests of different behavior can be detected. To see the problem of no test method names would require a complete code snippet, for example the sfFormTest.php, which is 900 lines of procedural code, testing 138 different behaviors, with no separation visible. The following snippet is an excerpt of this test suite:

```
$f = new FormTest();
$f->setValidatorSchema(new sfValidatorSchema(array(
    'first_name' => new sfValidatorString(array('min_length' => 2)),
    'last_name' => new sfValidatorString(array('min_length' => 2)),
)));
$t->ok(!$f->isBound(),
    '->isBound() returns false if the form is not bound');
$t->is($f->getValues(), array(),
    '->getValues() returns an empty array if the form is not bound');
$t->ok(!$f->isValid(),
    '->isValid() returns false if the form is not bound');
$t->ok(!$f->hasErrors(),
    '->hasErrors() returns false if the form is not bound');
$t->is($f->getValue('first_name'), null,
    '->getValue() returns null if the form is not bound');
$f->bind(array('first_name' => 'Fabien', 'last_name' => 'Potencier'));
$t->ok($f->isBound(), '->isBound() returns true if the form is bound');
$t->is($f->getValues(),
array('first_name' => 'Fabien', 'last_name' => 'Potencier'),
    '->getValues() returns an array of cleaned values if ...');
$t->ok($f->isValid(),
    '->isValid() returns true if the form passes the validation');
$t->ok(!$f->hasErrors(),
    '->hasErrors() returns false if the form passes the validation');
$t->is($f->getValue('first_name'), 'Fabien',
    '->getValue() returns the cleaned value for a field name ...');
$t->is($f->getValue('nonsense'), null,
    '->getValue() returns null when non-existant param is requested');
```

In defense of Symfony, the reformatting to fit the page made this snippet even more obscure, but it shows the problem of missing test method names. Lots of different behaviors of the given TestForm object are tested, with only little indication of what the general picture looks like.

You can avoid obscure test names by following this suggestion:

➤ Give your test methods good names, and don't hesitate to use an underscore to separate very long camel-case names.

Lying Test

Sometimes asserting a specific behavior for a piece of code is not very easy. A developer might resort to writing some interactions of some classes and assert nothing except the fact that no error or exception occurred. This is not a real unit test. It only serves to add some undeserved code coverage and false assurance of the component's functionality. Running random code does not verify that the component works correctly.

An example for a lying test is the following part of the `Zend_Db_Table` test suite:

```
abstract class Zend_Db_Table_TestCommon extends // [..]
{
    public function testTableConstructor()
    {
        $bugs = $this->_table['bugs'];
        $info = $bugs->info();
        $config = array('db'=> $this->_db,
                    'schema'          => $info['schema'],
                    'name'            => $info['name'],
                    'primary'         => $info['primary'],
                    'cols'            => $info['cols'],
                    'metadata'        => $info['metadata'],
                    'metadataCache'   => null,
                    'rowClass'        => $info['rowClass'],
                    'rowsetClass'     => $info['rowsetClass'],
                    'referenceMap'       => $info['referenceMap'],
                    'dependentTables' => $info['dependentTables'],
                    'sequence'           => $info['sequence'],
                    'unknownKey'         => 'testValue');
        $table = new Zend_Db_Table_TableBugs($config);\
    }
    // [..]
}
```

This test does nothing except assert that a new `Zend_Db_Table` instance can be created by passing an array as arguments. Worse, the input is taken from an already existing instance of the same class and the input, therefore, should be valid by definition. Moreover, a reader who knows the internals of `Zend_Db_Table` can see that this test generates lots of covered lines of code. In a worst-case scenario, the unit test writer wrongly assumes that a test was already written for those covered lines, although they are only executed by accident.

You can avoid a lying test by following this suggestion:

➤ Always make sure to assert a condition at the end of a test, either by calling a direct assertion on a condition or by defining indirect assertions via a Mock Object API. If you can't come up with an assertion, you can delete the test because it serves no purpose after all.

Slow Test

A great benefit of unit tests is their ability to quickly show you errors in your code. If the tests run slow, you are deprived of this benefit. Your tests run slow for several reasons:

➤ You are using lots of tests that talk with the database, file system, or any other external resource.

➤ Your code uses `sleep()` or `usleep()` often.

➤ Your code does very expensive computations.

You probably cannot do much against the third point except to find better algorithms, but good system architecture can help you avoid doing too much communication with external systems or sleeping during unit tests.

Separating domain logic and data access allows you to test the business logic of your application without having to set up and tear down a database fixture for each test. A good pattern to achieve this goal is Repository.

For the second point, the following example from `Zend_Service_Amazon` shows a case where sleep is necessary because of bad test design:

```
public function setUp()
{
    $this->_amazon = new Zend_Service_Amazon(
        constant('TESTS_ZEND_SERVICE_AMAZON_ONLINE_ACCESSKEYID')
    );
    $this->_query = new Zend_Service_Amazon_Query(
        constant('TESTS_ZEND_SERVICE_AMAZON_ONLINE_ACCESSKEYID')
    );
    $this->_httpClientAdapter = new Zend_Http_Client_Adapter_Socket();
    $this->_amazon->getRestClient()
                  ->getHttpClient()
                  ->setAdapter($this->_httpClientAdapter);
    // terms of use compliance: no more than one query per second
    sleep(1);
}
```

Because the Amazon service tests talk to the real Amazon instead of replacing its responses with predefined results, a `sleep()` call must be made to follow the terms of use compliance, which probably forbid flooding the service. A better test design would be to record a set of responses from the Web service and let a mocked HTTP client return these. This would save the expensive sleep and HTTP calls, which make this test suite run so long.

You can avoid slow tests in these ways:

➤ Separate code that is known to be slow from the business logic that relies on it, to be able to test the business logic without having to run the slow parts of the test.

➤ For database access, use the repository pattern or any other data mapping pattern to completely separate business logic from the persistence layer.

➤ For remote services, separate client, response, and parser into distinct objects, such that test responses can be easily injected into the Web service client.

Conditional Logic in Tests

Conditional logic in tests should be avoided completely. The argument for this rather strict statement is simple. Because tests are not themselves tested for their correctness, they should be as simple as possible. Conditional logic and loops add complexity and, therefore, should be avoided. This also reduces the possibility of introducing bugs into loops or creating conditions that cause erratic tests that pass although they should not.

Another argument against conditional logic is the possibility of different test paths running dependent on the preconditions. If preconditions control which part of a test is run, then there is no guarantee that the test covers the desired path when run. Furthermore, conditional logic introduces the possibility of tests failing when run alone but working when run in a group, or the other way around.

A nice example of why conditional logic should be avoided in tests is inside the test suite for
Zend_Session. Somewhat different functionality is tested depending on whether the session was
started before this test was run.

```php
class Zend_SessionTest extends PHPUnit_Framework_TestCase
{
// [..]
    public function testRegenerateId()
    {
        // Check if session hasn't already been started
        // by another test
        if (!Zend_Session::isStarted()) {
            Zend_Session::setId('myid123');
            Zend_Session::regenerateId();
            $this->assertFalse(Zend_Session::isRegenerated());
            $id = Zend_Session::getId();
            $this->assertTrue($id === 'myid123',
                'getId() reported something different '.
                'than set via setId("myid123")'
            );
            Zend_Session::start();
        } else {
            // Start session if it's not actually started
            // That may happen if Zend_Session::$_unitTestEnabled
            // is turned on while some other
            // Unit tests utilize Zend_Session functionality
            if (!defined('SID')) {
            session_start();
        }
        // only regenerate session id if session
        // has already been started
            Zend_Session::regenerateId();
        }
        $this->assertTrue(Zend_Session::isRegenerated());
            try {
                Zend_Session::setId('someo-therid-123');
                $this->fail(
                    'No exception was returned when trying to '.
                    'set the session id, after session_start()'
                );
            } catch (Zend_Session_Exception $e) {
                $this->assertRegexp('/already.*started/i', $e->getMessage());
            }
        }
    }
    // [..]
}
```

Although the nature of sessions probably requires this conditional logic, it is a good demonstration
of why conditional logic in tests can be dangerous.

You can avoid conditional logic in tests by following these suggestions:

➤   Extract fixture setup and assertions that require conditional logic or loops into their own test
    utility methods and test them for correctness.

➤   Avoid global state in your application that requires the use of conditional logic in tests.

Self-validating Tests

A convenient way to write a test is to let the class under test produce the output that is asserted to be correct. This is often the case when code is not developed by a test-driven approach and test code is written by the same developer as the production code.

Assume your system under testing generates some large XML output, parses some structure, and returns a PHP array or object or produces lots of output from other sources. Classes that generate complex return types are often tested by generating results from the unit tested class and using them to build assertions.

Tests designed in this way have the nasty side effect of proving bugs to be correct application behavior. If the generated output of a tested method is very complex, a developer can be tempted to create a test by copying this output without verifying that the output is actually correct.

It is very hard to show examples of self-validating tests in a book chapter, because they are often at least 50–100 lines of code. We will, however, refer to some examples for future reference.

In the CakePHP test suite, the `ModelTest` class has fixtures and expectations set up that span more than 400 lines of code. This test verifies the model component's correct behavior in regard to saving and retrieving data from the database. The method `testfindAllThreaded` is an example of a gigantic setup that looks like it was generated by applying `var_export()` on the given method's output and using that information to build up the assertion. It is unlikely that the test writer wrote this setup code himself or that he checked all the output and verified its correctness in detail.

In `Zend_Soap_AutoDiscoverTest`, the generation of WSDL XML files based on function or class input is verified. String equality of the complete WSDL output is asserted, and given the complexity of WSDL as a description language, it should be doubted that this was written or verified by someone. Accordingly, several bugs have already been found in earlier versions of `Zend_Soap_AutoDiscover`, which the self-validating tests asserted to be correct behavior.

You can avoid self-validating tests in these ways:

➤ Resist the generation of output for testing and assertion purposes, even if it is very convenient (and it probably is convenient very often).

➤ Test components that produce very complex output by asking a colleague to write tests for the components, or do the development test-drive by writing detailed tests up front.

Web-surfing Tests

A *surfing test* is a test that requires an HTTP connection to a foreign Web site to work. Because in PHP `file_get_contents()` and other functions allow us to retrieve a complete HTML site, RSS feed, or other content from the Web in a simple and convenient way, this functionality can easily be nested deep inside a class. It is not possible to replace or mock this external call. Any test of this class then retrieves content from a foreign location via a TCP/IP connection.

Calling external resources—networks, databases, or file systems—should be avoided in unit tests. These resources are expensive to talk to and considerably extend the test run time. A slow test suite is probably executed less and may therefore lose its benefits for the developer.

Another negative aspect of surfing tests is that you can't rely on the content of external sources, which makes it hard to test for specific return values of this resource. In fact, we can assert only some very general aspects that are independent of the content of the external source, rather than the specific functionality that is required to prove that the component works correctly.

A good example for this kind of test smell is, again, the `Zend_Service_Amazon_OnlineTest` test case, as shown in this code snippet:

```
class Zend_Service_Amazon_OnlineTest extends // [..]
{
    // [..]
    public function testItemSearchMusicMozart()
    {
        $resultSet = $this->_amazon->itemSearch(array(
            'SearchIndex' => 'Music',
            'Keywords'    => 'Mozart',
            'ResponseGroup' => 'Small,Tracks,Offers'
        ));
        foreach ($resultSet as $item) {
            $this->assertTrue(
            $item instanceof Zend_Service_Amazon_Item
            );
        }
    }
    // [..]
}
```

What is hidden from this listing is the fact that in the `setUp()` method of this PHPUnit test, a connection to the real Amazon Web Services is opened, such that the `itemSearch()` call makes a real request for products for Mozart in the music category of Amazon.

Because the content of this result is not the same between different test runs (different CDs with Mozart music can be returned), the only possible assertion for this test is the iteration over the result set. This verifies that the result parser worked correctly, but it does not verify that all the fields and values are injected correctly into the result items. This test fails to verify that the Amazon music search works correctly.

You can avoid web-surfing tests in these ways:

➤ Make sure you can mock calls to external resources, such as TCP/IP connections (or the file system and database). This requires the use of object-oriented abstraction layers or central gateways that can be reconfigured for testing purposes. Try to encapsulate PHP functions to access resources into objects, because functions cannot be exchanged at run time.

➤ Use sample responses of the external sources to test concrete use-cases of your code and assert its correct behavior.

Mock Overkill

Mocking calls to dependent objects is a common practice in unit testing that allows control of the environment and dependencies of the class under test. However, if many components must be mocked for a single test, it's difficult to understand how and why these mocks are used. Furthermore, you might end up testing nothing more than the fact that different mocks can pass parameters and return parameters to each other.

Generally, one can state that mocks are an underused feature of unit testing libraries. However, several examples of mock overuse also can be found, for example in the MVC Dispatcher in FLOW3:

```
class DispatcherTest extends \F3\Testing\BaseTestCase {
    //[..]
    public function dispatchCallsTheControllersProcessRequest...() {
        $mockRequest = $this->getMock('F3\FLOW3\MVC\Request');
        $mockRequest->expects($this->any())
            ->method('getControllerObjectName')
            ->will($this->returnValue('FooController'));
        $mockRequest->expects($this->at(0))
            ->method('isDispatched')
            ->will($this->returnValue(FALSE));
        $mockRequest->expects($this->at(2))
            ->method('isDispatched')
            ->will($this->returnValue(FALSE));
        $mockRequest->expects($this->at(4))
            ->method('isDispatched')
            ->will($this->returnValue(TRUE));

        $mockResponse = $this->getMock('F3\FLOW3\MVC\Response');

        $mockController =
            $this->getMock('F3\FLOW3\MVC\Controller\ControllerInterface',
                array('processRequest', 'canProcessRequest')
            );
        $mockController->expects($this->exactly(2))
            ->method('processRequest')
            ->with($mockRequest, $mockResponse);
        $mockObjectManager =
            $this->getMock('F3\FLOW3\Object\ManagerInterface',
                array(), array(), '', FALSE
            );
        $mockObjectManager->expects($this->exactly(2))
            ->method('getObject')
            ->with('FooController')
            ->will($this->returnValue($mockController));
        $dispatcher = $this->getMock('F3\FLOW3\MVC\Dispatcher',
            array('dummy'), array($mockObjectManager), '', TRUE
        );
        $dispatcher->dispatch($mockRequest, $mockResponse);
    }
    //[..]
}
```

In defense of FLOW3, it should be noted that reformatting of this code example made the code look even more complex. You can see in the last two statements that the actual test also is done through a mock object, which begs the question if there is some real code at test or only talking between mocks.

You can avoid mock overkill in these ways:

➤ Try to minimize dependencies of an object by creating a deep object graph. It is easier to mock dependencies of an object that has just three dependencies with three sub-dependencies each than it is to mock the total of nine objects to instantiate the class in a unit test environment.

➤ Delegate the generation of mocks to creation methods that have expressive names regarding their behavior. This tremendously shortens test code that needs several different mock objects. It also helps to reduce duplicate code.

➤ Make sure you leave at least some production code to be tested when using mocks. Otherwise, you may not truly test that the production code works as desired, but only that you configured your mocks correctly to pass parameters and output correctly to each other.

Skip Epidemic

If a test fails and the developer does not know why, he may decide to skip its execution for the time being. Obscure or fragile tests are often marked as skipped, because fixing their failures is a time-intensive task. Therefore, lots of skipped tests are an indicator for test smells in general. If programmers keep marking their tests as skipped, their test coverage slowly drops. Furthermore, it becomes increasingly difficult to realign a skipped test with the current behavior the longer it has been disabled.

PHPUnit counts the number of skipped tests on each test run. If this number is reasonably high, you should be warned that your test suite is becoming more and more like Swiss cheese, with large holes of missing test coverage.

CONCLUSION

This case study shows that bad practices in tests are common and even occur in large open-source frameworks. The specific consequences of poor test quality and test smells on maintenance, release cycles, and production code quality are described, as well as possible solutions. Avoiding most of these bad practices and test smells should become common sense to gain the greatest possible benefit from testing.

5

Quality Assurance at Digg Inc.

Robert Balousek, Matt Erkkila, Ian Eure, Bill Shupp, Jeremy McCarthy, and Brian O'Neill

WHAT'S IN THIS CHAPTER?

➤ Software development philosophies at Digg

➤ Overcoming the problems posed by legacy code

➤ Evaluating development team, project, and code base size issues

➤ The importance of unit testing

➤ Overcoming resistance to unit testing

➤ The characteristics of testable code

➤ Using mock objects

➤ Quality assurance in an agile environment

PROBLEMS WE ARE FACING

The first version of Digg launched in 2004. Written by a lone developer, Digg let people post and vote on links from around the Internet. Fast forward to 2009, and with more than 70 employees and more than 1.1 million lines of code, Digg serves about 39 million unique users and millions of page-views per month. With 16 developers split into four distinct teams, assisted by four QA engineers—one for each team—we push new code live to the site almost every single day. Sometimes those pushes are two to three lines of code to fix a bug, and sometimes they are 2,000 to 3,000 lines of code and a whole new site feature.

At the beginning of 2008, the engineering team at Digg was still relatively small, with eight developers and no QA team. We operated using a waterfall methodology and large requirement documents, moving through a single phase of the process at a time. Using this methodology, we were releasing feature sets every three to four months. Because our release cycle was so long, and the releases we were doing were extremely large and complicated, they often took much longer than planned and were rife with bugs.

These problems are nothing new in the software development world. Any team that has tried to create a product of any size or consists of more than three or four engineers has experienced similar pains. The solutions to these problems are well known and even well documented. Rather than pick a single approach, we decided to draw different lessons from all of them, chiefly from the agile and extreme programming disciplines.

In short, we knew we needed to speed up development, shorten the time between releases, and reduce the number of bugs. With all these things in mind, we decided to follow these six main philosophies:

➤ Smaller teams

➤ Smaller releases

➤ Code reviews

➤ Unit testing

➤ Build automation

➤ Continuous integration (CI)

Legacy Code Base

In the fast-moving tech industry, one is rarely afforded the time to do things right the first time. The initial version of any code is almost always bad, rigid, over-engineered, and poorly thought out. It is never easy to retrofit legacy code with new patterns, and a lack of forethought complicates the problem further.

This is the situation in which Digg found itself. The large base of legacy procedural code was written mostly in a reactionary mindset; when stuff broke, fixing it fast was more important than doing it right. Naturally, this led to some pretty hairy code. The paradox of the situation is that the code most in need of testing is the hardest to cover.

Much of Digg's legacy code was composed of monolithic functions. For example, a single 32KB file contained nine functions in 767 lines. That's nearly 100 lines per function, much too large to get a clear understanding of how they work. Other files had the opposite problem, with no fewer than 28 functions in 847 lines and 16 functions in 681 lines. This leads to problems during the unit testing process, where it's preferable to test the smallest possible area of code. When you have a 100-line method filled with dense conditionals, your test ends up becoming spaghetti.

The strategy we adopted was to create simple black-box tests for the legacy code that ensure the correct outputs were returned for known inputs. This allowed us to refactor the code and reuse the tests with minimal difficulty, while ensuring backward compatibility. From there, we were free to refactor or rewrite as necessary to produce clean code and handle test coverage one new method at a time.

There were still other problems with our legacy code, like the near-complete avoidance of object-oriented programming (OOP). In a language as rigid as PHP, procedural code is much harder to test. If the function you are testing calls another function, there is no way to change the called function to have it return a known value.

This is particularly hard when it comes to database code, because those functions are tightly coupled to the underlying database architecture, and there is no way to break the dependency. There are some ways around this, such as using Runkit (`http://pecl.php.net/runkit`) to replace functions on the fly, but this can result in dangerous, unintended consequences, so it's better to run tests in an environment that more closely mimics production deployment.

In contrast, when writing OOP, it is straightforward to inject a different object for that database connection into the code, and at that point the intended behavior can be simulated to achieve maximum test coverage.

There is really no good solution for this problem, so we had no choice but to refactor. Rather than port this code, we wrote entirely new OOP libraries for the functionality we needed, taking the opportunity to improve our core architecture at the same time.

Testing front-end code and testing the code in the back present similar difficulties. In this case, however, the dependencies are on the client request and server info. Most PHP coders have no problem touching superglobals, but it is really not behavior conducive to testing. It's a real pain to populate and repopulate those variables while running a test. Then, too, there is the matter of testing the generated markup. Again, most developers echo out the markup without a second thought. And again, this complicates the testing process, because the only way to capture and examine that output is by using output buffering. Worse still is the process of examining response headers, for example, to ensure that a certain request generates a redirect or that cache headers are set.

Instead of trying to hack around these problems, we took a page from Django and created request and response objects. Front-end code accepts a request object with the superglobals encapsulated and produces a response object in return that contains the necessary HTTP headers and payload. This way we can decouple the code from the Web environment, easily test handling of different requests, and examine the output directly.

How Do We Solve These Problems?

Size Does Matter

Bigger is not better, and it is not faster. More than six or seven engineers working on the same project is too many. Small teams of three to five people with the same objective produce better code, in fewer lines, and with fewer bugs than a team twice the size. We ran into this problem as soon as Digg's engineering team grew to eight.

It was difficult to manage that many people on a project. It led to our trying to fit too many new features in a release, which caused problems. The number of bugs we were producing started to increase, leading to a longer QA period and in turn pushing back the release date. It became clear we couldn't keep doing this and at the same time grow the business at the rate we needed.

Team Size

To fix the problem, we split the engineers into four smaller teams, each responsible for a specific area of the code. Currently, each team consists of a lead and three to five engineers. The lead runs the team on a day-to-day basis, answers questions, resolves roadblocks, keeps management informed, and makes sure people are on track.

Project Size

Our projects were also too big, so we made them smaller: What was a single three-month project was split into four three-week projects. We also reduced the number of lines of code written between releases, which cut down on the number of bugs and the time needed for QA. The result: We were better able to stay on schedule and meet our deadlines.

Code Size

When any system reaches a certain level of complexity, working on it becomes painful. What was once a simple task becomes much more complicated. Instead of grepping a single directory with a few dozen files, thousands of files in several locations must be searched.

There is also the problem of dependencies. In a monolithic code base, the dependencies tend to be internal and implicit, leading to code that is tightly coupled and difficult to refactor. It's even worse with legacy code written in a procedural style rather than object oriented.

We have experienced these problems in different ways at Digg, but it's most severe when it comes to the code. Fortunately, PHP already has a great system for this: PEAR (`http://pear.php.net`).

To solve these problems, we undertook a three-month project to refactor the code into more than 100 modular, self-contained packages. At the same time, we built a forward-looking infrastructure for adding functionality in a clean OOP style. We also ran an internal PEAR server, which allowed us to distribute our code to our staging and production servers.

Although it would be great to do something like this all at once, it's just not practical with a code base the size of ours. A large amount of the legacy code was refactored, but realistically it needs to be done in phases, preserving backward compatibility at each step.

Unit Testing and You

Unit testing works. Yes, you can spend as much as 30 percent (if not more) of your time writing unit tests, but you save much more in debugging later. When Digg made the decision to move to test-driven development, we spent a couple of weeks looking at various options for PHP. Our engineers had a mixed bag of previous experience when it came to unit testing; some had used PHPT, those from the Java world had used JUnit, and others had actually never once written a unit test.

With the large code base we have at Digg, engineers need to know that when they modify code, they are not breaking any of the dependencies. They also need to know that the contract between the module they are working on and the pieces of code that use it is still going to function. Unit tests signals where backward compatibility is broken and allows the code to be fixed or calling methods to be updated.

Choosing a Testing Framework

Digg didn't start from scratch with testing. We had some legacy tests written in PHPT, but they were more functional tests, rather than unit tests.

Tests in PHPT are extremely simple and offer nothing more than procedural code with output matching. If a test's output does not match its prerecorded output, it has failed. PHPT tests involve lots of echoing and dumping of variables to get that output. When a test fails, the only information you get is the output difference. If you were not forward-thinking enough to add some kind of identifier, you must sift through the test to determine which actual method failed.

After review, the superior features and formal approach convinced us that PHPUnit was the way to go. PHPUnit is a stark contrast to PHPT. When a test fails, it tells you precisely where the error occurred and prints a stack trace. Rather than output matching, you determine what a method is expected to do, what it should return if it throws an exception, and the method on other objects it should call. We found PHPT testing to be superficial, while PHPUnit allowed us to test the inner recesses of our code.

Working with an Expert

After we decided to bring in a consultant to assist us in setting up a unit testing framework and harness, we made calls to two consulting companies and one expert in the field. We weren't completely satisfied with either company. One had enough experience with unit testing, but did not have anyone available to work with us in PHP. The second company had a tremendous amount of PHP experience, but we did not believe they knew enough about unit testing. Eventually we decided to go with expert Sebastian Bergmann. He maintains the newest version of PHPUnit, which means he has the skills in both unit testing and PHP we required.

One Week in a Room

After we chose Sebastian to assist us in moving to PHPUnit and begin the process of using continuous integration (see Chapter 12), we booked him for his first available week. A month later, he flew from Germany to our office in San Francisco, where we spent a week with him in a meeting room massaging these new practices into our existing code base. The process itself wasn't terribly difficult, it simply required time, effort, and focus. At the end of the week, we had a functional test harness coupling our code to PHPUnit, and we created tests for a few of the classes from our core framework.

TRAINING OUR TEAM

After we had PHPUnit running in our continuous integration environment, it was time to get people to start using it. Only about 25 percent of our developers had prior experience with unit testing, and of those, some had only PHPT experience. Not everyone actually liked the idea of unit testing, so we had to spend some effort convincing the team. To get people started, we set up a three-hour workshop in late October 2008. The workshop included the following:

➤ Basic concepts of writing unit tests

➤ Generating code coverage

➤ Mocking objects for dependency injection

➤ Advanced options (data provider, methods of exception handling, manipulating code coverage)

➤ Practical help with writing tests

During the workshop, we displayed on a projector code examples that folks would have to type and execute. Although this was a useful way to get people's feet wet, we found that by the time people needed to write real tests for their projects, they needed further assistance. They often needed help with these things:

➤ Mocking objects and related refactoring

➤ Generating coverage (some folks forgot it was even available)

What we found most helpful was making sure developers used the PHPUnit documentation and encouraging them to take a couple of hours to read it. Because our development environment is more complex than perhaps most monolithic ones, it had to be easy to write and run tests. We wrote a PHPUnit shell wrapper that sets up the environment in "testing" mode, increases the memory limit, sets the include path, and finally invokes PHPUnit itself. We also wrote base case and suite classes from which all other tests extend. These classes provide helper functions such as easy mocking of `HttpMessage` objects and other reusable items.

Over the course of a few months, most developers got comfortable writing unit tests, mocking dependencies, and checking code coverage *before* code reviews. One or two are still reluctant and will not write tests unless reminded. Some participate but are openly against the idea, but most find value in unit testing and are becoming more proficient at it. All of this is ultimately raising the quality of the code base.

We have found that when an engineer first begins to write unit tests, the most common problem is that he misses most of the edge cases. An *edge case* is a possible scenario the code could be subjected to that is abnormal or unexpected, but still possible. If you write tests that cover all the possible scenarios, not only do you likely find existing bugs, but you protect yourself from refactors that mistakenly change the code's functionality.

Edge cases come in all varieties. What if the first parameter passed was null instead of an integer? What if no rows were returned from the database because you lost connection? Planning for these events that do not normally happen in a low-stress development environment takes practice, but it becomes second nature after writing tests for a while.

Here is an example function that adds two integers:

```
/**
 * Adds two integers and returns an integer
 *
 * @param int $a the first integer
 * @param int $b the second integer
 * @return int the result of $a and $b added together
 */
function add($a, $b)
{
    return $a + $b;
}
```

Some engineers may simply create one test, similar to the following, and assume they are finished:

```
function testAddition()
{
    $a = 2;
    $b = 3;
    $this->assertEquals($a + $b, add($a, $b));
}
```

But what about the many other cases, such as the addition of negative numbers, overflowing integers, or passing in strings instead of integers? Here is another test we can write to account for that which should pass just fine, but is still good practice to be sure:

```
function testNegativeAddition()
{
    $a = -12;
    $b = -10;
    assertEquals($a + $b, add($a , $b));

    $a = 14;
    $b = -9;
    assertEquals($a + b, add($a, $b));
}
```

Now, certain tests will not give the expected result from the intended parameters. It is expected that the function will return an integer. New tests need to be created to satisfy the edge cases, but the original function add() needs to be altered in order to pass. It's good practice in test-driven development to first create the tests that will fail and then create the code to make them pass.

```
/**
 * @expectedException Exception
 */
function testOverflow()
{
    $a = PHP_INT_MAX;
    $b = 1;
    add($a, $b);
}
/**
 * @expectedException Exception
 */
function testNegativeOverflow()
{
    $a = 0 - PHP_INT_MAX;
    $b = -1;
    add($a, $b);
}
/**
 * @expectedException Exception
 */
function testParameterOverflow()
{
    $a = PHP_INT_MAX + 100;
    $b = 1;
    add($a, $b);
}
```

```
/**
 * @expectedException Exception
 */
function testStrings()
{
    $a = 'RTFM';
    $b = 3;
    add($a, $b);
}
```

We've properly tested important edge cases, but they will fail. The original function should then be updated to allow these tests to pass:

```
function add($a, $b)
{
    if (is_int($a) && is_int($b)) {
        $result = $a + $b;
        if (is_int($result)) {
        return $result;
        }
    }
    throw new Exception('Invalid Integer');
}
```

All the tests written thus far should now pass. If a parameter or a result is not an integer, the function throws an exception.

WRITING TESTABLE CODE

Once in the right mindset, writing testable code becomes easier. Getting there, however, can be a struggle. At Digg, all of our development styles have changed since starting to unit test our code. For example, our code is much more explicit now; rather than exposing internals via public member variables, we tend to write accessors instead. Accessors are significantly easier to test because you can mock them to return different objects and values.

Avoid Static Methods

Code that uses static method calls is difficult to test because it is impossible to overload these methods in descendant classes. This has changed in PHP 5.3, but previously, it was a practical necessity to limit the number of static methods and calls.

In the following example, the self in Foo always refers to Foo and never to FooMock. This makes it impossible to change the behavior of doBar(), rendering it impossible to test both paths of the conditional in doFoo():

```
class Foo
{
    public function doFoo()
    {
        $res = self::doBar();
        if ($res) {
```

```
            // Path A
        } else {
            // Path B
        }
    }
}
class FooMock extends Foo
{
    public static function doBar()
    {
    }
}
```

PHP 5.3 solves this specific instance with late static binding, but static calls still can be problematic. A function can call to a static method in another class entirely, and there is no way to change the class it references.

Here is a good example:

```
class Foo
{
    function doFoo()
    {
        $res = DB::query('SELECT COUNT(*) FROM 'foo'');
        if ($res == 0) {
            // Do something
            return;
        }
        // Do something else
    }
}
```

This code is very hard to test because it is impossible to change what DB::query() returns in a test. Ideally, the DB class would have a mechanism to inject dependencies, allowing you to negate the use of the static call, as shown in the following code:

```
class DB
{
    private static $db;
    public static function acceptDB($db)
    {
        self::$db = $db;
    }
    public static function singleton()
    {
        if (!isset(self::$db)) {
            self::$db = DB::connect();
        }
        return self::$db
    }
    public static function query($q)
    {
        return self::$db->query($q);
    }
}
```

This enables you to mock the object, substituting different code for the `queryDB()` method. In this way, you can return responses appropriate to trigger the different paths of the conditional. However, this ties the testability of the code to the testability of the libraries in use. Perhaps a better implementation is to define a method that returns the DB object itself, as in this example:

```
class Foo
{
    protected function getDB($q)
    {
        return DB::singleton();
    }
    public function doFoo()
    {
        $res = $this->getDB()->query('SELECT COUNT(*) FROM 'foo'');
        if ($res == 0) {
            // Do something
            return;
        }
        // Do something else
    }
}
```

This keeps the number of methods in `Foo` down significantly, without needing to wrap every method in `DB`.

In summary, avoid static methods for anything except for trivial, easily tested operations. If static methods must be used, make sure the code is written in such a way as to allow mock objects to be injected.

Dependency Injection

As we have just seen, it is critical to extricate code from the normal run environment to reliably test it. This environment contains other code, which may or may not be reliable. Of course, the hope is that it's well tested and debugged, but it's impossible to know. Rather than rely on the behavior of the code it depends on, it's much better to write code that triggers specific behaviors in the code you are testing. And instead of using an external database or service, return canned success and failure responses to ensure that the code does the right thing.

If this seems like lots of work, it is. But after the support framework is in place, writing the actual code is not that difficult. We cover one approach to this in more depth in the next section.

MOCK OBJECTS

Overview

The biggest problems you have when testing involve how the code interacts with other objects. These fall into two areas:

➤ External dependencies you cannot (or do not want to) support in your test environment: databases, REST API calls, and caches, to name a few.

➤ Opaque interactions with other code: When certain conditions are met, the code calls out to some other code.

These problems can be solved with some forethought and application of design patterns. The following techniques are straightforward to implement.

Database

Breaking the database dependency was one of our biggest challenges, due to our legacy procedural database code. Testing this code is an ongoing process as code is refactored to work better. A traditional approach, where data from the database is replaced with mocked data, works in simple cases, but when the need arises to test complex interactions, something more sophisticated is required.

Our solution was to create a new driver for the database abstraction layer, which uses SQLite. When we test code, we set up a mock environment using SQLite databases and inject the classes with new database instances pointing to them. The setup is fairly complicated, involving at least a half-dozen mocked objects at different layers. Because this is desired specifically to test interactions, the setup is done only once, when the first test runs. The same environment is reused for the remainder of that test case and then destroyed. Subsequent cases in the suite create new environments. This is accomplished with a common test case class from which all cases in the suite extend. Its setUp() method creates the environment if it has not been created already for that case. The child classes call its setUp() before doing any other test case–specific setup.

There are still problems with this approach. In particular, it doesn't work while performing complex or MySQL-specific queries. For the right kind of code, though, it is an extremely effective way of testing.

Loosely Coupled Dependencies

One of the most effective testing strategies we have adopted is a loose adaptation of the Visitor pattern, which we call Acceptor. For classes with external dependencies, we have explicit methods to get the current instance and inject new instances. The code looks a little like this:

```php
class Tested extends Pattern_Acceptor_Common
{
    protected $acceptable = array('DB' => 'PDB_Common',
        'Cache' => 'Cache_Common');
    private function doWork()
    {
        $data = $this->getCache()->get('foo');.
        if ($data === false) {
            $data = $this->getDB()->getAll('SELECT * FROM 'foo'');
            $this->getCache()->set('foo', $data);
        }
        return $data;
    }
    protected function getDefaultCache()
    {
        return Cache::singleton('Memcache');
    }
    protected function getDefaultDB()
    {
        return DB::singleton();
    }
}
```

```
class TestedTest extends PHPUnit_Framework_TestCase {
    private $object;
    public function setUp()
    {
        $this->object = new Tested;
        $this->object->accept(Cache::singleton('Local'));
    }
}
```

`Pattern Acceptor Common` implements the `Pattern Acceptor` interface. It provides an `accept()` method, which accepts any object passing an `instanceof` test on a class listed in `$acceptable`. A `call()` method returns the objects when `getFoo()` (`Foo` being the key of `$acceptable`) is called. If no object has been accepted, `getDefaultFoo()` is called. In this manner, classes are allowed to define the objects they depend on so replacements can be injected easily. `Pattern Acceptor Common` also implements Subject/Observer (discussed in the following section), so the accepting instance can be notified of object acceptance. This is necessary in some cases to keep its internal state valid.

It is trivial to implement a simplified version of this with private `$db`, `$cache`, and similar variables and explicit `getDB()` and `getCache()` methods. It is a good way to get comfortable with the idiom, but after you start applying it on a larger scale, it pays to build a reusable implementation. Or you can use ours (see above).

Subject/Observer for Testing Class Internals

The Subject/Observer pattern also has been useful for testing and debugging. We wrote a simple interface for subjects and observers, which classes may implement.

There also are sample implementations that can be used where class structure permits. The addition of traits to PHP has made this approach significantly easier to implement.

The idea is to attach observers to an object, which then notifies all attached observers when actions of interest take place. This is particularly useful when you want to test interaction between two objects. This is a distillation of the essence of the interface:

```
interface Pattern_Subject
{
    /**
     * Attach an observer
     *
     * @param Observer $observer The observer to attach
     *
     * @return void
     */
    public function attach(Pattern_Observer $observer);
    /**
     * Notify observers of an event
     *
     * Each attached observer will have 'observe_$what' called,
     * passing $args as the first array.
     *
```

```
            * @param string $action The event, i.e. method name
            * @param array $args Additional information
            *
            * @return void
            */
           protected function observe($action, array $args = array());
       }
       interface Pattern_Observer
       {
           /**
            * Notify us that we were attached to a subject
            *
            * @param Subject $subject The subject we attached to
            *
            * @return void
            */
           public function attached(Pattern_Subject $subject);
       }
```

Consider the example of testing a primary object: When a specific action happens, it should call a method on a secondary object. For the purposes of the test, the secondary object needs to function normally, so mocking its methods is not feasible. If the secondary class supports Subject/Observer, a mock observer can be created and then attached. This is then injected into the primary instance with the approach previously outlined.

When mocking the observer, you can tell PHPUnit you expect certain methods to be called. The level of granularity this gives is very fine. You can specify the number of times methods should be called, as well as the arguments you expect it to pass.

We use this in a few places, but the database mocking is notable. Our databases are vertically partitioned into pools, each of which has one write master and a number of slaves (http://blog.digg.com/?p=213). When testing the database code, we can create mock read-only database connections and tell PHPUnit that they should never have their execute() methods called (we use query() for reads and execute() for writes). In this way, we can ensure that queries go to the correct places. It is also an excellent pattern for fine-grained logging. Rather than polluting the code with log statements, instead pollute it with $this->observe() statements.

Each one of those can serve multiple purposes, as many observers can be attached to each subject. One might log all queries at a low level, while another logs queries with specific characteristics to be found at a higher priority.

Memcached

Our caching layer was actually one of the easier things to work with. We already had an OOP interface around the PECL Memcached extension, and we had a few other drivers (APC, Local, and so on). We implemented a Chain of Responsibility pattern on top of these drivers, so a single request could check local cache, then APC, and then Memcached, and return a result from the one that was closest. This meant that all the cache drivers adhered to the same interface and could easily be substituted for one another. The cache drivers also follow Subject/Observer, so we have further access to its internals.

Again utilizing the Acceptor pattern, a local cache driver can be easily injected in place of Memcached. This gives the ability to take a deep look at the caching behavior of the code. Because our local cache driver keeps all cached data in its instance, we can reach inside and verify that the correct things are getting cached.

Taking it a step further, we can either mock our cache instances for specific tests or attach mocked observers to ensure that the cache is used in the ways we expect and that the correct code path is run depending on the cache contents. For example, we could inject a mocked Local driver with the cache primed, which throws an exception if any data is stored. This could reveal potential performance problems, as it would alert us to cases where we do more work than necessary. We also might inject the Void driver, which does not cache anything, to make sure that the queries run correctly without potential interference from cached results.

Caching code can be prone to strange behavior, so the ability to control it so thoroughly is a great benefit to us.

Mocking a Service-Oriented Architecture

Until recently, Digg's data access layer was tightly integrated to our front end application and used a simple master/slave configuration for MySQL. All writes went to a single master and that data was replicated to many slaves, which the application used to perform reads. This worked well for small or less write-intensive applications, but was quickly becoming a bottleneck in Digg's architecture. Because of that, we decided to move to a sharded dataset, splitting the writes across many machines, but each having only a percentage of the total dataset (http://en.wikipedia.org/wiki/Partition_(database)).

In order to keep the client applications simple, we created a data access layer in PHP that abstracted out the logic of determining which machine actually had which piece of data. In order to make all this available to more than just PHP applications, we put it behind a service-oriented architecture (SOA).

We decided early on that we wanted to have this system fully unit tested, both from the client side and on the server side. That meant we needed a way to abstract out the HTTP request/response portion of that stack. As it turned out, this was pretty simple.

Figure 5-1 shows what our stack looks like.

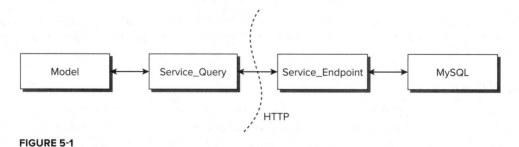

FIGURE 5-1

Model

We knew from past experience that hard coding the way data is retrieved in the client application is a bad idea, because it makes moving to another data access system extremely painful and time-consuming. With that in mind, we created the model layer. Its entire purpose is to abstract the SOA system, so the client does not even know what it is communicating with. It could be talking directly to MySQL, MemcacheDB, or Tokyo Cabinet, or to any of those systems over HTTP. We also can change which service it is talking to without changing any of the client code.

Service Query

Service Query is the proxy for the SOA system. It takes a few pieces of information from the model layer and builds up an HTTP request to the services layer. It can then send it and interpret the response when it is received.

Service Endpoint

The Service Endpoint receives the request from the HTTP server and performs whatever it was built to do, whether that is to insert a record into MySQL, send an email, or spawn a background process. It then builds up a response and sends that back to the client in whatever format was requested: PHP, JSON, or XML.

The Base Classes

The following code samples have been greatly simplified and have had lots of code removed, but the basic idea behind how to unit test them is the same. All requests to the service layer are made through the Service Query class; the run() method takes a Service Request object and returns a Service Response object. The request object actually contains four main pieces of information:

➤ The endpoint to use

➤ The parameters to pass to the endpoint

➤ The version of the endpoint

➤ The method (which will be one of the standard HTTP methods GET/POST/PUT/DELETE)

The response object contains all the information from the service layer, the list of results from the query, any possible error messages, and even some information about the total number of records matching the query (to be used for pagination).

```
class Service_Request
{
}
class Service_Response
{
}
class Service_Query
{
    public function run(Service_Request $request)
    {
        return new Service_Response;
    }
}
```

Regardless of what service it is communicating with in the background, each model supports two main methods: save(), and delete(). These methods build up and send a request to the service layer to save any changes made to the model or even delete it altogether. Right now they just throw an exception. Each class needs to implement those methods if the class is meant to support that functionality.

```
abstract class Model
{
    public function save()
    {
        throw new Exception('Method not supported');
    }
    public function delete()
    {
        throw new Exception('Method not supported');
    }
}
```

To communicate to the service layer, we have the Model Service class. That implements the abstract methods from the Model class and is composed mainly of convenience wrappers for the Model Service Query class, which actually makes the requests to the service layer.

```
abstract class Model_Service extends Model
{
    public function save()
    {
        return true;
    }
    public function delete()
    {
        return true;
    }
    protected static function getQuery($class)
    {
        return new Model_Service_Query($class, new Service_Query);
    }
}
```

Let's look at a specific example. This Model User class shown in the following code is used to represent a Digg user. It extends from model service and has a few annotations in its docblock to tell it which endpoint and version of the service layer to use. It also implements a public static method query(), which calls a method in the Model Service class that returns an instance of Model Service Query. We also give the caller the ability to pass this object in. Without this ability, we could not mock the response object later for unit testing. The reason we have to put this method in every child class is that PHP has a limitation with static methods where a common parent has no way of knowing which child class called it. This is not necessary in 5.3 due to the new late static bindings.

```
/**
 * @service_endpoint User
 * @service_version 1
 */
class Model_User extends Model_Service
{
    public static function query($query = null)
    {
        if ($query === null) {
```

```
        return parent::getQuery(__CLASS__);
      }
      return $query;
    }
  }
```

The only piece of code you have not seen yet is the `Model Service Query` class. Let's look at it more closely, because it is fairly complex. The constructor has two required parameters: the class name of the model that we will build up and give back to the caller, and a `Service Query` object that will send the request to the service layer. Using dependency injection for the `Service Query` object allows us to easily mock it later for unit testing.

```
class Model_Service_Query
{
    protected $class = null;
    protected $serviceQuery = null;
    public function __construct($class, $serviceQuery)
    {
        $this->class = $class;
        $this->serviceQuery = $serviceQuery;
    }
    public function get($field, $value)
    {
        //We just want the first user returned, there should be only one.
        return array_shift($this->runQuery(new Service_Request));
    }
    public function all()
    {
        return $this->runQuery(new Service_Request);
    }
    public function filter(array $params)
    {
        return $this->runQuery(new Service_Request);
    }
    protected function runQuery(Service_Request $request)
    {
        $response = $this->serviceQuery->run($request);
        //parse result from service layer, build up object to return
        return array(new $this->class, new $this->class);
    }
}
```

With just a little bit of reworking, we can mock the `Service Query` object and override the `run()` method to return a canned response based on a callback. This `getMockServiceQuery()` function can be used throughout unit testing to generate a mock response for any type of object.

DIGG'S QUALITY ASSURANCE PROCESS

The agile process significantly changes the way a QA team tests its software. The traditional software quality assurance function seen in waterfall models no longer applies. QA no longer has to wait until very late in the game for a build. As soon as a piece of development work is complete, QA can test that piece of code. Our agile process and tools allow us to test early and often. We have seen significant gains in the reduction of time to release, quality of product, and team efficiency since Digg's move to an agile model. The following sections show some of the successes as well as some of the challenges QA has faced at Digg.

Testing

Planning the Testing Effort

As part of the agile process, the quality assurance owner is part of the sprint from the very beginning. In order to achieve a successful testing effort, the QA owner needs to gather information from all the stakeholders, including product and development. It is important to work closely with product and development teams to fully understand the feature sets for sprints. From the product team, QA is looking for guidance and information on how the features should behave. From development, the QA owner receives information on how the features are built. This information is essential to accurately and thoroughly testing the software.

From this information, the product manager creates acceptance tests based on the features of the release. These acceptance tests are detailed steps intended to fully exercise the functionality in the feature, and each should do one verification. The QA team is responsible for further refining and defining those tests to ensure they have full coverage. Then from the acceptance tests, the QA owner can begin the process of creating tasks.

Tasks

Similar to development tasks for each sprint, there are also testing tasks. These tasks should follow the same guidelines as development tasks, including having clear start and end points. Although the goal is for the testing effort for each sprint to be fully automated, this is not always possible. There is often a combination of automated and manual testing tasks, and each of these is updated daily with the remaining work to be done. This allows the sprint lead to easily track the remaining work on the project. When determining when and what to automate, the goal is to choose scenarios that provide the greatest return. The items used when evaluating the priority of scenarios to automate are reusability, feature importance, and cost to implement.

Automation

Reusability is critical to determining the features to automate. The more frequently an automated script can be run—both in the current sprint and in future regression tests—the more attractive it is to automate. A script that logs in a user is an example of reusable automation. This script can be used repeatedly and added as a precondition to give other scripts more depth. A non-reusable script can be used if the tested functionality will not change in the near future and cannot be used to add onto other scripts. These types of scenarios are still useful to add to the regression suite.

It's also necessary to consider when the particular feature can be automated in the sprint. A feature that cannot be automated until very late in the sprint provides less benefit than one that can be automated at the beginning of the sprint. We have found that it is best to start automating at the very beginning of development of the current sprint. The QA team does not necessarily know what the final product will look like, which can be a struggle, but we have found it is best to outline our conditions in order to save time when development is closer to completion. Based on the acceptance tests, we can write out all the different cases that are needed to successfully test each feature. From there, we list each procedure for every test case. As mentioned before, we can reuse some of these procedures so we do not have to rewrite anything we have already written.

Feature importance is another factor to consider when making automation decisions. The "pain" associated with a particular feature not working correctly might mean the site is essentially unusable. We can use the user pain associated with a bug to help determine its priority. These types of failures can be catastrophic, so preparation is crucial. When testing these features, it is always important to ensure they work in the current release, and of course the most important features should always be tested with each release. It may even need to be part of a live monitoring suite.

The cost to implement automation varies significantly with each feature. Although some features are trivial, others can be very difficult and can lead to the question, "Is it really worth it?" Usually they fall somewhere in the middle of that spectrum. Nonetheless, it is important to be mindful of those features that carry with them an enormous cost to automate. Automation that was particularly difficult for us to complete had to do with implementing MySQL libraries into the automation suite and cookie modification. Even though they were difficult to automate, they ended up being very powerful and will be useful in later sprints.

An example of a function that we decided not to automate was syncing profile pictures and confirming that the actual picture was synced correctly. This would be very difficult to automate, and we determined that it was not worth the effort and that manual verification would suffice. The cost of implementation should be decided upon as soon as possible in order to avoid a loss of working cycles.

Benefits

Testing Early

When our continuous integration, or CI, environments matured to the point where we could rely on test results from it, we immediately saw huge gains. The CI environment automatically stages our code upon commits to Subversion. We can immediately test and verify new code changes as they are completed. As is always the case with QA, it takes a significant effort to build up the environments to resemble production. It is an iterative process. As we finish each release, we examine the bugs that were missed in the CI environments and take notes to make sure those types of bugs are discovered in the future.

The costs associated with finding a bug live rather than in early development are exponentially higher. A live bug not only has the obvious costs of a poor user experience, bad press, and security vulnerabilities, but also, releasing a patch is an expensive process. Developers must interrupt their current sprint work, and depending on the bug, much rework may need to be done in order to resolve the issue. Operations also must stage and push the code, and QA must verify the new functionality. The chance of regressions, or bugs that are fixed and reappear later, also increases.

Testing Often

With CI environments, bugs can be discovered and reported right away. Developers, having just checked in the code, can often resolve the problems quickly because they are still fresh in their minds.

The unit tests and code reviews have significantly increased the quality of the code that is staged. By the time the code reaches a CI or staging environment, it has already gone through a thorough set of tests and inspections. Although unit tests and code inspections work for many problems in the code, they do not take the place of the functional testing that allows code to interact. At Digg, we also run functional test automation using Selenium RC. The QA team has defined a set of "smoke" tests in our Selenium suite that runs on each build. This is a very rudimentary check of the major functional areas of the site, but we have found that it is important to focus on breadth and not depth of our tests. When we started this process, we found many cases where tests passed all the unit tests and other code inspections, but caused huge problems when pushed to the CI environment.

In a traditional waterfall approach, the task of creating automation often starts much too late for it to be useful. Automation becomes exponentially more valuable the more times a team runs it. For that reason, the goal of any software engineering team should be to automate as early as possible. When conversations with the product and development teams are complete, the QA team begins sketching out automated scenarios for the sprint. This collection of scenarios, both manual and automated, represents our full testing effort for each sprint. To help us with this, we use Twist, a product from Thoughtworks. Twist allows us to create easily readable scenarios with underpinnings in Java. The scenarios themselves are available in Wiki markup form and are easily accessible by product and development, so they have clear insight into what the testing effort includes.

Challenges

At the core of our agile process are the continuous integration environments. These environments allow us to perform functional testing early and often. When they are not available, due to either environmental or code problems, this can be very costly because developer and QA time is spent discovering and debugging the issues, and testing is often blocked until they are resolved. Initially, we saw lots of problems with the CI environments; however, with proper unit tests and discipline by development to ensure code works before committing it, we have been able to make them much more stable.

Integration testing is a key part of any software release process. It is performed as a serial process, in order to reduce complexity. By merging only one release into the trunk at a time, we reduce complex merges and risk; that way we can better focus the testing effort on the areas where code has changed. Integration testing becomes a challenge when one sprint is delayed and others are waiting in the queue, so the goal is to make this phase of the testing cycle very short because it can become a bottleneck. We try to always have one release in the integration testing phase of the cycle.

Although we are new to timeboxing and still getting better at determining our velocity, it can be difficult to know when a release is ready to enter the integration testing phase. When our integration environments are empty, it usually indicates trouble down the road, that several sprints will be ready at the same time. That's a problem because with the serial integration testing, we either must combine those releases or delay their release. Neither one is a good option, and the situation could have been avoided had we been better at understanding the end dates for sprints.

CONCLUSION

Moving to an agile process has resulted in tangible benefits. We have lowered our risk because of smaller code changes and have decreased the time to release. We have also found that having the right tools is crucial; for developers to adopt them, they need to work well and should be easy to use.

With our large PHP code base, PHPUnit made a perfect fit for a test-driven development process. In the act of creating unit tests, we discovered quite a few bugs that we fixed relatively quickly. Right now, the number of issues we encounter during the QA stage has reduced dramatically. Although we still face many challenges, the ability to release small amounts of code rapidly allows us to adapt to both internal and external factors. This model works very well for companies in an aggressive market.

Overall, the effects of unit testing have changed development and QA considerably and have brought Digg much more success.

PART III
Servers and Services

Testing Service-Oriented APIs

Matthew Weier O'Phinney

WHAT'S IN THIS CHAPTER?

➤ Recurring issues in Web service testing

➤ Testing an existing service that requires credentials

➤ Working around API limits

➤ Testing service protocols offline

➤ Testing Web service APIs without requiring network connectivity

One of Zend Framework's key strengths and differentiators in the crowded PHP framework arena is its offering of Web service consumer components. As of version 1.9, these include offerings for Adobe's AMF protocol, Akismet, Amazon (including EC2 and S3 support), Audioscrobbler from Last.fm, Delicious, Flickr, Google's GData services, Nirvanix, ReCAPTCHA, SimPy, SlideShare, StrikeIron, Technorati, Twitter, and Yahoo! — and more are planned or under development.

These services offer a myriad of functionalities:

➤ Add Spam filtering or CAPTCHA support to your forms (`Zend_Service_Akismet`, `Zend_Service_ReCaptcha`).

➤ Provide a listing of Amazon products matching particular criteria, or display individual Amazon products on your site (`Zend_Service_Amazon`).

➤ Scale your application using cloud services: offload file storage, utilize cloud databases, interact with queue services, or manage cloud server instances (`Zend_Service_Nirvanix`, `Zend_Service_Amazon_S3`, `Zend_Service_Amazon_Sqs`, `Zend_Service_Amazon_Ec2`).

➤ Manage or query social bookmarking services, search for music recommendations, create photo galleries from image services, embed your business presentations, or update social media statuses (`Zend_Service_Delicious`, `Zend_Service_Audioscrobbler`, `Zend_Service_Flickr`, `Zend_Service_Simpy`, `Zend_Service_SlideShare`, `Zend_Service_Technorati`, `Zend_Service_Twitter`)

➤ Interact with Enterprise Web service APIs (via `Zend_Service_StrikeIron`).

➤ Access and query Yahoo! search, images, and news (`Zend_Service_Yahoo`).

➤ Access Google GData (`http://code.google.com/apis/gdata/`) APIs, including Google Apps, Google Calendar, Blogger, and more (`Zend_Gdata`).

Offering components to interact with Web services is relatively trivial. A typical Web service is stateless and requires simply sending a request via HTTP (typically with some sort of identifying authentication token) and processing the response. Likewise, if you send the same request twice, you should expect either the same response or a response that retains the same structure.

Most Web service protocols fall under two umbrellas: resource-oriented services and RPC (Remote Procedure Call) services. REST is the most popular type of resource-oriented service due to its simplicity and flexibility; it utilizes HTTP verbs in order to interact with and manipulate a resource, and it provides the ability to list, view, create, update, and delete items within that resource. The resource representations may vary based on the service, but typically you use XML or JSON (Javascript Object Notation) for the resource representation; developers must rely on end-user documentation to know the structure of the representation in order to interact with it.

RPC-style services are more procedural in nature. Such services expose one or more methods that clients may then call. As an example, a search service typically exposes a `query()` method and defines one or more parameters that must be passed when invoked. Unlike RESTful services, most RPC services provide functionality for introspecting the service and its methods, including the method signatures, and are often self-documenting. This functionality provides incredible ease of use, but can also create limitations if the client and server are unable to provide the same variable types between implementations. Examples of generic RPC styles include XML-RPC and SOAP.

The various components in Zend Framework's `Zend_Service` tree provide clients a variety of services, both RESTful and RPC. At first glance, this task appears straightforward, but testing them offers a very different story.

For continuous integration (CI) purposes, it is typically better not to test against live services because this introduces network latency, and thus slows the testbed. Additionally, many services have API call limits, and automated test suites could easily rise far above these limits. As an example, the Twitter API allows 150 calls per hour, and the test suite contains around 70 discrete tests, several of which make multiple calls; clearly, running the tests more than once an hour will lead to overages. With a CI solution, this scenario is all too likely.

There are also concerns about keeping sensitive API keys or credentials in the repository; some services are paid services, and such information would present a breach of security or contracts. Some services offer rate exemptions for integrators or even special test services that integrators may sign up for and utilize. While this can solve many problems, it is not necessarily the best solution. Probably the biggest concern for continuous integration is that the tests should be capable of running in isolation and as fast as possible. Clearly, if the test suite relies on network connectivity, neither of these criteria is satisfied.

Over time, the Zend Framework team and contributors have developed a set of practices to address these issues that range from mocking the request and response payloads to offering different tests when credentials are provided via configuration. These practices can lead to well-tested service-oriented components and ensure that the end-user experience is as documented.

THE PROBLEMS

We have identified three recurring issues when testing Web services: security of API credentials, API request limits, and offline testing of services.

In the first case, many Web services require credentials of some kind, typically in the form of unique API keys. These credentials often are tied to specific user accounts, some of which may be paid services; as such, storing the credentials within the public test suite creates a potential security issue.

In a related vein, API request limits can cause issues. Good testing practices dictate that we test discrete behaviors, and this often leads to multiple identical requests. If a Web service imposes API request limits, this can lead to failed tests due to Web service throttling — either due to the shear number of requests the test suite makes or due to running the tests often.

This leads, of course, to the last issue: How can we test a Web service without network connectivity? As noted, we may want to limit network connectivity to ensure that we do not exceed API limits. Another factor is testing frequency; if we are testing frequently — perhaps using a continuous integration solution — in many cases, we do not want to impose the added time overhead of network latency into our testing.

Consider this: For each test, you need to make an HTTP connection to another server. This requires a DNS lookup, followed by requesting a connection, waiting for the connection handshake, sending the request payload, waiting for the response, and then closing the connection. This can take anywhere from fractions of a second to several seconds per request. Multiply this by dozens or hundreds of tests, and the aggregate can lead to many seconds or minutes of added time. Although this sort of integration testing is absolutely necessary from time to time, for routine continuous integration purposes, it's simply overhead.

In the case of established protocols, an existing service may not be feasibly available to test against. For example, Action Message Format (AMF)[1] is a binary format, and typically the transmission is from a Flex or Flash client to the server; developing a testing infrastructure to allow this is beyond the capabilities of most developers and practically begs for canned requests and responses to test against.

---

[1]AMF is the protocol used by Adobe Flash to communicate to remote servers; it is roughly modeled on SOAP and is generally considered an RPC-style service protocol.

SOLUTIONS

Now that we have defined the problems, namely the handling of API credentials, limits, and offline testing, we discuss effective solutions.

API Credentials

As noted earlier, API credentials typically should not be stored within a repository, particularly if the repository is publicly readable. How, then, can you test against an existing service that requires credentials?

Zend Framework's approach may not be the only solution, but it is one that has proven itself time and again. Its chief strength is its simplicity. In the Zend Framework test suite, we have defined two helper files: TestHelper.php and TestConfiguration.php.dist. TestHelper.php is a bootstrap file required by all component test suites. It sets up the PHPUnit environment, loading all typical PHPUnit classes used, setting up the include path, specifying files to be white- or blacklisted from coverage reports, enabling and configuring error reporting, and more. One of its directives is to look for a TestConfiguration.php file and load it if found; if not, it loads the TestConfiguration.php.dist file:

```
$configuration = $zfCoreTests . DIRECTORY_SEPARATOR .
'TestConfiguration.php';
if (is_readable($configuration)) {
require_once $configuration;
} else {
require_once $configuration . '.dist';
}
```

TestConfiguration.php.dist then simply defines a number of constants used within the test suites. Among these constants are various API credentials:

```
/**
* Zend_Service_Flickr online tests
*/
define(
'TESTS_ZEND_SERVICE_FLICKR_ONLINE_ENABLED',
false
);
define(
'TESTS_ZEND_SERVICE_FLICKR_ONLINE_APIKEY',
'Enter API key here'
);
```

Only TestConfiguration.php.dist is checked into the repository, and as you may note, the default values for these constants are such that they reveal no confidential information.

Users who want to test services need simply to copy TestConfiguration.php.dist to TestConfiguration.php and edit the appropriate constants. For example, users might override the above section to enable Flickr testing and provide Flickr credentials:

```
/**
* Zend_Service_Flickr online tests
*/
define(
```

```
        'TESTS_ZEND_SERVICE_FLICKR_ONLINE_ENABLED',
        true
    );
    define(
        'TESTS_ZEND_SERVICE_FLICKR_ONLINE_APIKEY',
        'some-made-up-key'
    );
```

But what about CI environments? In such environments, new constants may be added to the TestConfiguration at any point, which adds another point of failure in your tests. There are several ways to address this. First, you can create a version of the TestConfiguration specific to the CI environment; for example, you might create TestConfiguration.php.ci. In your build configuration, you add a prerequisite to copy this over to TestConfiguration.php prior to running tests. The problem with this method, however, is that you end up storing credentials in your repository — exactly the situation we were attempting to solve.

Another approach is to store the credentials in a separate repository. The CI build process then pulls the credentials from that repository and copies them to TestConfiguration.php. The following is one way to achieve this with ANT:

```
<target name="checkout">
<!-- primary repository being tested -->
<exec executable="svn" dir="${basedir}">
<arg line="co svn://server/primary-repository/trunk source" />
</exec>
<!-- build-specific repository -->
<exec executable="svn" dir="${basedir}">
<arg line="co svn://server/build-repository/trunk config" />
</exec>
</target>
<target name="test">
<!-- copy from build-specific repo to primary repository -->
<copy file="${basedir}/config/TestConfiguration.php"
todir="${basedir}/source/tests/"/>
<!-- ... -->
</target>
```

After we've established the constants and a process for defining and overriding them, we need to use them within our test suites. In many cases, we check for the ONLINE ENABLED constant for the given service and, when false, either mark all tests for the service as skipped or set a flag that is used in switch() cases, similar to the following:

```
if (constant('TESTS_ZEND_SERVICE_FLICKR_ONLINE_ENABLED')) {
    $this->onlineEnabled = true;
    // connect to service with stored credentials
    $apikey = constant(
        'TESTS_ZEND_SERVICE_FLICKR_ONLINE_APIKEY'
    );
    // ...
} else {
    $this->onlineEnabled = false;
    // specify mock adapter for connection, as well as expected
    // request/response payloads
}
```

In many cases, the various test methods delegate to protected methods to do the actual work of testing and delegate based on the status of the flag. For example:

```
class FooServiceTest extends PHPUnit_Framework_TestCase
{
    // ...
    public function testSomeServiceBehavior()
    {
        if ($this->onlineEnabled) {
            $method = '_' . __FUNCTION__ . 'Online';
        } else {
            $method = '_' . __FUNCTION__ . 'Offline';
        }
        $this->$method();
    }
    protected function _testSomeServiceBehaviorOnline()
    {
        // online tests
    }
    protected function _testSomeServiceBehaviorOffline()
    {
        // offline tests
    }
}
```

The problem with this approach is that it can lead to a disconnect between the online and offline tests; the developer may update the online tests and forget to update the offline version. A better approach is to have the two different versions make a given request, return a response, and make assertions on the response:

```
class FooServiceTest extends PHPUnit_Framework_TestCase
{
    // ...
    public function testSomeServiceBehavior()
    {
        if ($this->onlineEnabled) {
            $method = '_' . __FUNCTION__ . 'Online';
        } else {
            $method = '_' . __FUNCTION__ . 'Offline';
        }
        $response = $this->$method();
        $this->assertSame(200, $response->getStatus());
        // continue with assertions...
    }
    protected function _testSomeServiceBehaviorOnline()
    {
        // perform request to live service and return response
    }
    protected function _testSomeServiceBehaviorOffline()
    {
        // create and return mock response
    }
}
```

These strategies are not without their pitfalls. At times, developers have accidentally checked in their TestConfiguration.php files. In other cases, incorrect defaults have been supplied to the constants or constants have been omitted. However, the strategies generally work — very well.

API Limits

API limits are actually incredibly difficult to work around. If the test suite makes many discrete calls and has enough tests, it's easy to hit the limit. Additionally, if in active development of a component, you may be running the tests many times, which will have you hitting the limit due to the aggregate of tests run.

We have not entirely solved this issue, but two primary strategies have emerged. First, and often the least obvious, is to contact the API provider and ask for an exemption. In many situations, the API provider is quite willing to provide a limit-free account to those developing service classes so they can test. Developing the wrapper to their API provides them some free marketing, as well as a user base, so everyone involved benefits.

The second strategy we have used is to cache request/response pairs within the test suite. This can be accomplished rather trivially by simply concatenating the method name being invoked with the serialized arguments passed to it and then using that as a cache key within the class. Anytime a response is needed, you check first in the class for a matching cache key, and fetch a response only if none is found (storing it in the cache, of course).

For example, you can do the following:

```php
class SomeServiceTest extends PHPUnit_Framework_TestCase
{
    public $cachedResponses = array();
    public function getResponse($method, array $args)
    {
        $cachekey = md5($method . serialize($args));
        if (array_key_exists($cachekey, $this->cachedResponses)) {
            $response = $this->cachedResponses[$cachekey];
        } else {
            $response = call_user_func_array(
            array($this->service, $method),
            $args
            );
            $this->cachedResponses[$cachekey] = $response;
        }
        return $response;
    }
    public function testSomething()
    {
        $response = $this->getResponse(
            'someMethod', array('foo', 'bar')
        );
        // continue testing...
    }
}
```

In cases where you may be testing discrete behaviors of the service class based on identical requests, this often saves many round trips to the original Web service, thus reducing the number of actual calls that count against your API limit.

Offline Testing of Service Protocols

Several Zend Framework components implement generic service protocols, such as AMF (Adobe's Active Message Format, used with Flash and Flex), XML-RPC, JSON-RPC, and SOAP. Testing these protocols is typically easy, because each has one or more specifications detailing the expected request and response formats. However, these have not been completely without their challenges.

In the case of some binary formats, such as AMF, we found the only really reliable way to ensure compatibility was to have pregenerated request and response pairs that we could then compare against. To do this, we utilized Charles proxy (`http://www.charlesproxy.com`). Charles is an HTTP proxy that sits between your browser (specifically, Firefox) or other Web client and your server. It provides introspection into the requests and responses made, as well as the ability to capture and store them for later use or analysis.

Using Charles, we made requests from a Flex application to a known good AMF server, and we captured the request and response pairs. Within the unit tests, we could then pass the binary request to `Zend_Amf_Server`, pull the response, and compare it to the stored version. This process, while labor-intensive, ensured excellent binary compatibility. In fact, the lead on the component was able to identify and correct several bugs that had persisted from a previous incarnation of the code in the process.

Figure 6-1 shows Charles at work.

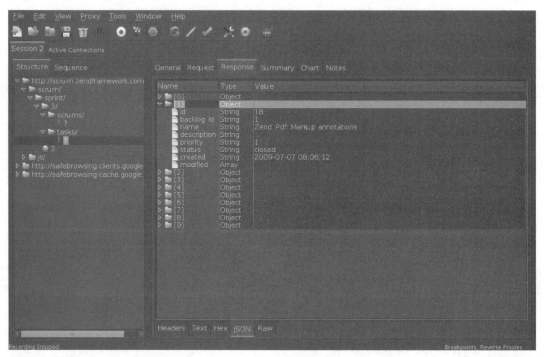

FIGURE 6-1: Charles proxy

The previous incarnation of the project had no unit tests and relied simply on the developers manually checking interactions between Flash applications (or their Flex or Flash IDE) and the server. One unresolved issue in that version had to do with processing nested objects. Under certain circumstances, the AMF response string generated was unreadable by Flash. This could lead to broken or stalled user interfaces on the client end — and sometimes worse. Because the developer was now writing tests, he was able to find a reproduce case by serializing a particular PHP structure that created it to AMF and comparing it to his expected AMF response. In doing so, he was finally able to isolate the source of the issue and correct it.

One issue arising from this style of testing is detecting and resolving API changes in the originating service. In most cases, service providers will version their APIs and have a unique URI endpoint for each distinct version of the API:

> `http://api.somehost.com/v1/` (explicit version)

> `http://somehost.com/api/20090701/` (date-based version)

Within our codebase, a service component typically is written to target the API current at the time of development. In a few cases, new versions of the API have been released that we then either need to adopt or provide functionality for. For example, Amazon changed its product search service in August 2009 to require an API key. For a period of several months, it had both versions of the API running in parallel, but Amazon strongly urged updating all code to send the API key in each request. We updated our Amazon component and released the new version before the cutoff deadline to ensure our users would be compliant. This, of course, necessitated a change in the unit tests to ensure that they failed if no API key was provided.

In other cases, we've needed to support different versions of the same API. The standard way to do this is to introduce adapters to the component. When instantiating the component, you then provide the version of the API you want to utilize, and the appropriate adapter is created; the main class then proxies to it for all functionality:

```php
class FooService{
    public function __construct($apiVersion, $apiKey)
    {
        $this->_apiKey = $apiKey;
        switch ($apiVersion) {
            case '1':
                $adapter = 'V1';
                break;
            case '2':
                $adapter = 'V2';
                break;
            default:
                throw new Exception('Invalid API version');
        }
        $adapter = 'FooService_' . $adapter;
        $this->setAdapter(new $adapter($this->_apiKey));
    }
    public function setAdapter(FooService_AdapterInterface $adapter)
    {
        $this->_adapter = $adapter;
        return $this;
    }
    // ...
}
```

This approach allows us to provide separate test suites per API version and makes it very simple to substitute mock adapters for testing the API offline.

When testing `Zend_Amf`, utilizing stored request and response pairs also provided another key benefit: The tests could be run entirely offline. This allowed us to refactor existing code safely, because we know that if the tests continue to pass, we have not altered the response format generated by the component.

Other protocols are much simpler to test. XML-RPC and JSON-RPC utilize XML and JSON under the hood, respectively, and PHP has native capabilities with these formats. As such, we have had excellent success in testing these formats because we can handcraft request and response payloads trivially for comparison purposes. With JSON, the native `json_encode()` and `json_decode()` functions can be used, and with XML, we have the DOM, SimpleXML, XMLReader, and XMLWriter extensions to choose from. In most cases, we utilize DOM or SimpleXML because they are present in vanilla installations of PHP and require no extra compilation switches or extensions.

As an example, consider the following PHP array:

```
array(
    'foo' => array(
        'subkey' => 'bat',
    ),
    'bar' => 'baz',
)
```

If this were a return value being serialized by `Zend_XmlRpc_Server`, we would want to verify that the XML generated matched expectations. The expected XML format is as follows:

```
<?xml version="1.0"?>
    <methodResponse>
        <params>
            <param>
                <struct>
                    <foo>
                        <subkey>bat</subkey>
                    </foo>
                    <bar>baz</bar>
                </struct>
            </param>
        </params>
    </methodResponse>
```

We could simply write out the XML in longhand, but we've discovered that this is problematic for several reasons. The principal reason is, quite simply, that the responses generated by the various Zend components usually do not retain any formatting. This is done primarily because the markup is intended to be machine readable; formatting is really only relevant for humans. Additionally, by stripping whitespace, we can make the payload smaller, reducing the overall size transmitted over the wire. The result is that creating mock XML payloads by hand can be troublesome to debug and can sometimes lead to errors due to inadvertent addition of whitespace.

As such, we might code the following to generate the XML we're expecting to receive:

```
$dom = new DOMDocument;
$response = $dom->createElement('methodResponse');
$params = $dom->createElement('params');
$param = $dom->createElement('param');
$struct = $dom->createElement('struct');
$foo = $dom->createElement('foo');
$subkey = $dom->createElement('subkey', 'bat');
$bar = $dom->createElement('bar', 'baz');
$foo->appendChild($subkey);
$struct->appendChild($foo);
$struct->appendChild($bar);
$param->appendChild($struct);
$params->appendChild($param);
$response->appendChild($params);
$dom->appendChild($response);
$xml = $dom->saveXML();
```

The above snippet creates the appropriate XML response, and we can then compare what was generated by `Zend_XmlRpc_Server` with this expectation:

```
$response = $this->server->getResponse();
$expected = $this->_getExpectedPayload(); // retrieves the expected XML
$this->assertEquals($expected, $response->saveXML());
```

We have similar issues with JSON. JSON can be written using formatting quite easily:

```
{
    "foo": {
        "subkey": "bat"
    },
    "bar": "baz"
}
```

However, `json_encode()` would write this with no extra whitespace whatsoever:

```
{"foo":{"subkey":"bat"},"bar":"baz"}
```

This makes comparisons more difficult. The answer, of course, is to simply use `json_encode()` on the representative PHP values:

```
$expected = json_encode(
    array(
        'foo' => array(
            'subkey' => 'bat'
        ),
    'bar' => 'baz'
    )
);
```

This value is now safe to compare against those generated by the given Zend component.

We can do the same general types of serialization operations for either requests or responses, and the approach is used extensively in our unit testing suite.

Offline Testing of Concrete Services

Now we get to perhaps the most difficult subject, which centers around testing Web service APIs without requiring network connectivity. The best solution is to do actual integration testing, and — as noted in a previous section — most of our service testbeds provide a way to do this already, by providing the option to specify credentials in the TestConfiguration.php file. However, testing should be simple, easily executed, and run with minimal dependencies — and the network is a dependency. So we have devised several strategies for offline testing of these services.

First, all the various service components utilize Zend_Http_Client to make the actual network requests. Zend_Http_Client is a lightweight component for performing HTTP requests and provides support for most HTTP features, including HTTP authentication and file uploads, PUT and POST requests, header manipulation, and more. It uses adapters for making the requests and includes one that uses PHP's native stream support, as well as another that uses the cURL extension.

A typical use case might look like the following:

```
$client = new Zend_Http_Client('http://example.org');
$response = $client->request();
if ($response->isSuccessful()) {
    $content = $response->getBody();
}
```

By default, the PHP stream adapter is used. If you wanted to use the cURL adapter, you'd simply tell the client to use that adapter:

```
$client = new Zend_Http_Client(
    'http://example.org',
    array(
        'adapter' => 'Zend_Http_Client_Adapter_Curl'
    )
);
$response = $client->request();
if ($response->isSuccessful()) {
    $content = $response->getBody();
}
```

Additionally, we have implemented a "mock" adapter, Zend_Http_Client adapter test, for the purpose of testing. The test adapter allows us to provide the expected response for a given request, which in turn allows us to test how the service component handles that response.

When using the test adapter with the HTTP client, you need to first instantiate it and then pass it to the client on creation:

```
$adapter = new Zend_Http_Client_Adapter_Test;
$client = new Zend_Http_Client(
    'http://example.org',
    array('adapter' => $adapter)
);
```

After you have the adapter and client instantiated, you can tell the adapter how to respond to a request using the setResponse(), addResponse(), and nextRequestWillFail() methods. The first and second allow you to specify the exact response payload that should be returned by the request:

```
$adapter->setResponse(
    "HTTP/1.1 200 OK" . "\r\n" .
    "Content-type: text/html" . "\r\n" .
                                "\r\n" .
    "<html>\n" .
    "<head>\n" .
      " <title>Test</title>\n" .
    "</head>\n<body>\n" .
    "<h1>Test</h1>\n" .
    "</body>\n</html>"
);
```

addResponse(), shown in the following code, is useful for when you want to test situations that include redirects. The HTTP client stores the number of redirections that occurred and returns the response from the page that finally returned a success or error status.

```
$adapter->setResponse(
    "HTTP/1.1 302 Found" . "\r\n" .
    "Location: /foo" . "\r\n" .
    "Content-type: text/html" . "\r\n" .
                                "\r\n" .
    "<html>\n" .
    "<head>\n" .
      " <title>Moved</title>\n" .
    "</head>\n<body>\n" .
    "<p>This page has moved.</p>\n" .
    "</body>\n</html>"
);
$adapter->addResponse(
    "HTTP/1.1 200 OK" . "\r\n" .
    "Content-type: text/html" . "\r\n" .
                                "\r\n" .
    "<html>\n" .
    "<head>\n" .
      " <title>Test</title>\n" .
    "</head>\n<body>\n" .
    "<h1>Test</h1>\n" .
    "</body>\n</html>"
);
$response = $client->request('GET');
$redirects = $client->getRedirectionsCount();
```

Similar to the situation with Zend_Amf, we have found that the best way to test the various situations is to make real, live requests to the API in question and to record the responses. This typically can be done using Zend_Http_Client directly or using more basic UNIX command line tools such as curl. After we have the responses, we can use them within our test cases.

When using curl, we found that using the -i switch was invaluable, because it includes the HTTP response headers in the output; these allow us to build accurate responses, as well as to test functionality that introspects the headers. By default, `curl` dumps to `stdout`, which is useful for checking to ensure that the request was successful; we often use the UNIX `tee` command to simultaneously redirect `stdout` to a file:

```
$ curl -i http://framework.zend.com/ | tee response.txt
HTTP/1.1 200 OK
Date: Wed, 11 Nov 2009 18:23:25 GMT
Server: Apache/2.2.12
Set-Cookie: PHPSESSID=XXXXXXXXXXXXXXXXXXXXXX; path=/
Expires: Thu, 12 Nov 1981 08:52:00 GMT
Cache-Control: no-store, no-cache, must-revalidate, post-check=0, pre-check=0
Pragma: no-cache
Content-Length: 3416
Content-Type: text/html

<!DOCTYPE html PUBLIC "-//W3C//DTD XHTML 1.0 Strict//EN"
    "http://www.w3.org/TR/xhtml1/DTD/xhtml1-strict.dtd">
<?xml version="1.0" standalone="true"?>
<html xmlns="http://www.w3.org/1999/xhtml" xml:lang="en" lang="en">
<head>
    <title>Zend Framework</title>
```

When using `Zend_Http_Client`, you need to inspect the response. To retrieve the received response headers, `getHeaders()` returns an associative array of header name/value pairs, and `getHeadersAsString()` returns the headers portion of the response as the verbatim string. Similarly, `getBody()` retrieves the readable version of the content body, while `getRawBody()` allows retrieving the body of the response as it was actually transmitted, which can be particularly useful for testing compressed or chunked responses. When creating response payloads for later use in mocking, it's easiest to use the methods that retrieve the raw versions.

```
$response = $adapter->request('GET');
$headers = $response->getHeadersAsString();
$body = $response->getRawBody();
```

One method used to get the responses has been to cache in a method similar to that which we have shown previously in the section on API limits. During the initial testing phase, instead of storing the response in memory within the class, we store it in a local file. Such a technique also ensures that for a given API version, the online and offline tests have parity. For example:

```
class SomeServiceTest extends PHPUnit_Framework_TestCase
{
    public function cacheResponse($method, array $args)
    {
        $cacheFile = $this->getCacheFile($method, $args);
        if (file_exists($cacheFile)) {
            return;
        }
        $client = $this->service->getHttpClient();
        $response = $client->getLastResponse();
        $headers = $response->getHeadersAsString();
        $body = $response->getRawBody();
```

```
            $content = $headers . "\r\n" . $body;
            file_put_contents($cacheFile, $content);
        }
        public function getCachedResponse($method, array $args)
        {
            $cacheFile = $this->getCacheFile($method, $args);
            if (!file_exists($cacheFile)) {
                throw new Exception(sprintf(
                    'Missing cache file for method "%s", args "%s"',
                    $method,
                    var_export($args, 1)
                ));
            }
            return file_get_contents($cacheFile);
        }
        public function getCacheFile($method, array $args)
        {
            $cachekey = md5($method . serialize($args));
            return dirname(__FILE__) . '/_responses/' . $cacheKey;
        }
        public function testSomething()
        {
            if (!$this->onlineEnabled) {
                $response = $this->getCachedResponse(
                    'someMethod', array('foo', 'bar')
                );
                $client = $this->service->getHttpClient();
                $adapter = $client->getAdapter();
                $adapter->setResponse($response);
            }
            $response = $this->service->someMethod('foo', 'bar');
            if ($this->onlineEnabled) {
                $this->cacheResponse(
                    'someMethod', array('foo', 'bar')
                );
            }
            $this->assertTrue($response);
        }
    }
```

The caching code is often removed after the tests have been completed, but keeping them around can be useful for testing future versions of an API or testing methods of the API unsupported in the original iteration of the component.

To pull a real-world example, let's look at Zend_Service_Akismet. Akismet (http://akismet.com/development/api/) is a service started by WordPress to help reduce spam comments in blogs. It basically acts as a huge honeypot[2] and allows users to flag submitted content as either "spam" (unwanted, unsolicited content) or "ham" (relevant content that should be kept), as well as to test whether given content should be flagged one way or the other. The API is a REST API (though not RESTful), supports limited methods, and is reasonably documented.

---

[2] A good description of "honeypot" in a computing context is available at http://en.wikipedia.org/wiki/Honeypot_%28computing%29.

To test the `isSpam()` method, we're primarily interested in determining whether the client parses the response correctly. As such, we create a POST payload and then simply call the relevant method. In order to test it, we must first build a mock response and then attach it to the HTTP client adapter; after we have done so, we can call the relevant method and assert against the results:

```
$response = "HTTP/1.0 200 OK\r\n"
          . "X-powered-by: PHP/4.4.2\r\n"
          . "Content-type: text/plain; charset=utf-8\r\n"
          . "X-akismet-server: 72.21.44.242\r\n"
          . "Content-length: 4\r\n"
          . "Server: LiteSpeed\r\n"
          . "Date: Tue, 06 Feb 2007 14:50:24 GMT\r\n"
          . "Connection: close\r\n"
          . "\r\n"
          . "true";
$this->adapter->setResponse($response);
$this->assertTrue($this->akismet->isSpam($this->comment));
```

We have a similar test showing an `assertFalse()` with a response that indicates the comment was not spam. Having the two separate tests allows us to ensure that the API behaves as expected when provided a given response, and it actually allows us to test different responses using the same requests, saving a number of coding contortions that may be necessary otherwise. (In the case of Akismet, for instance, it is hard to craft payloads that automatically are categorized as either spam or ham.)

CONCLUSION

Unit testing Web service components offers some unique challenges. On the one hand, testing these components is a prime example of integration testing, typically a difficult process due to the problems in reproducing the request environment and API limits and keeping the security of API credentials. On the other hand, it requires some thorough planning of test cases to ensure that all the various permutations of the API or protocol specification are covered, and it requires substantial effort to record the various request and response payloads necessary to execute those tests.

Fortunately, surmounting the difficulties can be relatively straightforward. Test configuration can be automated to provide the ability to switch online integration tests on or off, as well as to provide API credentials on demand. Caching, a topic all professional Web developers should already be intimately familiar with, can be used to solve a variety of problems as well, ranging from reducing the number of API calls made to creating response payloads that may be used in offline tests. Additionally, you also can turn to third-party tools, such as Charles Proxy, cURL, and others to create HTTP artifacts for use in your testbeds.

Overall, the choice of methodology depends largely on the protocols being tested and the tools with which an individual developer is most familiar. However, the end result has led to many well-tested and full-featured service components in the Zend Framework library.

7

Testing a WebDAV Server

Tobias Schlitt

WHAT'S IN THIS CHAPTER?

➤ Introduction to the WebDAV component

➤ Development of the WebDAV component

➤ Integrating different test methods into an existing unit testing setup

The goal of the eZ Components project is to provide a solid, well-documented, and unit-tested library for PHP application development. One part of these professionally developed components is a package to provide a generic WebDAV server to be integrated into custom applications.

In this chapter, I give you insight into the problems we faced during the development of the WebDAV component. Besides the violation of standards that almost every client performs, we had to deal with code that was very hard to test with the default way of unit testing. Integration and acceptance testing are two techniques discussed in this chapter.

ABOUT THE eZ WEBDAV COMPONENT

The eZ WebDAV component provides a modular and generic implementation of a WebDAV server for integration into custom Web applications. This section introduces you to WebDAV and the architecture of the component, to make it easier for you to follow the rest of this chapter.

WebDAV

Web-based Distributed Authoring and Versioning (WebDAV) is an extension to the HTTP protocol that enables users to edit Web content through their favorite Web or file browsers.

Initially, the Web was meant as a read/write medium, which can still be seen in the request methods PUT and DELETE that are part of the HTTP protocol definition. Nowadays, the Web is read-only for most users, if you do not consider the deficient possibilities of HTML form-based content editing used in most Content Management Systems (CMS), blogs, and forums.

In 1996, the W3C began discussing WebDAV as an extension to HTTP, which should provide interactive editing and publishing facilities. By 1999, a first official version of the protocol definition was released by the Internet Engineering Task Force (IETF) in RFC 2518.[1] This version is now obsolete and was replaced with the updated RFC 4918[2] in 2007. The newer RFC solves some of the basic design issues of the original version.

During the first discussions of WebDAV, the idea was to provide both authoring and versioning in the RFC. Because both topics turned out to be more complicated than expected, the latter part was left out, to be implemented in later additions. Only the authoring part was specified.

WebDAV basically adds new request methods to HTTP and refines existing ones, like PUT and DELETE. Using these extensions, a WebDAV client can provide authoring facilities to its user, if it connects to a WebDAV-enabled server. The user typically interacts with such a server through a file-system-browser-like Graphical User Interface (GUI) that allows him to create, delete, copy, and move directories and files.

To be independent from the file system analogy, the WebDAV standard uses a different terminology: Directories are called *collection resources* and files are called *noncollection resources*. I use the terms *files* and *collections* here, to avoid wasting too much space with terminology.

The following list gives you a short overview of the WebDAV request methods and what they are expected to do:

➤ **COPY**: This request copies a single file or a collection from one place to another. The source and destination of the COPY method must reside on the same server. COPY may potentially overwrite an existing destination.

➤ **DELETE**: The DELETE request is already specified in HTTP. WebDAV refines this request method slightly, but not enough to be significant for the purposes of this chapter. The purpose of the DELETE method, as you may already have guessed, is to permanently remove files or collections from the WebDAV server.

➤ **LOCK**: A WebDAV server can support locking, to avoid the "lost update problem."[3] A client may issue a LOCK request on a collection or file in order to gain exclusive access to it. Locks may be cleaned up by the server at any time, but they should normally be freed by the client through the UNLOCK method.

➤ **MKCOL**: Using this request, a client can create a new collection. The target for the new collection must not exist on the server.

---

[1]http://tools.ietf.org/html/rfc2518

[2]http://tools.ietf.org/html/rfc4918

[3]For a good description of "lock" in a computer science context, see http://en.wikipedia.org/wiki/Lock_(computer_science).

➤ **MOVE:** The MOVE request acts like the COPY request, followed by a DELETE request to the source of the COPY.

➤ **PROPFIND:** A WebDAV server maintains meta-information for each file and collection, called *properties* in the RFC. Two different kinds of properties exist: live properties, which are maintained by the server itself, and dead properties. For example, live properties are for the creation date of a file or collection or its content type. Dead properties can contain arbitrary information that a client wants to store. The PROPFIND method is used by a client to retrieve certain properties or to retrieve the names of all properties available on the server.

➤ **PROPPATCH:** Corresponding to the PROPFIND request, the PROPPATCH request is used to update property values on the server.

➤ **PUT:** The PUT request method is already defined in HTTP and is only slightly refined in WebDAV. Using this method, the client uploads a file to the server.

➤ **UNLOCK:** A lock acquired by the LOCK method should be released using the UNLOCK method. However, a server may release a LOCK at any time, for example, if the client crashes.

A WebDAV-compliant server must fulfill the requirements stated in the WebDAV RFC regarding these request methods as well as some other minor ones, like the OPTIONS request. The only exceptions are the LOCK and UNLOCK methods, which are not mandatory. In addition, the RFC defines many new request and response headers and bodies.

It should be noted that the RFC is not easy to read or understand. Its structure is similar to a plate of well-cooked Italian spaghetti, with lots of inconsistencies and elusive design decisions buried in it. Both factors greatly complicate the implementation of a WebDAV server or client.

Architecture

Four major requirements were defined for the eZ WebDAV component:

➤ **Flexibility:** A main purpose of the WebDAV component was to replace the old WebDAV implementation in our CMS "eZ Publish." But the goal was not a reimplementation of the existing functionality, exclusively for this purpose. The component should become a general purpose WebDAV server, which can be used in any Web application.

➤ **Client compatibility:** Many client programs claim to be WebDAV-compliant, but in fact they violate the standard in many ways. The WebDAV component should provide suitable mechanisms to work around such interoperability issues on a client-specific basis.

➤ **Modularity:** The most common way of storing WebDAV-accessible data is to use a file system. But there might be a use-case for storing such data in a different way, like in a database. Therefore, the component should allow flexible substitution of the storage mechanism without affecting other parts, like the client communication.

➤ **Extensibility:** Many additions to the WebDAV protocol exist, and custom extensions are possible. Therefore, the architecture of the component should allow for the later implementation of such additions without having to change the initial API. For example, locking functionality should optionally be implemented, without having to change already-implemented back ends drastically.

Finding the optimal architecture to satisfy these requirements was not trivial. Therefore, the design phase of the WebDAV component was quite long compared to other components. The final result of this process is shown in Figure 7-1.

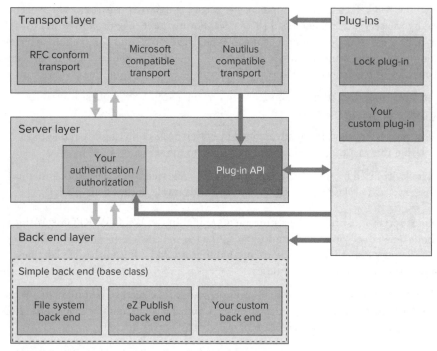

FIGURE 7-1: Architecture of the WebDAV component

As you can see, we decided on a three-layer architecture. The uppermost tier is the transport layer. This layer is responsible for communicating with the client and for ironing out any potential RFC compatibility issues. On an incoming request, the received information is parsed into data objects, which are then handed over to the next tier. After the request has been processed, the transport layer receives a data object back, containing the response information to send. It is then responsible for writing out this data in a format the client understands. Depending on the actual client, different classes are instantiated on the transport layer.

A typical example where client-specific handling is necessary is Microsoft Internet Explorer in various versions. This client sometimes sends broken PROPFIND requests, which require special headers to be present in every response. If these headers are not set, Internet Explorer refuses to talk to the server in WebDAV manner at all.

After the data objects that encapsulate the request information have been created, they are submitted to the second tier: the server layer. This layer represents the central control point, very much like the controller of the Model-View-Controller (MVC) pattern.[4] The object on this stage ties together the other layers, handles authentication, and contains the plug-in API. Typically, it hands the given request object over to the back end, if authentication succeeds.

---

[4]See http://en.wikipedia.org/wiki/Model_view_controller for a description of the Model-View-Controller pattern.

At the bottom level, the back end layer resides. This tier performs the processing of the request methods, given the corresponding data object. It accesses and potentially manipulates the data storage, creating a response object. This object is then handed back to the superjacent layers. By implementing a set of interfaces, custom data storage mechanisms can be integrated at this point, without taking care of client specialties or extended functionality.

Finally, you can see the so-called "Plug-in API" in the architecture chart. Through this API, plug-ins can hook into several events on the transport and server layers. For example, a client can parse and handle request methods that are not known by the transport and the back end. Plug-ins also may react on already handled methods and even manipulate request and response objects in some ways. To gather information from or manipulate information in the data storage, plug-ins may create request objects themselves and send these to the back end.

For example, locking is implemented as a plug-in. This plug-in parses and handles the LOCK and UNLOCK methods. The plug-in also reacts in several other methods and performs checks of the lock conditions. Furthermore, it is responsible for handling special headers in the scope of locking. To reflect locks in the back end, dead properties are used. The plug-in creates PROPFIND request objects to fetch these properties and PROPPATCH request objects to manipulate them in the back end.

DEVELOPMENT CHALLENGES

The eZ WebDAV component was initially developed by Kore Nordmann and me as a collaborative effort. On the one hand, this process was a prototypical development cycle in the eZ Components project, but on the other hand, it was very different from the other components we worked on before. We consequently stayed with test-driven development, as usual, but soon faced many unknown challenges.

I go into detail on only one test-specific issue later in this chapter. It is still important that I give you a little insight into the other problems with design, implementation, and testing that we faced during the development of this special component.

Requirements Analysis

The first stumbling block was the WebDAV RFC itself. Implementation of an RFC is not easy in general. In contrast to typical application development, the concepts you need to implement are not homemade. You need to read the RFC, understand the concepts described in it, find a sensible architecture, and design in your own environment to realize the concepts.

The first step is to get the big picture. What is the main purpose of the RFC? What are the main concepts, and what is just fluff? Which architecture fits these concepts best? In terms of WebDAV, this also involves known side effects, like client incompatibility.

With the WebDAV RFC, this was problematic. The document structure is really messy and information on specific topics is spread all over the roughly 100 pages. In addition, it is quite hard to make sense of some of the concepts, even for someone who has been in Web development for a long time. Some of the concepts are suboptimal, and others are just plain dumb. However, you need to stick to the RFC and cannot simply go your own way.

For these reasons, we first wrote a summary of the RFC in our own words. We structured this in a way that allowed us to get an overview about what was actually to be implemented. In addition, we added our notes, pointing to the main problems we had already discovered.

The next step was to create a design document, as was usual in the eZ Components project. This document first describes the overall architecture of the component, which you have already seen earlier in this chapter. In addition, it covers general design decisions and descriptions of the main classes and the basic workflow of the component to create.

TDD after RFC

The eZ Components development process uses a derivative of test-driven development (TDD): The first step after writing the design for a component is to write down a stub for the first class to implement. This stub contains only the signatures containing all public methods, but not method bodies. This defines the contract of the class against all other parts of the component and the user. While this may need to change during further development, it is the first incarnation of what the class is supposed to do.

After that, test cases against this interface are implemented, to fix the functionality the class must provide. Test cases must cover every behavior of each public method of the class, including exceptions in error cases. Error cases are especially important for a library/framework project, because you need to think about the errors that might be produced by faulty parameters provided by a user and error scenarios that might occur on the user's system, in every class.

When the test cases are finished, the class itself is filled with code, to make the test cases pass. Having the requirements for each method fixed in tests allows you to write only the code necessary.

Often, during my early days with this style of coding, I actually wrote too much code in a method. Back then, I sometimes implemented before doing the tests. However, when writing the tests afterward, I noticed that some code lines could never be reached or that checks were duplicated. I instantly needed to refactor the code, which was actually more work than doing it the right way to begin with.

For the WebDAV component, using the correct approach to writing testable code resulted in more than 80 classes to be created and tested. This was a problem: There was no possibility to validate the implementation in real life. Would the server finally run at all? Was the implementation conforming to the RFC? Would clients be able to communicate with it? We could not know until at least the basic server infrastructure was completed.

You can only create test cases based on your personal understanding of the RFC in this development phase. There is no way to ensure this understanding is correct until you reach the point where you can let a first client communicate with the server. The ambiguity of the WebDAV RFC made this even harder.

One way to validate parts of the implementation was provided by the request and response examples contained in the RFC. These allowed us to build integration tests after the first infrastructure bits were done. For example, we could test whether the transport layer was able to parse the requests correctly into data objects and whether it somewhat correctly serialized the response objects. Still, the examples delivered by the RFC were often incomplete or misleading, and there were not many of them.

The biggest advantage in a TDD approach was that we could refactor the code at any time easily. We could extract commonly needed functionality into new classes and introduce further abstraction steps without breaking the defined API. The test cases ensured this quite well.

However, we also needed to change APIs sometimes. In this case, the tests allowed us to spot all places where we needed to adjust additional code and saved us from a debugging hell.

Testing a Server

When the initial implementation of the design was done, the crucial point was reached: letting the first client access the server and see if it works. Developing a server is generally more challenging than a normal CLI (command line interface), GUI, or Web application. In those three other environments, you can usually perform manual acceptance tests on your code by hand. On the command line, you can run the application and see directly what it does and if errors occur. On the Web, you can use your browser. It gives you all generated output, which includes error messages. You can inspect HTML to spot errors easily. Front end debugging tools like Firebug are widely available and make things easier. In the GUI area, lots of toolkits exist to save you from endless debugging.

While developing a server against a special sort of client, you miss much of this functionality. WebDAV clients do not display the response data generated by the server directly. They interpret the response and react on it in their GUIs, if they understand the response, of course. If they do not, they usually show you a simple error message like "Action failed." Some clients even do not display an error; they simply refuse to work, or crash. For development, this is very difficult.

Luckily, WebDAV is only an extension to HTTP, so you can still test some of the request methods using a standard Web browser. The GET method is an example. This at least enabled us to check that the main server architecture was working. But, as you know from the WebDAV overview earlier in this chapter, this is only one of many methods supported in WebDAV, and most of them are not supported by Web browsers at all.

The first client we chose for testing is Cadaver,[5] which works on the UNIX/Linux command line. This client is well known for its RFC compliance. It provides somewhat useful error messages and supports all functionality defined in the main WebDAV RFC.

I admit that I was a bit astonished that large parts of functionality worked out of the box with Cadaver. However, even if many actions worked fine in Cadaver, not everything was perfect. So, what do you do if your server does not work as expected and you have no clue why?

I can recommend two basic techniques. First, you should inspect the communication of your server with the client. Second, and more importantly, try to reproduce the same scenario with another server implementation and inspect the communication there too.

The most important tool for this task is Wireshark.[6] This network sniffer allows you to capture all network packages that run through a specific network interface. Better yet, it allows you to filter on certain criteria, like the incoming and outgoing port numbers and types of packages, even matching on parts of a package.

---

[5]Cadaver's Web site is at http://www.webdav.org/cadaver/.

[6]The Wireshark Web page is at http://www.wireshark.org/.

Wireshark lets you inspect each single network package. It knows much about the many protocols on the different OSI[7] layers and formats the packages in each layer nicely for inspection.

Figure 7-2 shows a Wireshark dump of the communication between Cadaver and a WebDAV server setup using our component. The topmost area shows a list of all scanned packages in temporal order. The box below that shows detailed information about the selected package. You can see the HTTP headers and the content of the response. The third box shows the hex-encoded package. The tab list at the very bottom allows you to split between the typical package view and a de-chunked version. This is useful for chunked responses, so you can see the complete response information at once.

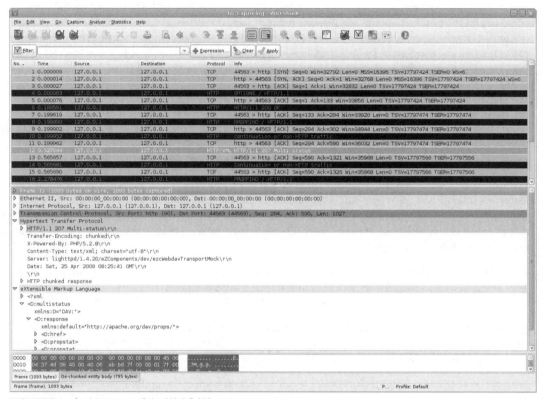

FIGURE 7-2: Architecture of the WebDAV component

In our case, we used Apache `mod_webdav`, together with different clients, to reproduce our error scenarios. By doing it this way, we were able to discover, for example, that some versions of MS Internet Explorer cannot cope with whitespaces between XML tags. Therefore, the WebDAV component now strips all non-significant whitespaces from XML response bodies, if it is talking to an Internet Explorer client.

---

[7]The OSI model is described here: `http://en.wikipedia.org/wiki/OSI_model`.

AUTOMATED ACCEPTANCE TESTS WITH PHPUNIT

PHPUnit, as the name states, is a unit testing framework. However, unit testing is not the full solution to all your problems. Integration and acceptance tests are an important part of your quality assurance too. Setting up a special test environment for each kind of test is not a desirable goal, so integrating different test methods into an existing unit testing setup is a much better solution.

In the case of the WebDAV component, we needed a mixture of acceptance and automated integration tests. Two major objectives needed to be met whenever a change was added to the source code:

➤ Ensure that every part of the server still works.

➤ Ensure that all clients still work.

Achieving these goals was the most challenging part of the development. In the Web environment, you usually use a tool like Selenium to ensure that your user interface contains all required control elements and that the application still works as expected. This kind of acceptance test is quite similar to the requirement that clients still work. However, there is no tool like Selenium for WebDAV clients, and writing one would be a life's work.

Our first idea was to research tools that can control GUI applications remotely. Using such a tool, we wanted to record the procedure of testing with a specific client and replay this from within our test environment. The idea failed for various reasons. Most of the tools we found could only operate on Windows, but the eZ WebDAV component supports clients on many different operating systems. Using many different tools for testing was not an option. This would require testers to install the needed tools in order to perform QA on their systems. Creating such a burden could potentially scare off voluntary testers. Furthermore, most of the remote control software is not open-source and not free of charge, which raises the burden for testing even more. Finally, the few tools that we tried did not perform their job well and were therefore useless for us.

We decided instead to implement a record-playback-based testing system on the basis of PHP, right inside PHPUnit. This system consists of two basic phases:

1. Capture the client-server communication data while testing with a certain client.

2. Replay the captured requests in temporal order and compare the actual response with the captured one.

This method actually represents a kind of black-box regression test. The functionality against a certain client is tested by hand. The input and output data of the system are recorded. During an automatic testing step, the input data is replayed and the generated output is compared to the captured variant. If it differs, the test fails.

In the WebDAV components language, we call a test run for a specific client a "test trail." A trail consists of an ordered number of data sets (test sets), which consist of a pair of request and response data. Each operation performed during the manual client test is reflected in one or more data sets of the test trail, because clients often perform multiple requests to reach a certain goal.

It is important to note that, in contrast to unit testing, the tests in a trail are not independent from each other. The order of the test sets is highly significant. Furthermore, the state of the server needs to be maintained between tests. In unit testing, both of these conditions are highly discouraged and heavily violate the basic idea.

If a test trail fails after a change, this does not necessarily mean that the corresponding client will not work anymore. Many changes are insignificant to the client. However, a failing test trail indicates that a manual test with the affected client is necessary. So this method of regression tests still involves manual work now and then. But it still gives us an indication when a certain client needs to be tested, and it avoids the need to test each client after each change or before every release. Furthermore, it saves us from debugging which change introduced a regression, in case a change broke a client that was previously working.

Capturing Test Trails

To dump a test trail, we use a specialized setup of the WebDAV component. This involves capturing the request and response data, on a common back end basis and infrastructure. This infrastructure also involves authentication, authorization, and potentially handling of lock information.

These steps are necessary steps here:

1. Wrap the transport layer to capture request and response data.

2. Set up a standardized server environment using a platform-independent back end.

3. Capture errors, notices, warnings, and exceptions for debugging.

4. Store the captured data for human examination and automated replaying.

Using this setup, testers can provide the development team with a successful test trail to be integrated into the test suite or with a failing one for debugging purposes. Furthermore, contributors can easily debug added functionality and new clients to be integrated.

I don't want to go into detail on the code of this script here, because it is very dependent on the WebDAV component. However, it is helpful to see that the generated test data makes sense in order to understand the next section.

The test setup generates a directory structure as follows:

```
Webdav/tests/clients/nautilus/
|-- 0001_PROPFIND_request_body.xml
|-- 0001_PROPFIND_request_server.php
|-- 0001_PROPFIND_response_body.xml
|-- 0001_PROPFIND_response_headers.php
|-- 0001_PROPFIND_response_status.txt
|-- 0002_PROPFIND_request_body.xml
|-- 0002_PROPFIND_request_server.php
|-- 0002_PROPFIND_response_body.xml
|-- 0002_PROPFIND_response_headers.php
|-- 0002_PROPFIND_response_status.txt
|-- 0003_OPTIONS_request_body.xml
|-- 0003_OPTIONS_request_server.php
|-- 0003_OPTIONS_response_body.xml
```

```
|-- 0003_OPTIONS_response_headers.php
|-- 0003_OPTIONS_response_status.txt
...
```

You can see test sets for the first three requests here. Each test set consists of five different files.

The request part of the test set is the request body and the $_SERVER[8] array. The request body is stored as plain text, and because it mostly contains XML (or no) data, we chose the specific file ending. The $_SERVER array, which contains the request headers and information about the requested URI and the environment, is stored as PHP code, using the var_export()[9] function.

Because the $_SERVER array contains some highly environment-specific information and lots of garbage (like environment variables) that is not significant for the tests, it is somewhat unified in the test script and unnecessary bloat is removed. It is important to note that this processing of the server variables happens before the WebDAV server comes into play at all. This way, potential flaws in the unification can be detected directly during manual testing and not only when running the test suite.

The response data is split up into three different files. The response body, although it might sometimes not contain XML data, is also saved as plain text. The generated headers are directly grabbed from the transport layer as an array of header name and value. Logically, this is stored as PHP code too. Finally, the response status is saved as plain text.

To ease debugging, the filenames for a test set are numbered in the order in which they occurred, and they contain the request method used by the server. This allows a quick overview of which kind of requests a server issued to achieve a certain result and potentially where it broke.

The example shown above is taken from a successful test trail. If a test trail fails, the test script also generates files that contain the occurred errors and exceptions for debugging purposes. Furthermore, it is possible to get a dump of the back end after each request, to inspect its status around the time when the client produced a failure.

Different clients produce different numbers of requests for the same tasks. This ranges from 50 generated files for the test recipe (as shown in the next section) up to about 600. Because the resulting number of files cannot easily be handled by our version control (Subversion), we needed to merge the test set files into a single file for each trail. Because we used only plain text and PHP code for the storage, the script to merge the debugging output into a single file is quite straightforward.

Test Recipe

Especially important for manual tests, and therefore also for the semi-automatic testing in the WebDAV case, is a well-defined test recipe. Such a recipe defines which steps to perform during a test. In a way, it's a checklist of what needs to be tested.

---

[8]The $_SERVER array is described at http://php.net/manual/en/reserved.variables.server.php.

[9]The var_export function is described at http://php.net/var_export.

Our test recipe looks like this:

1. Connect to the server without any username and password.

2. List the root directory.

   a. Make sure all files and directories are visible:

      ➤ `collection/`

      ➤ `file.xml`

      ➤ `file.bin`

   b. Run `/secure_collection/` with a hint that access is forbidden for you.

3. Enter directory `/collection/`.

4. List directory.

5. Download `file.txt` to your local machine.

6. Verify that the content is "Some content."

7. Create a new directory `/collection/subdir/newdir`, and make sure it was created.

8. Upload `file.txt`, and make sure it is there.

9. Delete `newdir/`, and make sure it is gone.

10. Rename `put_test_utf8_content.txt` to `put_test_öüß.txt` (or something similar, as long as it contains UTF-8 chars), and check that the client displays the change properly.

The list is shortened here because it is very extensive. The test recipe tries to ensure that every possible operation is tested. This ranges from listing directories to deleting directories recursively and using filenames with strange (UTF-8) characters. It is very important to define such a recipe for manual tests, like acceptance tests, to ensure that every client is completely tested. This way, the generated client test trail fully covers the client's behavior.

Integration into PHPUnit

PHPUnit makes implementing custom test concepts easy and therefore allows us to integrate the WebDAV acceptance tests. We basically needed to derive our own classes for two basic concepts of PHPUnit: a test case and a test suite class. With both together, we now run the client tests for each of the supported clients as part of our unit test suite.

A Custom Test Case

The class `PHPUnit_Framework_TestCase` is the very heart of every test run by PHPUnit. Whenever you write tests for a class, you commonly extend the base test case. For our acceptance tests, we do pretty much the same. Usually, you implement a `test*()` method for every test you want to combine into a test case. This is what we needed to change in our case, because writing a dedicated test method for each test set obviously would have been too much work.

Our test case class is named `ezcWebdavClientTest`, and each instance of this class represents exactly one data set of a test trail. That is, for each test trail, some test cases are instantiated and are set to be run in a specific order. Our custom test suite, explained later in this section, is responsible for instantiating, configuring, and executing these test cases. Note that this class does not extend `PHPUnit_Framework_TestCase` directly, but has `ezcTestCase` as its parent. This class extends the base test case class and provides some utility methods, like creating a temporary directory.

The most important information a test case needs is stored in the following attributes:

➤   `$server`: This variable holds the `ezcWebdavServer` instance to perform the test on. The attribute is public, because it is configured externally.

➤   `$backend`: The corresponding back end to use with the server is stored in this attribute. To run the server, this back end object is needed. This attribute is public too, for the same reason `$server` is.

➤   `$id`: This reflects the number of this test case or the number of the test set in the trail.

➤   `$testData`: This attribute holds the data of the test set to run. You saw this array of request and response data in the previous section.

As mentioned, the `$server` and `$backend` attributes are public. We made this to allow custom setups for these variables. For example, some clients need dedicated testing with locking or authentication enabled and disabled, because they behave differently in these cases. To achieve this, the attribute `$setup` holds an instance of `ezcWebdavClientTestSetup`, which performs the configuration of the test case.

This setup object is also responsible for keeping the `ezcWebdavServer` and `ezcWebdavBackend` instances between test cases. Remember that in unit testing, it is desirable to have each test case run independently from the others in a clean environment. This is different in our acceptance test because the data sets of a test trail need to be run in a continuous environment.

Besides these, the test case class has other attributes to store additional information. We do not go over these in depth, but you will see them as we go into detail on the code.

The creation of a new test case works as follows:

```
public function __construct( $id, ezcwebdavClientTestSetup $setup,
    array $testData )
{
    parent::__construct(
        sprintf(
            '%s %s',
            $id,
            $testData['request']['server']['REQUEST_METHOD']
        )
    );
    $this->id = $id;
    $this->testData = $testData;
    $this->setup = $setup;
}
```

The constructor receives the ID of the test case: in other words, the sequence number in the test trail to which it belongs. This is mainly used to give the test case a sound name. When calling the parent constructor, which receives the name of the test case, this ID is used together with the request method.

The second parameter is the setup object, which is responsible for configuring the test case. The last parameter is the actual data to be used for the test. You already know the structure of this data; it is the captured request and response information.

The ezcWebdavClientTest class also has the typical setUp() and tearDown() methods that you already know from your own test cases. In our case, these methods take care of setting up the actual server and its back end, as well as unifying the environment in which the test is to be run:

```
public function setUp()
{
    $this->oldLibxmlErrorSetting = libxml_use_internal_errors(true);
    $this->oldTimezoneSetting = date_default_timezone_get();
    date_default_timezone_set( 'UTC' );
    $this->setup->performSetup( $this, $this->id );
    $this->tmpDir = $this->createTempDir(
        get_class( $this )
    );
    $this->backend->options->lockFile = $this->tmpDir .
    '/backend.lock';
}
```

In the setUp() method, the current libxml error-handling setting is stored and overwritten to use internal errors. This is necessary because some clients use invalid XML, and loading this would cause ugly notices and warnings to be shown. Inside the server itself, this is done correctly already, but we also need this setting to avoid issues when loading the reference data. To avoid affecting other unit tests when they are run together with a client test, the original setting is stored to be reset in tearDown().

This is a habit you should generally get used to, to ensure your tests all run independently. Whenever you change something in the environment to run a test, do not forget to reset it after the test has finished. Otherwise, you'll end up in debugging hell, I promise! The code following these lines does basically the same with the time zone setting and unifies this to UTC.

The next code line makes the setup object perform the server setup. I don't go into detail on this process or show the setup classes here. All you need to know is that the setup object sets the public attributes $server and $backend.

In the final subsection of this chapter, you get some details on the different setups needed. It should be noted that the ezcWebdavServer is set up from scratch for each test set, as it is in real life. On each request, the PHP file is run independently, so we emulate this in the test too. The $backend, in contrast, is set up once for the first data set to be run. After that, it is kept in the setup object to make the changes persistent between test sets of a trail. Only for different trails are new back ends created.

Next, a temporary directory is created for the test case. As mentioned, the method used here is available in the base test class of the eZ Components project.

Finally, the newly created temporary directory is used to provide a lock filename for the $backend. This is needed by the back end to ensure that operations performed in a single request are atomic.

The `tearDown()` method is straightforward and just resets all environmental changes to their original values:

```
protected function tearDown()
{
    libxml_use_internal_errors( $this->oldLibxmlErrorSetting );
    date_default_timezone_set( $this->oldTimezoneSetting );
    $this->removeTempDir();
}
```

First, the original `libxml` error handling is reset and then the time zone setting. Finally, the temporary directory for this test case is removed again.

The method `runTest()` is used by PHPUnit to perform the actual test of this test case. For the typical unit test case, the framework clones the test case object to run each test method independently. In our case, the custom test suite already creates an object for each test. So we overwrote the `runTest()` method to perform our actual test run:

```
public function runTest()
{
    $this->setup->adjustRequest( $this->testData['request'] );
    $response = $this->performTestSetRun(
        $this->testData['request']
    );
    $this->setup->adjustResponse(
        $response, $this->testData['response']
    );
    $this->assertRunCorrect(
        $this->testData['response'], $response
    );
}
```

First of all, the setup object is requested to perform potential adjustments on the request data. This is especially important if locking is in the game. In this case, the setup object must keep track of lock tokens generated by the server and to replace the lock tokens from the original capturing with the actual ones.

Typically, you would extract the functionality of lock token creation in its own object and inject a custom object for testing, which does not create lock tokens randomly. We decided against this change for pure testability, because the generation of lock tokens would be replaceable only for this reason. So instead we adjusted the lock tokens in the test setup. Different test setups might also need further adjustments. You can see examples in the "Acceptance Tests by Example" section later in this chapter.

After the request data has been adjusted, the actual test run is performed by the `performTestSetRun()` method. This method actually injects the request data into the server and performs the run. The code here is very straightforward, so we don't go into detail.

Finally, the response data generated is also adjusted by the setup object. This happens for exactly the same reasons the request data is adjusted. The custom assertion method `assertRunCorrect()` looks like this:

```
protected function assertRunCorrect( array $expectedResponse,
        array $actualResponse )
```

```
    {
        $this->assertEquals(
                            $expectedResponse,
                            $actualResponse,
                            'Response sent by WebDAV server incorrect.'
        );
        $this->setup->assertCustomAssertions( $this );
    }
```

Basically, the equality of the response data is checked against the captured one. In addition to this, the setup object can perform additional assertions on the back end or the server itself, by delivering the test case to it. Again, you will see an example of this case later in this chapter.

This last method completed the custom test case class for the WebDAV acceptance tests. Let me summarize what you have seen so far: An instance of `ezcWebdavClientTest` represents a single test data set inside a trail. To customize test trails, the instance of `ezcWebdavClientTest` receives a setup object in its constructor, as well as the test data to work on. The test case instance is responsible for setting up the test environment, processing the actual test, and performing common assertions.

The setup object is responsible for bringing the server and the back end in place for the test. In addition to that, it can prepare request data and post-process response data, to adjust environmental dependencies. Finally, the setup object can inject custom assertions into the test run.

The Acceptance Test Suite

Now that I have presented the custom test set class to you, let me show the corresponding test suite. An instance of this class is used to set up all the test cases for a specific test trail, in correct order. It maintains the setup object (`ezcWebdavClientTestSetup`, which is common for the test cases and ensures that each test is executed).

Again, we take advantage of the PHPUnit framework here: `ezcWebdavClientTestSuite` extends `PHPUnit_Framework_TestSuite`. Most of the code in the base class is not overwritten, because it already performs the desired actions for us. The process looks like this:

1. Create a test case object for each test to run.

2. For each test, create a result object and run the test.

The latter step stays as is, but we need to overwrite the first one:

```
class ezcWebdavClientTestSuite extends PHPUnit_Framework_TestSuite
{
    protected $testSets;
    protected $setup;
    public function __construct( $name,
                                 $dataFile,
                                 ezcWebdavClientTestSetup $setup = null )
    {
        $this->name = "Client: $name";
        $this->testSets = new ezcWebdavTestSetContainer(
            dirname( __FILE__ ) . '/' . $dataFile
        );
```

```
        $this->setup = (
           $setup === null ?
              new ezcWebdavClientTestContinuousSetup() :
              $setup
        );
        foreach ( $this->testSets as $testId => $testData )
        {
           $this->addTest(
              new ezcWebdavClientTest(
                 $testId,
                 $this->setup,
                 $testData
              )
           );
        }
     }
   }
```

On construction, a test suite receives a name and the name of the data file to read. Remember that we merged all request/response files into a single data file, for storage in Subversion. Using the $name of the client, the test suite determines its own name. The base class from PHPUnit already knows the affected member variable and uses the suite name accordingly.

Optionally, the constructor receives a setup object. You saw this one in action in the previous section. If no such object is provided, a default object of class ezcWebdavClientTestContinuousSetup is created. This is appropriate for most tests, and only some exceptions need special setup objects.

The class ezcWebdavTestSetContainer is basically an ArrayObject, which reads the given test file and maintains it.

In the foreach loop, a new test case instance is created per test data set in the trail. The addTest() method is also provided by PHPUnit_Framework_TestSuite. It receives test case objects to be executed in the suite. Because the setup object already exists at this stage of the code flow, each test case receives the same setup object to maintain this certain amount of state between test case executions.

Let me summarize what we have discussed so far. The custom test case class we implemented takes care of executing the WebDAV server with a given set of request data and asserting that the generated response is correct. Each test case in an acceptance test suite receives the same setup object, to maintain state between test case executions. The test suite actually represents a test trail for a specific client.

Acceptance Tests by Example

You have seen lots of code in the last two sections, showing the infrastructure of WebDAV acceptance tests. In this section, I give you some insight into how this infrastructure is actually used.

The first example here is a typical setup for a typical client. Because I mentioned it before, I show the test file for Cadaver. To be able to run the test for a specific client independently from the whole components test suite, we create one file per client, setting up the test suite:

```
class ezcWebdavCadaverClientTest extends ezcTestCase
{
   public static function suite()
```

```
        {
            return new ezcWebdavClientTestSuite(
                'Cadaver',
                'clients/cadaver.php',
                new ezcWebdavClientTestContinuousSetup
            );
        }
    }
```

The new class `ezcWebdavCadaverClientTest`, created in this file, extends just the eZ Components base test case class. It is not necessary to extend the custom WebDAV test case here, because it is only a container to create a test suite. Therefore, the only method implemented here is the static `suite()` method, creating the test suite to execute.

As expected, a client test suite for the Cadaver client is created here. The corresponding data files location is given and, for clarity reasons, the setup object to use. This could actually be left out in this case, because `ezcWebdavClientTestContinuousSetup` is also the default for setup objects. This class is most commonly used to set up client tests. One exception is if the client supports locking. In this case, an instance of a derived class is used, setting up the lock plug-in properly in addition. The continuous setup class is shown below.

```
    class ezcWebdavClientTestContinuousSetup extends ezcWebdavClientTestSetup
    {
        protected $backend;
        public function performSetup( ezcWebdavClientTest $test, $testSetId )
        {
            if ( $this->backend === null )
            {
                $this->backend = $this->setupBackend();
            }
            $test->server = self::getServer(
                new ezcWebdavBasicPathFactory( 'http://webdav' )
            );
            $test->backend = $this->backend;
        }
        protected function setupBackend()
        {
            return require dirname( __FILE__ ) .
                '/scripts/test_generator_backend.php';
        }
    }
```

As you may have guessed, the methods in this class are pretty basic. The `performSetup()` method checks whether a back end has been instantiated. For the first test in a trail, this is usually not the case, so the `setupBackend()` method is called. For every subsequent test set, the existing back end is reused to maintain state.

A static method in the base setup class is used to set up a clean `ezcWebdavServer` instance. The path factory, which is responsible for translating URIs into local paths, is given here because this might vary for special tests. Both objects, the server and the back end, are used to configure the test case object through its public attributes.

The `setupBackend()` method requires a PHP file, which sets up a unified back end. The same file is used while capturing the test trails, to initialize the back end.

As you can see, the continuous setup does not introduce custom assertions. So I show you another, special client test:

```
class ezcWebdavRfcClientTest extends ezcTestCase
{
    public static function suite()
    {
        return new ezcWebdavClientTestSuite(
            'RFC',
            'clients/rfc.php',
            new ezcWebdavClientTestRfcSetup()
        );
    }
}
```

The RFC client test actually does not test the acceptance of a client, but performs regression tests against the WebDAV RFC. The data in this test trail contains the examples from the RFC. The purpose of this test trail is to verify that the server implementation still conforms to the RFC when changes are made.

Two problems exist with this test:

➤ The information given in the RFC examples is incomplete. For example, the full lot of request information is not given in every example, for clarity reasons.

➤ The examples use different server names and back end structures for illustration. Therefore, it is not possible to use a unified setup here.

The infrastructure for client tests can easily cope with these issues. We just implemented a different setup class for this test trail, and we were finished. For almost every test case, a custom back end and path factory must be created. This results in a huge switch-case statement in the `performSetup()` method and many methods to set up the single back ends.

What is important to note is that the infrastructure is capable of doing far more for us than just ensuring client acceptance. We also have a dedicated test trail, which tests the locking functionality from the RFC, and another one that performs functional tests against the locking facilities, ensuring that the edge cases work correctly.

CONCLUSION

Testing a server is hard, and PHPUnit can be used for unit testing and for system or acceptance tests, too. I know this seems like a short conclusion, but it's the basic essence of what we've discussed.

The eZ WebDAV component has (as this case study is written) almost 5,000 tests. About 4,000 of them are test trails for 16 clients and their variants, as well as functional test trails and regression tests for the RFC. These are integrated in our standard test environment. This also means that the component still has about 1,000 handwritten unit tests. Tests are written in a TDD-like manner before implementing the actual code.

Unit tests are very important for code quality and during development. They help you tremendously if you need to refactor, and ensure API stability. However, unit tests are not the Holy Grail and are not the full solution of your problems. Especially in highly integrated environments, like live applications, other test methods are also important. Unit tests can ensure that each class of your application works as expected, but they cannot tell you if the application as a whole works as your clients/users expect.

Still, you should try to find a way to automate tests as much as possible. Manual testing is long-winded, boring, and therefore error-prone. Unconventional methods in testing are not bad things. It is important to see that there is automated testing possible, beyond unit tests. Finally, although PHPUnit is a framework for unit testing, it is possible to integrate other types of tests into your existing test environment with very little effort.

These lessons should be learned from this case study:

➤ Test as much as you can, even if you need to go through unconventional ways.

➤ Automate your tests as much as you can.

➤ Although PHPUnit is the name of the framework, you can integrate other types of tests.

➤ Testing a server is a pain. WebDAV in itself is a pain for developers. However, it is still possible to test.

I hope that this chapter has brought you a bit nearer to practical testing.

PART IV
Architecture

8

Testing symfony and symfony Projects

Fabien Potencier

WHAT'S IN THIS CHAPTER?

➤ symfony release management

➤ Evolution of the symfony test suite

➤ Drawbacks of the singleton design pattern

➤ Advantages of dependency injection

➤ Using a dispatcher to reduce dependencies between objects

➤ Pragmatic approach to testing

➤ Unit testing and the lime testing library

➤ Functional tests for end-to-end application testing

➤ Debugging functional tests

Testing should be one of the main concerns of Web developers, but the truth is it's not yet as widespread as it ought to be. It is still the most neglected part of a Web development process. Most developers still think they cannot afford writing tests because the client budget is too tight or because the deadline is too short. But it's quite the opposite. A comprehensive test suite can save your day when you are under such a time constraint and/or a budget constraint. Because it is rather counterintuitive, we, as a community, need to educate developers and provide tools that ease testing.

Since the beginning of the project five years ago, the symfony framework project (`http://www .symfony-project.org/`) has tried to advocate Web development best practices, and as such, one of its main goals is to lower the barrier of entry to testing by providing pragmatic, simple, and easy-to-learn tools that speed up the creation of tests.

This case study is divided into two parts. In the first one, we see how the symfony framework itself is tested, what the specific challenges of testing such a large code base are, and how to ensure that no regression is introduced during the life cycle of a major release. In the second part, we focus on the tools the symfony framework provides to ease the testing of applications developed with the framework, from unit test tools to the browser simulator provided for functional tests.

TESTING A FRAMEWORK

Testing a framework can be quite challenging, and we learned it the hard way: from code that is too coupled to be tested thoroughly, to the usage of design patterns like the singleton or regressions because of some bug fix. Over the years, the symfony framework quickly evolved from the core team testing experience, and symfony now provides a well-decoupled but cohesive set of components. For symfony 2, the introduction of a dependency injection container greatly helps ease the testing process even more.

The symfony Release Management Process

To better understand why the symfony framework itself needs a good test suite, you first need to understand our release management process.

Like many other open-source software projects, we have major and minor releases. At the time of writing (July 2009), we have four major symfony releases: 1.0, 1.1, 1.2, and the upcoming 1.3. The first main difference compared to many other open-source software projects is the way we maintain these releases. They have their own life cycles, and they are maintained in parallel; even if the 1.2 release of symfony was released in November 2008, the 1.0 release is still maintained, so each major release has minor bug-fix releases (like the 1.0.20 release, which is the current 1.0 minor release).

Unlike many other frameworks, we also have so-called "enterprise" releases. For these enterprise releases (we have only one of them right now, the symfony 1.0 release), you get three years of maintenance. During three years, the symfony core team is committed to fixing bugs and to making the release compatible with the newest versions of the PHP language. However, we never add new features, even the smallest one; we even go one step further, because sometimes we can decide to not fix a small edge-case bug if the fix potentially introduces a regression in some existing projects. This means it is always safe and simple to upgrade to the next minor version of the framework and enjoy the latest bug fixes.

Even for non-enterprise releases, the symfony core team has a one-year maintenance commitment with the same level of support that we provide for enterprise releases.

Long-term Support

The symfony enterprise releases are the equivalent of the Ubuntu LTS (Long Term Support) provided for the Ubuntu "Hardy Heron" and "Lucid Lynx" releases. You also can compare them to the Red Hat Enterprise Linux (RHEL), versus the Fedora distribution. As for the Linux distribution, Sensio Labs, the main sponsor behind the symfony framework, also provides commercial support for the enterprise releases and extended support for all other releases.

To achieve such a high level of quality, the symfony core team must be sure to never break anything when fixing a bug. One of the great things about having a large community is the feedback you have in near-real time. If something breaks, a user will probably report the problem in the next few hours. But that's not the best way to handle non-regression. An automated test suite is, of course, much better.

Sometimes, the difference between fixing a bug and adding a new feature is not straightforward. For instance, in symfony 1.2, we made some changes between two minor releases to fix a performance problem associated with the routing system. We decided to include the fix because the improvement was significant. But for the fix to work, we refactored lots of code, and introduced two new settings to turn on the optimizations. So, by default, the behavior was the same as before, and people have the opportunity to turn on the optimizations to benefit from the changes. Because not all core team members were comfortable with the changes, even if the two new options were set to compatibility mode by default, we had a long talk about the issue on IRC. Eventually, we decided to accept the changes for the next minor release. However, we soon learned the hard way that we were wrong: The refactoring introduced a small and subtle bug for a very specific edge case. Of course, because of Murphy's law, one of Sensio Labs' customers discovered the problem just before the Web site needed to go live. It took us more than an hour to find the cause and apply a fix to the framework. Needless to say, the customer was quite upset.

For stable releases, stability is an order of magnitude more important than performance. And the problem was not related to the lack of tests. As a matter of fact, the symfony routing component is very well tested, with more than 250 unit tests and code coverage of nearly 90 percent. But don't be fooled by numbers! You never have enough tests, and the code coverage metric is a hard number to trust.

Based on this experience, the symfony core team has decided to follow our golden rule even more religiously:

Never add a new feature in a stable branch, even the smallest one.

Code Coverage

Having 100 percent code coverage does not mean that all your code is actually covered. Consider the following PHP snippet, which uses the PHP ternary operator:

```
$a = $b ? 1 : 0;
```

To achieve 100 percent code coverage, you just need to write a test that covers one of the two possible branches.

Tests versus Real Code

The symfony framework has had a test suite since the very beginning of the project, more than five years ago. The mythic 1.0 version of symfony (1.0.0), released in January 2007, was bundled with 3,896 tests. As we fix bugs in the 1.0 and greater branches, we add more tests. As of version 1.0.20, released in March 2009, there were 4,238 tests bundled with the release. As well, the newest releases of symfony have even more tests; for instance, the latest release of symfony 1.2 has 9,202 tests. The number of tests increased by more than 20 percent during the life cycle of the 1.0 stable release, where we add no new feature, even the smallest one. That means that the symfony 1.0 release becomes more and more stable, and we can be more and more confident about its stability and quality.

Testing is at the heart of the symfony evolution. As we write code, we add new tests. symfony 1.2 actually consists of about 15,000 lines of PHP code and about 12,000 lines of code that test the framework features. Even with such a large number of tests, we "only" have code coverage of 80 percent. But we don't consider it to be a problem. It's always better to have some tests, rather than none. Our philosophy is very pragmatic: We are aware that the framework is far from perfect, but we try to make it better, one step at a time.

Running the Test Suite

Another challenge when you have many tests is the time it takes to run the test suite. A good practice is to run all the tests before each commit, to be confident that no regression was introduced because of the new code. But with a large test suite, it can take lots of time to run all the tests (about 2 minutes for the symfony 1.2 branch test suite on a laptop). If it takes too much time, people stop running all the tests for each commit. They just run the tests related to the new code, and sometimes, of course, they forget some possible side effects from tests that have not been run.

To ensure the best speed possible for the symfony test suite, we continuously make optimizations to the test suite and to the lime tool in particular (more information about lime is available in the next section). We also benefit from PHP itself being faster with each release. Thanks to PHP 5.3, it takes 20 percent less time to run the symfony test suite than with PHP 5.2.8.

However, even with all these optimizations, the test suite still becomes slower to run as time passes and as we add more tests. That's one of the main reasons behind the introduction of a continuous integration server for symfony, named "Sismo."[1] Sismo, shown in Figure 8-1, is a simple and pure PHP continuous integration server. It runs the symfony test suite whenever someone commits new code to the project, and it immediately alerts the symfony core team if the build fails (Sismo provides notifications by email, Twitter, XMPP-Jabber, Growl for Mac users, and more). It has already proven several times to be very useful and ensured that broken code was fixed right away.

Main Lessons Learned

One of the main drawbacks of the current symfony test suite is the number of functional tests versus the number of unit tests. Having too many functional tests in a project probably means that the code is too coupled to be fully tested with unit tests. For symfony, we try to write as many unit tests as possible and fall back to write functional tests only when unit tests are not possible — and, of course, to test the integration of all features together.

Never Use the Singleton Design Pattern in PHP

We probably have too many functional tests because of the `sfContext` class. The `sfContext` class is a singleton (and a multiton since symfony 1.1). The singleton design pattern is one of the easiest design patterns to explain and understand, so it is one of the most documented and used. On the other hand, it also is probably one of the worst design patterns you can use in PHP. Because only one possible instance of the class is available, the unique instance can be retrieved with a static method like `sfContext::getInstance()`. That means the code contains lots of calls to the `sfContext::getInstance()` method, and it is then impossible to substitute another class for testing. The only possibility we found is to create a special `sfContext` class (a mock) to be used only for testing purposes, which is loaded in place of the original one.

---

[1]`http://ci.symfony-project.org/`

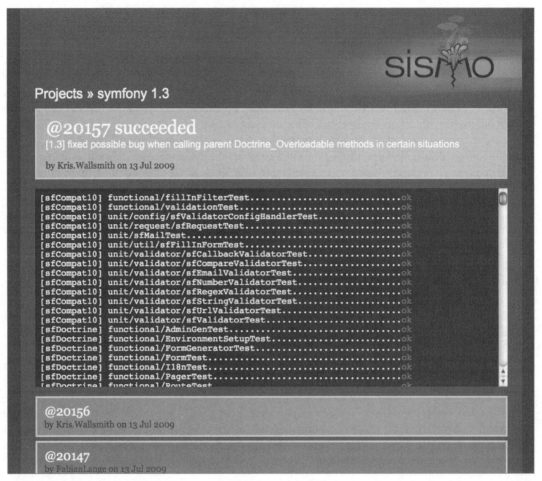

FIGURE 8-1: Sismo screenshot

SINGLETON VERSUS MULTITON

As read on Wikipedia,[2] "the multiton pattern is a design pattern similar to the singleton, which allows only one instance of a class to be created. The multiton pattern expands on the singleton concept to manage a map of named instances as key-value pairs."

In symfony 1.0, we had several other singleton classes: `sfConfigCache`, `sfRouting`, `sfWebDebug`, `sfI18N`, and `sfLoggersfConfigCache`. All but `sfContext` have been removed in symfony 1.1 and replaced with proper dependency injection; see the next section for an example.

---

[2]`http://en.wikipedia.org/wiki/Multiton_pattern`

The routing library is a great example of the singleton problem. In symfony 1.0, you were able to access the routing from anywhere by calling `sfRouting::getInstance()`. It was very convenient for developers using the framework, but it was next to impossible to replace the default symfony routing strategy by another one (except in a very hackish way). But the routing singleton was also accessible via the context: `sfContext::getInstance()->getRouting()`. So, as of symfony 1.1, the routing is not a singleton anymore; it now can be easily overridden to cope with the specificities of the project at hand, and it is still available easily from anywhere, thanks to the context. We also have made the routing object an argument of some core classes, so most of the time there is an accessor like `->getRouting()` in classes where it makes sense to use the routing (think of the MVC separation of concerns). It makes you think twice before using the more verbose and probably inappropriate `sfContext::getInstance()->getRouting()` call. The changes were definitely small steps in the right direction. And that's how the symfony framework evolves over time: We prefer to evolve the code step by step, instead of breaking the compatibility by doing a revolution in the code.

This sums up what I think about the singleton design pattern: Never use it if you want to write flexible and extensible code.

Decouple Your Code with Dependency Injection

The dependency injection concept is very widespread in the Java world. In the PHP world, it is also used very often in all modern libraries, but most people still don't know what it is exactly. I like the definition given by the PicoContainer website:[3] "Dependency Injection is where components are given their dependencies through their constructors, methods, or directly into fields."

As of the 1.1 release, the symfony framework uses dependency injection everywhere in its core classes. It helps so much in writing tests where we replace some objects with others to ease the testing.

For the sake of argument, here is one example taken from the symfony code base. I have tried to find a simple example, even if it is not the worst case we had to refactor. In symfony, the caching of the HTML generated by the view is managed by the `sfViewCacheManager` class. Below is the initialization code from the symfony 1.0 branch:

```
// in symfony 1.0
class sfViewCacheManager
{
    public function initialize($context, $cacheClass,
        $cacheParameters = array())
    {
        // create cache instance
        $this->cache = new $cacheClass();
        $this->cache->initialize($cacheParameters);
        // ...
    }
    // ...
}
```

It was not that bad, because we were able to change the cache class and the class parameters by passing them as arguments to the `initialize()` method. But we were implicitly forced to create cache classes that had an `initialize()` method.

---

[3]http://www.picocontainer.org/injection.html

As of PHP 5, there is a better way to enforce such a constraint: interfaces. So, for symfony 1.1, we refactored that code to read as follows:

```
// in symfony 1.2
class sfViewCacheManager
{
    public function initialize($context, sfCache $cache)
    {
        // cache instance
        $this->cache = $cache;
        // ...
    }
    // ...
}
```

Now, in a test, it is just a matter of creating a cache instance that implements the `sfCache` interface:

```
$cache = new sfMockCache();
$cacheManager = new sfViewCacheManager($context, $cache);
```

The astute reader will have noticed that even if the context is a singleton, it is still passed as an argument to the cache manager class. It will greatly ease the removal of the singleton if we decide to go that far some day.

> **DEPENDENCY INJECTION CONTAINER**
>
> For symfony 2, we go one step further by introducing a dependency injection container. You can read more about it on my personal blog.[4]

Lower the Number of Dependencies between Objects with an Event Dispatcher

Another problem during testing is creating a bunch of unrelated objects just to be able to test one of them. You end up testing too many things at a time, with some annoying side effects. We had this exact problem in symfony 1.0, where we had lots of dependencies between the main core classes, as shown in Figure 8-2.

For symfony 1.1, we worked very hard to decouple core classes as much as possible. The dependency graph for symfony 1.1 is much simpler, thanks to the introduction of an event dispatcher, as you can see for yourself in Figure 8-3.

The `sfEventDispatcher` class is based on the "Apple Cocoa Notification Center." It implements the observer design pattern[5] in a very lightweight and efficient way. The dispatcher class itself has less than 100 lines of code, and as you will read later in this section, it is now available as a standalone component[6] that you can use even if you don't use the symfony framework.

---

[4]http://fabien.potencier.org/

[5]http://en.wikipedia.org/wiki/Observer_pattern

[6]http://components.symfony-project.org/event_dispatcher/

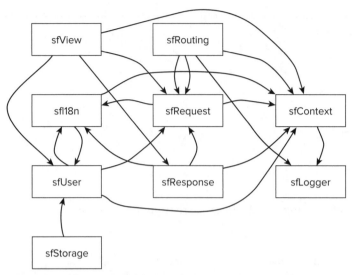

FIGURE 8-2: The symfony 1.0 class dependencies

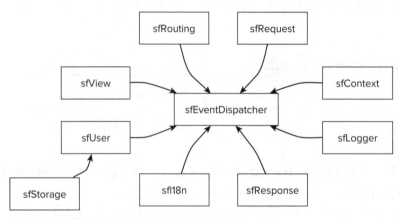

FIGURE 8-3: The symfony 1.1 class dependencies

To give you the gist of how the dispatcher works, here is a small usage example of the class that speaks for itself:

```
// sfI18N
$callback = array($this, 'listenToChangeCultureEvent');
$dispatcher->connect('user.change_culture', $callback);
// sfUser
$event = new sfEvent(
        $this,
        'user.change_culture',
        array('culture' => $culture)
);
$dispatcher->notify($event);
```

If you combine the usage of dependency injection and the observer pattern, you can easily create standalone libraries that are useful by themselves and become even more powerful when they are used together. The refactoring toward a totally decoupled framework was accomplished with the release of symfony 1.2, and the symfony core team makes available some of the most useful components as standalone libraries, under the symfony components website.[7]

TESTING WEB APPLICATIONS

Like many other frameworks, symfony supports two kinds of automated tests out of the box: unit tests and functional tests. Unit tests should verify that each method and function you write is working according to the requirements. Functional tests verify that the resulting application behaves correctly as a whole.

Lowering the Barrier of Entry of Testing

Writing tests is perhaps one of the hardest Web development best practices to put into action. Web developers are not used to testing their work, so lots of questions arise: Do I have to write tests before implementing a feature? What do I need to test? Do my tests need to cover every single edge case? How can I be sure that everything is well tested? But usually, the first question is much more basic: *Where to start?*

> ### DEFAULT PROJECT DIRECTORY STRUCTURE
>
> Testing is a first-class citizen in a symfony project, so the default directory structure created at project initialization has a `test/` directory to host your tests.
>
> The `test/unit/` directory contains unit test files; functional tests can be stored under the `test/functional/` one.

Even if we strongly advocate testing, the symfony approach is pragmatic: It's always better to have some tests than no tests at all. Do you already have lots of code without any tests? No problem. You don't need to have a full test suite to benefit from the advantages of having tests. Start by adding tests whenever you find a bug in your code. Over time, your code becomes better, the code coverage rises, and you become more confident about it. By starting with a pragmatic approach, you feel more comfortable with tests over time. The next step is to write tests for new features. In no time, you will become a test addict.

The problem with most testing libraries is their steep learning curve. That's why symfony provides a very simple but also very powerful testing library — lime — to make writing tests easy. As you see in the next section, using lime with some simple conventions helps you create relevant tests in a matter of minutes.

---

[7]`http://components.symfony-project.org/`

LIME VERSUS PHPUNIT

The lime tool was created in early 2004. Since then, PHPUnit has improved so much and is slowly becoming the de facto standard testing library for PHP applications and libraries. The upcoming PHPUnit 3.5 version is very promising and has most of the features and the simplicity we were aiming at with lime.

Those are a few of the reasons why we decided to switch from lime to PHPUnit for symfony 2. Using PHPUnit basically means we have less code to maintain ourselves. It's like having Sebastian Bergmann, the lead developer of PHPUnit, on board — one more great PHP developer helping us making symfony better. But using PHPUnit also has lots of other advantages:

➤ We play well with others (Zend Framework, Doctrine, Propel, and so on).

➤ Our users have better integration with IDEs, Continuous Integration servers, and so on.

➤ Our users benefit from features that are not available in lime.

➤ Our users have less symfony-specific things to learn.

Unit Tests

As said in the preceding section, the symfony framework is bundled with lime as its testing library. The symfony core team decided to write the lime testing library for two main reasons: First, we needed a library that could run tests in isolation; and second, none of the existing libraries could do so out of the box. We also wanted a library that gets out of the way and helps in the writing of relevant tests faster.

These were the main goals for lime:

➤ Easy to install and embed (only one file)

➤ Easy to learn (the API should be straightforward)

➤ Fast to run

➤ Runs tests in isolation (one process per test file)

➤ Allows each test file to be run separately

➤ Fun to use

I have a strong Perl background, so lime started as a port of the great `Test::More`[8] library.

Easy to Install

Installing the lime library is as simple as it can be, because lime consists of just one PHP file.[9] Using lime is as simple as requiring this PHP file in your test files.

---

[8]`http://search.cpan.org/~mschwern/Test-Simple-0.96/lib/Test/More.pm`

[9]`http://svn.symfony-project.com/tools/lime/trunk/lib/lime.php`

If you use lime with symfony, lime is already bundled with the framework, and a specific CLI tool allows it to run tests easily:

```
# Run all unit tests
$ symfony test:unit
# Run all functional tests
$ symfony test:functional
# Run all tests
$ symfony test:all
```

Easy to Learn

In a symfony project, all unit test files start with the same snippet of code:

```
require_once dirname(__FILE__).'/../bootstrap/unit.php';
$t = new lime_test(1, new lime_output_color());
```

First, the unit.php bootstrap file is included to initialize a few things. Then a new lime test object is created and the number of tests planned to be launched is passed as an argument. This allows for proper failure reporting if the PHP script halts prematurely.

> **TEST PLAN**
>
> The plan allows lime to output an error message in case too few tests are run — for instance, when a test generates a PHP fatal error.

Testing works by calling a method or a function with a set of predefined inputs and then comparing the results with the expected output. This comparison determines whether a test passes or fails.

To ease the comparison, the lime_test object provides several methods:

➤ ok($test): Tests a condition, and passes if it is true

➤ is($value1, $value2): Compares two values, and passes if they are equal

➤ isnt($value1, $value2): Compares two values, and passes if they are not equal

➤ like($string, $regexp): Tests a string against a regular expression

➤ unlike($string, $regexp): Checks that a string doesn't match a regular expression

➤ is deeply($array1, $array2): Checks that two arrays have the same values

You may wonder why lime defines so many test methods, because all tests can be written just by using the ok() method. The benefits of alternative methods are much more explicit error messages in case of a failed test and improved readability of the test script output, as shown in Figure 8-4.

Another great thing about lime is that it helps you to write relevant tests, thanks to some simple conventions. Each test method takes a last argument, which is a sentence describing the test. By convention, and to help people write good descriptions, you can always start the sentence with the method name you want to test and then add a verb and the thing you want to test:

```
$t->is(
    Jobeet::slugify('Sensio'),
```

```
        'sensio',
        '::slugify() converts all characters to lower case'
    );
```

```
1..9
# ::slugify()
not ok 1 - ::slugify() converts all characters to lower case
#     Failed test (./test/unit/JobeetTest.php at line 8)
#           got: 'sensio'
#      expected: 'sensiolabs'
ok 2 - ::slugify() replaces a white space by a -
ok 3 - ::slugify() replaces several white spaces by a single -
ok 4 - ::slugify() removes - at the beginning of a string
ok 5 - ::slugify() removes - at the end of a string
ok 6 - ::slugify() replaces non-ASCII characters by a -
ok 7 - ::slugify() converts the empty string to n-a
ok 8 - ::slugify() converts a string that only contains non-ASCII characters to n-a
ok 9 - ::slugify() removes accents
Looks like you failed 1 tests of 9.
```

FIGURE 8-4: Lime output in case of an error

If you cannot write such a sentence, it means you aren't really testing something useful or you are trying to test too many things at once. Also, the description acts as documentation for the class, and because the descriptions are automatically outputted alongside the test result when you run the tests, it makes it really easy to spot the failing tests and which feature is not behaving correctly.

The lime output is TAP-compliant,[10] which means you can integrate your tests easily as part of a continuous integration process; see the discussion of Sismo in the preceding section. Of course, lime also can generate an xUnit-compatible XML file (integrated as of symfony 1.3):

```
$ symfony test:all --xml=xml.log
```

Each file created the way we have seen in this section is autonomous, which means that running the tests is as simple as executing the file.

When part of a larger test suite, the CLI tools provide a way to run a test harness, where each test file is run one after the other and the output is parsed to report possible problems. The output is then something similar to Figure 8-5.

```
functional/frontend/affiliateActionsTest...........................ok
functional/frontend/apiActionsTest.................................ok
functional/frontend/categoryActionsTest............................ok
functional/frontend/jobActionsTest.................................not ok
    Failed tests: 10
functional/frontend/languageActionsTest............................not ok
    Failed tests: 1, 2, 3
unit/JobeetTest....................................................ok
unit/model/JobeetJobTest...........................................ok
Failed Test             Stat  Total   Fail  List of Failed
---------------------------------------------------------------
tional/frontend/jobActionsTest    0     1      1  10
l/frontend/languageActionsTest    0     3      3  1 2 3
Failed 2/7 test scripts, 71.43% okay. 4/93 subtests failed, 95.70% okay.
```

FIGURE 8-5: Test harness with symfony

---

[10]http://testanything.org/wiki/index.php/Main_Page

CODE COVERAGE

When you write tests, it is easy to forget a portion of the code. To help you check that all your code is well tested, symfony provides the `test:coverage` task. Pass this task a test file or directory and a lib file or directory as arguments, and it tells you the code coverage of your code:

```
$ symfony test:coverage test/unit/SomeTest.php
```

If you want to know which lines are not covered by your tests, pass the `--detailed` option:

```
$ symfony test:coverage --detailed test/unit/SomeTest.php
```

Keep in mind that when the task indicates that your code is fully unit tested, it just means that each line has been executed, not that all the edge cases have been tested. Because `test:coverage` relies on Xdebug2 to collect its information, you need to install it and enable it first.

Lime also is very well integrated with symfony and provides a simple way to test the project model (Propel or Doctrine objects) and to write fixture files in the YAML format:

```
JobeetCategory:
   design: { }
   programming: { }
JobeetAffiliate:
   sensio_labs:
       url: http://www.sensio-labs.com/
       email: fabien.potencier@example.com
       is_active: true
       token: sensio_labs
       jobeet_category_affiliates: [programming]
   symfony:
       url: http://www.symfony-project.org/
       email: fabien.potencier@example.org
       is_active: false
       token: symfony
       jobeet_category_affiliates: [design, programming]
```

Fun to Use

Writing tests is quite boring, but it is a full part of a developer's job. So lime tries to be fun to use. Where available, it colorizes the output to give the developer immediate feedback and make it easier to spot the problems, as you can see in Figure 8-6. Whenever you see the green bar at the end, it is safe to say that all the tests pass. If not, you see the infamous red bar, which means you need to fix the failing tests right away.

Functional Tests

Functional tests are a great tool to test your application from end to end: from the request made by a browser to the response sent by the server. They test all the layers of an application: the routing, the model, the actions, and the templates.

```
1..9
# ::slugify()
ok 1 - ::slugify() converts all characters to lower case
ok 2 - ::slugify() replaces a white space by a -
ok 3 - ::slugify() replaces several white spaces by a single -
ok 4 - ::slugify() removes - at the beginning of a string
ok 5 - ::slugify() removes - at the end of a string
ok 6 - ::slugify() replaces non-ASCII characters by a -
ok 7 - ::slugify() converts the empty string to n-a
ok 8 - ::slugify() converts a string that only contains non-ASCII characters to n-a
ok 9 - ::slugify() removes accents
Looks like everything went fine.
```

FIGURE 8-6: Lime output

They are very similar to what you probably already do manually: Each time you add or modify some code, you need to go to the browser and check that everything works as expected, by clicking links and checking elements on the rendered page. In other words, you run a scenario corresponding to the use case you have just implemented.

If the process is manual, it is tedious and error prone. Each time you change something in your code, you must step through all the scenarios to ensure that you did not break something. That's insane. Functional tests in symfony provide a way to easily describe scenarios. Each scenario can then be played over and over automatically by simulating the experience a user has in a browser. Like unit tests, they give you the confidence to code in peace.

> **SELENIUM**
>
> The functional test framework does not replace tools like Selenium.[11] Selenium runs directly in the browser to automate testing across many platforms and browsers, and as such, it can test your application's JavaScript.

The Browser Simulator

In symfony, functional tests are run through a special browser, implemented by the sfBrowser class. It acts as a browser tailored for your application and directly connected to it, without the need for a web server. It is fast because there is no HTTP-layer overhead, and it gives the developer access to all symfony objects before and after each request, giving the opportunity to introspect them and do the needed checks programmatically.

The sfBrowser class provides methods that simulate navigation done in a classic browser:

- ➤ get(): Gets a URL
- ➤ post(): Posts to a URL
- ➤ call(): Calls a URL (used for PUT and DELETE methods)
- ➤ back(): Goes back one page in the history
- ➤ forward(): Goes forward one page in the history
- ➤ reload(): Reloads the current page

---

[11]http://seleniumhq.org/

➤ `click()`: Clicks a link or a button

➤ `select()`: Selects a radio button or check box

➤ `deselect()`: Deselects a radio button or check box

➤ `restart()`: Restarts the browser

Here are some usage examples of the `sfBrowser` methods:

```
$browser = new sfBrowser();

$browser->
  get('/')->
  click('Design')->
  get('/category/programming?page=2')->
  post('search', array('keywords' => 'php'))
;
```

To facilitate the introspection of the symfony objects, the `sfTestFunctional` class provides some specific test methods and takes a `sfBrowser` instance as an argument. The `sfTestFunctional` class delegates the actual tests to tester objects. Several testers are bundled with symfony (request, response, form, i18n, user, Propel, Doctrine, and some more), and you can create your own.

```
// test/functional/frontend/categoryActionsTest.php
include(dirname(__FILE__).'/../../bootstrap/functional.php');

$browser = new sfTestFunctional(new sfBrowser());
$browser->
  get('/category/index')->
  with('request')->begin()->
  isParameter('module', 'category')->
  isParameter('action', 'index')->
  end()->

with('response')->begin()->
  isStatusCode(200)->
  checkElement('body', '!/This is a temporary page/')->
  end()
;
```

FLUENT INTERFACE

At first, the script above may look a bit strange. That's because methods of `sfBrowser` and `sfTestFunctional` implement a fluent interface by always returning `$this`. It allows you to chain the method calls for better readability.

As for the unit tests, executing the functional tests can be done by using some CLI commands:

```
$ symfony test:functional
```

Also, each test file is autonomous and can be run directly without any other tool. Behind the scenes, `sfTestFunctional` converts your calls to lime calls and automatically generates relevant test descriptions, as shown in Figure 8-7.

```
> 1 - The homepage
# get /en/
ok 1 - request parameter module is sfJobeetJob
ok 2 - request parameter action is index
>   1.1 - Expired jobs are not listed
ok 3 - response selector .jobs td.position:contains(expired) does not exist
> 1 - The homepage
>   1.2 - Only 10 jobs are listed for a category
ok 4 - response selector .category_programming tr matches 10 times
> 1 - The homepage
# get /en/
>   1.3 - A category has a link to the category page only if too many jobs
ok 5 - response selector .category_design .more_jobs does not exist
ok 6 - response selector .category_programming .more_jobs exists
> 1 - The homepage
>   1.4 - Jobs are sorted by date
ok 7 - response selector .category_programming tr:first a[href*=/2371/] exists
```

FIGURE 8-7: Output of a symfony functional test

The Fixtures

Each time you launch your tests, you need to put your database in a known state. You can do this in several ways, but symfony provides a simple and effective tool: fixtures. Fixtures in symfony are test data described in the YAML format; see the preceding section for an example of such a file.

The symfony functional test features benefits from the symfony environments system to provide a specific database for testing. Each time you execute a functional test, the fixtures are used to put the test database in a known state. It's a very simple and powerful mechanism. If performance is a problem, such as when you need lots of fixtures to bootstrap a test, you can wrap all your tests in a transaction and rollback at the end. It is very fast, and the database state is not altered by your tests anymore:

```
$pdo->beginTransaction();
// some tests
$pdo->rollback();
```

It also works if a test crashes the PHP script before the end, because the transaction is automatically rolled back by PHP.

The CSS3 Selectors

Most of the time, when you write functional tests for a web application, you need to test that the HTML outputted in the browser follows the client requirements.

The most naïve way of testing HTML is to use regular expressions. If you want to be more precise, you need a better tool. Using XPath is one possibility, because it can be very expressive; but some web developers do not know how to use Xpath very well. That's why in symfony, we decided to use CSS3 selectors, a technology known by all web developers, as a way to check elements in an HTML page.

Symfony supports most advanced CSS3 selectors, as in the following example:

```
$browser->
    with('response')->
    checkElement('.blog_comment dd:last p:contains("Some comment")');
```

If you develop semantic websites, the resulting tests are not fragile, because your tests use the "ids" and the "classes" defined in the HTML, and these rarely change.

Testing Forms

Even if testing the outputted HTML is a good way to ensure that your website behaves correctly, symfony provides specific tools to ease testing things that you will use again and again. One such example is the way we handle form testing.

The form tester object provides a very efficient way to test the behavior of your forms (the error messages, for instance), without parsing the HTML output at all:

```
$browser->
info('Submit a Job with invalid values')->

get('/job/new')->
    click('Preview your job', array('job' => array(
        'company' => 'Sensio Labs',
        'position' => 'Developer',
        'location' => 'Atlanta, USA',
        'email' => 'not.an.email',
)))->
with('form')->begin()->
    hasErrors(3)->
    isError('description', 'required')->
    isError('how_to_apply', 'required')->
    isError('email', 'invalid')->
end()
;
```

Debugging

Last, but not least, when your functional tests do not work as expected, you need a way to debug them. Outputting the whole HTML on the screen is not necessarily the best way to debug. So, symfony provides special debugging tools to help you find the problems. For instance, when testing a form, you can call the ->debug() method:

```
$browser->
    info('Submit a Job with invalid values')->
    get('/job/new')->
    click('Preview your job')->
    with('form')->debug()
;
```

The method outputs all the submitted values and the associated error messages, as shown in Figure 8-8.

```
>   3.2 - Submit a Job with invalid values
# get /en/job/new
# post /en/job
 Form debug
Submitted values: array ( 'category_id' => '257', 'type' => 'full-time', 'company' =>
'Sensio Labs', 'url' => '', 'position' => 'Developer', 'location' => 'Atlanta, USA',
'description' => '', 'how_to_apply' => '', 'is_public' => '1', 'email' => 'not.an.emai
l', 'id' => '',)
Errors: description [Required.] how_to_apply [Required.] email [Invalid.]
1..26
 Looks like you failed 1 tests of 26.
```

FIGURE 8-8: Form debugging in a functional test

CONCLUSION

As you may have noticed in this case study, testing is at the center of the symfony framework, and we have barely scratched the surface of the tools provided by symfony for testing.

On the one hand, we try to provide simple tools that lower the barrier of entry of testing to get the developer started faster with testing; we also give the developer powerful means of testing that boost his productivity.

On the other hand, the framework itself is well tested, and most of its internal evolution is the result of this testing experience. Testing your code is also a great way to test and refine your API.

9
Testing the ezcGraph Component

Kore Nordmann

WHAT'S IN THIS CHAPTER?

➤ Overview of the ezcGraph component

➤ Testing requirements for image-generating components

➤ Using mock drivers to test the render class

➤ Testing the output drivers

➤ Working with SVG images

➤ Working with bitmap images

➤ Working with Adobe Flash graphics

In early 2007, I was asked to design and develop a component to generate graphs for the eZ Components project,[1] for several reasons. I already had lots of experience with image generation, I had already developed a chart library, and a chart library had been requested by the users of eZ Publish several times.

The requirements for components in the eZ Components were a bit different compared to the image libraries I developed before. The eZ Components project focuses on full backward compatibility, ease of use of all APIs, and stability. Backward compatibility and stability can be ensured by well-written unit tests, so all components are intended to be developed via

---

[1]http://ezcomponents.org

test-driven methodology. Test-driven development of a component purely intended to generate images, which are nothing but binary data, resulted in some problems that had to be solved:

➤ Test expectations are hard to craft beforehand.

➤ The generated binary data may depend on aspects not defined in the test, such as library versions, dates, or some internal state in the library.

➤ Proper comparison methods on binary data can be quite time-consuming.

This chapter shows how these problems were solved while developing the graph component.

DEVELOPMENT PHILOSOPHY

The eZ Components project was designed to build the foundation for future releases of the popular open source content management system eZ Publish; both were developed by eZ Systems. The main intention was to extract single components, which could be reused by other projects, under open source licenses, so they could be maintained outside of the normal eZ Publish release cycle. Single components are not only easier for its developers to test, but also can be used and live-tested by external users.

The eZ Components started with the extraction of existing components, but quickly added new components that were not yet part of eZ Publish, but still are required in many projects. All its components can be used independently from each other and can ease the general development of applications with PHP. The list of available components includes components for handling mail, templating, database abstraction, caching, full text search, image transformation, authentication, and many more. Another component that is especially interesting, because of the way it is tested, is the WebDAV component, covered by Tobias Schlitt in Chapter 7.

GRAPH COMPONENT

The graph component has been developed to offer users a simple and intuitive way to generate good-looking charts from their data. From the very beginning, it supported pie, line, and bar charts. Nowadays, it also supports radar charts and simple odometers.

There are various ways of generating images with PHP; probably the best known uses the GD library. Because the GD library offers only low image quality and still needs a relatively long time to render images, other libraries should be supported as well. For charts, vector-based image formats fit particularly well, so the graph component also supports SVG and Flash as output formats. Since 2008, it can use the cairo library through the cairowrapper PHP extension, hosted at `http://pecl .php.net`, which is faster than GD and produces images of a far better quality.

One of the key requirements is that the user of the component should be able to influence the way the charts look in every possible way. This means being able to not only configure colors and backgrounds, but also to change the overall way a chart is rendered. This was solved by introducing another layer between the data representation of the chart and the output drivers: the renderer. By default, different renderers are available, which, for example, produce two- or three-dimensional views of that chart, both using the same data source and the same output drivers. If you don't like the way the charts are rendered, now you can write your own renderer that transforms the chart data into completely different images.

Supporting different output formats requires some kind of "driver" infrastructure so the user can freely choose the generated image type and the library used to generate the image. This is especially useful because the available image creation libraries may differ in each PHP environment. By default, the SVG driver is used because only the default PHP extensions for XML creation are required, since SVG is a XML-based 2D vector image format.

The internals of renderer and drivers are completely transparent to the user and can be switched at any point during the chart generation. A simple example for generating a pie chart using a different renderer can look like this:

```
$chart = new ezcGraphPieChart();
$chart->title = 'Access statistics';
$chart->data['Browser'] = new ezcGraphArrayDataSet(
    array(
        'Mozilla' => 19113,
        'Explorer' => 10917,
        'Opera' => 1464
    )
);
$chart->renderer = new ezcGraphRenderer3d();
$chart->render( 300, 150, 'pie_chart.svg' );
```

The output is shown in Figure 9-1. Setting a chart title and a renderer is optional.

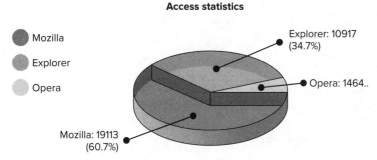

FIGURE 9-1: Example three-dimensional pie chart

The example shows the simplicity of the API. More details on usage and an in-depth guide to customization can be found in the ezcGraph tutorial at http://ezcomponents.org/docs/tutorials/Graph.

Architecture

To explain the requirements for testing the chart component, a rough architectural overview is required. The chart class aggregates a renderer class, which implements the visualization of the data, as mentioned before. The renderer class again uses the driver to generate an image from the visualization of the renderer.

To keep the driver implementations small and testable, their only responsibility is to handle *image primitives*. Image primitives are basically circles, circle sectors, polygons, and text boxes. An abstract driver class defines method headers for each image primitive, and they are implemented in their concrete implementations for each output format, such as SVG or GD, to handle.

The renderer is called to render chart primitives, which are self-contained elements in the visual representation of a chart, such as the chart title, its legend, a single axis, or a pie chart segment. The renderer then transforms such a chart primitive into the proper calls to the driver to render a set of image primitives visually representing the chart primitive. This can, of course, differ significantly between renderers, in order to accomplish different looks of the chart. Currently, the graph component implements two- and three-dimensional renderers. For a pie chart segment, this means that it renders an ellipse sector, optionally a text box placed next to the ellipse sector, and maybe some kind of outline for the ellipse sector.

Figure 9-2 shows a basic overview of the rendering architecture. Besides the mentioned elements, there are data representations, configurations, and layout information, which are not shown in the diagram. All rendering calls, after the initial preparation of the chart, end in calls to the driver, which are the only ones generating output. The renderer layer, and thus the chart layer, therefore completely depend on the driver, which makes selective testing of single components harder.

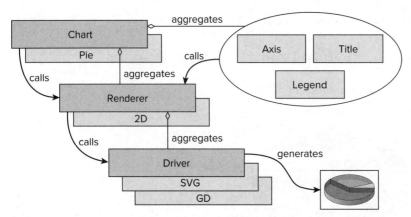

FIGURE 9-2: Rendering architecture of the chart component

Test Requirements

In a chart-generating component, basically all operations result in rendered images. As mentioned before, comparisons of binary data can be expensive and inaccurate, so they should be used as seldom as possible. Still, the actual generation of images must be checked, which is covered later in this chapter.

To detect errors early in your unit test runs and keep the complexity of tests and tested implementation low, you always want to test small, independent bits of code. To verify the functionality of the renderer, for example, it is sufficient to verify the calls from the renderer to the driver implementations, assuming the driver will render the image primitives correctly. Because the renderer aggregates the driver, only one object must be replaced by a "mock object."

DRIVER MOCKING

The output drivers are replaced by mock objects, so the conversion from chart primitives into image primitives can be tested without needing to compare binary data. The drivers themselves are not tested during this process, because their functionality is not touched at all.

As explained in Chapter 2, mock objects can record calls and return canned data for the mocked methods. The recorded calls can then be verified at the end of the test.

Mock the Driver

To be able to test renderers and drivers themselves, they must be decoupled, so the renderer aggregates only a driver object, on which it calls the relevant methods. The renderer itself again can be instantiated without the context of the chart, if the required driver is passed to it.

To test the calls to the driver executed by the renderer, we first must assign a mocked driver instead of a real implementation or instantiation of the renderer:

```
$renderer = new ezcGraphRenderer2d;
$driver = $this->getMock(
    'ezcGraphSvgDriver',
    array( 'drawCircleSector' )
);
$renderer->setDriver( $driver );

$driver->options->width = 400;
$driver->options->height = 200;
```

The renderer is the class we want to test in this test case, and by default it already knows an instance of the default SVG driver. Because the driver can be changed at any point during the creation process of a chart, it is not set directly in the constructor, but changed using the setDriver() method.

The getMock() method, which is part of the PHPUnit test case class, returns an instance of a class extending the class given as the first argument, where the methods given in the array are replaced by mocks. It ensures the creation of a unique class for each request, so you can mock different methods in different tests.

Only the methods listed in the passed array are mocked; all other methods keep their original implementation. Because mocking works by dynamically creating code for an extending class and executing it, you cannot mock final methods or final classes. On the other hand, you could mock the abstract driver class ezcGraphDriver instead of the concrete SVG driver, but in this case, you would have to mock all methods that are abstract in the abstract base class. You will see why you would not want to do that in a moment.

For all mocked methods, you can formulate expectations, when they are called, and what parameters are expected on each call, as the following example shows:

```
$driver->expects( $this->at( 0 ) )
       ->method( 'drawCircleSector' )
       ->with(
            $this->equalTo(
                new ezcGraphCoordinate( 200, 100 ), 1.
```

```
        ),
        $this->equalTo( 180, 1. ),
        $this->equalTo( 180, 1. ),
        $this->equalTo( 15, 1. ),
        $this->equalTo( 156, 1. ),
        $this->equalTo(
            ezcGraphColor::fromHex( '#FF0000' )
        ),
        $this->equalTo( true )
    );
```

This assertion defines that the first call to any mocked method, defined by at(0), is a call to the drawCircleSector method. You may optionally define expectations on the passed parameter values. The method parameter value expectations, defined by equalTo, are defined in the same order as the method expects its parameters. The first parameter passed to equalTo is always the expected value, and the second a maximum delta, to handle common floating-point inaccuracies.

Because of the internal representation of floating-point numbers in nearly all programming languages (including PHP), slight variations in the value might occur, depending on the platform used or even the current version of PHP. Simple calculations like 12 / 3, for example, might lead to 4, or a number very close to 4. Because of that, floating point numbers should never be compared for equality; instead, compare using a small delta value. In this case, a delta value of 1 is sufficient to ensure the test meets its expectations. Even possible variations are probably much smaller in the used value ranges.

FLOATING-POINT NUMBERS

Integer numbers are far more familiar to most people, because they have a defined range and accuracy. But because they can't naturally represent decimal numbers, floating-point numbers are used for such data. Floating-point numbers normally use just the same amount of bits to represent numbers, thus they cannot represent more different distinct values than integer numbers can. The representation of very small and very large numbers is accomplished at the costs of inaccuracy in calculations and variable steps between two representable numbers. For more details, see "What Every Computer Scientist Should Know About Floating-Point Arithmetic" (ACM Computing Surveys, Volume 23, Issue 1, March 1991, 5-48, ISSN 0360-0300) by David Goldberg.

Because complex data types are required in ezcGraph (like the coordinates in the example above), PHPUnit has been extended so the application of delta values also works recursively for checks of properties inside objects, up to defined depth. This defaults to 10. This way, the delta value for the comparison is also applied to the x and y coordinate values of the first parameter value assertion.

Multiple Assertions

If the tested renderer method issues only one call to the tested class, assertions like ->expects($this->once()) would also work. But in the case of ezcGraph, the renderer issues multiple calls, even to the same method of the mocked class, so we use at(). This defines assertions on a specific method call in the sequence of all mocked calls to the mocked object. If multiple methods are mocked, all methods influence the counter; the counter is not per method name.

Several people argue for one single assertion per test, so that failing assertions are not hidden by the first failing assertion and thus are easier to maintain. But to test one aspect of the implementation, it might be useful to still assert on multiple method calls to the mocked object, even on multiple different methods. In the case of the rendered pie chart segment, this could mean also including assertions on the line, which links the description label with the circle sector of the pie chart and the label text box itself.

```
// [...]
$this->driver
    ->expects( $this->at( 2 ) )
    ->method( 'drawLine' )
    ->with(
        $this->equalTo(
            new ezcGraphCoordinate( 205., 166. ), 1.
        ),
        $this->equalTo(
            new ezcGraphCoordinate( 250., 190. ), 1.
        ),
        $this->equalTo(
            ezcGraphColor::fromHex( '#000000' )
        ),
        $this->equalTo( 1 ));

// [...]

$this->driver
    ->expects( $this->at( 5 ) )
    ->method( 'drawTextBox' )
    ->with(
        $this->equalTo( 'Testlabel' ),
        $this->equalTo(
            new ezcGraphCoordinate( 256., 180. ), 1.
        ),
        $this->equalTo( 144.5, 1. ),
        $this->equalTo( 20., 1. ),
        $this->equalTo( 36 ));
```

For this test case, the list of mocked methods in the driver class has been extended to also cover at least the methods `drawLine()` and `drawTextBox()`. As mentioned before, all calls to any of the mocked methods are recorded in one global caller list. The assertions on the call order of the mocked methods need to respect this, which is obvious from the calls to `at()` in this example test case.

Structs

The last example again shows assertions on non-scalar data structures, such as the coordinate classes. On the eZ Components team, we call these small classes, mostly containing properties, "structs," just like they are called in C. We agreed on their usage in a very early stage of the project, because we think they make reading and maintaining the code much easier. With them, you can easily detect what kind of data you are dealing with and optionally implement trivial validations for the contained data in these struct classes.

You could also use PHP arrays to represent such data, which would be slightly faster for creation and data read access. However, doing so means you don't have a name for a given data structure, nor can you easily ensure that the contained data matches a predefined structure.

Programming languages like C# introduced dedicated struct classes in their language specification, to solve one problem you get in PHP when using struct classes extensively. Each object is referenced on assignment in PHP (since PHP 5) and not copied like scalar values. This means that struct classes, which are modified in some methods, are required to be explicitly cloned because the caller class might still expect the original unmodified struct to further work with. Structs in C# solve this by acting like classes in most aspects, but they are always copied instead of referenced.

The same problem affects mock object support in PHPUnit, because the assertions are not verified before tearing the test down. You can, for example, verify if a method has been called at all during the test execution only at the very end of the test. If an object is passed to a mocked method, it therefore must be cloned, because it might be modified during the further execution of the calling method.

This is especially important for values like coordinates or vectors, which are often transformed during further geometric calculations. Cloning of passed object parameter values is one of the extensions I contributed to PHPUnit's Mock-Object support during the testing of the graph component. This is much like the recursive application of delta comparisons for object properties, which were mentioned in the "Mock the Driver" section earlier in this chapter and were required for proper handling of struct classes.

Expectation Generation

For the simple renderer tests, it is possible to go for the test-driven approach and write the mock assertions before running the test and the code the first time. Again, complex calculations happen in the renderer, such as the labels on rotated axes, which could be very time-consuming.

For the generation of those mocks, a simple driver has been created that just echoes the parameters of the calls, so these could be verified manually and then transformed into the mock expectations. Checking those values should happen with care, of course; otherwise, the expectations might be useless or even lead to wrong assumptions about the tested code.

Conclusion

Mocking the back end made it possible to test even complex logic, without any dependency on comparisons of binary data, which would have been generated by the tested library otherwise. The definition of expectations for mocked calls is quite verbose and lengthy, so testing methods generating lots of calls to the back end may be tedious. On the other hand, it seems sufficient to define assertions on only a subset of these calls, like the first and last ones. If these calls are correct and depend on each other, most probably all calls in between are also correct. As always, knowledge about the tested code is required, to justify such assumptions.

If the back end is mocked in the tests using the back end, the back end must be tested separately. Testing the back ends separately ensures that they follow the defined interface only and do not implement additional assumptions.

In the tests for ezcGraph, we always implement at least one test for the "full stack," so we ensure that everything works smoothly together.

TESTING BINARY DATA

Because the drivers are not even touched in the other tests, they also need to be tested themselves in dedicated tests. The drivers are directly generating the output, so basically two options exist for ensuring they work correctly:

➤ Define assertions on the generated binary data.

➤ Overwrite and mock the internal PHP functions.

Mocking the internal functions would require a PHP extension such as `pecl/runkit`[2] to be available during the test runs. `pecl/runkit` is an experimental extension, which allows overwriting and redefining of functions and classes, among other things. It is generally considered "dangerous," and there are normally no distribution packages for it.

In the case of the driver mocking shown above, the renderers already caused quite a few calls to the driver. The driver might again multiply the number of calls. The GD extension, for example, does not support some of the required shapes directly. For instance, their curved lines need to be simulated by lots of short straight lines, which might cause hundreds of calls to the respective method. Due to the verbosity of the mock definitions and their sheer amount in such cases, this approach seems impractical. Additionally, it would be very hard to even verify hundreds of calls to the driver, not to mention generating such expectations beforehand.

Some of the libraries used by the tested output drivers, such as ext/ming, are still in an alpha state and might change their API in future releases. By comparing the calls to only these libraries, API violations wouldn't be caught by our test suite, and as such, we wouldn't be able to react.

Because of all these points, we decided to test the generated binary data. This caused quite a few problems, which differed depending on the format. This part of the case study discusses the problems and how they were solved during the development of the ezcGraph component.

The Drivers

As previously discussed, the drivers render simple image primitives, such as lines and circles. There is no complex state in the drivers, and the most complex operation is to fit text in designated boxes. Therefore, the tests for the drivers are generally very simple. For example, we would test just the render of a line, a filled circle, or the border of a simple polygon. The driver itself is not expected to have any state that's modified, except for the canvas on which all shapes are drawn. The style aspects of the primitives are always defined completely in the respective method call.

Expectation Generation

Test-driven development normally asks you to write the test and the expectation first and then start implementing the functionality. While this often is the best approach, it is nearly impossible when it comes to binary data generation.

Even a small generated bitmap image consists of hundreds of pixels, which nobody wants to draw by hand in some image-processing software. On the other hand, it is quite easy to see whether the image is correct after an image has been generated.

---

[2]`http://pecl.php.net/package/runkit`

In the graph component tests, each image is stored in a temporary test directory when a test fails. A test also fails if the comparison image does not exist yet. In the case of a failed test, the generated image can be introspected and the test author can decide whether it is correct. Correctly rendered images are then moved into the folder for the expected results and used for future comparisons. For this, the implementation already must be complete.

SVG

SVG is a W3C standard for XML-based "Scalable Vector Graphics." It is an open standard, and because it's XML, it's easy to generate and sometimes even user readable. Because SVG is XML, you may include stuff from other namespaces directly in your SVG document or even define your own extensions. You may, for example, use data URLs to directly include other documents, such as bitmap images.

When displayed in a browser, you may also include ECMAScript to interactively modify the DOM tree, creating animations or user interfaces. Some other displaying clients may also be capable of interpreting ECMAScript, but you shouldn't expect that from the average image viewer.

There are two real drawbacks when it comes to SVG rendering in image viewers. The subset of supported SVG elements may differ. The W3C defines a standard called SVG Tiny,[3] which contains a small subset common to nearly all clients, and it's a good base for estimations, what some clients may support, and which ones may even be displayed on mobile clients. The ezcGraph library uses only the TinySVG standard, so the generated images should be displayed properly everywhere.

The largest issue with those different clients is the rendering of text. There is no way to know which fonts may be available on the client, so you can't know how much space some text will consume or what it will look like. To bypass this issue, you may convert text to paths, which is supported by some editors. However, this increases the complexity of rendering for the client and the size of your SVG document. In ezcGraph, you can optionally embed a converted font definition file, which contains the glyph definitions for all characters, allowing exact font width estimations. However, this may not be supported by all image viewers.

XML Comparison

Comparison of SVG basically boils down to comparing XML. XML files can be considered just as normal strings, and that was where we started the comparisons. However, the PHP DOM extension by default does not apply any formatting to XML documents, and two files — each consisting of only one line, with slight differences in some float values — are very hard for the human brain to compare. Always applying output formatting to the generated XML files does not really make sense either, because it would increase the file size only for testing purposes.

To properly compare XML files or strings, special assertions were implemented in PHPUnit. By adding line breaks and proper indentation and stripping out irrelevant white spaces, the assertions reload the XML using proper options for DOM to normalize the XML string representation as follows:

```
<svg xmlns="http://www.w3.org/2000/svg" width="200" height="100" version="1.0"
    id="ezcGraph">
<defs/>
```

---

[3]http://www.w3.org/TR/SVGTiny12/

```
<g id="ezcGraphChart">
- <path d=" M 12.0000,45.0000 L 134.0000,12.0000" style="..." id="ezcGraphLine_1"/>
+ <Path d=" M 12.0000,45.0000 L 134.0000,12.0000" style="..." id="ezcGraphLine_1"/>
</g>
</svg>
```

With such formatting, the common line-based diff algorithms work just fine in PHPUnit for most cases, as the example above shows. Each XML element is echoed in a distinct line, and modified lines are printed next to each other, so even slight variations are directly visible. Therefore, SVG images are quite easily testable. The expected output still cannot really be pregenerated by hand, so test output must be verified by a human and then stored as the expectation for future tests.

Floating-point Problems

Floating-point numbers again cause problems, just like when mocking the back end. The values handled in the graph component are always floating-point numbers, and there is no way around that. In SVG, these floating-point numbers must be converted into string representations. To make the results more predictable, and the files smaller and less platform-dependent, all values are rounded to four digits. This is generally a sufficient resolution, because the values are given in pixels.

On 64-bit platforms, PHP also uses 64-bit to represent floating-point numbers, which results in slightly more accurate calculations. This difference is invisible when viewing a SVG image, but still may change the generated SVG. The difference of .49994 and .49995, rounded to two digits, results in two different values:

```
$ php -r 'var_dump( round( .49994, 4 ), round( .49995, 4 ) );'
float(0.4999)
float(0.5)
```

We see that even a minor inaccuracy in floating-point numbers may result in different results in the SVG file. Because of this, two tests of the graph test suite always fail on 64-bit platforms, and you really can't do anything about this.

Bitmap Creation

The graph component implements two different drivers to create bitmap images. *Bitmap images* means in this case any of the following: PNG, JPEG, or GIF. Those are basically two-dimensional arrays of pixels, encoded in one or another form. In bitmap-based formats, the original shapes are not preserved, but the generating library transforms them into pixels visualizing the original shape. Thus, the generated output totally depends on the used driver.

The two implemented drivers are based on different bitmap generation libraries in PHP. The GD extension is the best known PHP library for image generation, and it has been in use for years now. It is very well documented, and you can find examples for nearly everything you may want to do using the GD library. However, there are still several major drawbacks. As said previously, when it comes to bitmaps, the generating library has to take care of the rendering, so the decision about the used library will have a major effect on the quality of the resulting image. ext/GD does not support anti-aliasing in most cases, so each line you draw has bad aliasing steps, as well as each circle and each polygon. The aliasing of fonts depends on the back-end library you use. For PS type 1 fonts, you get no anti-aliasing, while TTF fonts, rendered with FreeType 2, are anti-aliased. There is no native support for gradients, and some shapes, such as circle sectors, may look very bad when used with transparent colors. Trying to emulate gradients fails, because setting lots of single pixels in an image is just far too slow. The only real benefit from using GD is that it is available nearly everywhere, so a driver for GD still must be implemented.

On the other hand, there is Cairo, a fantastic 2D graphic library. This, for example, has been used by Gnome since 2.8 to draw the GUI, by Firefox 2 to render SVGs, and by Firefox 3 to render the whole view. It has native support for paths, gradients, anti-aliasing, and nearly everything you could demand from a 2D graphics library. It also is very fast and uses established libraries like Pango for text rendering.

The original Cairo library outputs not only bitmap formats, but also SVG, PDF, or PS. Additionally, it may render directly to X windows or use OpenGL through Glitz for hardware acceleration. Hartmut Holzgraefe wrote a PHP extension for the Cairo library using his pear/CodeGen PECL package for extension generation, which is used by the graph component to render images.

Bitmap Comparison

Comparing generated bitmaps is a non-trivial task. Most bitmap formats contain additional headers, which may contain library versions, generation date, or similar information. Simply comparing the hash of the file leads to failures after minor updates.

The intuitive approach would be to compare each pixel of the image and to store the difference in an additional file. But, as said before, iterating pixel by pixel over an image is very slow in PHP, especially using the GD library. Applying this comparison for each test would make each test run unbearably slowly. Additionally, each very slight variation could make the tests fail, and because libraries tend to improve image generation, this might also give lots of test failures over time.

We needed a way to test for images that still are sufficiently similar to be perceptually the same. ImageMagick provided us with an amazingly fast way to calculate the mean average error (MAE) over all channels between two images:

```
$ time compare -metric MAE expectation.png result.png null:
13390.6 (0.204327) @ 0,0
real 0m0.021s
user 0m0.012s
sys 0m0.004s
```

The `compare` command is part of the ImageMagick software package and used to compare images, as the name indicates. The first parameter is the metric to use, where MAE (mean average error) was selected. The mean average error aggregates the absolute difference for each pixel in the images and returns the mean value of all those differences throughout the whole image. Besides the metric, you specify the two images to be compared. The last parameter `null:` defines an output image, which visualizes the differences between the two images. This can be very helpful for debugging. The `null:` value in this case tells ImageMagick to omit the comparison image.

As you can see, the comparison took far less than a second for an image 200×100 pixels in size. Bigger images would, of course, consume more time and especially more memory for the comparisons. However, because only the very basic driver operations are tested, and because the more complex stuff uses mocked drivers, small images should be sufficient for such comparisons.

For the assertions on the differences, the eZ Components test suite uses only the first value from the returned string by ImageMagick, which is the sum of the average distance for each color channel, using the current internal color representation inside ImageMagick. The value stays constant on different platforms in different versions of ImageMagick, so the real unit of the value is not that relevant. For the tests inside the eZ Components, a threshold of 2000 proved valid for the comparisons. It works very well, especially for the Cairo driver.

GD Version Differences

With the GD driver testing comes a bigger, not yet completely solved, problem. The rendering quality of the GD extension tends to change quite drastically between different library versions. The difference is the distance between a simple image generated with PHP 5.2.9 versus PHP 5.3-beta1. The comparison image in Figure 9-3 shows the differences calculated by ImageMagick.

FIGURE 9-3: Image difference between different GD versions

The graph component by default uses supersampling to improve the image quality of graphics generated with GD. This means that the image is first generated in twice the destination size (or even more) and resampled to the destination dimensions on output. This resampling then combines four pixels into one pixel, which results in anti-aliasing, at the cost of more memory consumption.

The resampling algorithm has changed slightly between these different versions of PHP, so there are slight changes all over the image. This then causes a high average pixel distance value. Such changes happen and will happen again inside libraries, and it is nearly impossible to find a comparison metric that will cover those changes and still correctly inform about real changes in the images.

The only way we found to deal with it is to regenerate the images to match the current development version of PHP and deal with the failures when testing with older PHP versions. Even if the whole QA team knows about these failures, they are still there, but at least you can deal with them. Another way would be to pregenerate the comparison images for each PHP version, but because the changes might even occur between different beta versions of a PHP release, this seems impractical, because it would involve lots of images to generate and verify.

Flash

Flash is a closed standard defined by Adobe for animated and interactive web graphics. When it comes to image generation, you can consider this a vector graphics format, by omitting all possibility to add animation frames or user interaction.

The ming extension is still in an alpha state and is designed to create Flash's SWF files. It currently supports a subset of functions, which does not match any specific Flash version, but you can expect support for texts, gradients, basic shapes, a very limited set of bitmaps, and action script. Even the documentation is often missing or may contain broken examples. Some of the documented functions and methods do not work as expected, or at all, but that is something you have to live with when using an alpha extension. It is still the only real way to create Flash images or animations with PHP.

Because Flash is a vector-based format, just like SVG, testing generated Flash files should be easy; even the files are compressed by default. The assertion for similar Flash files first started by comparing a hash of the file, which worked quite well until one test was moved around in the test suite, which caused all subsequent tests to fail.

After reviewing the source code of the ming extension, it was discovered that it is using a global static ID to number all generated shapes. This ID is not reset for each new Flash image, but steadily increased during one request. Because the tests are executed in one single executor run by default, the IDs in the Flash files depended on the number of tests run before the current test.

To properly compare the Flash files, these IDs had to be stripped from the files, but because Flash is a closed source binary format, this wasn't such an easy task. What helped was a tool to read existing Flash files and generate PHP code that recreates the same Flash file again. This way, a "normalized" representation of the Flash file could be created, which also was far easier to debug.

A changed file hash in a failed test would tell you that something changed, but you would have no idea what exactly this would be. A diff of two PHP files might tell you much more, such as a call to draw a line is missing or its parameter values are wrong. The tool used is called swftophp and is part of libming, the library used by the PHP ming extension.

The Assertion

The graph base test case class contains a custom function that performs the conversion and assertion on two Flash files, the expected and the generated:

```
protected function swfCompare( $expected, $generated )
{
    // [ .. Assertions, that both files exist .. ]
    $executeable = ezcBaseFeatures::findExecutableInPath( 'swftophp' );
    if ( !$executeable )
    {
        $this->markTestSkipped(
            'Could not find swftophp executeable to compare flash files.' .
            ' Please check your $PATH.'
        );
    }
    $this->assertEquals(
        $this->normalizeFlashCode(
            shell_exec(
                $executeable . ' ' . escapeshellarg( $expected )
            )
        ),
        $this->normalizeFlashCode(
            shell_exec(
                $executeable . ' ' . escapeshellarg( $generated )
            )
        ),
        'Rendered image is not correct.'
    );
}
```

The code generated by `swftophp` still contains the original IDs of the elements in the Flash file in comments and variable names. To ensure that nothing is messed up just because of these comments, some regular expressions are executed on the generated source code in the method `normalizeFlashCode()`. The method is quite simple and looks like this:

```
protected function normalizeFlashCode( $code )
{
    return preg_replace(
        array(
            '/\$[sf]\d+/',
            '[/\\*.*\\*/]i',
            '(BitmapID:.*?,SWFFILL_RADIAL_GRADIENT\\);)s'
        ),
        array(
            '$var',
            '/* Comment irrelevant */',
            '/* Inserted bitmap fill */'
        ),
        $code
    );
}
```

This method strips all irrelevant bits from the Flash file, such as the mentioned variable names, which are all replaced by `$var`. This breaks the script execution, but it is, of course, sufficient for the pure comparison and the comments, which are all replaced by a dummy comment. Also the bitmaps are replaced, because they also get a global ID assigned.

CONCLUSION

Testing libraries that generate binary data and that might depend on more than the actual generation script may seem impossible at first glance. But with mock object support in PHPUnit, most parts of the library can be tested without even touching any of the binary data generation.

However, the binary data generation must be tested, and there may be many format-specific caveats. During the development of the tests for the graph component, binary data comparison has been solved for the used image formats, and the component currently has a test coverage of more than 95 percent. Considering the complexity of the geometric calculations necessary in graph creation and the diversity of the used back-end drivers, the number of found bugs in the previous years is surprisingly low. The test-driven approach was definitely the right way to go and rewarded us with a very solid graph creation library.

10

Testing Database Interaction

Michael Lively, Jr.

INTRODUCTION

In the application development process, we need to be certain that we are correctly working with our data. One of the best tools we have as developers to ensure that we are doing this is unit tests. Despite the usefulness of unit tests, my experience in reviewing code, writing code, and talking to other developers is that we tend to ignore the complete persistence of data when writing unit tests.

Although we test what we can with mock objects and stubs, we can sometimes completely ignore the actual code that stores the data into the database for later use. We can come up with a wealth of excuses for why we do this:

➤ It makes tests take too long to run.

➤ It is no longer testing a single unit; it is testing the database engine as well.

➤ We assume the database works, so we do not need to test it.

➤ Database testing is a pain in the neck, and those stupid fixtures take forever to write.

Those statements are true, but they do not take into account the entire picture. Sure, database tests may take a while, but would you rather an automated test suite take a few more minutes to write and a few seconds longer to run, and test a little more than the "experts" would like? Or, would you rather be blind-sided when you discover that the database doesn't quite work exactly like you thought it did?

What happens if we fail to adequately protect our database interaction and a bug is introduced to the system under test (SUT)? Ideally, someone will catch the issue elsewhere in the quality assurance process. We hope the issue doesn't make it into a released version of the software, only to be discovered by the end user. If this occurs, it often results in lost time toward your next release, loss of confidence in your product, and in many cases loss of revenue. Even in the best case, you have wasted time diagnosing the problem and fixing it. If we can detect potential issues with our database interaction early in the development process with automated unit tests, then we can save an incredible amount of time and reduce the risk that changes to the system late in the development process bring.

Testing data interaction is difficult because we have very little control. Database interaction creates many different areas where you can very easily introduce bugs. You open a connection to a database, you send the database instructions on what you would like the database to do, and then you do something with the results. This seems like a straightforward process. However, each step creates additional risk that flaws will be introduced to the system. The area where the greatest danger lies is in the step of telling the database what to do. Incorrectly instantiating database connections and misusing results from the database are certainly problematic, but this code is incredibly easy to test and almost certainly will get significant testing attention. However, the difficulty of testing database interaction often presents a seemingly insurmountable barrier to complete and thorough testing.

REASONS NOT TO WRITE DATABASE TESTS

Creating and maintaining the fixtures necessary to perform repeated, isolated database tests takes time. And getting databases set up for all your developers to use when they are running tests against their own changes also requires time. Running the tests themselves requires a measurable amount of time as well. Databases are frequently a performance bottleneck in applications, and tests are no different.

The more you interact with the database, the more time your tests take. Is database testing really worth it? To answer this question, we must understand the risks of not testing our database interaction. To understand the risks, we must understand the purpose of database testing. The purpose of database testing is to ensure that we are communicating the appropriate instructions to the database to achieve the results needed for our application to run properly. Database testing protects us from misunderstanding how SQL works. Databases are complex systems that follow a complex language, one that many developers do not fully understand. Many PHP developers are much more fluent in PHP than they are in SQL. If we are experienced with PHP and yet still feel the necessity to test the PHP code that we write, then we should think it even more important to test the SQL statements that we write in a real and tangible way. If we write a statement to retrieve a list of all states that contributed more than 2% to your overall revenue through the sales of thumb drives, we can only truly ensure that we are using the right SQL statement using a real database with real data.

There are certainly legitimate and even somewhat compelling problems in attempting to test your database interaction. However, I do not think they are serious enough that they should dissuade you entirely from database testing. You simply need to be smart about your testing. More importantly, you must be smart about your development. The less code you have that interacts directly with the database, the fewer tests you need testing that interaction.

The easiest way to get out of creating database tests without greatly increasing risk in your SUT is to use a database access layer or even an object-relational mapping (ORM) framework. This allows you to focus your database tests toward those frameworks, and in most cases, you can minimize the need for database fixtures.

WHY WE SHOULD WRITE DATABASE TESTS

There are many reasons why you may want to test your database interaction as a part of your unit test suite. Some of them are very apparent, such as helping ensure that you are storing and loading your data correctly. There are other reasons that aren't nearly as apparent. One of the most unappreciated aspects of database testing is that it provides a path for guaranteeing that your code works correctly with new versions of your RDBMS. I have often upgraded versions of MySQL only to discover that the most mundane aspects of functionality have changed. One particular upgrade I did from MySQL 5.0.17 to MySQL 5.0.24 resulted in a large number of completely unexpected errors. The errors were all very legitimate. Several of our older queries were not indicating which table a particular column belonged to, and then another table would be joined into the query containing a column with the same name. This should have resulted in errors all along, but MySQL 5.0.17 in some cases assumed that it was the first matching column that should be used. While this is not correct behavior, some code was written to depend on this behavior. When they fixed the problem in MySQL 5.0.24, suddenly we received a large number of errors stating that the column name 'x' is ambiguous. We ended up rolling back the upgrade, running extensive manual testing on a QA environment of the critical components in the system, fixing the problems, releasing the code, and rereleasing the MySQL server upgrade. We then had to deal with the same error in the remaining portions of our application because they slowly trickled in from the end users. It took several weeks to completely resolve the problem. If we had had a reliable set of database unit tests, we could have simply run those tests against a database on the new version and we would not have gone through the time-wasting rollback routine and the embarrassing bug reports from our end users. As much as you may trust your database vendor, you have no way to ensure that they are not introducing bugs or changes in behavior even in minor, bug-fix releases.

Another often unrealized benefit from database testing is that it allows you to certify your code and applications against multiple RDBMSs. Several open-source software projects are attempting to target support on multiple database platforms. The largest challenge to this is ensuring that the queries you are issuing against the database will work against all the different targeted database platforms. Database tests can be engineered in a way that makes them very easy to run on multiple RDBMSs. The PHPUnit database testing extension is written utilizing PHP Data Objects (PDO) and provides a well-defined interface to allow for the ability to create tests for practically any RDBMS supported by PHP.

The most important benefit of database testing is ensuring that your data is kept safe and used properly. In the world of programming today, most of our applications are data driven, in one form or another. This often means that there is some level of database interaction with our code. We usually are loading and displaying the data to our end users. Often, we allow them to add to and modify that data. Occasionally, we may even provide some insight into that data in the form of reporting and analysis modules. Our applications do not work without this data. If data is important to the proper operation of our application, then that importance should be reflected in the amount of attention retrieving and storing data is given inside of our test suites.

WHAT WE SHOULD TEST

One of the questions we must ask ourselves when we write database tests is "What should we test?" If we can take the time to test everything, then that is fantastic and we may as well go for it. Often, we have to focus our efforts on specific pieces of code initially. This is especially true with database tests because we not only have to consider the time it takes to develop the tests, but we also have to consider the time it takes to run the tests. A balance must be achieved in order to keep our tests easy and sane to run.

The most important aspect to consider when identifying what code we are writing tests for is ensuring that any data in our application that is considered to be critical receives an adequate amount of attention. We must also consider the overall impact to our software and our business if a particular piece of code breaks. In many cases, ensuring that the proper data is saved to the database at a particular time is far more important than ensuring that the data is retrieved correctly from the database. If we load the data incorrectly, we can simply fix the code and everything then works as it should. However, if we are saving data incorrectly, then it is possible and even likely that we have inaccurate data. We may not be able to correct this data. In the fortunate event that it can be corrected, it takes more effort to fix the invalid data than it would to fix data that is just displayed incorrectly.

We also need to consider what eventually happens with the retrieved data. If we retrieve data and then send it to an external e-mail address, then the importance level of that data goes up. For example, if we are retrieving an order from our database and then e-mailing it to our shipping department, we have significant problems on our hands if the application is sending incorrect orders out for each customer.

A good litmus test for how much attention should be paid to the database interaction of various units is business value. Whatever we consider to be the most important data in our system should not have any code loading or saving to it that is not covered by database testing. If we are maintaining a shopping cart system, then the most important data in that system is likely the order data and our products. Without those two sets of data, we cannot sell to or fulfill orders from our customers. On the other hand, comments and product ratings are something we could live without for a few hours, so they don't need as much attention.

This is especially important to understand if we are not employing test-driven development and/or we are limited in time for writing database test cases. After we have adequately tested the money-making data, the next level of data we may want to test is the data that is used to make any kind of financial decision.

If we take the same shopping cart application, we might have a bricks-and-mortar portion of the software that allows salespeople to enter orders. It is very likely that we need to associate the salesperson with particular orders so we can pay commissions. Obviously, it is important that this data is represented properly or we will have some very unhappy (or possibly incredibly happy) salespeople when they view their commission checks. Another scenario is financial reporting. If we have reporting built in that shows sales of products over time, then that data could very likely be used to forecast sales, ramp up inventory, or drive numerous other business decisions. If business decisions are made on invalid data, that could cause serious, long lasting problems.

WRITING TESTS: MOCKING DATABASE CONNECTIONS

After the decision has been made to implement database tests against our SUT, we need to determine how to write those tests. There are multiple ways you can test database interaction in your software. The two most prevalent and common ways are (1) to mock your database connection and assert calls made to it, and (2) to utilize a real database and have a framework to insert data for you before a test runs, and to validate that particular data exists when a test completes.

The first time I tried to provide test coverage for code that was working with databases, I actually took the steps of creating a mock MySQLi object, creating a dummy connect call that did nothing, and then using that to assert that I was calling the query method with the correct SQL statement as a parameter. Although it did a great job at helping me add coverage to my database classes, it really did not do a great deal to protect me from errors. The only thing it really did was make sure that my database classes were generating the queries I thought should be generated. What if I had the wrong query in place?

When you are testing your database interaction, you need to do more than just ensure you are using the SQL statement you expect. You need to ensure that you are using the SQL statement that will return or modify the data that you expect. When unit testing, you should be testing a unit's behavior as a whole. The testing should not always stop as soon as direct control leaves the unit you are testing. For example, you wouldn't want to mock PHP's in_array() function just because your unit test "shouldn't care" whether in_array() is working. Doing this would create many useless tests, and then what would you do if in_array() ever did break? Direct interaction with the database should be treated much the same way. It should be allowed to occur and then verified to make sure it did what you expected.

The arguments for mocking a database connection are that it allows your tests to run faster and it keeps your tests protected from external dependencies (the database). The problems with mocking a database connection are that it results in tests having increased knowledge of the implementation, does not test the actual correctness of the queries issued, and does not allow changes to schema to be revealed by tests.

WRITING TESTS: PHPUNIT DATABASE EXTENSION

It is now common to utilize a database testing framework when testing database interaction in your unit tests. These frameworks can be full-fledged third-party frameworks or simply small tools generated by developers specifically for the project they are working on at the time. The general goal and use of these frameworks is all the same, however. They allow a specified set of data to be inserted into a test database at the beginning of a test. The test itself then runs against that same database. The data remaining in the database is checked to be sure it is in an expected state. Finally, the data is removed from the database. The details of each step may differ and in some cases even the order may differ, but that is the general flow of a database test when using a framework of some sort.

A simple example of this is if you are writing a test for the user management module of your software. You may have an addUser() method that takes a username and a group name as a parameter. You would write code in the fixture portion of your test to insert the group into the group table of the database. You would then execute the addUser() method. Finally, you could select out of the database to ensure that the user is indeed added using the correct group ID.

I created the PHPUnit database extension in response to a need I had to be able to quickly test data modeling layers to ensure that they were working properly. A tool already existed in Java called DBUnit that did just this. It allowed developers to put their databases into a known state between test runs. It allowed for creating data sets and for validating existing data against a predefined data set. I took the functionality of this tool and created a port of it for the PHPUnit testing framework. PHPUnit 3.2 was the first version to see database testing support. PHPUnit 3.3 added several useful features based on feedback from the initial release of database testing. PHPUnit 3.4 has brought even more features focused on easing the pain of creating database tests. Development is ongoing, and although many improvements still need to be made, overall it allows all the functionality necessary to get started quickly with database testing.

The Database Test Case Class

The foundation for creating a database test in PHPUnit is the PHPUnit_Extensions_Database_TestCase class. This class provides the base functionality you need to create tests capable of populating a database with fixture data. If you want to create a database test, you normally ensure that your test case extends this class. The only additional data required by a database test case is the database connection you want to use in your test and the data set you want to use as the fixture data for your database.

The database connection is provided by implementing the getConnection() abstract method. This method must return an implementation of the PHPUnit_Extensions_Database_DB_IDatabaseConnection interface. This interface defines the method calls necessary to allow the database extension to correctly return data from the database by tables and queries, properly escape queries, return row counts, and return metadata from the database. The default implementation of this is called PHPUnit_Extensions_Database_DB_DefaultDatabaseConnection, and it utilizes an existing PDO connection. The constructor for this class requires a PDO object as well as a schema. This may seem slightly redundant, but with good reason. As of PHP 5.3.0, there is no way to retrieve the data specified in the DSN after a PDO instance is constructed. There is also no standard way in SQL to retrieve the current connected database. It should be noted that some database engines (namely SQLite) do not require a schema. In these cases, you can pass an empty string for the second parameter. An example of getConnection() to connect to a SQLite database can be found below.

```php
<?php
    include_once 'PHPUnit/Extensions/Database/TestCase.php ' ;
    abstract class MySQLDatabaseTest
    extends PHPUnit_Extensions_Database_TestCase
```

```
    {
        protected function getConnection ( )
        {
            return
                new PHPUnit_Extensions_Database_DB_DefaultDatabaseConnection (
                    new PDO(
                        'mysql:host=localhost; dbname=testdb' ,
                        'root' ,
                        'password'
                    ),
                    'testdb'
                );
        }
    }
?>
```

This `getConnection()` implementation returns a database connection to the SQLite database in memory. This is a simple example that reveals a common bad practice worth mentioning. One thing we should always avoid is hard-coding the database connection information inside of tests. Doing this makes it incredibly difficult to change the database connection information should the test database move. It also decreases flexibility when allowing multiple test databases. A good way to centralize this information to a single location is through creating your own base database test class. If you convert the above class to an abstract class, this allows you to extend it for all your database tests. The advantage this provides, of course, is that it allows you to keep your database connection information in a single location. It also prevents you from needing to repeatedly re-declare your database connection. An example of how to do this is discussed later.

One benefit of using PDO for the connections made by PHPUnit is that it provides a wealth of drivers for different database engines. The engines that have known support for the database testing in PHPUnit are MySQL, PostgreSQL, Oracle, and SQLite. Although PHPUnit utilizes PDO for making the database connections required to set up and validate your test database, you still can use your preferred connection method within your code. So if your code utilizes the mysqli extension, you can still easily test the database code using PHPUnit.

Establishing the Test Database Connection

A decision that you must make when you begin creating database tests is what database you will run the tests against. The foremost rule when choosing a test database is to never choose a production database. The reason is that you will not have the ability to completely reset the database without disrupting service for your users. If you accidentally did something like reset the database, it could have disastrous consequences. It is always best to have at least one separate database that is used only for testing. Ideally, you would be able to place the database on a separate development server to further reduce the chance of accidentally running against the production database. There are few things customers hate more than having all the data removed from their databases.

If you are working on a project with multiple developers, I recommend having a separate test database for each developer. Each developer having a test database allows developers to run the tests at any time without having to worry about multiple developers' test cases colliding and causing tests to report as failures when it was simply a matter of two tests simultaneously writing to and reading from the same tables. These databases can all reside on a single development server or even on each developer's local development work station. If you do provide separate test databases for each developer, you want to provide a way for developers to quickly create their test database schemas as well as keep them up to date with changes. A common practice (and something I have done in multiple projects) is to create a script that exports the schema from a central development database to any database on a developer's local box. This allows each developer to quickly create his own instance of the database. This not only helps with testing but also with development as a whole. To keep our schemas in sync with day-to-day changes, developers could send out files containing the required schema changes whenever their code is completed and committed to the software configuration management (SCM) system. Tools such as dbdeploy and phing can be used to help with this process.

If you do have multiple test databases, you face an additional challenge with your database test cases. You must have a way to configure database connections in your test case. This is made easier by providing a single location from which your database connection is served. This could be extended slightly to utilize the PHPUnit configuration system to specify the database connection information you need.

PHPUnit provides a --configuration option that allows you to specify an XML configuration file that contains several different options and capabilities. One of the capabilities of this XML file is to allow you to specify global variables for tests. As shown in the following code, we could create a configuration file that defines global variables containing the database DSN, username, password, and schema name as globals:

```xml
<?xml version="1.0" charset="utf-8" ?>
    <phpunit>
        <php>
            <var name="TESTDB_DSN" value="mysql:host=localhost; dbname=testdb" />
            <var name="TESTDB_USERNAME" value="test" />
            <var name="TESTDB_PASSWORD" value="password" />
            <var name="TESTDB_SCHEMA" value="testdb" />
        </php>
    </phpunit>
```

If you then pass this file name to the --configuration argument of the phpunit command, these globals are available in your test fixtures.

Another very convenient trick is naming this XML file phpunit.XML. As long as this file is in the working directory when the phpunit command is run, the configuration automatically reads from that file. After this configuration file is loaded, you can use the defined globals in your base test class to create the database connection, as shown in this code:

```php
<?php
    include_once 'PHPUnit/Extensions/Database/TestCase.php';
    abstract class MySQLDatabaseTest
        extends PHPUnit_Extensions_Database_TestCase
    {
        protected function getConnection( )
        {
            return
                new PHPUnit_Extensions_Database_DB_DefaultDatabaseConnection (
                    new PDO(
```

```
                    $GLOBALS[ 'TESTDB_DSN' ] ,
                    $GLOBALS[ 'TESTDB_USERNAME ' ] ,
                    $GLOBALS[ 'TESTDB_PASSWORD' ]
                )
                $GLOBALS[ 'TESTDB_SCHEMA' ]
            ) ;
    }
  }
?>
```

If a particular developer in your group prefers not to use the test account on his database for testing or wants to run his testing against a different database schema, then he can simply create his own configuration file and pass it to the `--configuration` argument of the `phpunit` command. Another way this could be accomplished is by utilizing the `--bootstrap` argument of the `phpunit` command. This feature allows you to create a PHP file that is executed prior to any tests being run. It could be used as shown in the following code to define a class containing the information necessary to construct a default database connection:

```php
<?php
    class MyBootstrapClass
    {
        public function getTestDbDsn( )
        {
            return 'mysql:host=localhost; dbname=testdb';
        }
        public function getTestDbUsername( )
        {
            return 'root';
        }
        public function getTestDbPassword( )
        {
            return 'password';
        }
        public function getTestDbSchema( )
        {
            return 'testdb';
        }
    }
?>
```

Now in your base test case, you can instantiate this class as shown next to get the information necessary to create your database connection. This allows you to avoid using globals:

```php
<?php
    include_once 'PHPUnit/Extensions/Database/TestCase.php';
    abstract class MySQLDatabaseTest
        extends PHPUnit_Extensions_Database_TestCase
    {
        protected function getConnection( )
        {
            $bootstrap = new MyBootstrapClass( );
            return
                new PHPUnit_Extensions_Database_DB_DefaultDatabaseConnection (
```

```
                    new PDO(
                        $bootstrap->getTestDbDsn( ),
                        $bootstrap->getTestDbUsername( ),
                        $bootstrap->getTestDbPassword( )
                    ),
                    $bootstrap->getTestDbSchema( )
                );
            }
        }
    ?>
```

With this method, if a particular developer in your group prefers to customize the database configuration, then they can simply create their own bootstrap file containing an implementation of this class and pass it to the –bootstrap argument of the phpunit command. These are two very effective techniques for allowing your test database connections to be configurable.

Creating Data Sets

In the previous example of a simple database test, the established fixture was essentially a single SQL query executed against our test database to add a single row. This works well and is adequate for small tests. However, as your tests begin to grow and you start needing to test more data, this could become very cumbersome. The ratio of code establishing your fixture to code in your SUT begins to grow immensely. One of the goals of the PHPUnit Database Extension is to abstract out the task of setting up your database fixture. In order to accomplish this, PHPUnit uses the same concept of interchangeable data sets introduced in DBUnit.

Currently, only a single data set is tied to each database test case. This means all tests in a single test case must utilize the same data fixture. There is an open feature being worked on to allow data sets to be defined for individual tests in a test case. This new feature is planned for a future release of PHPUnit.

To define your data set you must implement the getDataSet() method in your database test case. This method must return an implementation of the PHPUnit_Extensions_Database_DataSet_ IDataSet interface. These data sets provide the fixtures that will be used in your database for each of your test cases. Below is a simple example declaring an empty data set. Provided PHPUnit resides in your include path, you would be able to execute this test case with the phpunit command and receive no errors.

```php
<?php
    include_once 'PHPUnit/Extensions/Database/TestCase.php';
    include_once 'PHPUnit/Extensions/Database/DataSet/DefaultDataSet.php';
    class SQLiteDatabaseTest extends PHPUnit_Extensions_Database_TestCase
    {
        protected function getConnection( )
        {
            return
                new PHPUnit_Extensions_Database_DB_DefaultDatabaseConnection (
                    new PDO('sqlite::memory:') ,
                    ' '
                ) ;
        }
```

```php
        protected function getDataSet( )
        {
            return
                new PHPUnit_Extensions_Database_DataSet_DefaultDataSet(array ( ) ) ;
        }
        public function testMyCode( )
        {
        }
    }
?>
```

You will notice a few things that are different in this code when compared with the previous examples. Again, we are using a SQLite memory database. This is a very convenient database to write tests against if your code utilizes SQLite or is intended to be database-platform-agnostic. Also notice the newly defined `getDataSet()` method. It is currently returning a basic data implementation that requires manually setting up tables and data via PHP code. Although it is very convenient for this particular example, I would recommend that you not use this data set implementation for your actual tests. The last method is `testMyCode()`, which is a simple test that is not doing anything useful.

The data sets can be represented in a variety of formats. They can be XML files, CSV files, or YAML files. They also can be programmatically created from PHP or even imported in from other databases. There are benefits and drawbacks to each type of data set. I would generally recommend starting out using the YAML format. YAML is considered by many to be a far cleaner format than XML, and I would tend to agree. Also some data set decorators can be used to further enhance the capability and flexibility of your data sets. For the examples in this book, I use the standard XML format. However, it is important that you understand the various data set formats available.

Most of your tests use at least one of the "format" data sets that PHPUnit has to offer. As we discuss each of the formats in the following sections, I show an example of how to use that format to represent data in the following table named user:

```
date created table1 id username password notes
2009-01-01 00:00:00 1 mikelively 3858f62230ac3c915f300c664312c63f NULL
2009-01-02 00:00:00 2 johnsmith 73cf88a0b4a18c88a3996fa3d5b69a46 I have no idea
[...]
```

I also show how to specify a table called `empty_table` with no rows.

XML Data Sets

The standard XML format is a verbose XML format that allows you to precisely indicate the tables in your data set and the columns and data contained in those tables. The `PHPUnit_Extensions_Database_DataSet_XmlDataSet` class accepts the path of the XML file relative to the current working directory as the first and only parameter to the constructor. You can create a new standard XML data set using this code:

```php
<?php
$xml_data_set =
new PHPUnit_Extensions_Database_DataSet_XmlDataSet( 'mydataset.xml' ) ;
?>
```

The root element of the XML file is the `<dataset>` element. This element can then contain zero or more `<table>` elements. Each `<table>` element has a name attribute containing the name of the table. The `<table>` element contains zero or more `<column>` elements. The `<column>` elements contain text nodes with the name of the column. The `<table>` element also contains one or more `<row>` elements. Each `<row>` element represents a single row in the current table. Each `<row>` element is expected to contain the same number of child elements as there are `<column>` elements for that table, and they are interpreted in the same order as the column elements are defined. The children of the `<row>` element are one of two elements: either `<value>` or `<null>`. The `<value>` element can contain a text node indicating the value in the identical column for the row. If there is no text node, then the value for that column is a blank string. The `<null>` element is used to indicate a true NULL value for that column. Here's an example of a simple standard XML file for our sample data set:

```xml
<?xml version="1.0" charset="utf-8" ?>
<dataset>
    <table name="user">
        <column>date_created</column>
        <column>user_id</column>
        <column>username</column>
        <column>password</column>
        <column>notes</column>
        <row>
            <value>2009-01-01 00:00:00</ value>
            <value>1</value>
            <value>mikelively</value>
            <value>3858f62230ac3c915f300c664312c63f</value>
            <null/>
        </row>
        <row>
            <value>2009-01-02 00:00:00</column>
            <value>2</value>
            <value>johnsmith</value>
            <value>73cf88a0b4a18c88a3996fa3d5b69a46</value>
            <value>I have no idea who this is</value>
        </row>
    </table>
    <table name="empty_table">
        <column>date_created</column>
        <column>empty_table_id</column>
        <column>data</column>
    </table>
</dataset>
```

As you can see, we have used the `<null>` element to specify that the notes column contains a NULL value in the first row. Also note that the `<value>` and `<null>` elements in each row are ordered the same as the `<column>` elements for the table. There is no rule saying that the `<column>` elements must come first, but I have found that it is a useful standard and it provides clarity on what data is contained in the table. This is especially true when you are using an XML editor capable of collapsing elements.

Also note that white space inside the `<value>` and `<column>` elements is important. If there is a line break inside your `<value>` element, it is translated as that same line break in the database after the data set is loaded to the database.

The last issue to be aware of is that if you have any special XML characters in your values, you need to use entities in the XML data set. For instance, if you were to store a full anchor tag in the notes column, you would want to use the following <value> element as an example:

```
<value>&lt;a href=&quot;http://www.google.com&quot;/&gt;</value>
```

Flat XML Data Sets

There is also a lighter weight XML format that can be used to specify simple data sets. This format is called the "flat XML" format. The class that implements this format is PHPUnit_Extensions_ Database_DataSet_FlatXmlDataSet. Like the standard XML data set's class, the flat XML data set's class accepts a file relative to the current working directory. You can create a new flat XML data set using this code:

```
<?php
$xml_data_set=
new PHPUnit_Extensions_Database_DataSet_FlatXmlDataSet ('flat.xml');
?>
```

The root element of the flat XML format is again the <dataset> element. The <dataset> element then contains a child element for every row and empty table you want in the data set. If you want to specify a row in your data set, the element name must be identical to the name of the table to which the row belongs.

Each column in that row is then represented as an attribute of the element. The name of the attribute is the name of the column, and the value of the attribute is the value in the row for that column. It is important to understand that the first row defined for each table is depended on to define the columns for that table. If a row further down in the file contains columns not found in the first row, those columns are ignored. If a column that is defined in the first row is not defined in a future row for that table, then it is given a NULL value. If you want to specify an empty table, you simply create an element with the same name as the table and do not specify any attributes for that element.

```
<?xml version="1.0" charset="utf-8" ?>
<dataset>
    <user
        date_created="2009-01-01 00:00:00"
        user_id="1"
        username="mikelively"
        password="3858f62230ac3c915f300c664312c63f"
    />
    <user
        date_created="2009-01-02 00:00:00"
        user_id="2"
        username="mikelively"
        password="73cf88a0b4a18c88a3996fa3d5b69a46"
        notes="I have no idea who this is"
    />
    <empty_table /><!-- the empty table contains no data -->
</dataset>
```

This data set has a big problem. The "notes" attribute is not defined in the first <user> element. This means that it is ignored in all future <user> elements in that data set. So in the earlier example, the "notes" column for both rows in the user table is NULL. This reveals a major limitation of the flat XML data set. The flat XML data set alone cannot explicitly set a column to NULL. You have to depend on the implicit behavior of including and not including attributes in each element. If you need to have a null column in your first row, you cannot just use a flat XML data set.

One way to work around this problem is to use PHPUnit's replacement data set decorator. This allows you to define a token that can be used in your data set to represent NULL values. We cover the details regarding how you can use the replacement decorator later in this chapter.

CSV Data Sets

In PHPUnit 3.3, the CSV data set format was introduced. It is implemented using the PHPUnit_ Extensions_Database_DataSet_CsvDataSet class. The constructor of this class takes several optional parameters to define the exact format of the files passed to the CSV data set. The parameters are $delimiter, $enclosure, and $escape. Their roles are very similar to the parameters for the fgetcsv() PHP function. The CSV data set is implemented using the fgetcsv() function. The default parameters for this data set are for comma-delimited files where columns are enclosed by double quotes. If a value for a column contains double quotes, it is escaped by another double quote. This is in line with the common format definition for CSV files laid out in IETF RFC4180 (http://tools.ietf.org/html/rfc4180). After the PHPUnit_Extensions_Database_DataSet_ CsvDataSet object is created, you can use the addTable() method to add a CSV file as a particular table. The first parameter to the addTable() method is the table name, and the second parameter is the file path. As with the constructors in the XML data sets, the file path passed to the addTable() method is relative to the current working directory. If you call addTable() twice with the same table name, the later call overwrites the first. The following code could be used to create a data set containing our user and empty_table tables:

```php
<?php
require_once 'PHPUnit/Extensions/Database/DataSet/CsvDataSet.php';
$csv_data_set=
    new PHPUnit_Extensions_Database_DataSet_CsvDataSet ( ' , ' , ' " ' , ' " ' ) ;
$csv_data_set->addTable ( 'user' , 'user.csv' ) ;
$csv_data_set->addTable ( 'empty_table' , 'empty_table.csv' ) ;
?>
```

The layout of the CSV files is very simple. The first row must contain the column names, and all other rows must contain the values in row order. If you want an empty table, you must still specify at least one column in the first row. The CSV format suffers from a similar deficiency as the flat XML format. Again, there's no way to explicitly set a column to NULL. In fact, there is not even an implicit way to set a NULL column for CSV formats. Again, you can use the replacement decorator to define a NULL token:

```
date_created, user_id , username , password , notes
"2009-01-01 00:00:00" , "1" , "mikelively " , "3858f62230ac3c915f300c664312c63f " ,
"2009-01-02 00:00:00" , "2" , "johnsmith" , "73cf88a0b4a18c88a3996fa3d5b69a46 " ,
                                            " I have no idea who this is"
empty_table_id
```

These two files define our example data set with the exception that the first row's notes column is an empty string instead of a NULL value. Also notice that the second file simply has empty_table_id and no more.

YAML Data Sets

In PHPUnit 3.4, the YAML data set was introduced. YAML is a hierarchical data format that aims to "provide a human friendly data serialization standard for all programming languages" (http://www.yaml.org/). This data format provides all the flexibility and capability of the standard XML format in a significantly easier-to-read format. The YAML data set is implemented by the PHPUnit_Extensions_Database_DataSet_YamlDataSet class. Similarly to both of the XML data set classes, the YAML data set class accepts a file path relative to the current working directory. One useful feature of the YAML data set class is that it also provides an addYamlFile() method that allows you to merge an additional YAML file into your existing YAML data set. If the additional file has records for a table that already exists, unlike the CSV format, it continues to add the data as additional rows to that table. This allows you to segregate your YAML files according to purpose and then, if necessary, combine the files to build a larger data set for your more intense tests. A YAML data set can be created using the following code:

```
<?php
require_once 'PHPUnit/Extensions/Database/DataSet/YamlDataSet.php';
$yaml_data_set =
 new PHPUnit_Extensions_Database_DataSet_YamlDataSet( 'data.yaml' ) ;
?>
```

The YAML specification is very flexible, and I highly recommend taking the time to read about it online. In this chapter, I go over some of the basics as they relate to building data sets. In YAML, there is a concept of mapping. This is essentially associating a piece of data to a string much like an associative array in PHP. This is accomplished by specifying your key suffixed with a colon and followed by the value for that key. An example of this is "key name: value." There is also a concept of sequences. This equates to a numerically indexed array of values in PHP. Sequences have each element prefixed with a single dash. A YAML data set maps a sequence of column-value mappings to a table name.

```
user:
    -
        date_created: 2009-01-01 00:00:00
        user_id: 1
        username: mikelively
        password: 3858f62230ac3c915f300c664312c63f
        notes: null

    -
        date_created: 2009-01-01 00:00:00
        user_id: 1
        username: johnsmith
        password: 73cf88a0b4a18c88a3996fa3d5b69a46
        notes: I have no idea who this is
empty table:
```

You can see that the user table key is followed by a single indented dash. Indentation in YAML is very important. It is how hierarchy is depicted. The two user table rows are both started by a single indented dash, and both dashes are indented by the same amount. You should always use spaces for this indention. After each dash, the individual column values are defined and indented one level further. Again, each column is indented by the same amount. Note that in the first row, the notes column's value is set to NULL. When this value is specified with no quotes, it is interpreted as a literal NULL by virtue of the YAML standard. If you want to comment your data set, you can use the # (pound sign) character.

There are some escaping issues in YAML that you must be aware of. If a column value ever contains tabs or the : (colon) or # character, you must use either single quotes or double quotes to delimit that string. If you delimit a string with a double quote, you can then use escape sequences. If you have a large block of text that you need to insert into a column, you can break that text into multiple lines, each having the same level of indentation. Here's an example of this:

```
user:
    -
        date_created: 2009-01-01 00:00:00
        user_id: 1
        username: mikelively
        password: 3858f62230ac3c915f300c664312c63f
        notes:
            This is a slightly larger block of text
            than you have seen
            in our previous examples.
```

When you have an indented block of text, each new line is folded into a space.

If you want to allow empty lines to represent line breaks, you can prefix your block of text with the > character (greater than).

```
user:
    -
        date_created: 2009-01-01 00:00:00
        user_id: 1
        username: mikelively
        password: 3858f62230ac3c915f300c664312c63f
        notes:
            This is a slightly larger block of text
            than you have seen
            in our previous examples.

            We can also create additional paragraphs with
                an empty line
                or a further indented line
```

Also, if you have a block of text where you want all line breaks to be interpreted literally, you can use the | (pipe) character.

```
user :
    -
        date_created: 2009-01-01 00:00:00
        user_id: 1
        username: mikelively
        password: 3858f62230ac3c915f300c664312c63f
        notes : |
            This block will
            be interpreted as having
            three lines.
```

You also can specify that the trailing line break be deleted in this example by replacing | with |-.

Database Data Sets

You also can generate a data set from a database connection. The PHPUnit_Extensions_Database_ DB_IDatabaseConnection class provides two different ways to create data sets directly from data in the database. The first is the createDataSet() method, which takes an array of table names that you want to export into a data set. It exports all data in those tables. For this reason, I do not recommend calling this method for anything but small tables. If you do not provide an array of table names as a parameter, then all data from all tables is dumped into your data set. Following is an example of using the createDataSet() method to create a data set containing all data from the user table:

```php
<?php
$db_connection =
    new PHPUnit_Extensions_Database_DB_DefaultDatabaseConnection (
        new PDO(
            'mysql:host=localhost; dbname=testdb',
            'root',
            'password'
        ) ,
        'testdb'
    );
$user_data_set=$db_connection->createDataSet(array( 'user' ) ) ;
?>
```

The second method available to you is the createQueryTable() method. This does not actually return a data set. It simply returns a table that you must then add to a data set. The createQueryTable() takes two parameters. The first parameter is used as the table name in the returned table. The second parameter is a query that is used to select data into the table. The columns of the table are determined by the names of each column specified in the query. This is useful for extracting a limited set of data out of a single table or combining data from different tables into a single table.

After you have created a table using the createQueryTable() method, you likely need to add it to a data set. The easiest way to do this is by using the PHPUnit_Extensions_Database_DataSet_ DefaultDataSet class. This class provides all the methods necessary to build a data set programmatically. The constructor simply takes an array of table objects. If you need to add more tables after the data set is constructed, you can always call the addTable() method.

Here's an example of how you can use the createQueryTable() method to extract a data set containing the newest 10 rows out of the user table:

```php
<?php
$db_connection =
    new PHPUnit_Extensions_Database_DB_DefaultDatabaseConnection (
        new PDO(
            'mysql:host=localhost; dbname=testdb',
            'root',
            'password'
        ) ,
        'testdb'
    );
$user_table=$db_connection->createQueryTable (
    'user' ,
```

```
        'SELECT * FROM user ORDER BY date_created DESC LIMIT 10 '
    ) ;
$user_data_set =
    new PHPUnit_Extensions_Database_DataSet_DefaultDataSet (
        array($user_table)
    ) ;
?>
```

Data Set Decorators

To provide more flexibility and versatility in the data sets, PHPUnit provides three decorators that can be used to enhance the functionality of the data sets. The first is the data set filter. It can be used to filter columns and tables that you do not need from existing data sets. The second is a composite data set. This allows you to combine multiple data sets with different tables into a single data set. The last decorator is the replacement data set, which we mentioned earlier in this chapter. It can be used to provide tokenized replacement for data in your data set.

Filter Decorator

The data set filter is implemented by the PHPUnit_Extensions_Database_DataSet_ DataSetFilter class. It accepts an existing data set object as the first parameter and a specially formatted array containing a list of tables and columns that you want to exclude from your tests. The array is keyed by table name, and each table name is then set to one of three things. It includes either an array of column names that you want to exclude from the data set, the * character (which indicates that the entire table should be excluded), or a string containing a single column to exclude from the data set. Here's an example of a data set filter that filters out the date created and user id columns from user, the empty table id column from empty_table, and the entire useless table:

```
<?php
$xml_data_set=
new PHPUnit_Extensions_Database_DataSet_XmlDataSet( 'mydataset.xml' ) ;
$filtered_data_set=
new PHPUnit_Extensions_Database_DataSet_DataSetFilter (
    $xml_data_set ,
    array(
        'user' => array('date_created','user_id') ,
        'empty_table' => 'empty_table_id',
        'useless_table' => '*'
    )
) ;
?>
```

You rarely use this class on a data set that is being used as a fixture. It is very common, however, to use this as a way to protect your database assertions from indeterminate values. When asserting data existing in your database, you may frequently find that auto increment columns and time stamping columns give you trouble. Using the data set filter, you can remove these columns from the data set generated by your database. We cover this in more detail later.

You also can use the data set filter when attempting to generate a new data set file from an existing data set file. Again, we cover this in more detail later in this chapter.

Composite Decorator

The composite data set can be used to combine one or more data sets of potentially varying types into a single data set. The composite data set is implemented by the PHPUnit_Extensions_ Database_DataSet_CompositeDataSet class. This class takes an array of data set objects. After a composite data set object is created, you can add additional data sets using the addDataSet() method. When adding data sets, the composite data set does not allow you to add a data set that contains rows for a table that already exists inside of the composite data set. This likely will be changed in a future version. Here's an example combining a flat XML, standard XML, and CSV data all set into one single data set.

```php
<?php
$xml_data_set=
    new PHPUnit_Extensions_Database_DataSet_XmlDataSet('xmldata.xml');

$flat_xml_data_set=
    new PHPUnit_Extensions_Database_DataSet_FlatXmlDataSet('flat.xml');
$composite_data_set=
    new PHPUnit_Extensions_Database_DataSet_CompositeDataSet(
        array(
            $xml_data_set,
            $flat_xml_data_set
        )
    );
$csv_data_set=
    new PHPUnit_Extensions_Database_DataSet_CsvDataSet( ' , ' , ' " ' , ' " ' ) ;
$csv_data_set->addTable ('user','user.csv');
$csv_data_set->addTable ('empty_table','empty_table.csv');
$composite_data_set->addDataSet($csv_data_set);
?>
```

This provides a convenient and easy way for you to break your data sets into small reusable chunks. This prevents you from having to create the same XML, YAML, or CSV files repeatedly and also lends your fixtures much more flexibility. For instance, if you have reference tables in your database that for most tests need to be populated with the same data, you can define these data sets as separate fixtures returned from various methods in your base class.

```php
<?php
include_once 'PHPUnit/Extensions/Database/TestCase.php';
abstract class MySQLDatabaseTest
    extends PHPUnit_Extensions_Database_TestCase
    {
        protected function getConnection( )
        {
            return
                new PHPUnit_Extensions_Database_DB_DefaultDatabaseConnection(
                    new PDO(
                        'mysql:host=localhost; dbname=testdb,
                        'root',
                        'password'
                    ),
                    'testdb'
                ) ;
        }
```

```php
        protected function getUserTypeDataSet( )
        {
            return
                new PHPUnit_Extensions_Database_DataSet_XmlDataSet('utype.xml');
        }
        protected function getGroupDataSet( )
        {
            return
                new PHPUnit_Extensions_Database_DataSet_XmlDataSet('group.xml');
        }
        protected function getCategoryDataSet()
        {
            return
                new PHPUnit_Extensions_Database_DataSet_XmlDataSet('cat.xml');
        }
    }
?>
```

If you create a new database test case that requires group and category data in order to run its tests, you can use the following code in your new test case:

```php
<?php
include_once 'PHPUnit/Extensions/Database/TestCase.php';
class GroupCategoryTest extends MySQLDatabaseTest
{
    protected function getDataSet ( )
    {
        return new PHPUnit_Extensions_Database_DataSet_CompositeDataSet (
            array (
                $this->getGroupDataSet( ) ,
                $this->getCategoryDataSet( )
            )
        );
    }
}
?>
```

You could take it one step further and remove the need for you to worry about setting up the composite data in each test case by also implementing getDataSet() in your base test case class and then calling an abstract method to determine what you will pass to your composite data set:

```php
<?php
include_once 'PHPUnit/Extensions/Database/TestCase.php';
abstract class MySQLDatabaseTest
    extends PHPUnit_Extensions_Database_TestCase
    {
        protected function getConnection( )
        {
            return
                new PHPUnit_Extensions_Database_DB_DefaultDatabaseConnection(
                    new PDO(
                        'mysql:host=localhost; dbname=testdb' ,
                        'root' ,
                        'password'
                    ),
```

```
                'testdb'
            );
    }
    protected function getDataSet()
    {
        return
        new PHPUnit_Extensions_Database_DataSet_CompositeDataSet(
            $this->getDataSetList( )
        );
    }
    abstract protected function getDataSetList();
    protected function getUserTypeDataSet()
    {
        return
            new PHPUnit_Extensions_Database_DataSet_XmlDataSet('utype.xml');
    }
    protected function getGroupDataSet()
    {
        return
            new PHPUnit_Extensions_Database_DataSet_XmlDataSet('group.xml');
    }
    protected function getCategoryDataSet()
    {
        return
            new PHPUnit_Extensions_Database_DataSet_XmlDataSet('cat.xml');
    }
    }
?>
```

Your previous test case class can then be simplified down to the following:

```
<?php
include_once 'PHPUnit/Extensions/Database/TestCase.php';
class GroupCategoryTest extends MySQLDatabaseTest
{
    protected function getDataSetList()
    {
        return array (
            $this->getGroupDataSet(),
            $this->getCategoryDataSet()
        );
    }
}
?>
```

Replacement Decorator

The last data set decorator we discuss is the replacement data set decorator. This decorator is implemented by the PHPUnit_Extensions_Database_DataSet_ReplacementDataSet class. As mentioned in the overview of the flat XML data set and the CSV data set, the replacement data set decorator can be used to simulate NULL values. It does this by allowing you to specify a token and the data with which you want to replace that token. You can use either full column replacements or sub-string replacements. The constructor for the PHPUnit_Extensions_Database_DataSet_ReplacementDataSet takes an existing data set object and two associative arrays. The arrays are keyed by the strings that you want to replace. The values are what you want to replace the keys with. The first array specifies full column replacements. These match and replace the column value only if the entire column value is a match for the key. The values for this array can feasibly be any type, including NULL. The second array specifies sub-string replacements. These replace any occurrence of the key in every column in the database. Again, you can specify any type, but it is cast as a string before it is inserted into the column. Here's an example of how you could set up the previous flat XML file to be used with the replacement data set decorator in order to create a true NULL value in the first notes column:

```xml
<?xml version="1.0" charset="utf-8" ?>
<dataset>
    <user
        date_created="2009-01-01 00:00:00"
        user_id="1"
        username="mikelively"
        password="3858f62230ac3c915f300c664312c63f"
        notes="[[[NULL]]]"
    />
    <user
        date_created="2009-01-02 00:00:00"
        user_id="2"
        username="mikelively"
        password="73cf88a0b4a18c88a3996fa3d5b69a46"
        notes="I have no idea who this is"
    />
    <empty table /><!-- the empty table contains no data -->
</dataset>
```

The only difference is that we have actually specified the notes column as an attribute and given it the value of [[[NULL]]]. You can now use the following code to cause that string to be replaced by a true null value:

```php
<?php
$xml_data_set=
    new PHPUnit_Extensions_Database_DataSet_FlatXmlDataSet('data.xml');
$replaced_data_set=
    new PHPUnit_Extensions_Database_DataSet_ReplacementDataSet(
        $xml_data_set ,
        array('[[[NULL]]]'=>NULL)
    ) ;
?>
```

There are many other uses for replacement data sets. Suppose you have a table called "article" containing a list of blog postings, and you are testing a method that is used to retrieve all blog posts for the current month based on a date stored in YYYY-MM-DD format in a column labeled "date published." You could create a data set similar to this one:

```xml
<?xml version="1.0" charset="utf-8" ?>
<dataset>
    <article
        article_id="1"
        date_published="[[[CURDATE]]]"
        author="mike lively"
```

```
        subject="Cool story #1"
        content="The coolest stories are short!"
    />
</dataset>
```

You could then use the following code to ensure that whenever your test case runs, you are populating that table with a day that allows this method to pull the article:

```php
<?php
$xml_data_set=
    new PHPUnit_Extensions_Database_DataSet_FlatXmlDataSet('data.xml');
$replaced_data_set=
    new PHPUnit_Extensions_Database_DataSet_ReplacementDataSet(
        $xml_data_set,
        array('[[[CURDATE]]]'=>date('Y-m-d'))
    ) ;
?>
```

Generating Data Sets

One of the keys to being able to deploy database tests quickly using PHPUnit is the capability to quickly establish data sets. For small tables and data sets, it is often quicker to write the data set in your preferred table format. For others, it may be much easier to work with an existing development database to generate your data sets. This is especially useful if you have several rows that you need to insert into your fixture or if you have a table with a particularly large number of columns.

The current formats that can be persisted are the flat XML, standard XML, and YAML data set formats. Each of these formats has a static `write()` method on its data set class. Each of the `write()` methods takes a data set as its first parameter and a path to a file relative to the current directory as the second parameter. You can pass any type of data set to these methods. This means it can be used to convert from CSV to XML, XML to YAML, from a database generated data set to YAML, even from a replacement or composite data set to XML.

As your application grows and you continue to add more tests, you may find that you need an easier way to set up and track data sets. Due to the interchangeability of data sets in PHPUnit, you can easily set up a central database to manage your data sets. This allows you to reduce the amount of code and time spent associating the correct data set to the correct test case. It centralizes the data in fixtures. It also allows you to easily represent the test data you are using in your test cases in a visual way.

To implement this, you need an additional database holding your test fixtures. I recommend utilizing SQLite. This allows for somewhat easier distribution of the test fixtures. It also allows you to maintain the test database in your source control systems such as subversion.

Data Operations

After you have created your data fixture, you need to determine how PHPUnit should use that fixture to set up your database for the test. Many different operations are supported by PHPUnit out of the box, and it is fairly easy to create your own if necessary.

The default setup operation is called a CLEAN INSERT. It essentially deletes all records in the tables involved in the data set using a TRUNCATE command. If the RDBMS in question does not support

TRUNCATE, then DELETE FROM is used instead. It then inserts each row defined in the data set in the order in which it was defined. CLEAN INSERT is used as the default setup operation because it allows you to see the full resulting data of failed tests. When this operation is used in conjunction with the —stop-on-failure option of PHPUnit, you can inspect the database and see the exact state of the data at the point at which the test failed.

You also can define a tear-down operation. You have the same choices of operations. The default tear-down operation is essentially a NULL operation. The reason for this is that the default setup operation is intended to clean out the database prior to inserting the necessary data.

The default operations work in most cases, although if your data sets are not complete, problems can arise. For example, default operations can cause problems when you do not add a table to your data set that is written to as a part of the test. This results in potentially unpredictable data being in the database that could cause further inserts into that database to fail. If you have a large number of tables and cannot predict which tables will be affected by a particular piece of code, I recommend changing your default tear-down operation to a TRUNCATE. This helps minimize the risk of data flowing from one test and affecting another.

Two methods in the PHPUnit_Extensions_Database_TestCase class can be overridden to change the default behavior regarding the database on setup and tear-down. The first method is getSetUpOperation(). This method defines the setup operation for the test case. The second method is getTearDownOperation(). This method defines the tear-down operation for the test case.

All the built-in operations can be instantiated using the PHPUnit_Extensions_Database_ Operation_Factory class. The following list itemizes all the static methods available for these operations and what they do:

➤ PHPUnit_Extensions_Database_Operation_Factory::NONE(): This represents a null operation. This means that no action is taken on the database.

➤ PHPUnit_Extensions_Database_Operation_Factory::INSERT(): This inserts all rows in the data set into the appropriate tables.

➤ PHPUnit_Extensions_Database_Operation_Factory::TRUNCATE(): This truncates all tables in the data set. If the database platform being used does not support TRUNCATE, then a DELETE FROM table is issued instead.

➤ PHPUnit_Extensions_Database_Operation_Factory::DELETE(): This deletes all rows that have a matching primary key with a row in the same table in the data set.

➤ PHPUnit_Extensions_Database_Operation_Factory::DELETE_ALL(): This is similar to a TRUNCATE operation, but it uses the DELETE FROM syntax instead.

➤ PHPUnit_Extensions_Database_Operation_Factory::UPDATE(): This updates all rows with matching primary keys in the data set with the data for that table.

➤ PHPUnit_Extensions_Database_Operation_Factory::CLEAN_INSERT(): This is a composite operation consisting of a TRUNCATE operation followed by an INSERT operation. You can optionally pass TRUE to this method to indicate that you want to force truncates to cascade.

One additional operation that is not exposed by PHPUnit_Extensions_Database_Operation_ Factory is the PHPUnit_Extensions_Database_Operation_Replace operation. This operation works much like the REPLACE statement in MySQL. If a row in the data set matches a row in the database based on a primary key, it updates that row. If the row cannot be found, it is created. This is an effective way to quickly refresh the database without having to completely empty the table.

Any of the existing operations can be combined with another operation utilizing the PHPUnit_ Extensions_Database_Operation_Composite operation. The constructor for this operation accepts an array of operations, which then are executed in the order defined in the array.

Here's an example of modifying the base test class to always perform a REPLACE operation in the table setup:

```php
<?php
include_once 'PHPUnit/Extensions/Database/TestCase.php';
abstract class MySQLDatabaseTest
    extends PHPUnit_Extensions_Database_TestCase
    {
        protected function getConnection()
        {
            return
                new PHPUnit_Extensions_Database_DB_DefaultDatabaseConnection(
                    new PDO(
                        'mysql:host=localhost; dbname=testdb',
                        'root',
                        'password'
                    ),
                    'testdb'
                );
        }
        protected function getSetUpOperation()
        {
            return new PHPUnit_Extensions_Database_Operation_Replace();
        }
    }
?>
```

Any test case that extends MySQLDatabaseTest now performs a REPLACE operation using the database specified.

Creating Tests

Testing the Loading of Data

The last aspect of database testing that needs to be addressed is how to assert that your code is interacting with the database correctly. You can check this interaction in two ways. The first is testing that code correctly retrieves data from the database. One of the abilities required by our User_Model class is to load a user by username and password. As shown in the following code, the method to load the user accepts two string parameters containing the username and password, respectively, and a third parameter containing a PDO database connection. If it can successfully find a user, it returns TRUE and the correct data for that user is populated on the model itself.

```php
<?php
class User Model
{
    /**
   * Loads the model with data found by the user and plain text
   * password.
   *
   * The password in the database should be md5 hash
   * @param string $username
  * @param string $password
  * @param PDO $db
  * @return bool True if the user is found, false otherwise
  */
    public function loadByUserPass($username, $password, PDO $db)
    {
    // functionality here
    }
}
?>
```

To test this method, we need to ensure that our test database has a row in the user table that can be retrieved by this method. I use the YAML data set format for this. Notice that the password is an md5 string. This allows us to meet the requirements denoted in the method comments.

```yaml
user:
    -
        date_created: 2009-01-01 00:00:00
        user_id: 1
        username: mikelively
        password: 3858f62230ac3c915f300c664312c63f
        notes: This is my account.
```

Finally, utilizing our base test class, I write a new test case class for testing the user model. The test case class initially needs to contain a single test that calls loadByUserPass() with the data in the fixture and asserts that the method returns true and that the model is populated with the correct data. We use the createPDO() method that we defined earlier to pull the database connection. This allows our tests to be moved easily to a separate database with little or no problem.

```php
<?php
class User_ModelTest extends MySQLDatabaseTest
{
    public function getDataSet()
    {
        return new PHPUnit_Extensions_Database_DataSet_YamlDataSet (
            'fixtures/usermodeltest.yaml'
        ) ;
    }
    public function testLoadByUserPass()
    {
        $usermodel = new User_Model() ;
        $successful = $usermodel->loadByUserPass (
            'mikelively',
            'password',
            $this->createPDO()
        ) ;
```

```
            $this->assertTrue($successful);
            $this->assertEquals('mikelively',$usermodel->getUsername());
            $this->assertEquals('This is my account.',$usermodel->getNotes());
        }
    }
    ?>
```

We now have a test that verifies the behavior exhibited by the `loadByUserPass()` method when the requested data exists. It also is appropriate to have a test that verifies the behavior when the requested data does not exist. I must add another test to the test case to accomplish this. That test should call `loadByUserPass()` with data that does not already exist. Because this is our second test, I also move the common fixture code into a custom `setUp()` method. For now, that common code simply sets up the `User_Model` instance. I also slightly rename the `testLoadByUserPass()` test to something more indicative of what is being tested.

```php
<?php
class User_ModelTest extends MySQLDatabaseTest
{
    //code truncated...
    public function testSuccessfulLoadByUserPass()
    {
        $usermodel=new User_Model();
        $successful=$usermodel->loadByUserPass(
            'mikelively',
            'password',
            $this->createPDO()
        );
        $this->assertTrue($successful);
        $this->assertEquals('mikelively',$usermodel->getUsername());
        $this->assertEquals('This is my account.',$usermodel->getNotes());
    }
    public function testFailedLoadByUserPass()
    {
        $usermodel=new User_Model();
        $successful=$usermodel->loadByUserPass (
            'mikelively',
            'password',
            $this->createPDO()
        );
        $this->assertFalse($successful);
        $this->assertNull($usermodel->getUsername());
        $this->assertNull($usermodel->getNotes());
    }
}
?>
```

Now the primary two behaviors of the `loadByUserPass()` method are being tested.

There are other tests you could do as well. For example, you could verify that values are properly escaped before being inserted into the query. I recommend caution when developing tests for things like ensuring data is escaped. You will quickly find your tests becoming cumbersome to write and lengthy to run. Instead, limit them to your more important classes where data is most likely to break, or enforce proper escaping through code reviews and coding guidelines. You also can encapsulate the code that builds queries so it can be tested separately, one at a time, to ensure that it is escaping data properly.

In this case, we did not manipulate data in the database, so I did not do any assertions of the data inside of the database. Occasionally, you may work with code that you need to verify is not manipulating data in the database. Perhaps the code interacts with sensitive data or you had a bug in the past with the code in question actually manipulating data. I have encountered scenarios where a method that was responsible for retrieving data on an individual record in a system was inadvertently changed to actually start modifying that same record. This caused several problems and was not detected for several days because the fallout of the problem could be seen only on edge cases. The issue was missed all the way through acceptance testing, and the database was never checked for modifications in the unit tests. When issues like this occur once in that area of code, it is quite likely to occur again. It is wise to introduce a new test to ensure that calls to this code do not edit the database. This is often as simple as asserting against the fixture you used to set up your test, as shown in the following code:

```php
<?php
class User_ModelTest extends MySQLDatabaseTest
{
    //code truncated...
    public function testSuccessfulLoadByUserPass()
    {
        $usermodel=new User_Model();
        $successful=$usermodel->loadByUserPass(
            'mikelively',
            'password',
            $this->createPDO()
        );
        $this->assertTrue($successful);
        $this->assertEquals('mikelively',$usermodel->getUsername());
        $this->assertEquals('This is my account.',$usermodel->getNotes());
        $this->assertDataSetsEqual(
            $this->getDataSet(),
            $this->getConnection()->createDataSet(array('user'))
        );
    }
    public function testFailedLoadByUserPass()
    {
        $usermodel=new User_Model();
        $successful=$usermodel->loadByUserPass (
            'mikelively',
            'password',
            $this->createPDO()
        );
        $this->assertFalse($successful);
        $this->assertNull($usermodel->getUsername());
        $this->assertNull($usermodel->getNotes());
        $this->assertDataSetsEqual(
            $this->getDataSet(),
            $this->getConnection()->createDataSet(array('user'))
        );
    }
}
?>
```

These tests now use `assertDataSetsEqual()` to verify that the data in the database still matches the data provided by the fixture. Essentially, it is verifying that your data has not changed. It may not always be desirable to do this additional testing due to the amount of runtime it adds to your test cases. You need to make a case-by-case judgment call on how important it is to protect yourself from the data changing.

Testing the Modification of Data

We have covered how to test methods that load data from the database. We now need to explore how we can test methods that manipulate data in the database. To do this effectively without having to test several behaviors at once, we need to compare data existing in our database with a known data set. We have already explored how we can extract PHPUnit data sets out of our database and how we can create data sets with files. All that remains to discuss is how we can compare them.

The `PHPUnit_Extensions_Database_TestCase` class provides two methods that can be used to assert the data in your database: `assertDataSetsEqual()` and `assertTablesEqual()`. The first method accepts two data sets of any type. It then verifies that the data sets contain the same tables, each table in the data set contains the same number of rows, and the rows in the data sets are identical. It is important to note that the order of data in each data set is going to be considered. In many cases, this makes the `createQueryTable()` method that was discussed in the data sets section very appealing. We can enforce the order using an `ORDER BY` clause, and then we do not need to be concerned about how each database orders data by default.

The problem with `createQueryTable()`, however, is that it does not actually create a data set for you; it simply returns a table. That is where the usefulness of `assertTablesEqual()` is revealed. The `assertTablesEqual()` method accepts two tables and verifies that they have the same number of rows and the rows in the table are identical.

The next behavior of our `User_Model` class that we test is adding a new user. The `User_Model` class has a method called `insert()` that accepts a single parameter containing a PDO database connection. It is then responsible for inserting a new user row into the database using the username, password, and notes that are currently set for the instance of the user model. If it can add the user to the database, it returns TRUE. The model's internal ID also is changed to represent the new row.

```php
<?php
class User_Model
{
  /**
   * Inserts the data in the model as a new row in the database
   * @return bool True if the user is successfully inserted, false otherwise
   */
   public function loadByUserPass($username, $password , PDO $db)
   {
      // functionality here...
   }
}
?>
```

To test this particular method, we actually do not necessarily need any data existing in the database. However, for simplicity's sake, we can just use the test data set that we created for testing the loadByUserPass() method. This allows us to put this new test in our existing test case. This is by no means a requirement. We could just as easily make a new test case with an empty data set. The determining factor for whether you create a new test case class should balance the number of separate test case classes you want to manage with the performance implications of setting up data in the database that you do not strictly need. In this particular case, we are setting up a single row of data, so we stick with the existing data set and test case.

To accurately test the insert() method, we need to do some setup of a User_Model class. That setup involves calling methods to set the username, password, and notes to known values. After this is done, we can call the insert() method. To assert that insert() did what we expected, we must compare the data in the database with what we think the data should look like and we need to verify that the new ID of the user row is set in the User_Model class. This is shown in the following code:

```
user :
    -
        user_id: 2
        username: anotheruser
        password: 5ebe2294ecd0e0f08eab7690d2a6ee69
        notes: This user's being added for testing.
```

```php
<?php
class User_ModelTest extends MySQLDatabaseTest
{
    public function getDataSet()
    {
        return new PHPUnit_Extensions_Database_DataSet_YamlDataSet (
            'fixtures/usermodeltest.yaml'
        );
    }
    public function testInsert()
    {
        $usermodel=new User_Model();
        $usermodel->setUsername('anotheruser');
        $usermodel->setPassword('$ecr3tP4ss');
        $usermodel->setNotes('This user\'s being added for testing.');
        $this->assertTrue($usermodel->insert());
        $this->assertEquals(2, $usermodel->get_Id());
        $expected_data =
            new PHPUnit_Extensions_Database_DataSet_YamlDataSet (
                'expected/usermodeltest_insert.yaml'
            ) ;
        $this->assertTablesEqual(
            $expected data->getTable('user'),
            $this->createQueryTable(
                'user',
                'SELECT user_id, username, password, notes
                    FROM user WHERE username="anotheruser" '
            )
        );
    }
}
?>
```

We have created a new YAML data set to compare the data in the database. The data set in this particular file looks slightly different than our fixture because we are not comparing the date_ created. The date_created column is a time stamp that is set upon inserting the object into the database. There is currently no way in the database to directly compare values with a delta. This means that if your test was run while your clock rolled over to the next second, your test would likely fail due to a difference in the date_created value. We are using the assertTablesEqual() method to do our comparison in the database. This allows us to select the row that we believe should have been inserted and keeps the size of our data set relatively small. Notice that we have passed the table name of user to createQueryTable(). The table name you provide to createQueryTable() must match the name used for the table in your data set. Otherwise, the assertTablesEqual() fails due to the table names being different.

If you feel it is important to test your date_created column as well, you can slightly modify the test. Because the likelihood of this test taking more than one second is extremely low, you can add another column to the data set and createQueryTable() to test that the value in date_created is no more than one second less than the current time:

```
user:
    -
        date_created_check: 1
        user_id: 2
        username: anotheruser
        password: 5ebe2294ecd0e0f08eab7690d2a6ee69
        notes: This user's being added for testing.

<?php
class User_ModelTest extends MySQLDatabaseTest
{
    public function getDataSet()
    {
        return new PHPUnit_Extensions_Database_DataSet_YamlDataSet(
            'fixtures/usermodeltest.yaml'
        ) ;
    }
    public function testInsert()
    {
        $usermodel = new User_Model();
        $usermodel->setUsername('anotheruser');
        $usermodel->setPassword('$ecr3tP4ss');
        $usermodel->setNotes('This user\'s being added for testing.');
        $this->assertTrue($usermodel->insert());
        $this->assertEquals(2, $usermodel->get_Id());
        $expected_data =
            new PHPUnit_Extensions_Database_DataSet_YamlDataSet(
                'expected/usermodeltestinsert.yaml'
            );
        $now = time();
        $this->assertTablesEqual(
            $expected_data->getTable('user'),
            $this->createQueryTable (
                'user',
                'SELECT
```

```
                    (' . $now . ' - date_created) <= 1 as date_created_check,
                        user_id , username , password , notes
                    FROM user WHERE username = " anotheruser " '
                )
            );
        }
    }
?>
```

This validates that the date_created is within one second of what the value should be. This should be more than enough accuracy to validate that you are properly setting date_created when you insert new rows. This change shows more of the power and flexibility that can be achieved using the createQueryTable() method of comparing data in the database. I must caution you against introducing much complexity into the queries, however, because you should never find yourself in a position where your tests are becoming as complicated as the code they were meant to test. After all, we have enough to test without having to test our tests!

Using the Database Tester

If you are in the middle of transitioning to using database tests or if you are using a framework other than PHPUnit for your unit testing, you may wonder if you can even utilize the database testing PHPUnit provides. The good news is that with a little bit of code, you certainly can. The database test case class in PHPUnit is essentially a wrapper for a standalone class that performs all the essential fixture operations for database testing. It is pretty trivial to integrate this class into a simple test, PHPT, or even your own framework as long as you follow the general order of operations for testing: set up test, run test, assert data, tear down tests.

PHPUnit provides the PHPUnit_Extensions_Database_DefaultTester class. This class does not have any dependencies to PHPUnit outside of the database extension class and is suitable for integration into other frameworks and projects. Essentially, for each isolated test, you should create a new instance of PHPUnit_Extensions_Database_DefaultTester and pass in an instance of your PDO class. You can then set your setup and tear-down operations respectively using the setSetUpOperation() and setTearDownOperation(). You also can set the data set you want to use as a fixture using the setDataSet() method. Then, before the test is run, you simply call the onSetUp() method, and when the test is finished running, you call onTearDown(). To assert your data sets and tables, you can utilize the assertEquals() methods that are defined for each table and data set. If I wanted to create a quick test for the insert() method in my User_Model class outside of the PHPUnit framework, I could do the following:

```php
<?php
/* Set up the tester with the correct database, operations, and dataset. */
$db = new PDO('sqlite::memory:');
$test_conn = new PHPUnit_Extensions_Database_DB_DefaultDatabaseConnection
    ( $db , ' ' );
$db_tester = new PHPUnit_Extensions_Database_DefaultTester($test_conn);
$db_tester->setSetUpOperation(
    new PHPUnit_Extensions_Database_Operations_CleanInsert()
);
$db_tester->setTearDownOperation(
    new PHPUnit_Extensions_Database_Operations_Null()
);
```

```
$db_tester->setDataSet(
    new PHPUnit_Extensions_Database_DataSet_YamlDataSet(
        'fixtures/usermodeltest.yaml'
    )
);
/* Inserts data into the database */
$db_testerdb->onSetUp();
try
{
    $usermodel=new User_Model();
    $usermodel->setUsername('anotheruser');
    $usermodel->setPassword('$ecr3tP4ss');
    $usermodel->setNotes('This user\'s being added for testing.');
    if($usermodel->insert($db)!= TRUE)
    {
        throw new Exception("insert() did not equal true.");
    }
    if($usermodel->getId()!= 2)
    {
        throw new Exception ("getId() did not equal 2.");
    }
    $expected_data =
        new PHPUnit_Extensions_Database_DataSet_YamlDataSet(
            'expected/usermodeltest_insert.yaml'
        ) ;
    $expected data->getTable('user')->assertEquals(
        $test_conn->createQueryTable (
            'user',
            'SELECT user_id , username , password , notes
            FROM user WHERE username = "anotheruser"'
        )
    );
    $db_tester->onTearDown();
}
catch (Exception $e)
{
    $db_tester->onTearDown();
    throw $e ;
}
?>
```

There is not much inherent value in creating a test like this, because it adds a significant amount of duplication to your tests, but it provides a good view of how the database tester in PHPUnit can be used from outside of PHPUnit. The first portion of this code is setting up the database connection and the database tester with the correct operations and data set. We then call `$db->onSetup()`.

These two sections of the preceding code encompass the database portion of the fixture. They are the equivalent to implementing `getConnection()`, `getDataSet()`, and optionally `getSetUpOperation()` and `tearDownOperation()` in a normal PHPUnit database test case. We then start a try/catch block that contains the test itself. I have chosen to throw exceptions to indicate test failures so we can easily short circuit the test on any failure. When validating the data in the database, we use the `assertEquals()` method on the YAML table that we created. You can see that even without utilizing PHPUnit test cases, you have a significant amount of functionality at your fingertips. If `assertEquals()` fails, it throws an exception. Finally, we call onTearDown(). Notice that we call onTearDown() if we catch an exception as well. This ensures that regardless of whether the test passes or fails, we clean up the database.

APPLYING TEST-DRIVEN DESIGN TO DATABASE TESTING

If you are working with a team that employs test-driven development (TDD), then you should find some immediate use for database testing. It allows you to iteratively set up your database schema and interaction through tests, much like you would your code. After you have identified that a new feature for your current iteration requires interaction with your database, you can immediately begin establishing database fixtures and assertions to determine the completion of that feature.

Consider a project to develop an authorization service. The requirements we need to work on inevitably include adding a user to the database. One test case for this requirement may include a test case against our user database model to insert a new user. As part of making that test case work, we need to create the user table schema. We may then have an additional requirement to force users to change their passwords the first time they log in. If the design decision is made to retrieve this flag using the same model, we would introduce another test case against that model to ensure that this flag can be set and unset correctly inside of the database. As a part of making that test case work, we would then need to modify the user table schema.

USING DATABASE TESTS FOR REGRESSION TESTING

We must make sure we are writing database tests whenever we find a problem with the data in our code. Regression database testing is similar to normal regression unit testing. We still need to isolate the root of the problem, create a test that exposes the problem, and create code to fix the test; in the process, we fix the problem. The hardest part of this process is identifying the root of the problem.

We must understand the source of any bug. Most often, it is an issue with one of two things: either the logic in the code or the data on which the logic is operating. If the issue you are experiencing is purely a logic issue and any data being utilized by the method with the bad logic is loaded and saved in a different method, then there is no reason to introduce database fixtures or database assertions in the regression test. For regression tests, we want to focus on testing what is broken. If the code that loads or saves the data is directly in the same method, then we need to use fixtures, assertions, or possibly both. If data is loaded from the database, then it is appropriate to use database fixtures. If data is saved back to the database, then it is appropriate to use database assertions. I do not recommend refactoring the code prior to writing the unit tests. It is almost always best to create our tests prior to any code changes because it helps us to be certain we have identified the problem.

The condition of our data often has a large impact on our software's ability to function correctly. The bottom line is that it is hard to completely understand what data is going to look like. There are always variants on the data that we do not expect. When they are found and dealt with, we should protect ourselves with tests against that data to ensure that the problem does not come up again.

In some senses, when we find an unexpected problem, we should be happy. We can't prevent situations we are unaware of. Unexpected bugs are the perfect opportunity for us to learn from mistakes.

The key is making sure we learn from the mistake and protect ourselves from making that same mistake in the future. As developers, we often introduce bugs into the system. We are simply human. We all make mistakes. If you did not think this were true, you likely would not be reading this book. Something I do not think is realized enough is that if a mistake is made once, it can certainly be made again. This happens even more often when you are working in large teams.

When we create a solution for a given programming problem, we are making the assumption that we not only understand the problem enough to say that we are solving it, but also that our solution will not introduce unacceptable problems anywhere else in the system. Essentially, we depend on having a perfect understanding of the software we are working on. This is, in most cases, an unrealistic goal. As developers, most of our time is spent dealing with those "gotcha" moments that can be introduced by everything from misunderstood project requirements to not considering the functionality of external systems.

We have all experienced occasions where a mistake is made in code due to a misunderstanding of the requirements. The mistake is then fixed, but due to time constraints, an attitude of thinking that it is not important, or the thought that "I won't make this mistake again," a regression test is not written. Then another developer comes along. Working with the code again, he or she decides to rework the code for some reason, and again misunderstands the original requirements in likely the same way as the original developer, and reintroduces the same defect.

Testing Problems with Data

Problems with the data itself can be the result of errors by developers when manually inserting data or errors in the application stemming from not validating the data, manipulating data incorrectly, or incorrectly translating data from a user or external service. Most often, regression tests involving these kinds of bugs involve asserting that data in the database is correct after the code we are testing is executed.

Isolating what data is causing our problem is not always easy. However, often it has a large impact in how our tests are written. What we may think is a problem with how data is pulled from the database may actually be a problem with how the data is inserted into the database. What if the data being inserted is coming from a web service and is incorrect? Where you previously thought there was an issue with database interaction, you now have a problem with how data is retrieved from an external service. The regression test for this may wind up not having any database fixture at all; we may just have the test asserting that data was inserted into our test database correctly based on a corrected web service call.

After we have isolated the problem data, the ideal next step is to develop a test to expose the problematic data. It is important that whenever possible, we expose the problem with tests before we fix the problem. There are two reasons for this. The first reason is that it allows us to have confidence that we fixed the problem.

The second reason is that once code is fixed, we are generally very lazy about doing anything else with that code, like creating unit tests. As much as we may always want to write tests first, we always need to balance the need to fix a problem quickly with the need to make sure the problem doesn't happen again. In some cases, especially for severe bugs, we cannot take the time to create tests before we actually create and release a fix for the bug.

Any company with a product that is provided as a service with any kind of a semi-frequent release cycle is going to have this problem. Making our customers happy should always be our first priority. This does not mean, however, that getting a fix out quickly is mutually exclusive to protecting ourselves with unit tests. It just means that we need to have the additional discipline to make sure that even though we don't currently have a problem, we still take the added step of writing a test to expose the broken code or data.

Testing Problems Revealed by Data

If a bug is being revealed by data in the database, there are two possible ways to create a test for that bug. The first and most ideal way requires that the code loading the data is well encapsulated and isolated from the logic that has the problem. As long as the data itself is correct and not the actual problem, we can isolate out the method with the bad logic and test it. The key is to make sure our data access is fully encapsulated. If this is the case, then you shouldn't need to worry about creating database fixtures or asserting any of the data in the database.

The second way is to create a database fixture containing the data that is triggering the errors in logic. If our database access code is tightly coupled to the logic in question, then we are forced to test in this manner. We must make sure the bad data is in our test database before we can adequately test the logic. In the event that the same method results in more data being written back into the database, we must assert the data in the database as well.

CONCLUSION

Database testing can be a powerful tool when used properly. When used correctly, it allows you to protect and ensure correct operation of parts of your system that often go unnoticed with standard unit testing. We hope you can walk away from this chapter with a better knowledge of how to utilize the functionality provided by PHPUnit's database testing extension. Although applying database tests to your system is not an easily learned task, the rewards you experience from doing so are valuable. You can have peace of mind when testing a new RDBMS version because you know your critical queries are being run. You can ensure that query optimizations do not cause new bugs in your system. You also can ensure that old bugs do not reappear.

PART V
Q&A in the Large

11

Quality Assurance at studiVZ

Christiane Philipps and Max Horváth

INTRODUCTION

"The software tests at studiVZ are complete, error-free, stable, and tremendously elegant."
This is the legend we would love to tell you. studiVZ performs only rudimentary testing before
we deploy new features; after all, we have millions of testers (that is, users). At least, this
might be what outside observers with little insight into our work would say.

The truth always lies somewhere in the middle. Certainly, not everything we do is perfect,
but we invest lots of time, money, and effort to make our software a little better every day.
studiVZ has a quality assurance team with up to 10 members, which is something that only
a few web companies can afford. But we also are really busy with three platforms that deliver
13 billion page impressions to over 15 million members. Even with a team twice the size,
we would certainly not be bored. Our features have to work, they must be easy to use, and
they must be available with short loading time. Despite the application's high complexity, no
side effects may occur, and performance is always an important topic for our server farm.

The privacy of our users and the required data protection are very sensitive topics, where any issue quickly leads to lots of public scrutiny. Software quality is not a luxury for us; it's a bare necessity, an insight that many companies still have to gain.

All these requirements cannot be fulfilled by manual testing. This would require hundreds of humans to test one single release. Test automation thus plays an important role at studiVZ. Next to classical unit tests, we put a strong emphasis on end-to-end tests using Selenium, which has been a part of our testing strategy from very early on. We started to write front-end tests with Selenium in mid-2007, when Selenium started to get attention, but only a few companies used it in production, so no one had much experience with it.

A case study about testing with Selenium should not talk about an ideal state, because this is just not the reality when dealing with web front-end testing. Just talking about our progress and our success, while leaving out how often we went off track, would be an incomplete and rather worthless case study.

Thus, we also talk about the numerous painful detours we had to take, only to find the right next step. Our own experience is that other people's problem reports and their learning experiences were extremely useful to us.

Christiane visited the Google Test Automation Conference (GTAC) in Fall 2008. During the two days, she had a chance to talk to several colleagues of other companies—some of them very big web companies. She had originally expected to find answers to some of the problems with end-to-end tests with Selenium and other tools that we faced at the time. The bottom line was that most attendees had gone though a similar learning curve or even were ahead of it. All teams had faced similar problems and pretty much gained the same experiences. Many attendees were relieved that all the others were fellows in misery. Quite often, however, talking about the common problems led to a new approach to a solution.

Our goal with this case study is to show the full bandwidth of our experiences with Selenium front-end tests. We hope this leads to a shorter learning curve for our readers.

First, we introduce special kinds of tests that have a different approach from unit testing. We explain what a Selenium test suite is and what role the PHPUnit extension for Selenium plays. Following this, we introduce our own development and test environment, so you can get an impression of how we work and what our test team needs are. Mainly, however, we want to talk about our experience with Selenium: We want to point out the advantages of this kind of test, as well as the stumbling blocks. For those we have not yet overcome, we are still searching for solutions. We do not intend to present a panacea; our goal is to give an overview of our best practices. The phase we talk about stretches from mid-2007, when Max introduced the brand-new Selenium, until Fall 2009. We also take a short peek into the future and discuss our next steps.

About studiVZ

studiVZ is one of the largest and fastest growing social networks in Europe. Originally targeted for students, today the three platforms, studiVZ, schülerVZ, and meinVZ (for everybody who is not a student), have over 15 million members.

schülerVZ and studiVZ are German networks, while meinVZ is available in German and English. meinVZ and studiVZ are connected, so their members can communicate with each other, while the platform and data of schülerVZ is separated from the others for purposes of youth protection. The company VZnet Netzwerke Ltd. was originally founded as studiVZ Ltd. in 2005 and is part of the Verlagsgruppe Georg Holtzbrinck. Approximately 250 people work for the platforms; about 60 are technical personnel. The QA team, comprised of 8 to 10 people, includes testers, QA engineers, and security experts. Max Horváth originally built the team and led it until October 2008. Christiane Philipps, who had been a member of the team since 2008, took over Max's job when he focused on building the mobile VZ platforms. She led the team until Fall 2009.

ACCEPTANCE TESTS

Acceptance tests are so-called black box tests. This means that software is being tested without knowing the actual code. Although unit tests make sure that individual components of the software work as expected, regardless of how they are actually used in the product, acceptance tests take the perspective of the end user or the customer and look at the whole application. Any customer requirement can be documented in the form of an acceptance test. When the acceptance test passes, the customer's requirement is met. One big advantage is that the customer, the tester, and the developer speak the same language when writing an acceptance test. Misunderstandings can be swept out of the way in the early planning phase.

For studiVZ, an acceptance test for our messaging functionality could read as follows:

> *When Max sends a message to Christiane, she will see the number "1" behind the menu item "Messages" to indicate that there is a new message.*

An acceptance test can either pass or fail. There is no notion of "50% done." It is crucial to phrase the test case as precisely as possible and to break it down to simple facts. In case of doubt, create more than one test case per feature. In our example, we could add a second test case:

> *When Max sends a message to Christiane, she can access that message from her inbox.*

We can run an acceptance test manually. Automation is a better idea, of course, because you can then use the test to repeatedly make sure the software works as expected from an end user's point of view—for example, prior to rolling a release. This is where Selenium comes into play.

Acceptance Tests in Agile Environments

Although developers write unit tests, writing acceptance tests was initially the QA team's exclusive responsibility. This way, we can be sure that the tests do justice to the intended functionality. We all know of unit tests that have not been developed through test-driven development, but after writing the production code. Many of these tests are not useful, because they primarily serve the purpose of confirming the production code, instead of testing it. We can write an acceptance test this way, but a tester who is testing early in development (before the application is ready for customers) will not make the mistake of writing a test that confirms rather than tests the production code.

The disadvantage is that the QA team cannot start writing tests until the developers have finished their work, instead of trying to break the application right after code freeze.

In early 2009, studiVZ switched to agile development, using a development process called Scrum. The main difference to a waterfall process is that the development steps are much smaller. This creates transparency and makes writing tests for the user interface much easier. "Done" means that no more work is required on a feature, which makes writing acceptance tests much easier. A so-called "level of done" defines which quality attributes—for instance, automated acceptance tests—are required for a certain feature.

Thanks to Scrum, testers are more involved in the creation process and work together with the developer much more closely.

Agile processes also stress the significance of acceptance tests. Features are not written down in complex specification documents anymore, but in the form of lean user stories that are broken down into tasks. Documenting all requirements that stem from the users' stories in the form of acceptance tests is a good practice. This is done by the product owner, the tester, and the developers together. This makes clear what needs to be done by the end of the iteration. This is also a first step to writing Selenium tests, which are automatically put into focus—which is important when you are trying to involve developers more in writing acceptance tests. We have just started to take this step. Ideally, this leads to acceptance test – driven development.

SELENIUM

Among other things, Selenium is a framework that helps you create automated acceptance tests for web applications. Its big advantage over other frameworks is that the test is run in an actual browser rather than against libraries like `htmlUnit`. This makes it possible to test the real behavior of most browsers, including their bugs and oddities.

Behind the scenes, Selenium controls the browser using JavaScript. Selenium uses its own language, Selenese, to control the test process. Selenese is not very complex and rather easy to learn. From an outside viewpoint, most actions are the same for each browser, but behind the scenes, the Selenium Core often translates the API command into a browser-specific dialect.

Elements to test are chosen using so-called *locators*. A locator specifies which button or link is clicked or whether a certain element in some navigation bar must be present. Locators can be specified using XPath or DOM or with CSS selectors.

It is always great fun to demonstrate the running of acceptance tests to first-time Selenium users: The browser starts as if by magic, and an invisible user clicks through a web application, writes tests into form fields, and uploads profile photos. It may not be magic, but even developers usually watch with some degree of astonishment.

The heart of all Selenium applications is Selenium Core. It provides the API with the test commands and a test runner capable of executing the tests. All other tools of the Selenium suite are based on Selenium Core.

Selenium Remote Control, Selenium RC for short, is a proxy server that can be accessed from a client driver via HTTP. A PHP driver implementation is available.

Selenium RC supports the following:

➤   Starting and stopping browser instances

➤   Sending Selenese commands to control the browser

➤   Injecting the Selenium Core application into the application under test

We use Selenium RC to run the automated front-end tests in our continuous integration environment. The structure is shown in Figure 11.1.

Selenium Remote Control

FIGURE 11-1: Selenium RC architecture

Usually, several months pass between two official releases of Selenium RC, so we recommend that you use nightly builds. They are usually quite stable and work well for us, so we can get access to bug fixes and improvements months ahead of the official release.

Selenium IDE is a capture and replay extension for Firefox that can record the test steps manually executed in the browser. These tests can be saved as HTML tables with Selenese commands in "command – target – value" format, or they can be exported to another language—for example, PHP. At studiVZ, we do not use Selenium IDE very frequently.

Another tool in the Selenium family is Selenium Grid. Based on Selenium RC, it can execute multiple tests in parallel, which greatly reduces the test execution time. Because PHPUnit did not support process isolation before version 3.4, you cannot use Selenium Grid from PHP. When using test suites and a continuous integration server that supports parallel test execution, using Selenium Grid has some advantages, but it also causes a few problems.

The Selenium Extension of PHPUnit

Even though you can use the Selenium tools alone, it does make sense to use the Selenium extension of PHPUnit, especially in large projects. This extension allows testers and developers to write Selenium tests in an environment they are familiar with. The class `PHPUnit_Extensions_SeleniumTestCase` provides the communication interface to Selenium RC and offers quite a few assertions specific to Selenium—for example, `assertElementContainsText()` or `assertLocationEquals()`. Next to this, all other unit test assertions can be used, of course.

It is mandatory to write a setUp() method where parameters required by Selenium (for example, browser, URL, and host) must be set.

The online documentation of PHPUnit shows a simple example for a Selenium test with PHPUnit:

```php
<?php
require_once 'PHPUnit/Extensions/SeleniumTestCase.php';
class WebTest extends PHPUnit_Extensions_SeleniumTestCase
{
    protected function setUp()
    {
        $this->setBrowser('*firefox');
        $this->setBrowserUrl('http://www.example.com/');
    }
    public function testTitle()
    {
        $this->open('http://www.example.com/');
        $this->assertTitleEquals('Example WWW Page');
    }
}
```

Today, the Selenium extension of PHPUnit even has some additional features, like the possibility to capture screenshots on error. We get back to this later.

You can collect code coverage information, and PHPUnit can directly execute Selenese/HTML files recorded by the Selenium IDE. This is a useful feature for teams that started using the IDE and want to switch now without losing their existing tests. For teams starting from scratch, we recommend not using the IDE, as we further detail in the section titled "Capture and Replay versus Programming Tests."

There is one feature, however, that the testing community is still waiting for: the full support of parallel test execution in PHPUnit. When every test is executed in a separate PHP process, a fatal error occurring in one of the tests would not stop the whole test run, like it does today. The release of PHPUnit 3.4 with the option --process-isolation and the @runInSeparateProcess and @runTestsInSeparateProcesses annotations, respectively, showed a big step in this direction. This feature makes it possible to execute individual tests, test suites, or all tests in general in their own processes. Future plans for parallelizing tests and the problems that must be solved are described by Sebastian Bergmann in his blog.[1] Especially in large test suites, speed is crucial, so parallel test execution in conjunction with Selenium Grid would be great. We are very much looking forward to this feature, which will probably unfold its full potential in PHPUnit 4.0, or maybe even earlier.

THE TECHNICAL SETUP OF STUDIVZ

Development Environment

Because studiVZ is a system that grew rapidly in a very dynamic environment, in early 2007 we had reached a point where we realized that the old code was too hard to maintain. We opted for a complete re-engineering and rewrote the whole code base under the code name Phoenix.

---

[1]Sebastian Bergmann, "Isolated (and Parallel) Test Execution in PHPUnit 4," December 19, 2007, accessed April 17, 2010, http://sebastian-bergmann.de/archives/730-Isolated-and-Parallel-Test-Execution-in-PHPUnit-4.html.

As we started, we used Zend Framework, which at that time was in a very early development stage (version 0.4), but we had to realize at some point that it would not work for the immense load of three million users that we had to deal with at the time. We reused some of the design concepts of Zend Framework in Phoenix, but we removed the Zend code itself, adapted performance-critical parts, or rewrote them to suit the special needs of the studiVZ platform. We are quite happy with this decision, because we are pretty sure that our platform would not be able to deal with 15 million members if it were based on the Zend Framework.

Over the turn of the year 2007/2008, several months and a few hundred thousand lines of code later, the new system was ready. After a few test runs, the new system went into production. Our new, MVC-based framework ran all platforms with one code base, something that wasn't possible with the old code. So in early 2008, we launched the new portal meinVZ.

The system today has about 1.5 to 2 million lines of code and templates and is based on a classical LAMP stack with PHP 5.2, APC, and memcached to handle the load, and in peak times it uses 750 servers to send out up to 5.400 Mbits per second of dynamically generated pages to the user.

All features are module-based and can be enabled and disabled individually and can be configured for each platform.

Test Environment

As we mentioned, our testing strategy does not rely only on manual tests, but it strongly relies on automated tests. In addition to special API tests, we have about 3,000 unit tests to test our models. Our front-end tests comprise about 1,500 acceptance tests with Selenium.

The core of our test system is an Atlassian Bamboo Continuous Integration Server that tests the code and displays errors whenever code has been committed into our subversion repository. We chose the commercial Bamboo in 2007 because `phpUnderControl` did not exist back then and adapting CruiseControl seemed too time-consuming.

All in all, we are still happy with our choice, because Bamboo has a feature that we really fell in love with: You can set up a Continuous Integration Grid. Our server, though rather powerful with 4 Xeon CPUs with 3.8 GHz and 8 GB RAM, could not run all tests in a decent amount of time, so we set up three additional servers with the same configuration. Thanks to the Grid feature, Bamboo distributes all tests that must be executed to the available servers. Using the so-called agents, we can configure which server should run which of our test suites. This allows us to run the tests in a decent amount of time.

Another advantage is the good integration with all other Atlassian products—for example, the SVN browser FishEye, the code review tool Crucible, and the project and bugtracker Jira.

The target host of the application under test is our acceptance test server. It runs the current version of our VZ platforms. Aside from a few configuration settings that make testing easier for us, we try to stay as close as possible to the production conditions. Selenium RC runs on the test clients that Bamboo uses. On every test run, Bamboo fetches the current version of our code and the tests and starts the front-end tests using PHPUnit.

In short, the PHPUnit tests are executed in Bamboo and Selenium, and the browser is running on the test clients, which calls the application under test on our acceptance test server. This three-way structure sometimes causes confusion with people who are new to Selenium. The test results are displayed to the developers on large monitors that are located close to the coffeemaker and sitting area. This makes testing as transparent as possible for everybody.

Successful tests are the basis for our 14-day release cycle and provide information about the quality of our trunk and the current release branch.

BEST PRACTICES

We started to automate tests using Selenium rather early, in mid-2007. In the last two and a half years, we adapted the way we write tests several times. As we gained more experience, it became clearer how our tests should look. As a consequence, our front-end tests changed quite a bit.

Much of what we have learned can be generalized. Some of it is not new and can be found as ground rules in programming or testing.

Sins of Our Youth

Monolithic Tests

The first tests we wrote were monolithic. This means that each test case was a block of various tests that were run together. This way, we intended to save time on executing the tests by starting a browser session once per test case. In addition, we ran a setup just once for each test case and built each subsequent test on top of the previous test, because they all tested one feature that required similar click paths.

As an example of how you should not do things, here are monolithic tests from our early times:

```
class AcceptanceTests_Modules_Migration_MigrationBasicsTest
    extends PhoenixSeleniumTestCase
{
    private $_testUser = 'ATMigrationFriend92@studivz.net';
    public function setUp()
    {
        parent::setUp();
        $this->setAutoStop(false);
    }
    public function testLinkToMigration()
    {
        $this->login($this->_testUser);
        $this->open('Profile/EditGeneral');
        $this->assertElementPresent(
            "xpath=id('ProfileEditGeneral')/fieldset/div[1]/div[2]/a"
        );
        $this->clickAndWait(
            "xpath=id('ProfileEditGeneral')/fieldset/div[1]/div[2]/a"
        );
        $this->assertLocationEquals(
            PHX_PLATFORM_URL_1 . 'Migration/MigrationInfo'
        );
        $this->clickAndWait(
```

```
            "xpath=id('MigrationInfo')/div[3]/a[1]"
        );
    }
    public function testMigrationPhotoPage ()
    {
        $this->assertLocationEquals(
            PHX_PLATFORM_URL_1 . 'Migration/PhotoInfo'
        );
        $this->assertEquals(
            PHX_PLATFORM_URL_1 . 'Img/step1.jpg',
            $this->getAttribute(
                "xpath=id('Migration')/div[1]/img/@src"
            )
        );
        // links and button
        $this->assertElementPresent(
            "xpath=id('MigrationInfo')/div[3]/a[1]"
        );
        $this->assertEquals(
            Phx_I18n_GetText::get(
                'Migration', 'page.migrationInfo.back'
            ),
            $this->getText(
                "xpath=id('MigrationInfo')/div[3]/a[2]"
            )
        );
    }
}
```

These kinds of tests run much faster than the tests we write today, but they brought lots of misery, because tests like this are really fragile and hard to maintain. One failed test was enough to make all subsequent tests fail as well. Worse, sometimes the third test would behave differently than planned, but we would not notice, so maybe the fifth test failed. Debugging these kinds of problems was quite a challenge. Another disadvantage was that tests always had to be run as a whole, and we could not run individual tests using filter or group parameters in PHPUnit.

You might ask why we violated the ground rule of atomic, independent tests that we know. The fact that we created front-end tests made us believe that they had different requirements and that different rules would apply, but experience has taught us that the general rules of programming and automated testing do apply to front-end tests.

Static Users

Another strategy was the creation of static test users. These test users had a profile that suited the test case. For example, this could be a studiVZ user who had not agreed to publish his data in meinVZ, so we could make sure the data would not appear in the meinVZ member search. Other examples are a pupil from Berlin whose profile was visible only to friends attending the same school and a studiVZ user with a certain number of friends in both platforms and 30 messages in his inbox. These users were hard-coded in the test code and in the database, as we saw in the previous example:

```
private $_testUser = 'ATMigrationFriend92@studivz.net';
```

We did this primarily because creating these users and the appropriate scenarios would have taken lots of effort, and back then we did not have any helper classes that would assist us in doing the job. All this made the tests very fragile.

The users in our common test database were used in multiple tests run in parallel. Of course, they failed because tests would affect each other due to user settings being stored in the database. It was especially nerve-stretching when the tests were accidentally executed manually by two testers. In that case, it was almost impossible to debug the resulting error, until you heard a colleague cursing as well.

Strategy Change

Atomic Tests with Dynamic Test Data

In mid-2008, we started to change the way we did front-end testing: We created test fixtures that were used by multiple tests, initially still with static users. They prepared the system to test the actual production code snippet. The individual tests, grouped together by common test fixtures, now were completely independent from each other and could be executed in arbitrary order. Just like with unit tests, the setUp() method created the test fixture that tearDown() cleaned up after the test. This made it much easier to create and debug tests, but it made our tests run much longer. Still, we quickly realized that this switch was the right decision.

The next step to clean up our tests was moving to dynamic test data. We used a few service classes that one of our developers had written for unit tests in the meantime. These services dynamically created test data, suited to various typical test scenarios of our platform, and deleted it again at the end of the test. These services covered about 80% of our test fixture requirements. This, again, made the test run much slower, but it made tests more stable and maintainable.

Over time, we realized that stability and maintainability are the most important criteria for our front-end tests, even more than with unit tests. We even sacrifice test execution speed and speed of test development for this.

The following listing shows an example for an atomic test with dynamic test data created by unit test services:

```
class AcceptanceTests_Modules_Gruscheln_GruschelFriends
extends PhoenixSeleniumTestCase
{
    //declare UnitTestServices
    protected $_userService;
    protected $_friendsService;
    protected $_user;
    protected $_friend;
    function setUp() {
        parent::setUp();
        $this->_userService =
            Test_Models_PhpUnitService_Manager::registerService(
                'Test_Models_PhpUnitService_User'
            );
        $this->_friendsService =
            Test_Models_PhpUnitService_Manager::registerService(
                'Test_Models_PhpUnitService_Friends'
            );
```

```
        $this->_user = $this->_userService->createObject(
            $this->platformId
        );
        $this->_friend = $this->_userService->createObject(
            $this->platformId
        );
        $this->_friendsService->setFriendship(
            $this->_user->ids, $this->_friend->ids
        );
$       this->login($this->_user->emailAcct);
    }
    public function testIsGruschelnLinkAvailableOnFriendsProfile()
    {
        $this->open(
            ACCEPTANCE_TESTS_URI . '/Profile/' . $this->_friend->ids
        );
        $this->assertElementPresent(
            "xpath=id('gruscheln')"
        );
    }
    public function testIsGruschelnLinkAvailableOnFriendsList()
    {
        $this->open(
            ACCEPTANCE_TESTS_URI . '/Friends/All/'
        );
        $this->assertElementPresent(
            "xpath=//a[contains(@href,'/Gruscheln/DialogGruscheln/'" .
            $this->_friend->ids . ')]'
        );
    }
    public function tearDown() {
        Test_Models_PhpUnitService_Manager::unloadServices();
        $this->stop();
    }
  }
}
```

Robust Selenium Tests

Front-end tests are usually more fragile than unit tests. This is because they are integration tests and thus must deal with the many components of the system. In addition, the web interface of popular websites like the VZ platforms are under continuous development, and sometimes small details change, so the locators that Selenium uses to find its way through the page change, and the test breaks.

This was particularly painful for us in a phase when the platforms changed often, so many tests failed. The workload of the QA team was too high, so they did not have time to fix all the broken tests. During that time, which lasted a few months, we lost a three-digit number of tests and are still working on refactoring all these broken tests.

Test Scope Must Be Clear

Due to these problems, we changed our strategy yet again. Our initial goal had been to achieve high code coverage with automated acceptance tests, which included trying to cover all edge cases as well. We then realized that we did not have the manpower to maintain all the tests. Therefore, we decided to set some ground rules for selecting tests for automation:

➤ Test only the important functionality of a feature.

➤ Test important edge cases—for example, those that influence the user's privacy. Test important functionality requiring a complex test fixture, which makes a manual test too time-consuming.

A few working tests are worth much more than a multitude of detailed tests that do not work properly, requiring you to constantly refactor them.

Common Functionality or Browser Compatibility as Well?

Due to our changed strategy, we asked ourselves whether our Selenium tests should mainly test general functionality or also browser compatibility. One of Selenium's advantages is that it can test JavaScript and AJAX-intensive applications against various browser instances.

First, we ran our tests against Firefox and Internet Explorer clients on Windows, plus Firefox on Linux and Mac hosts. However, we soon realized that this meant lots of maintenance effort, with little additional gain. We suggest that you not invest in this additional effort, unless manpower is available in excess. So today we run our Selenium tests in Firefox only, while we run additional browser compatibility tests manually based on a checklist.

A multi-browser strategy with Selenium gets expensive due to the small differences between the various browsers that must be taken into account. There are some XPath statements that work well in Firefox, but not in Internet Explorer. Generally, our experience is that Internet Explorer causes more trouble than Firefox when it comes to the XPath implementation. AJAX-intensive tests often cause problems.

We also had quite some trouble with keyboard commands like keyPress and typeKeys. Although they work in Firefox in most cases, Internet Explorer had trouble handling them. Some commands just do not work in this browser, and others seemed to cause problems only in certain test scenarios. Mouse and keyboard simulations are less robust than other operations in Selenium. Making tests multibrowser-compatible significantly increases the effort for the test implementations.

A last big difference between browsers is how they deal with file uploads. Some features of our platform offer the possibility of uploading photos. For security reasons, it is generally not possible to execute a file upload via JavaScript. When running Firefox in Chrome mode, file uploads are still possible:

```
$this->setBrowser("*chrome");
```

We always use the Chrome mode, and our experiences with it are really good.

Today, workarounds for Internet Explorer are available, but when it comes to creating one implementation for multiple browsers, the devil is often in the details.

Fix Tests Right Away!

A major mistake that we have made was to delay fixing of broken tests in times of high workload, for the sake of manual testing. When our workload was above 100%, as mentioned earlier, we decided to leave broken tests unfixed, with the intent of fixing them later, and we focused on our daily business—a vicious circle, as we should soon find out. Because fewer automated tests were available to us, the manual test effort increased, which in turn gave us less time to fix old tests. In addition, the failed acceptance tests were quite demotivating for our team. It felt like a tilt at windmills.

Later, when the workload went down to normal, some modules had changed so much that we had to rewrite the tests, because understanding the old code would have been too much effort. We could have avoided that by regularly refactoring the code. As well, debugging is much easier when you still can track individual changes to the features.

Therefore, one of our suggestions for QA teams suffering from chronic overload is this: Even when it is difficult to prioritize the daily business, never delay fixing of broken tests. And to be perfectly honest, the hope for a future with enough surplus capacity is just an illusion in times of Web x.0. Therefore, it is especially important to dedicate enough time for the refactoring of broken tests. We have to spend about 10% of our time on refactoring.

One of the main difficulties when debugging and fixing Selenium tests is to identify the exact location and circumstances where the test fails. Quite often, the error messages are not obvious, because they report the ramification and not the cause of the problem. For better orientation, we used to work with screenshots for a while, when tests failed. Today, this feature is a part of the PHPUnit Selenium extension. If the variables $captureScreenshotOnFailure, $screenshotPath, and $screenshotUrl are set, PHPUnit shows an error message along with a reference to the screenshot.

Stabilize Locators, and Use IDs

Based on our experiences with broken tests, we asked ourselves how we could make our tests more robust. We had already worked on the architecture of the tests and which tests we actually wanted to automate.

We saw great optimization potential in working on the locator that Selenium uses to access page elements. Different notations for these locators are available: DOM, XPath, CSS selectors, or just the ID of an element:

```
<a href="http://www.studivz.net/Start"
alt="Startseite"
id="startlink">
```

Whenever possible, you should use the ID. As long as the ID does not change, the locator never breaks. Especially in small and medium-sized projects, it should not be a problem to agree with the front-end team that every element that must be accessed in a test gets such an ID. In projects of the size of studiVZ, and especially projects with the amount of traffic we get, it is almost impossible to assign an ID to every element; it would mean bloated source code. Many elements, though, were assigned an ID for testability reasons.

Where we were unable to use IDs, we used XPath for quite a long time. One advantage of XPath is that good add-ons like XPath Checker are available for Firefox. They make using XPath very quick and simple, but the drawback is that XPath statements are hard to read and understand:

```
"xpath=id('news_staticContent')/div[2]/div/p[4]/a"
```

Starting from the left, this statement means: Access the element with ID `news_staticContent`, then the second `div` container following it, then the first container, then the fourth paragraph (`p`), and use the contained link (`a`).

This shows another disadvantage: The closer to the page's root element the locator starts, the more fragile it becomes. If we had no ID in the preceding example, we would have to start at the page beginning, and thus the XPath statement would look like this:

```
"xpath=/html/body/div[3]/div[2]/div[3]/div[4]/div[2]/div/p[4]/a"
```

As soon as another `div` is added, the test breaks, because the number of `div`s on the page does not match the locator any more.

You should try to reduce the XPath statement to the shortest possible path:

```
"xpath=//div[@id='box']/p[4]/a"
```

It does not matter whether you use CSS selectors, DOM, or XPath; the problem is that locators are hard to read and fragile.

Some ground rules for creating assertions make your work easier:

➤ Use IDs whenever possible.

➤ Use patterns for the elements to test, and use functions that XPath offers, like `contains()` `text()`: `$this->click("xpath=//a[contains(@href, 'editProfile')");` instead of `$this->click("xpath=id('profile')/div[2]/div/p[4]/a");`.

➤ When an element has no unique ID, make the assertion more general to make it more robust. It is better, for example, to check whether a link is present: `$this->assertTextPresent('Profil bearbeiten')` instead of using `$this->assertEquals('Profil bearbeiten', $this->getText("xpath=id('news_staticContent')/p[4]/a");` to check for the exact location.

➤ Define all locator paths in a central location, on top of the test, or in a separate file. Comment them liberally, and use speaking variables instead of a locator: This makes tests much easier to understand and maintain. `$this->click($locator['linkToEditProfile']);` is much easier to understand in a test than `$this->click("xpath=id('profile')/div[2]/div/p[4]/a");`.

 Using a UI element that is integrated into Selenium as an extension is a good idea.

Speed, the Sore Subject

Regarding the speed of Selenium tests, if you are used to the execution time of unit tests, you will probably be shocked by the execution time of Selenium tests. Although a suite of component tests usually runs in tenths of seconds or a few seconds, a Selenium test suite might well run for a few minutes.

One reason for this is that tests are executed through the web interface. Another reason is that, depending on the configuration, the browser is restarted after each individual test with a fresh session and closed after the test. This takes time, which usually is not a problem in smaller projects, but when running a four-digit number of tests, execution time can quickly add up to a couple of hours. Selenium tests can thus quickly become a bottleneck when testing.

The following measures can help:

➤ **Run concurrent tests.** We have already talked about this topic; even when PHP does not allow a fully concurrent test execution, continuous integration servers offer grid functionality out of the box. In conjunction with hardware and Selenium Grid, this can really speed up your tests.[2]

➤ **Adapt test runs to the time of day.** If it takes hours to run the tests, nightly builds are the right option to execute all tests. During the day, when developers need quick feedback, a downsized version of the Selenium test suite can be run—for example, the automated version of an otherwise manually executed release checklist.

➤ **Avoid unnecessary stopping of the browser.** Selenium offers a flag, `browser- SessionReuse`, that prevents the browser from being stopped after each test run. This saves lots of time, because starting and stopping the browser makes up for most of the execution time in atomic tests. There are a few gotchas, however. Because cookies and cache are not deleted between tests, side effects can occur. You should thus be extra careful when creating tests.

➤ **Clearly separate setup and tests.** Especially beginners often put actions that prepare the actual tests into the test itself. Instead, move them where they belong—into the test setup. Also, it is not necessary to perform all preparations—for example, creating a user—via the browser. Instead, helper classes do a great job in the background. Selenium and the browser should come into play only when the actual testing takes place.

Recipes for Last-Minute Features

The devil takes the hindmost. This is a proverb that every tester should have heard of. Which strategies does a QA team have to deal with last-minute features?

➤ **Front-end first.** First, developers created the back-end and front-end of a new feature at the same time, and in the end, our HTML team cleaned up the source code. This forced us to refactor all tests we had already written, because we had used XPath statements and did not have many element IDs. After we had changed our approach, a large portion of the views were created by the front-end team before the actual functionality was written. This made our tests more reliable.

➤ **Mock-ups and predefined IDs.** If you cannot create the views first, mock-ups are a great help. If every element that will be accessed in a test additionally has a CSS ID, there is not much left that can go wrong. It helps to stick to a common naming scheme when it comes to IDs, to make sure that every team member knows in advance how an element will be named.

---

[2]Dirk Pahl, "Automated acceptance tests using Selenium Grid without parallelization," August 17, 2009, accessed February 9, 2010, `http://developer.studivz.net/2009/08/17/automated-acceptance-tests-using-selenium-grid-without-parallelization/`.

➤ **Agile method of operation.** One of the advantages of agile methods over conventional methods is that they offer more transparency. This also holds true for big features that are broken down into smaller sub-features. With a waterfall process, the QA team would get access to a big feature after weeks; with agile processes, they get to access smaller parts that require less testing effort. Ideally, the tester is part of the agile team and thus gets to know the feature as it is being developed. The less head start developers have over QA, the better.

Tests Are Software Too

When writing tests, especially front-end tests, an old rule is often forgotten: Test code is software as well. The same rules that apply to development of production code should be applied to test code:

➤ **Use speaking test and variable names.** Test names should tell colleagues right away what the test does. PHPUnit supports this with the built-in TestDox functionality that is easy to use:

➤ Every test name starts with the word test.

➤ **The actual name is appended in camel case.** (For example, `testPageIsAccessibleWithoutLogin`, when running PHPUnit, is displayed as "Page is accessible without login.")

This feature can be used to create agile test documentation on demand. This approach, as we found out, has another advantage: If it is difficult to find a speaking name for the test that is straight and to the point, this is usually a test smell—a sign that the test is too complex and should be split.

➤ **Keep commenting to a minimum.** Excessive comments, especially in places where selectors come into play, make understanding the tests more difficult.

➤ **Stick to coding conventions.** Coding conventions make the test code much more readable, just like all the other code.

➤ **Use inheritance.** Especially when testing big features, `setUp` classes that can extend and adapt to the individual needs of each test case can be extremely useful.

➤ **Create a library of test helpers, ideally from day one.** This way, commonly used functionality that can be used in multiple tests or even features can be outsourced, which helps to avoid redundant code.

➤ **Keep it simple.** The golden rule of software development holds true: KISS—Keep It Simple, Stupid! The simpler the structure of a test is, the easier it is to read and maintain.

Capture and Replay versus Programming Tests

For quite some time, we have exclusively programmed our tests. But how about these common capture and replay tools that make it so easy to record tests? The Selenium tool suite offers this functionality through Selenium IDE. You can even export recorded tests to PHP and other languages. With some effort, you can even execute them in a continuous integration server. So why do we code our tests then? For one, our software requires it: Our tests must work for three platforms and in two languages. Of course, it does not make sense to record six tests for each test case. For large projects, recording tests usually just does not work.

From our viewpoint, there are more reasons that offer advantages also for smaller projects:

➤ **Thanks to the Selenium extension of PHPUnit, tests can be executed in the same way.** The advantage is that you only have to deal with and maintain one infrastructure and technology. Especially in complex test environments like ours, this is a big plus.

➤ It is not very difficult for developers to get started with Selenium tests, because they already know PHPUnit. This increases the willingness to cooperate, because they can build upon their PHPUnit know-how.

➤ **The framework of your own applications can be used for helper functions in the tests.** That way, we use hundreds of functions that make it easier for us to write tests. Tests can quickly be executed locally by every developer during a refactoring.

➤ **Test data can be created dynamically.** After running the tests, they are deleted. There are no dependencies to existing data and no dependencies to other tests.

➤ **Setup is clearly separated from the actual test.** Selenium IDE does not know about this separation and produces long, monolithic tests.

Still, the short development time of a capture and replay test is compelling. We thus wrote a small CLI application that we call `Selenium_Transformer`. It does the following:

➤ `Selenium_Transformer` creates a setup from a pool of standard scenarios that we have predefined and that cover a large part of the simple test scenarios of our platform.

➤ After that, a studiVZ.net test case is recorded with the user of the newly created scenario using Selenium IDE. It is exported to PHP using the IDE.

➤ Now `Selenium_Transformer` adapts the test case to our environment: The class extends our test framework; all studiVz.net strings that occur in the tests are being replaced by our own identifiers (we assume that the strings have been sanity checked while recording the test). The user that Selenium IDE has hard-coded into the test is removed and replaced by a dynamic user, whose attributes are known based on the underlying scenario.

➤ In addition, we make use of the fact that Selenium IDE can include a custom Selenium Code JavaScript file. We use this to add more assertions to the IDE's context menu.

The result is much more advanced than a regular test created with Selenium IDE. It can be executed just like our handwritten automated tests. However, there are a few drawbacks: A test case comprises just one monolithic block. This contradicts all ground rules of good testing and our own best practices. Discipline is required to create short and neatly arranged tests. What's more, the locators that Selenium IDE creates are not always as robust as they could be. So this approach pays off only when elements can be tested that are accessible by ID. Manual rework over-compensates the time savings and thus does not pay off.

So for simple, neatly arranged tests with default setup scenarios, creating such a quick test can pay off. The transformer is not an alternative to the programming of tests. The more complex the test setups and adaptations in tests are, the more it pays off to code the tests.

The Team: a Good Mix

When we talk about test automation, we often forget the fact that these tests are automated by humans. We should never underestimate the value of humans in our development processes. After all, they make all the difference in how good software is written and tested. Thus a word to the QA team members: The dream of every QA manager is the thoroughbred tester with 10 years of development background. Except for very few exceptions, this usually remains a dream. Usually, people tend to have an affinity for one or the other. If it is almost impossible to unify these qualities in one person, the team members should have these combined qualities on average. According to our experience, a good mix of testers and developers in QA of our project has moved our project forward, which was indispensable for our testing strategy and the development of our test framework.

We know of other QA departments that have little developer potential. In this case, it is even more important to collaborate with the developers. Especially when using Selenium RC in large-scale projects, solid programming know-how is vital to being able to set up sensible testing processes.

On the other hand, the classical tester has a completely different perspective on the application than a developer, and he often has a way of finding potential trouble spots. Teams that solely rely on developers and do not have testers will forego this advantage. Automated acceptance tests unify the requirements from both worlds, because they are the link between classical manual testing and automated component tests. Collaboration between classical testers and developers can greatly enhance the quality of Selenium tests.

WE NEED A DSL

In late 2008, we considered the preliminary results based on our experiences: We had mastered a long learning curve, but still had lots of work ahead of us. Our tests were much more readable, maintainable, and stable than in the beginning, but we were still not happy. Above all, we pondered how to avoid code and content redundancies and to take advantage of them. After all, we constantly accessed and used the same elements. We briefly experimented with Fitnesse, a software testing tool, but back then it did not seem suited for our needs. Without knowing, we still started to work our way toward a Domain Specific Language (DSL).

A Domain Specific Language is a language created for a very specific domain. This has the advantage that the language models and describes the domain very accurately. A DSL does not care about anything outside of the scope it was created for. Depending on the DSL characteristics, even non-programmers can describe facts and circumstances. Another advantage is the improved readability of DSL code versus universal programming languages.

There are two approaches to creating a DSL:

➤ **Internal DSL:** An internal DSL is based on an existing language—for example, PHP. This greatly reduces the required implementation effort, but an internal DSL is usually rather technical in its terms, thus it limits the user base to people with good technical insight. Examples of an internal DSL are rake (the Ruby make) or the xUnit frameworks.

➤ **External DSL:** An external DSL is a language designed from the ground up. There are no restrictions with regard to formulations, so the language can be adapted to the domain requirements in a more flexible way and can be closer to natural language. This is a big advantage for domain experts without technical skills. A famous example of an external DSL is SQL.

When Max started to write the first version of what later became Testing SeleniumDSL, he did not even intend to create a DSL, but he created a framework for some helper methods for common functionality of our platform and our tests, respectively. Over time, the project turned more and more into a DSL framework.

Internal DSL

Due to the history of our DSL framework, the question of whether to create an internal or external DSL did not even arise for us. Still, an internal DSL has some advantages:

➤   We can build on our existing tools, PHP, and our studiVZ platform.

➤   Our test framework is still PHPUnit, which is a very powerful tool that our developers are experienced with. There is no need to reinvent the wheel. The PHPUnit assertions can be used in `Testing_SeleniumDSL`; additional assertions do not exist in the DSL framework.

➤   Another important advantage that we benefit from is that PHPUnit can already run Selenium. `Testing_SeleniumDSL` is an extension of PHPUnit's Selenium driver and is completely based on PHPUnit, so we wasted no time thinking about running Selenium. Because PHPUnit is object-oriented, our DSL framework can easily be integrated into PHPUnit.

We accepted the disadvantage of less readability for non-developers, because our tests are read only by tech people anyway. Readability for testers and developers was greatly increased thanks to the DSL approach.

Testing_SeleniumDSL 1.0

When we realized that development was heading toward a DSL, new requirements came up: Practical migration was most important to us. Because we did not want to run two test environments in parallel, old tests still had to execute, while new ones would be written with `Testing_SeleniumDSL`. This was not a problem, because the software is based on PHPUnit.

The whole framework concept was based on a "work in progress" approach. As we wrote new tests or refactored existing tests, new requirements appeared, but we adapted the DSL rather easily.

So how does a DSL work? Because we only deal with testing of web applications, we can focus on typical HTML elements and stick to the DOM (Document Object Model). In web applications, you usually test titles, forms, input fields, control elements like buttons, links, tables, images, and <div> containers with content. This content can be described with HTML elements and their names, IDs, and attributes.

The DSL is a built-in analogy to DOM: Starting with the root element, the page is indexed, and child and grandchild elements are accessed. Internally, XPath is used for identification, but this is hidden from the user. The DSL provides a method—for example, "RadioButton"—that defines how a radio button can be identified via XPath. The methods are embedded in an object-oriented relationship to each other. To stick with the radio button example, a radio button always has a "Form" element as parent. The code reflects this through fluent interfaces.

What is a fluent interface? Cal Evans gives a good explanation:

> ...*fluent interfaces is a way of chaining methods of an object together. By having a method return a reference to the object itself* (return $this;) *you chain methods together like this*
>
> ```
> $this->methodOne()->methodTwo()->methodThree();
> ```
>
> *This can make your code easier to read, and that is the point of using fluent interfaces: making your code easier to read.*
>
> —CAL EVANS, "FLUENT INTERFACES IN PHP," DECEMBER 20, 2006, ACCESSED FEBRUARY 9, 2010, HTTP://DEVZONE.ZEND.COM/ARTICLE/1362.

Martin Fowler talks about fluent interfaces and DSLs:

> *Probably the most important thing to notice about this style is that the intent is to do something along the lines of an internal Domain Specific Language. Indeed this is why we chose the term "fluent" to describe it; in many ways the two terms are synonyms. The API is primarily designed to be readable and to flow. The price of this fluency is more effort, both in thinking and in the API construction itself. The simple API of constructor, setter, and addition methods is much easier to write. Coming up with a nice fluent API requires a good bit of thought.*
>
> —MARTIN FOWLER, "FLUENT INTERFACE," DECEMBER 20, 2005, ACCESSED FEBRUARY 9, 2010, HTTP://MARTINFOWLER.COM/BLIKI/FLUENTINTERFACE.HTML.

Fluent interfaces make code much more readable. Let's look at an example test implemented with Testing_SeleniumDSL:

```
// Check for message box with specific error message.
$this->assertTrue(
    $this->dsl->currentPage()
        ->div(withId('errors'))
        ->contains('Invalid login!')
);
```

The same test implemented without a DSL would look like this:

```
// Check for message box with specific error message.
$this->assertEquals("xpath=id('errors')/div/p[4]", 'Invalid login!');
```

The more assertions a test has (and many assertions are usually unavoidable in front-end tests), the better the description of a DSL is.

We reused the same principle that applies to classical HTML elements for custom elements that kept occurring in our web application. We can use a method "Dialog," for example, that describes how a dialog box appears and can be accessed on every page. This way, we have reached one of our main goals, namely not to repeat ourselves. This leads to more stability and less refactoring effort.

Problem: Context Sensitivity

To make use of the full potential of a description language, context-sensitive matchers and constraints are important. We have already used them in the above example. We quickly had a collection of functions like `exists()`, `click()`, `withName()`, `withId()`, and so on that we could use to detail an element or link to an action:

```
$page->link(withName('test'))->click();
```

In the first version of `Testing_SeleniumDSL`, these functions were not available for every element (check box, radio button, table, button, div, and so on), but unfortunately they were also implemented separately for each element for which they were available. It soon became clear that this led to lots of redundant code. What's more, methods with identical names sometimes had little differences, depending on the element they had been implemented for. This made the DSL logic hard to understand and caused confusion over which methods to use in which order. This affected developers when extending the DSL and testers when writing tests.

We had worked with `Testing_SeleniumDSL` 1.0 for a few months when we realized that we were basically on the right track. Because the framework originally had been developed in another direction, our framework still did not provide us with what we expected from a DSL.

Testing_SeleniumDSL 2.0 — a Draft

The experiences with version 1.0 helped us to find a notion of how `Testing_SeleniumDSL` should look. It must be more powerful and more maintainable, and first and foremost it must be easier to learn and understand for developers and testers.

In `Testing_SeleniumDSL` 2.0, not every method has a strict parameter set, but each method is implemented in such a way that it can be applied to an arbitrary object. The object to check is accessed with the appropriate method that represents a matcher, a constraint, or an action. In the end, the DSL framework puts everything together and executes it.

For better orientation, a new class hierarchy will be introduced in version 2.0. The following categories seem appropriate to simplify the design and make the code more testable:

- Element description (check box, radio button, page)
- Differentiating the target element (`withFileName`, `endsWith`, `withId`, `withName`)
- Actions (`click()`, `clickLink()`, `navigate()`, `insertText()`)
- Checks (was the radio button clicked?)

Other changes are planned for `Testing_SeleniumDSL 2.0`. For example, PHP 5.3 will be a requirement. Why is that so? Because we can use namespaces and the Phar extension. Using namespaces is important to us because up to version 5.2, there was only one global namespace. To avoid name conflicts with other method names, long method names would have to be used. This certainly does not conform with the goal of a DSL, namely to be linguistically simple.

This is more difficult to read:

```
TestingDSL_withName(TestingDSL_endsWithFileName)
```

than this:

```
withName(endsWithFileName)
```

Another drawback is bound to disappear from the source code: using $this->. Again, this:

```
radioButton(withName(endsWith("test")))
```

is easier to read than this:

```
radioButton($this->withName($this->endsWith("test")))
```

In version 1.0, the methods were in part realized as functions in the global namespace to avoid using $this. In version 2.0, all methods are implemented in an object-oriented fashion.

Finally, we also started using Phar, which is a main part of PHP 5.3. Phar makes it easier to use SeleniumDSL just by loading a Phar file and without implementing and setting up DSL in the test method. The Phar archive takes care of bootstrapping and including all additional files.

State and Outlook on Version 2.0

Just like many good projects, Testing_SeleniumDSL 2.0 suffers from a lack of resources. We have introduced the concept, which is based on our experiences with version 1.0. We also started to write code, but the new framework is not ready for production yet; we still need to do lots of work. One alternative is to open-source Testing_SeleniumDSL even before we finish it, so version 2.0 can be created by more hands. Alternatively, perhaps somebody is willing to take up our ideas and experiences and write their own software.

While already available in the Ruby community, domain specific languages are still in short supply in the PHP community. DSL would certainly be an advantage for many users of Selenium in large-scale setups. After all, more stability and readability in practice means that two main problems of front-end testing are solved.

CONCLUSION

When we talk to programmers and testers who do not—or not yet—do front-end tests, we are often asked: Is it worth the effort to write front-end tests? Would unit tests and manual testing not suffice for quality assurance of our application? Because we have talked about our learning curve in detail, it should be obvious that we have asked ourselves the same question from time to time, with the answer switching back and forth between yes and no. Today, our answer is: Yes, it does pay off to put in the additional effort. However, you should pay close attention to the requirements of the tested system.

Selenium tests lead to a sensible ratio of cost and benefit when you work toward a concrete goal. Before you start, you should answer the following questions:

➤ **Goal:** What is the goal that we want to reach? Do we want to make sure that our features are functional, do we want to have integrated the software successfully, or do we also want to test browser compatibility?

➤ **Scope:** Which functionalities should be tested? Do we only want to test the most important features, or are we looking for extensive coverage of all functionality, including seldom used ones?

➤ **Time frame:** How fast-moving is the application under test? How many changes to the front end are to be expected?

➤ **Approach:** Will we have to program the tests, or will it suffice to record and possibly adapt them?

➤ **General conditions:** What is the concept of creating setups? How is test data being generated?

➤ **Continuous integration:** Do we have a strategy for continuous integration? How can we make sure that all tests are frequently executed?

➤ **Resources:** Can we afford the amount of maintenance required? Have we planned for enough time to refactor Selenium tests?

If you have decided to write Selenium tests, you should remind yourself of the following two goals:

➤ It is crucial for maintainability that tests are easy to read and understand.

➤ The robustness of tests is the main criterion for success of front-end tests.

If the project is large enough and the number of tests reaches several thousands, you should consider integrating a DSL as early as possible. We have talked about the advantages of an internal DSL. In other cases, when you want to put more focus on integrating other business units in production and test, an external DSL can be a better solution. In both cases, additional effort is required in the beginning, but the larger the project, the more this effort pays off. Thanks to agile practices and influences from languages like Ruby, DSLs will be a hot topic for PHP, especially in Enterprise environments.

We have tried to give you an insight into the interesting topic of testing with Selenium and to extract some rules that have proven themselves as true for us in the last two and a half years. If you stick to these rules and adapt them to your environment, you will thoroughly enjoy testing with Selenium. The tests can serve as integration tests, browser compatibility tests, and acceptance tests, and they can complement unit tests and help to improve the code and release quality.

12

Continuous Integration

Manuel Pichler and Sebastian Nohn

WHAT'S IN THIS CHAPTER?

➤ Configuring continuous integration

➤ Automating build processes

➤ Using version management

➤ Refactoring code clones

➤ Gathering information with software metrics

➤ Detecting security issues with RATS

➤ Installing CruiseControl and phpUnderControl

➤ Configuring CruiseControl

➤ Implementing continuous deployment

INTRODUCTION

After the success of dynamic testing techniques (such as unit testing), static testing techniques (such as static code analysis) and continuous integration are getting more attention in the PHP world.

Static code analysis belongs to the family of static testing techniques. In contrast to the dynamic testing techniques discussed in Chapter 2, these static techniques perform their tests without actually executing the code. Static analysis looks at its test object—the code—and evaluates it with regard to formal quality criteria such as correct code formatting or the absence of code duplication. Furthermore, simple metrics such as the number of executable lines of code and more complex metrics such as Cyclomatic Complexity and code rank are calculated to provide key indicators about the code. Because a complete automation of these checks is not only possible but also easy, static testing techniques can be used to prove the absence of errors, whereas dynamic testing techniques can only show the presence of errors. Impeccable code is a requirement for high-quality software. Static analysis facilitates the cheap discovery of stylistic errors that commonly hint at semantic errors.

Continuous integration ideally integrates all components of the software system after each change to the code. This means automatically producing a state of the software that can be checked using dynamic and static tests for all quality criteria as well as a build artifact that can be deployed or shipped. Thanks to the prompt execution of these tests after each change and in a controlled environment, as well as providing the build artifact for further (maybe manual) testing, the introduction of continuous integration improves the quality of the project. Once set up, continuous integration plays a vital role in improving the software's quality, and by keeping records of each build's metrics and statistics, it facilitates long-run analysis about the quality of the development processes.

The process of introducing static analysis and continuous integration described in this chapter is based on the experience from a software project that originally began in 2003 and was supposed to run for two years. The technical foundation for this project was a library that had already been in use within the company for a couple of years. This library provided infrastructure function such as object persistence, templating, and session management. The origins of this library can be traced back to PHP 3. The library was extended over the course of multiple projects, often using Copy and Paste or Copy, Paste, Adapt. Over the years, many different developers worked on the library, and due to the lack of clear programming conventions, they all left their distinctive marks on the code base.

In 2005, when the first quality assurance measures were implemented, the size of the project was about 50,000 lines of code that were mostly undocumented. A first analysis quickly showed that one of the central problems was the frequent copying (and adapting) of functionality. This had led to a situation in which a simple requirement from the customer could not be implemented at one single place in the code, but rather in multiple places scattered all over the code base. This scattering of identical logic frequently caused unforeseen problems in other parts of the software system.

The main reason for the frequent use of Copy, Paste, Adapt probably was the high complexity of many methods and classes. In many cases, they were a couple of hundred lines long. In the absence of automated tests, each change to the code required elaborate manual testing to prevent side effects. This testing had to be repeated after discovering and fixing each bug, of course. This process was both cumbersome and error-prone and led to increased costs for the client and the contractor. Usually, there was an overhead of 40% over the originally estimated time for a change request.

All these factors led to dissatisfaction with the project for all stakeholders. The end users often felt like software testers in the beta testing stage, and the developers, whose work was now actually good, were frustrated by the fact that unforeseen side effects impeded their effort to produce high-quality software. The gradual introduction of quality assurance processes, such as continuous integration, static code analysis, and automated tests, remedied the dissatisfaction of all stakeholders with the projects over time.

Continuous Integration

In software engineering terms, integration means the joining of components into a known configuration.[1]

Configuration

A combination of known versions of components that has been produced through integration is called a *configuration*. We can distinguish between configurations that fulfill our quality requirements and those that do not. Known configurations can be produced in a reproducible way for the deployment to production systems or for reproducing regressions in a development environment, for instance.

A common part of an integration is the compiling and linking of the different components and libraries into an executable and installable system. This step is omitted for an interpreted language such as PHP.

Known versions of the components that are to be integrated are a prerequisite to achieve an added value with regard to quality criteria. This known configuration can be tested. When these tests reveal a regression, the changes since the last configuration that is known to work can be used to analyze the root cause of the regression. A developer can also use the first configuration that exhibits the regression for debugging.

The four pillars of configuration management[2] are amalgamating (not discussed in this chapter), continuous integration, version management, and build management. The process of integration is usually called building. The value of such a build can be considerably increased by additional measures: Automated tests help with increasing the quality of the build. If developers may claim that they are "done" only when the build is successful—after committing the changes to the repository, this leads to an environment where a working state of the software is always available. The actual building should not take more than a couple of minutes so it doesn't impede the developers' work.

Build Management and Automated Tests

Build tools such as Make, Ant, or Phing can be used to automate the build process. Automated build processes are easy to reproduce and vital for continuous integration.

A typical PHP project is comprised of PHP source code files directly belonging to the project as well as external PHP libraries and configuration files. Software versions are restorable and retraceable when all files that belong to the project are managed in a version control system such as Git or Subversion, including build scripts that automate integration. In particular, this means that historic versions cannot be changed and consistent systems can be produced.

---

[1]Helmut Balzert, *Lehrbuch der Softwaretechnik. Bd. 1. Software-Entwicklung* (Spektrum Akademischer Verlag, 2005, ISBN 3-8274-0480-0).

[2]David Whitgift, *Methods and Tools for Software Configuration Management* (John Wiley & Sons, 1991, ISBN 0-4719-2940-6).

Version Management

The use of a version control system such as Git or Subversion for all components of the software is an essential prerequisite for continuous integration.

We now have everything in place to automatically integrate our software—for instance, integration can be time-controlled (that is, regularly scheduled) or done whenever a file that is under version control is changed. One of the advantages of continuous integration is the immediate feedback on changes that do or do not break the build. This feedback is particularly useful for identifying problems earlier and finding their root causes faster than would be possible during traditional "code freezes" where no changes may be made.

The easiest (and probably most common) way to practice regular integration is to use a cronjob (or a similar mechanism) to produce a "daily build." For continuous integration, however, we need more refined mechanisms and specialized tools. For this case study, we use phpUnderControl, which is based on CruiseControl.

Continuous Integration

Continuous integration means triggering an automated build by external events—for instance, when the code changes. One of the advantages of continuous integration is immediate feedback on the consequences of changes made to the software.

Continuous integration is more than just setting up a couple of tools, and it demands discipline from everyone involved with the code. Thanks to the prompt feedback from the continuous integration server, the change that caused a build to fail can be not only localized, but localized quickly. This requires the early and frequent committing of changes to the version control system by the developers. For the advantages of continuous integration to persist, failures must be detected as soon as possible. Fixing the root cause of a failed build must be the highest priority. Test-driven development, as well as automated acceptance and integration tests, makes mistakes detectable the moment they are committed to version control. This almost automatically leads the developers to test their code changes before each commit.

Formal criteria of software quality are checked with each change; the results are recorded and are thus available for analysis. Violations of these criteria are reported via e-mail, for instance. This increases the inhibition threshold to commit such violations of quality criteria. Repetitive tasks are automated and executed reproducibly. This induces the desire to automate further steps of the production cycle. Recurring tasks of the software development life cycle that can be automated should be, in order to relieve everyone involved in the project. This ensures that the process that is manifested in the build script is always adhered to.

Last but not least, the continuous integration system always provides the most recent state of the software that can be delivered or deployed. Newer approaches go in the direction of real continuous deployment systems. These demand more adaptations of the development and testing processes. We give a brief overview on this later in this chapter.

Altogether, continuous integration provides all project stakeholders an increased surety in their daily work.

Static Analysis

Code Clones

One of the biggest problems in software projects is that of duplicated source code. The term "code clone" describes identical or strongly correlated code fragments that occur multiple times in the source code.

The main problem caused by duplicated code is that you can never be sure that a change to one part of the code has no unintended side effects in another part of the code. This is because the behavior of the application is not encapsulated but rather scattered throughout the system. This quickly leads to new errors because the software as a whole is hard to comprehend. The situation is worsened by the fact that the copied source code usually does not come with a comment that it has been copied. In the worst case, the adverse effects of these code clones are discovered by the end user only when the application behaves inconsistently.

According to Martin Fowler,[3] code duplication is the Number One Bad Smell as an error in code that has been copied (or developed multiple times) and dramatically increases the cost of maintenance. The preferred way of dealing with the problem of code clones is to refactor.

Refactoring

Refactoring means to make enhancements to existing code in order to make it more readable or easier to extend. No functionality is added or changed while refactoring; the external behavior must not be changed.

Code clones were not uncommon in the software on which this case study is based. A large part of the library was copied and adapted countless times over the years. But code clones had also crept into various parts of the software itself.

The most striking (and easiest to find) form of code duplication was in the component that is responsible for template processing. In total, there were three different implementations of template handling. The only difference among them was the data source being used. Apart from the data source, the actual functionality was almost identical. A code clone like this is easy to find with the appropriate tools—for instance, using PMD-CPD[4] or phpcpd.[5]

```
$ phpcpd /home/case-study/lib/template
phpcpd 1.3.0 by Sebastian Bergmann.
Found 7 exact clones with 99 duplicated lines in 3 files:
- /home/case-study/lib/template/db.php:24-30
/home/case-study/lib/template/string.php:19-25
- /home/case-study/lib/template/db.php:28-36
/home/case-study/lib/template/string.php:45-53
```

---

[3]Martin Fowler, *Refactoring: Improving the Design of Existing Code* (Addison-Wesley, 1999, ISBN 978-0201485677).

[4]http://pmd.sf.net/cpd.html

[5]http://github.com/sebastianbergmann/phpcpd

```
  - /home/case-study/lib/template/db.php:167-193
/home/case-study/lib/template/string.php:71-97
  - /home/case-study/lib/template/db.php:79-88
/home/case-study/lib/template/file.php:65-74
  - /home/case-study/lib/template/string.php:127-142
/home/case-study/lib/template/file.php:85-100
  - /home/case-study/lib/template/db.php:132-149
/home/case-study/lib/template/file.php:130-147
  - /home/case-study/lib/template/db.php:244-262
/home/case-study/lib/template/file.php:170-188
  14.73% duplicated lines out of 672 total lines of code.
```

The example shows how easy it was to find the exact code duplicates in the code base using `phpcpd`. In our case study project, we wrote test cases for these code duplicates that enabled us to safely refactor the code and eliminate the duplication by factoring out identical code fragments into a common abstract base class.

Detection of code duplicates is no longer easy when the duplicates are not exact copies anymore. This happens when one of the code duplicates is modified. A very simple yet often found case of this in real life is the renaming of iteration variables—for instance, inside a `for` loop. When the code in the body of the loop uses such a variable, it becomes hard to detect duplication. To alleviate this problem, most duplication detection tools offer further options, such as the number of identical tokens[6] required to classify two code fragments as identical. Another option is the fuzzing or normalization of the names of classes, functions, methods, and variables.

Software Metrics

Software metrics provide statically measured values that can be used to assess and verify the quality of software. One of the main goals is the detection of all parts of the software that are prone to defects or make maintenance harder. Because software metrics can be calculated using tools, they are well suited for use in an automated build process. The information gathered can be used as the foundation for a manual code review. During such a code review, the focus is on the code areas highlighted by the software metrics.

Besides supporting code reviews, the use of analysis tools has further advantages:

➤ An analysis tool can process large amounts of source code in the shortest amount of time possible.

➤ The tool-based analysis is cost-effective and repeatable.

➤ The tool is always impartial. Subjective or personal factors do not matter.

➤ Careless mistakes that commonly occur when performing repetitive tasks are not an issue when a tool is used.

The software metrics gathered during an automated build process can be used to continuously control the quality of the software. They help to detect negative developments in a project as early as possible. The calculated key indicators enable software architects and developers alike to identify parts of the software that should be the focus of a code review or refactoring.

---

[6]A token can be a single character, such as the plus sign or a single brace, or it can be a sequence of characters that makes up a single keyword of the language.

Classic Metrics

Software metrics are not a new topic. The idea of detecting error-prone software artifacts based on measurements goes back to the 1960s. The Cyclomatic Complexity, for instance, was described by Thomas J. McCabe[7] in 1976. The following sections use the term *software artifact* as a general term for a set of parts of the software such as files, functions, methods, or classes.

Lines of Code

The Lines of Code (LOC) metric is a classic that easily calculates the number of lines of code in a software artifact. Because long code fragments have a negative impact on readability and comprehensibility, the Lines of Code (LOC) metric is a first indicator that a software artifact should be refactored. It is common to find a tangling of different functionalities in such software artifacts. This is contrary to the separation of concerns as a principle for testable software.[8]

On UNIX and Linux systems, the wc tool can be used to count the lines of a file:

```
$ wc --lines /home/case-study/libs/base/*
283 /home/case-study/libs/base/array.php
103 /home/case-study/libs/base/date.php
3210 /home/case-study/libs/base/func.php
179 /home/case-study/libs/base/session.php
3775 total
```

This example shows the Lines of Code results for a directory of the case study project. Looking at these results, we immediately notice the outlier file func.php that contains 3,210 lines of code, much more than the rest of the files. Software artifacts that differ this much from other software artifacts in their vicinity should be added to a list of "suspect" objects that require closer investigation.

In principle, the use of a specialized tool to calculate the Lines of Code metric is recommended. Such a tool can provide more details than just the plain number of lines of code, such as Comment Lines of Code (CLOC) and Non-Comment Lines of Code (NCLOC). In addition, these specialized tools usually provide a breakdown of the numbers by software artifact category. phploc[9] and PHP_Depend[10] are two such tools that cater to PHP code.

phploc calculates, among other software metrics, the LOC, CLOC, and NCLOC metrics for the whole project or individual directories. Furthermore, it reports the number of detected classes (NOC), interfaces (NOI), and methods (NOM). A truly unique feature of phploc is its functionality to count the ELOC metric. This metric measures the number of lines of code that contain executable statements as regarded by the PHP interpreter's compiler. This feature requires the Bytekit[11] extension for the PHP interpreter to work.

---

[7]Thomas J. McCabe, "A Complexity Measure," *IEEE Transactions on Software Engineering*, Vol. 2, No. 4 (IEEE Computer Society Press, Los Alamitos, CA, USA, 1976).

[8]Kent Beck, *Test-Driven Development*: *By Example* (Addison-Wesley, 2003, ISBN 0-3211-4653-0).

[9]http://github.com/sebastianbergmann/phploc

[10]http://pdepend.org/

[11]http://www.bytekit.org/

```
$ phploc /home/case-study/libs/base/
phploc 1.5.0 by Sebastian Bergmann.

Directories:                                                    474
Files:                                                         2206
Lines of Code (LOC):                                        441274
   Cyclomatic Complexity / Lines of Code:                     0.17
Executable Lines of Code (ELOC):                            159233
Comment Lines of Code (CLOC):                               204514
Non-Comment Lines of Code (NCLOC):                          236760

Namespaces:                                                       0
Interfaces:                                                     104
Classes:                                                       2094
   Abstract:                                           189 (9.03%)
   Concrete:                                         1905 (90.97%)
   Lines of Code / Number of Classes:                         168
Methods:                                                      14990
   Scope:
      Non-Static:                                    13996 (93.37%)
      Static:                                          994 (6.63%)
   Visibility:
      Public:                                        12105 (80.75%)
      Non-Public:                                      2885 (19.25%)
   Lines of Code / Number of Methods:                          23
   Cyclomatic Complexity / Number of Methods:                2.84

Anonymous Functions:                                             0
Functions:                                                       1

Constants:                                                    3623
   Global constants:                                            7
   Class constants:                                          3616
```

In addition to a plethora of other software metrics, PHP_Depend offers a similar amount of line-based metrics as phploc. PHP_Depend breaks down these line-based metrics not only by directory and file but also by software artifacts in general. Furthermore, PHP_Depend supports the export of all gathered metrics to an XML document, making it a prime candidate for inclusion in a build process.

In the case study project, we detected quite a few suspect software artifacts just by looking at the Lines of Code metric. Later code reviews showed that large parts of the code could actually be deleted, because they were no longer relevant to the project. The remaining code was then split up into multiple files based on the Separation of Concerns principle. A tool such as phpdcd[12] can help detect code that is no longer used.

Number of Classes, Methods, and Functions in a System

Other classic software metrics are gathered by simply counting the number of classes, interfaces, methods, and functions in the system. Although these metrics are very easy to calculate, they help

---

[12]http://github.com/sebastianbergmann/phpdcd

with getting a deep insight into a system quickly and without the need for a time-consuming code review. Just like with the Lines of Code metrics, a software artifact is suspect (for instance, in terms of comprehensibility and maintainability) if it differs too much from other artifacts in its vicinity with regard to these metrics. This list shows the most common of these metrics:

➤ NOC, Number of Classes: Classes in a package or file

➤ NOI, Number of Interfaces: Interfaces in a package or file

➤ NOM, Number of Methods: Methods in a package or file

➤ NOF, Number of Functions: Functions in a package or file

For instance, when a subsystem contains many classes but relatively few methods (or no methods at all), it is safe to assume that these are pure data objects with no logic or very little logic of their own. They are used by other classes as data stores or transport mediums instead. This architecture violates a basic rule of object-oriented software design: the encapsulation of data and behavior. The context of the class needs to be taken into account for this assessment, of course. Data objects that are used only for communication do have a right to exist in distributed software systems. Good examples of this type of class are the Data Transfer Objects that Martin Fowler describes.[13]

Another extreme is classes with many more methods than other classes in their vicinity. This type of class is prone to provide more logic than would be required to implement a single responsibility. They usually interoperate with a multitude of data objects that are used to store data between transactions. Because this type of class concentrates lots of logic in a single place in the system, they are commonly referred to as "God Classes." A software system that contains classes that exhibit these criteria is said to have a "design disharmony," or more specifically an "identity disharmony," in its architecture. The latter means a clustering of functionality that prohibits a subject-specific classification of the class.[14]

PHP_Depend is a tool that can calculate the NOC, NOM, and NOF software metrics for PHP code. In the following example, we use PHP_Depend to analyze all source code files found in /home/case-study/libs/data and write the results to an XML document:

```
$ pdepend --bad-documentation \
        --suffix=php,inc
        --summary-xml=/tmp/summary.xml \
        /home/case-study/libs/data
```

Here we show an excerpt of the produced XML document:

```
<?xml version="1.0" encoding="UTF-8"?>
<metrics noc="3" nof="0" noi="0" nom="6">
    <package name="+global" noc="17" nof="0" noi="0" nom="237">
        <class name="data_container"nom="55">
            <file name="/home/case-study/libs/data/container.php"/>
        </class>
```

---

[13]Martin Fowler, *Patterns of Enterprise Application Architecture* (Addison-Wesley, 2002, ISBN 0-3211-2742-0).

[14]Michele Lanza and Radu Marinescu describe approaches to resolve design disharmonies using refactoring in *Object-Oriented Metrics in Practice: Using Software Metrics to Characterize, Evaluate, and Improve the Design of Object-Oriented Systems* (Springer, 2006, ISBN 978-3-540-24429-5).

```
        <class name="data_download" nom="10">
            <file name="/home/case-study/libs/data/download.php"/>
        </class>
        <class name="data_element" nom="61">
            <file name="/home/case-study/libs/data/element.php"/>
        </class>
        <class name="data_file" nom="8">
            <file name="/home/case-study/libs/data/file.php"/>
        </class>
        <class name="data_link" nom="10">
            <file name="/home/case-study/libs/data/link.php"/>
        </class>
        <class name="data_text" nom="7">
            <file name="/home/case-study/libs/data/text.php"/>
        </class>
    </package>
</metrics>
```

Looking at the report, we see that the NOM values for the classes `data_container` and `data_element` are outliers compared to the other classes. A code review showed that these two classes contained lots of management logic for the other classes. In addition to the large number of methods, these two classes also shared lots of duplicate code due to their similar functionality.

During a later refactoring, we first wrote test cases for the affected parts. Then we moved functionality into separate methods of the related classes. We even moved some methods to newly created classes.

Cyclomatic Complexity

A large number of lines of code makes a method hard to understand, but a large number of control structures or a deep nesting thereof is also problematic. This problem, which at first glance seems like a purely human problem, can in many cases have a negative impact on the software. Statistically speaking, code with complex logic is more prone to undetected bugs that occur only under certain conditions. Furthermore, there is an increased risk of introducing new bugs with future changes because the correlations, dependencies, and related implications are not obvious to the developers.

One approach to detecting complex code structures in an automated way is the Cyclomatic Complexity Number (CCN). This software metric was described for the first time by Thomas J. McCabe[15] in 1976. It is a numerical value that counts the number of possible decision branches within a software artifact such as a function or method. Three variants of the software metric exist:

➤ CCN1 counts all control structures within a function or method. Each case statement within a switch is taken into account.

➤ CCN2 counts Boolean operators such as || and && in addition to control structures.

➤ CCN3 counts all control structures, but in contrast to CCN1, the case statements are not counted.

---

[15]McCabe, "A Complexity Measure."

CCN2 is the most commonly used metric and is supported by tools such as PMD,[16] Checkstyle,[17] JavaNCSS,[18] and PHP Depend.[19] A threshold of 10 has emerged for this variant of Cyclomatic Complexity. Functions and methods that violate this threshold should be examined closely. At the time of this writing, two tools exist to measure the Cyclomatic Complexity of PHP code: PHP_CodeSniffer and PHP_Depend.

Object-Oriented Metrics

One problem of object-oriented software is the interconnectedness between different software artifacts within the application. This sometimes complicated mesh of dependencies can make changes in one area of the system cause unanticipated side effects in other parts of the system. The growing pervasiveness of object-oriented programming since the 1990s led to a demand for new software metrics. Their goal was to make the complex network of objects analyzable and break down their dependencies into understandable key indicators.

Instability, Abstraction, and Distance

The Instability and Abstraction software metrics, as well as the Distance that is derived from them, are useful tools to easily detect parts of the software that pose a risk to future changes.

The foundations of the Instability software metric are Afferent Coupling and Efferent Coupling. These are simple counting metrics for the number of incoming and outgoing dependencies, respectively, of a software artifact. A high Efferent Coupling is a first indicator that a software artifact is prone to unanticipated side effects of changes made to other software artifacts due to its high coupling. A high Afferent Coupling indicates that changes made to the software artifact are likely to have adverse effects on other parts of the system. Software artifacts with a high Afferent Coupling should be particularly well tested using automated tests.

The Instability of a software artifact is calculated based on its Afferent Coupling and Efferent Coupling. The value for this derived metric is always between 0 and 1, and is calculated using the following formula:

Instability = Efferent Coupling / (Efferent Coupling + Afferent Coupling)

A software artifact is considered stable when its Instability is close to 0 and unstable when its Instability is close to 1. It is important to understand that this value does not quantify the actual state of the software artifact, but rather postulates a requirement: This software artifact must be stable!

Similar to the Instability, the Abstraction of a software artifact is also calculated based on two simple counting metrics: the number of abstract and concrete artifacts within the context of the

---

[16]http://pmd.sf.net

[17]http://checkstyle.sf.net/

[18]http://www.kclee.de/clemens/java/javancss

[19]http://pdepend.org/

software artifact. These can be the methods of a class or the classes within a package. Based on these values, the Abstraction of a software artifact is calculated using the following formula:

Abstraction = Abstract Artifacts / (Abstract Artifacts + Concrete Artifacts)

A value of 0 means that the software artifact contains only concrete classes or methods, whereas a value of 1 means that the software artifact contains only abstract classes (including interfaces) or methods.

If we denote abstraction and instability in a two-dimensional coordinate system and then draw a diagonal between the maximum values, we see a line for the ideal hypothesis of Abstraction + Instability = 1. In this context, the Distance describes the distance of a software artifact from this diagonal. It is calculated using this formula:

Distance = |Abstraction + Instability| − 1

This distance is an indicator for the balance between abstraction and instability.

Software artifacts that are close to the diagonal are, in most cases, a good compromise between abstraction and instability.[20]

PHP_Depend can be used to measure the software metrics that were discussed in this section. For output, PHP_Depend supports both an XML format and a chart that visualizes abstraction, instability, and distance.

```
$ pdepend --bad-documentation \
          --suffix=php,inc
          --jdepend-xml=/tmp/jdepend.xml \
          --jdepend-chart=/tmp/jdepend.svg \
          /home/case-study
```

Figure 12.1 shows the PHP_Depend chart for abstraction, instability, and distance for the case study project.

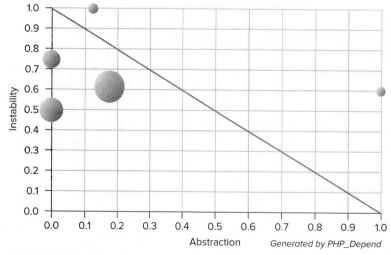

FIGURE 12-1: PHP_Depend chart for instability, abstraction, and distance

---

[20]André Fleischer, "Metriken im Praktischen Einsatz" (Objekt Spektrum 03/2007).

Code Rank

The Code Rank metric belongs to the newest generation of object-oriented software metrics. Concepts from modern search engines have been adapted for this metric to evaluate the coupling between software artifacts. Even if this approach may make no sense on first glance, the explanation is quite simple. Modern search engines such as Google can find the information relevant to a search term in a boundless number of documents and show the results in a ranked way. This ranking is based on the links between all documents found. This is similar to an object-oriented software with its components, classes, and methods and the complex mesh of dependencies between those software artifacts.

This section gives a brief introduction to the algorithm used to measure the code rank metric. A more detailed explanation can be found in "CodeRank: A New Family of Software Metrics" by Blair Neate, Warwick Irwin, and Neville Churcher (IEEE Software Engineering Conference, Australia, 2006), as well as in the Wikipedia article on Google's PageRank algorithm.[21]

Each class in the system gets an initial value that describes its relevance to the system as a whole before the actual software metric is calculated. One approach to determine this initial relevance value is to divide one by the number of all classes in the system. After the assignment of the initial value, the relevance of all classes is updated based on the outgoing edges. This process is repeated until, after a couple of iterations, the values converge. Using this approach, the relevance of a class is not only based on its immediate dependencies but also on indirect connections, possibly spanning multiple architecture layers, to other parts of the system. That makes this software metric well suited to detect classes that are potential sources for problems when changes are made.

Equivalent to the described algorithm is working the other way around. This way, classes with many direct or indirect dependencies can be detected:

```
$ pdepend --bad-documentation \
        --suffix=php,inc
        --summary-xml=/tmp/summary.xml \
        --coderank-mode=inheritance,property,method \
        /home/case-study
```

PHP_Depend supports both variants of the code rank metric for classes using different analysis strategies. The default strategy takes only the inheritance hierarchy into account. It is easily possible, though, to include attributes, methods, and method arguments in the measurement. This is done via the `--coderank-mode` switch that accepts a comma-separated list of analysis strategies.

Getting a Quick Overview

PHP_Depend provides the functionality to generate a software overview pyramid for a whole project or a single package of a project. This type of visualization is a condensed summary of the measured software metrics. The idea here is that various software metrics such as Lines of Code and Cyclomatic Complexity can be shown in a single chart while also showing additional information, such as the relation between different pairs. Using the background color for this additional information allows a quick grading into low, medium, and high. This visualization provides a quick overview of the complexity and structure of the project without the need for an in-depth code review.

---

[21]Wikipedia, "PageRank," accessed April 18, 2009, http://en.wikipedia.org/wiki/PageRank.

Figure 12.2 shows an example of such a software overview pyramid.

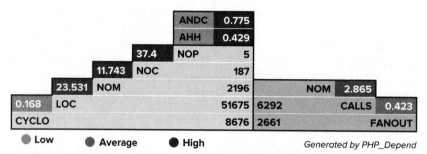

				ANDC	0.775				
				AHH	0.429				
			37.4	NOP	5				
		11.743	NOC		187				
	23.531	NOM			2196		NOM	2.865	
0.168	LOC				51675	6292		CALLS	0.423
CYCLO					8676	2661			FANOUT

● Low ● Average ● High   Generated by PHP_Depend

FIGURE 12-2: Software overview pyramid generated by PHP_Depend

RATS

A simple, yet useful tool to automatically detect security issues early in a project is RATS.[22] It is used to find function calls that are critical from a security point of view. In addition to strongly typed programming languages such as C and C++, RATS also supports a variety of dynamic programming languages such as PHP.

The acronym RATS stands for Rough Auditing Tool for Security, which describes the tool's functionality well. Although in some cases RATS takes the context of a function call into account, it does not perform an in-depth analysis of all possible execution paths. Instead, it simply looks at the source code and tries to find calls to potentially dangerous functions. After this analysis, it lists all function calls that are relevant to security. This report gives an assessment about the potential risk for each function call listed.

The example below shows the output of RATS for the template component of the case study project:[23]

```
$ rats --language php --warning 3 \
       --input /home/case-study/libs/template/
Entries in perl database: 33
Entries in python database: 62
Entries in c database: 334
Entries in php database: 55
Analyzing /home/case-study/libs/template/db.php
Analyzing /home/case-study/libs/template/string.php
Analyzing /home/case-study/libs/template/file.php
/home/case-study/libs/template/string.php:155: High: eval
/home/case-study/libs/template/string.php:227: High: eval
/home/case-study/libs/template/string.php:249: High: eval
Argument 1 to this function call should be checked to ensure that it does not come
from an untrusted source without first verifying that it contains nothing
dangerous.
/home/case-study/libs/template/file.php:43: Medium: is_readable
```

---

[22]http://www.fortify.com/

[23]The output was reformatted for print.

```
A potential TOCTOU (Time Of Check, Time Of Use) vulnerability exists.
This is the first line where a check has occurred.
The following line(s) contain uses that may match up with this check:
48 (dirname)

/home/case-study/libs/template/file.php:51: High: fopen
Argument 1 to this function call should be checked to ensure that it does not come
from an untrusted source without first verifying that it contains nothing
dangerous.

/home/case-study/libs/template/file.php:51: Low: fopen
A potential race condition vulnerability exists here. Normally a
call to this function is vulnerable only when a match check
precedes it. No check was detected, however one could still exist
that could not be detected.
Total lines analyzed: 3026
Total time 0.014804 seconds
204404 lines per second
```

Based on this analysis, six potential security issues were found, three of which affected PHP's `eval()` function that is commonly considered a security risk. The other three pointed at potential dangers with regard to file system operations.

In addition to the textual output shown earlier, RATS can alternatively produce its report in HTML or XML format. This makes an integration of the tool into an automated build process straightforward.

Another use case for RATS stems from the XML format for vulnerability databases. Using a custom vulnerability database and a fast RATS parser, you can implement a blacklist of unwanted function calls in a very efficient way.

INSTALLATION

CruiseControl[24] requires a JDK; phpUnderControl requires the PHP tools discussed in the preceding section. A client for the version control system used is also required. For the following, we assume that Java, PHP, and Subversion are already installed. For a first test installation, even a weakly equipped machine is sufficient; however, it should not have less than 1 GB of memory. In general, you do not want to save on the integration server's hardware. Every investment made here means shorter build times and thus faster feedback. We can now install CruiseControl and phpUnderControl:

```
$ sudo pear channel-discover components.ez.no
$ sudo pear channel-discover pear.phpundercontrol.org
$ sudo pear upgrade-all
$ sudo pear install --alldeps phpuc/phpundercontrol-beta
$ unzip cruisecontrol-bin-2.8.3.zip
$ phpuc install cruisecontrol-bin-2.8.3
```

Now phpUnderControl is ready to use. Before we start it the first time, we delete the connect four example project and replace it with our own.

---

[24]http://cruisecontrol.sourceforge.net/download.html

CONFIGURATION

Continuous integration happens with CruiseControl in the Build Loop, as shown in Figure 12-3. The system polls the version control system at regular intervals for changes. When a change is discovered, it triggers a build—for instance, by invoking Apache Ant and running a build script. In the end, it publishes the build results. This is where phpUnderControl comes into play: It formats the results in a format suitable for PHP projects.

The configuration is done in two files: the build script and the base configuration for CruiseControl. The build script consists of "targets" that can depend on each other.

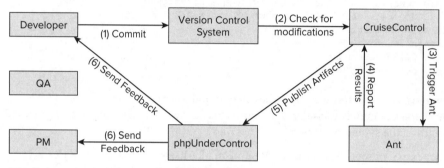

FIGURE 12-3: The build loop of phpUnderControl

The following shows a common structure for such an Apache Ant build script:

```
<project name="case-study" default="build" basedir="../">
  <target name="build"
    depends="update, prepare, test, deliv"/>
  <target name="clean">
    <delete dir="${basedir}/build"/>
  </target>
  <target name="prepare" depends="clean">
    <tstamp>
      <format property="build.tstamp" pattern="yyyyddmmhhmmss" />
    </tstamp>
    <mkdir dir="${basedir}/build/logs"/>
    <mkdir dir="${basedir}/build/deliv"/>
  </target>
  <target name="update" depends="prepare">
    <exec dir="${basedir}/src" executable="svn">
      <arg line="up"/>
    </exec>
  </target>
  <target name="test"
    depends="prepare, test_static, test_unit"/>
  <target name="test_static" depends="prepare"/>
  <target name="test_unit" depends="prepare"/>
  <target name="test_acceptance" depends="prepare, test"/>
  <target name="tag"/>
  <target name="deliv" depends="test, tag"/>
```

```
    <target name="deploy" depends="test_acceptance, deliv"/>
</project>
```

We flesh out this script over the course of the following sections. Saved as `build.xml`, this script can already be executed:

```
$ ant
Buildfile: build.xml
clean:
    [delete] Deleting directory .../projects/case-study/build
prepare:
    [mkdir] Created dir: .../projects/case-study/build/logs
    [mkdir] Created dir: .../projects/case-study/build/deliv
update:
    [exec] Update to revision 1.
test_static:
test_unit:
test:
tag:
deliv:
build:
BUILD SUCCESSFUL
Total time: 0 seconds
```

Now we can configure CruiseControl itself:

```
<cruisecontrol>
    <project name="case-study" buildafterfailed="false">
        <listeners>
          <currentbuildstatuslistener
            file="logs/${project.name}/status.txt"/>
        </listeners>
        <modificationset quietperiod="60">
          <svn
            repositoryLocation="http://svn.example.com/case/trunk"
            username="cruisecontrol"
            password="secret" />
        </modificationset>
        <schedule interval="60">
            <ant buildfile="projects/${project.name}/src/build.xml"
                target="build"/>
        </schedule>
        <log dir="logs/${project.name}/">
            <merge dir="projects/${project.name}/build/logs"/>
        </log>
        <publishers>
            <artifactspublisher dir="projects/${project.name}/build/logs"
                dest="artifacts/${project.name}" />
            <execute command="phpuc graph logs/${project.name}"/>


<currentbuildstatuspublisher
file="logs/${project.name}/status.txt"/>
<htmlemail
```

```
     mailhost="localhost" xslDir="webapps/cruisecontrol/xsl"
     returnaddress="noreply@example.com" spamwhilebroken="true"
     buildresultsurl="http://cruise.example.com/cruisecontrol">
     <always address="qa@example.com" />
     <failure address="dev@example.com" />
     </htmlemail>
     </publishers>
     </project>
     </cruisecontrol>
```

Finally we delete the connect four example project:

```
$ phpuc delete --project-name connectfour .
```

After the initial checkout of the source code from the version control repository, it is time to start CruiseControl:

```
$ mkdir projects/case-study
$ svn checkout http://svn.example.com/case/trunk \
    projects/case-study/src
$ ./cruisecontrol.sh
```

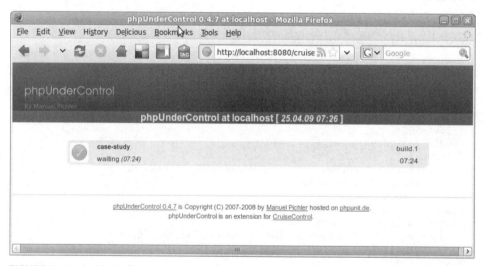

FIGURE 12-4: phpUnderControl after the basic configuration for the case study project

Static Tests

In addition to the static testing techniques discussed earlier in this chapter, another important criterion for software quality is ensuring the adherence to programming conventions.

Programming Conventions

An important, yet too often underestimated aspect for the quality of software is the programming conventions. The developers of a team (or ideally, all developers of a company) decide on common rules for naming and code formatting. These rules can have a broad spectrum, from very simple rules—such as using spaces instead of tabs—to exact specifications on indentation, line breaks, and additional rules on how to structure the code. The big advantage of such strict rules for formatting is that developers can more easily read and understand the code. For this, it doesn't matter whether it's a developer new to the team or a long-time team member who needs to work on a part of the code that he or she did not write.[25]

For a long time, the case study project did not have any form of programming conventions. This led to a multitude of indentation variants (tabs or two, four, or in some cases even three spaces), different naming schemes (CamelCase, underscores, combinations of both, or no visual separation at all), and different positioning of braces (with line break, without line break, or even without a brace). Due to this rank growth of different styles, people were afraid to change code that was written by others. They knew from experience that even the smallest change could produce an error in the system.

```php
<?php
for ($i=0;$i<count($ItemList);++$i)
   if($i%2==0)
      if($th<$ItemList[$i]->value) { /* ... */
      }
      else if($th==$ItemList[$i]->value){ /* ... */
      }elseif($th>$ItemList[$i]->value)
        if($highlight_value==c_green) $c='#00ff00';
        elseif($highlight_value==c_red) $c='#ff0000';
          elseif($highlight_value==c_blue) $c='#0000ff';
      else $c='#000000';
echo $c;
?>
```

As you can see in this example, mixing different formatting and programming styles leads to a situation in which the intent of the code is not obvious.

In addition to the different usage of braces and the creative naming, this example also exhibits further stylistic errors. Names such as $th and $c are too short to convey what they are used for, which can lead to problems when the code is changed later—especially when the original developer is no longer with the company.

A widely used tool in the PHP world to automatically validate the adherence of code to programming conventions is PHP_CodeSniffer.[26] It can easily be installed via PEAR. The following example shows its output for the case study project.[27]

```
$ phpcs /home/case-study/examples/coding_conventions.php
FILE: /home/case-study/examples/coding_conventions.php
-----------------------------------------------------------------
FOUND 10 ERROR(S) AND 8 WARNING(S) AFFECTING 9 LINE(S)
-----------------------------------------------------------------
   2 | WARNING | Inline control structures are discouraged
   2 | ERROR   | Missing file doc comment
```

---

[25]Paul M. Duvall, *Continuous Integration – Improving Software Quality and Reducing Risks* (Addison-Wesley, 2007, ISBN 978-0-321-33638-5).

[26]http://pear.php.net/package/PHP_CodeSniffer

[27]The output was reformatted for print.

```
  3 | WARNING | Inline control structures are discouraged
  4 | ERROR   | Expected "if (...) {\n"; found
    |         | "if(...) { /* ... */\n"
  4 | ERROR   | Line indented incorrectly; expected 0 spaces,
    |         | found 6
  6 | ERROR   | Expected "} else if (...) {\n"; found "}\n
    |         | else if(...){ /* ... */\n"
  6 | ERROR   | Expected "if (...) {\n"; found
    |         | "if(...){ /* ... */\n"
  6 | ERROR   | Line indented incorrectly; expected 0 spaces,
    |         | found 6
  7 | ERROR   | Closing brace indented incorrectly; expected
    |         | 6 spaces, found 5
  8 | ERROR   | Constants must be uppercase; expected C_GREEN but
    |         | found c_green
  8 | WARNING | Inline control structures are discouraged
  8 | WARNING | Equals sign not aligned with surrounding
    |         | assignments; expected 5 spaces but found 0 spaces
  9 | ERROR   | Constants must be uppercase; expected C_RED but
    |         | found c_red
  9 | WARNING | Equals sign not aligned with surrounding
    |         | assignments; expected 3 spaces but found 0 spaces
 10 | ERROR   | Constants must be uppercase; expected C_BLUE but
    |         | found c_blue
 10 | WARNING | Equals sign not aligned with surrounding
    |         | assignments; expected 1
    |         | space but found 0 spaces
 11 | WARNING | Inline control structures are discouraged
 11 | WARNING | Equals sign not aligned with surrounding
    |         | assignments; expected 32 spaces but found 0 spaces
------------------------------------------------------------------
```

Without using the `--standard` switch, PHP_CodeSniffer uses the PEAR Coding Standard[28] by default. As you can see from the output above, the case study project's code violated this coding standard in multiple places.

Coding Guidelines

Before we introduced programming conventions to the case study project, there was one important question that we asked ourselves: Do we define our own set of rules, or do we use an established standard instead? The result of a lengthy discussion was the decision to use the widely used PEAR standard. This decision was based on two pragmatic reasons. On the one hand, defining our own set of rules would have exceeded our budget. On the other hand, many developers had already used the PEAR standard and were used to it. In hindsight, this decision was of great advantage to the project as the introduction of programming conventions based on an established and well-documented standard was easy for the developers.

The existence of a rule set for PHP_CodeSniffer should be criteria when choosing a coding standard. But even if you choose to define your own coding standard, you can still customize or extend an

---

[28]http://pear.php.net/manual/en/standards.php

existing rule set, and you can add completely new ones. In its default installation, PHP_CodeSniffer comes with a couple of rule sets, including one for the Zend Framework.[29]

PHP_CodeSniffer can be installed using the PEAR Installer:

```
$ sudo pear install PHP_CodeSniffer
```

It also can be integrated into our build script so phpUnderControl can generate reports on coding standard violations:

```
<target name="phpcs">
   <exec dir="${basedir}" executable="phpcs"
        output="${basedir}/build/logs/checkstyle.xml"
        failonerror="false">
           <arg line="--report=checkstyle --ignore=build ."/>
   </exec>
</target>
```

Gradual Introduction into Legacy Projects

As you can see, we are invoking all tools using the `failonerror` option in such a way that errors do not fail the build. Whether a build should be marked as a failure when an inspection finds an error depends on company or project guidelines. This can change during the project life cycle. Especially in the case of brownfield software redevelopment projects such as our case study project, most software metrics have critical values for long periods of time. Failing the build in such a scenario is not very helpful.

When we started to introduce quality assurance processes, we asked ourselves how the adoption of the PEAR standard would fit into our daily work. Because we had no rules for formatting and structuring code, the initial violation reports were far too extensive to find violations in newly developed parts of the application.

This is why we opted for a two-step approach: We defined a trimmed-down version of the PEAR standard that we used for our legacy code and applied the full PEAR standard only to newly written code. Initially, this trimmed-down standard only contained rules that demanded a comment block before each class and basic indentation rules.

```
<target name="phpcs">
   <exec dir="${basedir}" executable="phpcs"
        output="${basedir}/build/logs/checkstyle.xml"
        failonerror="false">
        <arg line="--report=checkstyle --ignore=build ."/>
   </exec>
</target>
<?php
require_once 'PHP/CodeSniffer/CommentParser/PairElement.php';
require_once 'PHP/CodeSniffer/Standards/CodingStandard.php';
class PHP_CodeSniffer_Standards_PEARLight_PEARLightCodingStandard
   extends PHP_CodeSniffer_Standards_CodingStandard
{
```

---

[29]http://framework.zend.com/

```php
    public function getIncludedSniffs()
    {
        return array(
          'PEAR/Sniffs/Commenting/ClassCommentSniff',
          'PEAR/Sniffs/WhiteSpace/ScopeIndentSniff',
          'Generic/Sniffs/PHP/LowerCaseConstantSniff',
          'Generic/Sniffs/PHP/DisallowShortOpenTagSniff',
        );
    }
}
?>
```

Within three months, the number of violations went down drastically, and we added more rules to the legacy code coding standard during a second phase. An additional benefit of writing comment blocks for each class was that the knowledge about the legacy code increased in the current development team.

After a year and a half, we reached a compliance with the PEAR coding standard for the whole project of about 95%. At this point, we stopped using a separate set of rules for the legacy code.

Coding Standards in the Daily Work

Although it should be natural to continuously verify the adherence to a coding standard, it took a while until the new tool was integrated into the daily routine of our developers. In the beginning, for instance, it commonly occurred that unverified code was checked into our version control system. This unintended negligence was countered with an automated verification before each commit to version control. We chose the pragmatic approach of using pre-commit hooks with our Subversion environment. This way, we made sure that no files with coding standard violations could be checked in.

```sh
#!/bin/sh
# Check coding conventions for committed files
/opt/pear/bin/phpcs-svn-pre-commit "$1" -t "$2" \
    --standard=PEARLight >&2 || exit 1
```

Newer versions of PHP_CodeSniffer come with a ready-to-use shell script that can be used as a pre-commit hook. As you can see in the preceding example, this can be done with very little effort.

We now install additional tools that were discussed earlier in this chapter:

```
$ sudo pear channel-discover pear.phpmd.org
$ sudo pear channel-discover pear.pdepend.org
$ sudo pear install phpmd/PHPMD-alpha
$ sudo pear install phpunit/phpcpd
$ sudo pear install pdepend/PHP_Depend-beta
```

And we integrate them into our build script:

```xml
<target name="test_static"
        depends="prepare, phpcs, phpmd, phpcpd, pdepend">
</target>
<target name="phpmd">
    <exec dir="${basedir}" executable="phpmd" failonerror="false">
        <arg line=". xml codesize
            --reportfile ${basedir}/build/logs/pmd.xml"/>
```

```
      </exec>
  </target>
  <target name="phpcpd">
      <exec dir="${basedir}" executable="phpcpd" failonerror="false">
          <arg line="--log-pmd=${basedir}/build/logs/phpcpd.xml ."/>
      </exec>
  </target>
  <target name="pdepend">
      <exec dir="${basedir}" executable="pdepend" failonerror="false">
          <arg line="--jdepend-xml=${basedir}/build/logs/pdepend.xml ."/>
      </exec>
  </target>
```

Syntax Analysis

The most widespread, yet rarely known tool for static analysis is the linter. The origin of this type of tool goes back to a compiler for the C programming language developed at Bell Labs in 1979.[30] Since then, linters have served the purpose of performing lexical and syntactical analysis of source code before the actual compilation or execution. In the beginning, a separate tool was necessary for this; now the process is implemented as part of the compilers or interpreters themselves.

```
1 <?php
2 echo 'start';
3 require_once 'not_existant.php';
4     echo 'hello '
5 echo 'world!';
6 ?>
```

A linter for PHP is already built into the PHP binary. It can be executed using the -l switch:

```
$ php -l test.php
Parse error: syntax error, unexpected T_ECHO,
expecting ',' or ';' in test.php on line 5
Errors parsing test.php
```

As you can see, the linter performs a syntax check of the source code only. The missing file not_existent.php is not detected, and neither is the creative indenting in line 4. One of the most important aspects of using a linter is that you do not have to try to execute the code to detect syntax errors.

In a broader sense of the term, validators for CSS, HTML, and XML are also lint checkers. These also check the code for syntactical errors. Contrary to programming languages, these markup languages still suffer from portability issues, making automatic detection of all syntactical issues non-trivial. Especially when using the modern AJAX interface, it is essential to ensure syntactical correctness of the HTML and JavaScript code used.

Modern compilers can perform deeper analysis and checks of the compiled code to provide more detailed and semantic analysis than is possible with language interpreters out of the box. These checks include checks for the consistency of function and method calls or for undeclared variables. At the time of this writing, no such tool exists to deeply analyze PHP source before its execution.

---

[30]Wikipedia, "Lint (Programmierwerkzeug)", accessed April 21, 2009, http://de.wikipedia.org/wiki/Lint_(Programmierwerkzeug).

Dynamic Tests

Contrary to static tests, we want to abort the build when a dynamic test fails:

```
<target name="test_unit" depends="prepare">
    <exec dir="${basedir}" executable="phpunit" failonerror="true">
        <arg line="--log-xml ${basedir}/build/logs/phpunit.xml
                   --coverage-clover ${basedir}/build/logs/clover.xml
                   --coverage-xml ${basedir}/build/logs/coverage.xml
                   --coverage-html ${basedir}/build/deliv/coverage
                   --stop-on-failure
                   AllTests src/tests/AllTests.php"/>
    </exec>
</target>
<target name="test_acceptance" depends="prepare, test">
    <exec dir="${basedir}" executable="phpunit" failonerror="true">
        <arg line="--log-xml ${basedir}/build/logs/selenium.xml
                   --stop-on-failure
                   AllTests src/acceptance-tests/AllTests.php"/>
    </exec>
</target>
```

Reporting

Notification in the Case of Errors

One of the most important results of introducing continuous integration into a project is that all stakeholders have access to information about the state of the project at all times. It is important that (only) the information that is relevant to each project role is pushed—for instance, via e-mail—to the stakeholders. All information is available to all stakeholders through the web interface or via RSS.

Our phpUnderControl instance is already configured like this: Developers are notified in the case of build failures, and the quality assurance team is notified about the status of every build. For this we use the `htmlemailpublisher` to send e-mails about the build results. Additional notification services that are supported are SMS or special hardware for audio/visual feedback,[31] for instance. At any time, the web interface of phpUnderControl can be used to access information about the current state of the project as well as statistical information.

Statistics

Under pressure, the team has to cut down on reviews first—and then on the tests. Using the techniques and practices of static analysis and continuous integration, these deficits can be detected and the development can be observed over time. Code Smells[32] can be monitored and remedied using static analysis and continuous integration. The individual software metrics were discussed earlier in this chapter. The processing of the results of the static tests is performed by phpUnderControl. These results are available in the Metrics tab of the web interface.

---

[31]These are discussed in *Continuous Integration – Improving Software Quality and Reducing Risks* by Paul M. Duvall (Addison-Wesley, 2007, ISBN 978-0-321-33638-5).

[32]Fowler, *Refactoring.*

PHP_CodeBrowser

The PHP_CodeBrowser provides a code browser for PHP files with syntax highlighting and colored error sections found by quality assurance tools such as PHPUnit and PHP_CodeSniffer. It can be installed like this:

```
$ pear install --alldeps phpunit/PHP_CodeBrowser
```

To integrate PHP_CodeBrowser into phpUnderControl, we need to amend the publisher's section of CruiseControl's `config.xml` configuration file again:

```
<execute
    command="phpcb --log projects/${project.name}/build/logs
                   --source projects/${project.name}/src
                   --output projects/${project.name}/build/php-code-browser"/>
    <artifactspublisher
        dir="projects/${project.name}/build/php-code-browser"
        dest="artifacts/${project.name}"
        subdirectory="php-code-browser"/>
```

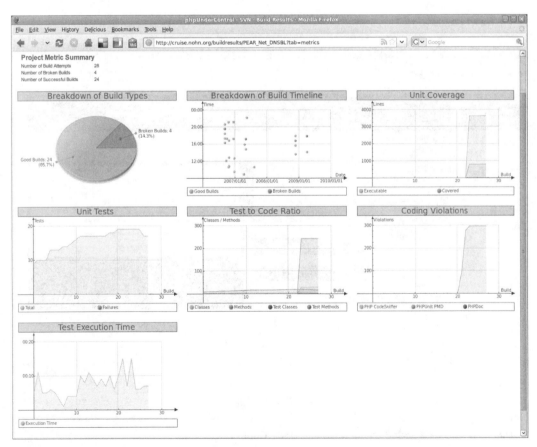

FIGURE 12-5: The metrics tab of phpUnderControl

Deliverables

The deliverables—installable software packages, documentation, and reports—are produced in the `deliv` target of our build script. In our example, we create a PEAR package.[33] Of course, all package formats that can be created on the command line are also possible.

```
<target name="tag">
    <exec dir="${basedir}/src" executable="svn" failonerror="true">
        <arg line="cp .
            http://svn.example.com/case/tags/build_${build.tstamp}"/>
    </exec>
</target>
<target name="deliv" depends="test, tag">
    <exec dir="${basedir}" executable="pear" failonerror="true">
        <arg line="package" />
    </exec>
    <move todir="build/deliv/">
        <fileset dir="${basedir}">
            <include name="*.tgz"/>
        </fileset>
    </move>
</target>
```

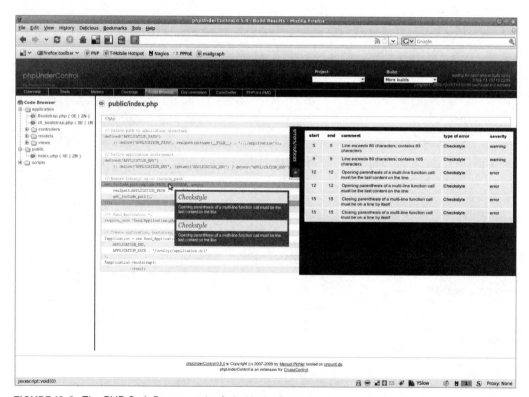

FIGURE 12-6: The PHP CodeBrowser tab of phpUnderControl

---

[33]*PEAR Manual*, PHP Group, `http://pear.php.net/manual/`.

We copy the generated PEAR package to CruiseControl's build artifact directory using the `<move>` task. This directory is configured in the `<publishers>` section of CruiseControl's configuration file:

```
<artifactspublisher
    dir="projects/${project.name}/build/deliv/"
    dest="artifacts/case-study/" />
```

Additional deliverables could be API documentation produced by phpDocumentor[34] or Doxygen.[35] We use phpDocumentor to generate up-to-date API documentation for each build:

```
<target name="phpdoc">
    <exec dir="${basedir}" executable="phpdoc" failonerror="true">
        <arg line="-ct type -ue on -t ${basedir}/build/deliv/doc -d ."/>
    </exec>
</target>
```

For this to work, we need to amend the `deliv` target in our build script as follows:

```
<target name="deliv" depends="test, phpdoc, tag">
    <!-- ... -->
</target>
```

OPERATIONS

With regard to operations, CruiseControl unfortunately is a product of low quality. Maintainability and stability, for instance, leave much to be desired. Approaches to upgrade an existing CruiseControl installation exist,[36] but at the time of this writing, they do not actually work. This means upgrades need to be performed manually.

The most feasible way of doing so is to copy the new version to a new directory and move the configuration and projects to the new directory:

```
$ unzip cruisecontrol-bin-2.8.3.zip
$ phpuc install cruisecontrol-bin-2.8.3
$ rm -rf ./cruisecontrol-bin-2.8.3/logs/connectfour
$ rm -rf ./cruisecontrol-bin-2.8.3/artifacts/connectfour
$ rm -rf ./cruisecontrol-bin-2.8.3/projects/connectfour
$ rm ./cruisecontrol-bin-2.8.3/connectfour.ser
$ cp -r ./cruisecontrol-bin-2.8.2/logs \
        ./cruisecontrol-bin-2.8.2/artifacts \
        ./cruisecontrol-bin-2.8.2/projects \
        ./cruisecontrol-bin-2.8.2/config.xml \
        ./cruisecontrol-bin-2.8.2/*.ser \
        ./cruisecontrol-bin-2.8.3/
```

Because the syntax of the `config.xml` file is prone to change, you should upgrade CruiseControl only when the new version brings bug fixes or features that are really relevant to your needs.

---

[34]http://www.phpdoc.org/

[35]http://www.doxygen.org/

[36]http://confluence.public.thoughtworks.org/download/attachments/5234/install.tgz

On the other hand, upgrading phpUnderControl is easy:

```
$ sudo pear upgrade phpunit/phpundercontrol-beta
$ phpuc install cruisecontrol/
```

ADVANCED TOPICS

Continuous Deployment

The continuous deployment of the software—for instance, to test or demo systems—after each successful build for use by the development team is straightforward to implement: From the perspective of the developers, who write tests for their code that are run during each build, the software is ready for use by other stakeholders in the team—for instance, the quality assurance team.

In most cases, however, project stakeholders such as the quality assurance department or the customer will not be satisfied by this and will demand additional (manual) acceptance testing before taking the software into production. The developers could have misunderstood requirements or specifications. The quality assurance team could want additional acceptance, load, or system tests.

Introducing continuous deployment while sticking to the principles of quality assurance and acceptance requires a more agile approach to configuration management. At the core of this is version control strategy as outlined in "Version Control for Multiple Agile Teams."[37]

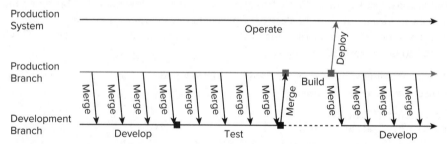

FIGURE 12-7: Branching strategy for continuous deployment according to "Version Control for Multiple Agile Teams"

All changes are made in separate development branches—for instance, one branch per team, per task, per planned release. Only when all criteria for the deployment in the production environment are ensured via automated tests in such a branch may it be merged into the production branch, which is continuously integrated, as shown in Figure 12-7.

Every configuration we want to install—and that's every configuration for which all automated tests have passed—gets a unique version number. We have implemented this in our build script using the tag `target`. This allows us to trigger the deployment based on the success of the acceptance tests:

```
<target name="deploy" depends="test_acceptance, deliv">
    <exec dir="${basedir}/build/deliv" executable="scp"
```

---

[37]Henrik Kniberg, "Version Control for Multiple Agile Teams," *InfoQ*, March 31, 2008, accessed April 15, 2009, http://www.infoq.com/articles/agile-version-control.

```
            failonerror="true">
            <arg line="case-study.tgz user@deployment.case-study.local:"/>
    </exec>
    <exec dir="${basedir}" executable="ssh" failonerror="true">
            <arg line="ssh user@deployment.case-study.local \
                       'pear install case-study.tgz'"/>
    </exec>
  </target>
```

In addition to an appropriate branching strategy, continuous deployment also requires fully automated deployment and rollback mechanisms and strategies. In complex systems with multiple database servers, web services, and distributed yet interdependent systems, fully backward and forward compatible interfaces are one important piece of the puzzle. More important than technologies and tools such as dbdeploy[38] or Capistrano,[39] however, are working processes.

Using a Reverse Proxy

In most cases, especially when a phpUnderControl instance is to be made available to a large group of users—on the Internet or an intranet—it is prudent (because of security concerns, for example) to operate the service behind a proxy.

On the one hand, the access to critical areas such as the dashboard can be limited in a better way than is possible with CruiseControl's own mechanisms. On the other hand, CruiseControl's web server can thus be operated on a port that is not privileged and does not require root permissions.

The operation behind a proxy is easy with phpUnderControl and Apache HTTPD:

```
<VirtualHost *:80>
    DocumentRoot /opt/cruisecontrol/webapps/cruisecontrol/
    ServerName cruise.example.com
    # VirtualHost is Reverse Proxy for http://localhost:8080/
    ProxyRequests Off
    <Proxy *>
       Order deny,allow
       Allow from all
    </Proxy>
    ProxyPass / http://localhost:8080/
    ProxyPassReverse / http://localhost:8080/
    # Allow everything
    <Location />
       Order allow,deny
       Allow from all
    </Location>
  # But disallow the dashboard
    <Location /dashboard>
       Order deny,allow
       Deny from all
    </Location>
</VirtualHost>
```

---

[38]http://dbdeploy.com/

[39]http://capify.org/

Continuous Integration and Agile Paradigms

Continuous integration supports many ideas from agile process models: The efficacy of unit tests is increased. The whole test suite is run for each changeset. Refactorings can be performed without the fear of breaking something and not noticing it. With its statistics on code hygiene, continuous integration also can help determine the right focus and the right time for such a refactoring. Early and frequent builds are another agile method, and they're often the reason to introduce continuous integration in the first place.

However, there are also conflicting goals with regard to continuous integration: High test coverage often leads to longer build times, which is contrary to most agile models. The choice between build time and test coverage is the worst solution possible here. It is better to accelerate the test execution instead. Acceptance tests through the user interface are especially hard to accelerate, even with parallel test execution.[40] These tests also require a highly complex test environment.[41]

In practice, it makes sense to set up cascading or parallel continuous integration systems, especially when you want to implement Continuous Deployment. The static tests can be made parallel quite easily using Apache Ant and its `<parallel>` task:

```
<target name="test_static" depends="prepare">
    <parallel>
        <antcall target="phpcs" />
        <antcall target="phpmd" />
        <antcall target="phpcpd" />
        <antcall target="pdepend" />
    </parallel>
</target>
```

CONCLUSION

In the course of time, continuous integration, retroactively added unit tests, software metrics, and other static testing techniques have become vital parts for the case study project discussed in this chapter. They contributed to improving the software quality of a legacy application. A drastic reduction of the costs for development and testing was achieved within two years. The actual introduction of the aforementioned processes did not happen overnight or in a new project; they were introduced gradually into the daily work on the existing project. The changes were introduced parallel to our day-to-day business and did not yield any additional costs for our customer.

The average overhead for functional tests and rework was reduced from an initial 40% to less than 5%. This measurable positive development did not include additional time savings that were the result of the improved maintainability of the software. It made clear, though, that changes could be performed with significantly lower effort and that new requirements for the product could be

---

[40]Jason Huggins and Jen Bevan, "Extending Selenium Into the Browser and Out to the Grid," *Vortrag auf der Google Testing Automatic Conference*, New York, 2007, accessed April 9, 2009, http://www.youtube.com/watch?v=qxBatJ1N_Og.

[41]Paul M. Duvall, *Continuous Integration – Improving Software Quality and Reducing Risks* (Addison-Wesley, 2007, ISBN 978-0-321-33638-5).

implemented more easily and quickly. Thanks to automated testing techniques and a clean modularization of the application, we were able to dramatically reduce the amount of manual testing.

We have shown in this chapter that software metrics can be a very useful tool to perform quality tests of software in an automated way. It is key to choose appropriate metrics for different use cases. Often, not a single metric is used, but a combination of various values to gain an even deeper insight into the system. It is important to keep in mind that automated and manual code reviews are not mutually exclusive. The result from a tool-based analysis should rather be used to guide a manual code review.

Another important aspect for an impartial assessment of the measurements was the definition of appropriate thresholds. Only with well-defined thresholds is it possible to determine whether a critical violation has been found. This is even more important with legacy software for which too many violations would be reported otherwise. This would bear the risk of not seeing the relevant violations among the vast number of violations. Because of this, it is advisable to use higher thresholds or simpler rules in the beginning that are then continuously adapted in the direction of the desired values.

The retroactively introduced requirement to document classes and methods leads to another, initially undervalued, side effect. Over time, the team developed a profound knowledge about the functionality already implemented in the system. Based on this information, it was possible to identify even more parts of the code that no longer had any relevance to the project. Following the agile principle of Single Source of Information,[42] the automatically generated and well-structured API documentation was used to amend either missing or insufficient documentation.

The most positive effect of introducing quality assurance measures was that the satisfaction with the actual product and the collaboration among all project stakeholders continuously improved. The customer can be sure now that new features will not require weeks of bug fixing and rework, and the software vendor is now in a position to give better estimates on how long it will take to implement a new requirement.

---

[42]Scott W. Ambler, *Agile Modeling: Effective Practices for Extreme Programming and the Unified Process* (Wiley & Sons, 2002, ISBN 0-4712-0282-7).

13

swoodoo: A True Agile Story

Lars Jankowfsky

INTRODUCTION

Before we start with our agile story, let us throw some light on the swoodoo company so you have a better idea about us. The swoodoo flight search engine is being developed in Germany and Lithuania. The project is managed from our Munich office in Bavaria. There we have a few people who take care of the user interface design, product management, and software architecture of the swoodoo project. Our development team of more than 10 developers is located in Kaunas, Lithuania. The development in Lithuania is not a usual offshoring because we founded our own company there. The advantage of running our own team is vital compared to pure contractor work, which is widespread in the IT industry. When you have such a small team, the team spirit and dedication to the project become extremely important.

Over the last few years, our team has gradually grown from 4 to 13 members. This slow increase has helped us in integrating new members efficiently. Now let's go back in history and learn more about the evolution of swoodoo.

EVOLUTION: ONLY THE STRONG SURVIVE

Back in 2003, the first low-cost carriers showed up with really cheap flight offers. In those days, there was no simple way to find the best deals, besides browsing the websites of the low-cost airlines. You had to manually try many departure and return date combinations to find the cheapest flights. The swoodoo founders came up with an idea of creating a database with all the flight prices of the low-cost carriers. Having such a database would provide grounds for building a very fast flight search engine with many more search options than any other search engine at that time. A totally new experience of searching for the cheapest flights without entering an exact departure date or inputting departure and destination airports would come true. For instance, searching for the cheapest flights from Germany to Asia at any time within a one-year date range would be a piece of cake. Therefore, we decided to start the project and give it a try.

In our former company, we had a few Java developers who were running out of work, so we asked them to try to screen scrape the flight prices from several low-cost airline websites. The team decided to build a Java desktop application that parses flight information from HTML pages. The project was not yet seriously driven by management, and neither agile development nor test-driven development was involved. Nevertheless, we realized that the potential of such an application was enormous, so we decided to carry on.

One year later, in 2004, we realized that the airlines might not be amused by massive amounts of requests coming from a single system and producing a load on their websites. To avoid such problems, the decision was made to refactor the whole application and use a peer-to-peer architecture. So we developed a C++ ActiveX component for the Internet Explorer browser, which could be downloaded and installed from our website. When a user initiated a flight search request, the ActiveX component sent a request to our central Java server, which distributed tasks to fetch flight data from airline websites to all our Internet Explorer users out there. The gathered flight data was sent back to the Java server, which stored it into a PostgreSQL database for later reuse and sent the data to the Internet Explorer user who had initiated the request. Besides using C++ and moving the parsing of airline websites from the server side to the client side, that approach was similar to the previous one.

The refactoring to ActiveX was hard—kind of like Sisyphus's work from the old Greek story. There were no unit tests for the existing code base, so safe refactoring appeared to be simply impossible. We had to learn it the hard way. If you try to do a big system refactoring without tests, you can expect many bugs and problems, all of which results in a poor software quality and broken functionality. During that refactoring phase, our management frequently changed feature requirements, which made our life even more complicated. All that led to a situation where nearly all our available manpower was eaten by maintenance and bug-fixing tasks. After every change, bugs occurred in various places in the system and the overall quality dropped. That was very annoying for the management and frustrating for the developers.

In the end, we made the ActiveX approach work. Unfortunately, we encountered new problems. We used XSLT for parsing HTML pages from airline websites. The maintenance of XSL stylesheets was lots of work because they were really complex and airline websites changed their layouts frequently.

The following code is an excerpt of the XSLT used to scrape the Ryanair website in 2003:

```
<xsl:template match="form">
<xsl:if
    test="contains(table[1]/tr/td/table/tr/td,'Going Out')">
    <flight>
        <xsl:variable
            name="out"
            select="table[1]/tr[2]/td/table/tr"/>
        <xsl:variable
            name="outflight"
            select="normalize-space(
                substring-after($out/td[3],'Flight  ')
            )"/>
        <price>
            <xsl:value-of
                select="table[3]/tr[3]/td/table/tr[2]/td/table/tr[1]/td[4]"/>
        </price>
        <oneway airline="ryanair" flightnumber="{$outflight}">
            <xsl:call-template name="parse-way">
                <xsl:with-param name="p" select="$out"/>
            </xsl:call-template>
        </oneway>
        <xsl:if
            test="contains(table[2]/tr/td/table/tr/td,'Coming Back')">
        <xsl:variable
            name="in"
            select="table[2]/tr[2]/td/table/tr"/>
        <xsl:variable
            name="inflight"
            select="normalize-space(
                substring-after($in/td[3],'Flight  ')
            )"/>
        <backway airline="ryanair" flightnumber="{$inflight}">
            <xsl:call-template name="parse-way">
            <xsl:with-param name="p" select="$in"/>
            </xsl:call-template>
        </backway>
        </xsl:if>
    </flight>
</xsl:if>
</xsl:template>
```

Furthermore, the flight data quality in the database was linearly proportionate to the number of online users, because our central server could send tasks to fetch flights only to the online users. Without having some critical number of users, the flight data quality suffered. It became clear that we needed to take another step in the evolution of swoodoo. As you can see, the term *evolution* definitely suits the swoodoo project!

It was clear that we had to change not only the software architecture but also our project management and development processes. After a long discussion, we decided to introduce Extreme Programming (XP) methodology. We harnessed continuous integration, test-driven development

(TDD) practices and all the fancy agile stuff that helps to develop good quality software. The whole system was rewritten almost from scratch. We threw away C++ as the language for our screen scrapers in favor of PHP, but we left Java for the central controlling engine. The very first publicly available version of the swoodoo system consisted of the following components:

➤ A frontend website, written in PHP and providing users with a GUI to the flight search engine. As the Zend Framework was not born yet, we had to use some other framework for the website. We chose our own framework, which was also used by the online shopping cart solution OXID eShop. Like the Zend Framework MVC library, that framework was—and still is—based on MVC design pattern and used Smarty as a template engine. We had extremely good feature coverage by Selenium acceptance tests. Unlike the acceptance tests, our class level functionality was not fully unit-tested. This happened for historical reasons. Many website parts had not been written from scratch, but were reused from our old website. Unit tests could be written only for truly isolated or loosely coupled classes, but at that time some of our website components were still showing symptoms of the Big Ball of Mud. We kept refactoring such parts and writing unit tests for them. We regularly reviewed Xdebug reports on code coverage and were constantly increasing the unit test coverage. Because of the Selenium tests, all our refactoring changes became safe, even though the swoodoo build time on our integration server took almost half an hour. If any internal change broke a previously defined requirement, the integration server let us know about it immediately. That feeling of safety gave our team a lot of confidence and comfort.

➤ A database server, a decent server running MySQL.

➤ The components that gathered flight data were called *agents*. Those modules imported flight data using different approaches for each airline. Some airlines were offering exports by csv or xml, others needed to be screen scraped. Unfortunately, for the latter it was either impossible to write good automatic tests or, if it was possible, then those tests would not have been worth the effort.

➤ Our engine was called *LCA* (Low Cost Airline) Engine. It was written in Java using the JBoss application server and could be considered as the brain of swoodoo. The engine generated tasks for each airline agent, defined the import timeframes, and was responsible for gathering flight data from the agents and importing it into the flight database. In the swoodoo Java world we wrote unit tests using JUnit.

➤ Our aggregation server was also built in Java. Its major job was to read all the imported flights into a local database and aggregate the flight data every six hours. The aggregation resulted in so-called summary tables, which contained the information about the cheapest routes, prices, and airlines on every region level, e.g. the cheapest flights from Munich, Bavaria, Germany, Western Europe, Europe, etc. That information was needed for our "PowerSearch," and it enabled us to search through millions of flight records in a fraction of a second.

The system served us successfully for nearly two years, but then we slowly began running into problems and hitting the limits of our architecture. In the end, we realized that once again we had to start drastic changes. Even though we were heavily using TDD and the code coverage was over 90%, we were stuck because our architecture would not allow us to further extend the software. The implementation of new features started to take too long as rather small changes rippled through the whole system. Many components were interconnected too closely. The GUI accessed the database directly so a change on the database side usually had an impact on the GUI. Maintenance costs kept increasing and it became obvious that we would soon reach a dead end. Also with time success came and this led to new challenges, the most important of which was scaling. The number of swoodoo users, as well as the traffic, kept increasing. As our architecture was more or less monolithic, we had difficulties in scaling the system.

Et voilà—evolution kicked in and another swoodoo refactoring started. And there we could benefit a lot from our test driven development. As we had tests for nearly everything, we could refactor safely and mercilessly. The tests screamed immediately if we broke any functionality. To solve the maintenance and scaling problems we decided to utilize a service-oriented architecture.

The database was refactored into a flight server—a standalone Java server with multiple sharded MySQL databases in the backend. The flight server communicated with the rest of the system using a self-made TCP/IP protocol. The aggregation server was replaced by PHP processes which were doing the aggregation job on a continuous basis. Our front end website went the Zend Framework way, still using Smarty, and the Java engine was refactored into separate components, called "AI3," which—to reflect our evolution over the last years—means Airline Information System 3rd Generation.

During the last six years swoodoo technologies and architecture have frequently changed. Besides massive changes due to market needs, we have added a lot of new functionality and become the market leaders in the German-speaking countries: a true love story for Extreme Programming and test-driven development. Without TDD, now we would most probably be among the market outsiders, as we would have wasted our energy on maintenance and bug fixing instead of inventing new cool features. Evolution is a natural, inevitable companion of any long-term software project. Just get it under control, and take time not only for adding new features, but also for refactoring your software to keep it clean of any hacks.

Don't allow your software to evolve into a Frankenstein. It is worth it to remember that refactoring is not rebuilding from scratch. Rebuilding usually takes too much time, which you most likely never get from your management.

The next sections will reveal the techniques, that enabled us to refactor successfully so often and helped to maintain good software quality.

How We Reached the eXtreme Side

The introduction of Extreme Programming into the swoodoo team was an interesting experience for all of us. After management decided and confirmed that swoodoo had to go the XP way, our development team leader stayed locked up in a room with all our developers (at that time there were five of them) for two days to give an initial introduction into XP and have a discussion within the team about how we should proceed. XP requires a change in mindset, and demands the voluntary involvement, initiative, and commitment of all team members. So it was absolutely necessary to get the approval of everyone.

A few developers, who heard words like *agile*, *XP*, and *automatic tests* for the first time in their lives, looked reserved and a bit suspicious. Others, who already knew something about TDD and unit tests, were ready for a change.

They had been exhausted by fixing recurring bugs and quite enthusiastically agreed to XP. In the end, everybody agreed to go the XP way. swoodoo's journey on the eXtreme side of the road started, and it seems like it is never going to end.

Rome was not built in a day, and the same is valid for switching into XP. It is a process of constant self-improving. Some practices, like TDD, need a while until they are fully understood and accepted. Developers who are not prepared for this methodology often respond with something like: "Writing tests before code? What's this? Noooo, I write code first and then, if there is some time left, I add tests." I've forgotten how many times I heard that song. Most often this song ends with clumsy code, additional obsolete functionality, and miserable or absent tests, and it requires a gentle (or not so gentle) kick in the rear and writing everything from scratch. Actually, we experienced that practicing the TDD mantra—"Red. Green. Refactor."—is one of the most difficult habits in the world. The temptation to write code first is so difficult to resist that we are still trying to conquer it. There are cases when TDD does not pay off or does not make sense. For example, writing Selenium tests for website pages that are not yet created is senseless, because you don't know yet the names and structure of HTML elements. Thus, the xpath locators can't be used; you cannot always use just id locators! But if you need to make a change in an existing web page, then TDD with Selenium works like a charm! One developer writes tests and another implements requested functionality until the tests are passed!

Let's have a deeper look into the tools we use to utilize test-driven development. We use PHPUnit when we write unit and integration tests for our PHP components. Selenium tests are also written in PHP, using the PHP driver for Selenium RC, which is a part of the PHPUnit framework. Because our backend engine, AI3, is written in Java, we write Java tests using JUnit. Last but not least, there is Crosscheck, a unit testing tool for JavaScript that emulates the most common browsers. Because swoodoo heavily uses JavaScript, Crosscheck has proven to be a great help in testing our JavaScript code.

Luckily, all these testing frameworks generate test reports in similar formats. Our continuous integration server runs CruiseControl, which can merge test reports from these different testing frameworks and present a uniform test report for each swoodoo system build.

Actually, we do not use a standalone version of CruiseControl. We have installed a whole set of tools that comes with Buildix on a ready-to-use Ubuntu-based live CD. Buildix helped us to introduce agile methods into our project. Besides CruiseControl, Buildix includes Subversion, a version control system, and Trac, a Python-based bugtracker and wiki. Trac integrates well with CruiseControl and Subversion. All our internal project information, concepts, and specifications are in Trac wiki. Trac bugtracker has a highly customizable workflow and permission system. After having customized it to our needs, we use Trac bugtracker not only for bug handling. It has become our project management tool, which we use for planning of new features or tasks and organizing them into iterations and milestones.

For the first few years, we customized CruiseControl ourselves, which is not easy. The configuration is a bit tricky, and there are many pitfalls when you start integrating other tools for copy-and-paste detection, coding standard rules, and so on. Luckily, phpUnderControl is available now, which saves us lots of time.

One tool is really worth mentioning: PHP_CodeSniffer. This small, handy tool checks whether all the developers adhere to the defined coding standard. We use a subset of the Zend Framework coding standard and adopted PHP_CodeSniffer according to our rules. PHP_CodeSniffer is usually run in CruiseControl during the build time. Therefore, if you commit a piece of code that violates the standards, you do break the build. We take a broken build very seriously, so such incidents make the whole team nervous. Therefore, we added PHP_CodeSniffer into a Subversion pre-commit hook. Now it is simply impossible to commit any piece of code that is not compliant with our coding standards.

We do have a focus on naming classes and methods consistently. It is very important to choose meaningful names for classes and methods, so everyone can understand their purpose, which increases code readability and saves time. Unfortunately, there is no existing efficient tool to enforce meaningful names—at least not yet. Using PHP_CodeSniffer rules is not a good idea, because they are too dumb for this.

Test-driven development helped us kill another bad developer habit: adding functionality that was not asked for by management. Developers tend to think too much about the future and to implement additional fancy features to make code "more extendable" and "more scalable": They may say "I also additionally implemented sorting. I am sure you will need it soon," even though we don't need it now or in the near future. So you have wasted time on some feature that has never been requested. Remember YAGNI! (You Ain't Gonna Need It). KISS! (Keep It Simple Stupid). When tests must be written first, the desire to implement additional functionality is reduced to a minimum immediately. Who wants to write tests for a feature that is not needed yet? You? None from our team, for sure!

Currently, our team is using almost all XP practices with just a few exceptions, which we discuss later. The whole team sits in one large room. It was not so easy to find the right place where we could stuff 11 developers inside and give them enough space. We have also borrowed some practices from Scrum, another agile flavor, the most important of which is daily stand-up meetings. Every morning at 9:30 the team starts the day with an obligatory stand-up meeting. The guys really had to stand in the first years. But swoodoo has gone through evolution, and that evolution has made an impact on our developers as well. Most probably some of them have grown old, and it has become too tough to stand in the morning; every now and then someone is sitting. (Such small annoyances are not welcome in swoodoo, but are not punished.) These stand-up meetings usually take around 10 minutes and developers report their task status, expose encountered problems, and share their plans for today. These standard questions should be asked in such a stand-up meeting: What did you do yesterday? Are there any showstoppers? What do you plan to do today? It may sound obvious, but you need to make sure the team understands things such as these:

➤ Leaving early or coming in late is important information to all your colleagues.

➤ Having trouble with your PC or Mac is a showstopper as well and also must be mentioned.

➤ Feeling sick is also important, and it does not make much sense to work with a headache. You will only add bugs rather than fix them.

Exposing encountered problems sounds easy, but it is not. It is not so easy for juniors to speak up about their problems. The word *courage* is often mentioned in Extreme Programming and is exactly what is needed in these situations. Team members need to communicate and say what they think, even if management or co-workers do not like to hear the truth. It took a while until everyone on our team felt comfortable to speak openly without fearing punishment, but in the end we succeeded.

Our management once asked for a brand new "absolutely small" feature—to filter flights by the time of day: morning, afternoon, evening. They thought it would be just a "small change" and expected it to take no longer than two days. Our team checked what changes this "small" feature implied. Turns out, it was a few serious changes in the database, summary table, and algorithms, and required adjusting all existing queries to the flight summary database. Finally, our developers said that this feature was worth 12 story points and that there was no way it could be done in two days. The swoodoo developers had the courage to say that the expectations of management were unrealistic. Management agreed and got the feature after a week.

It is a general rule that management tends to shrink estimates, while developers tend to overestimate. The key to mutual understanding is that management should trust developers' estimations and developers should stop overestimating.

Developers must not be punished for wrong estimates, and with time their estimates are going to improve. If a team member realizes that he underestimated a feature, he should have the courage to inform management immediately and should not keep waiting until the deadline comes and some marketing campaign, carefully planned by the management, is ruined.

It may sound easy, but it was a long time before we reached the current understanding between the team and the management. A few key practices helped us more than others.

AND WHILE WE ARE WORKING...

The planning and proper estimation of new features is one of the most difficult tasks for developers. Extreme Programming helps here with the planning game.

Our team consists of more than 10 developers, which is already a bit too much for everyone to take part in each planning game. Our whole team is split into several sub-teams that are responsible for certain areas: Java server-side, frontend, agents. All new features and requirement changes are estimated by sub-team leaders. Other sub-team members provide their own estimations only if the sub-team leader feels uncertain. Most often, simpler stories are estimated by a sub-team leader, and for more complex user stories, he consults his sub-team or even other sub-teams. This is a clear violation of the Extreme Programming process defined in the books, but it works better for us and saves us lots of time and discussions.

The planning of new features involves lots of communication. The team gets feature requirements from the Chief Technology Officer (CTO), who acts as a customer. For the planning of large-scale features, which have a big impact on the whole system, we use meetings, via Skype or face to face, where our CTO presents to the team leaders what management expects. After it becomes clear what management *wants*, we think about *how* we can implement it. The implementation concepts are initiated by the team leaders with assistance from other team members. While discussing the architecture or workflows, we often write and draw on two big whiteboards in our room. These whiteboards are probably the most important tool we use in our processes. If you do not have any yet, think about getting some! Having a few large whiteboards helps to build a better mutual understanding about the problems or concepts during discussions.

After the implementation concept is finished and approved by the CTO, the estimation phase starts. In some cases, feature requests are too complex to be estimated easily. Then we split user stories into smaller parts until the team feels confident enough and can estimate the work that needs to be done. If developers are still very uncertain about their estimates, then we create a prototype "spike solution," which usually clears our open questions. This kicks in especially if we have to solve technically complex problems, when we are not sure whether the chosen approach delivers the result we need. Estimations are done in *story points*, the base for all estimations in Extreme Programming. One story point is equal to one ideal man day—8 hours—when you are not disturbed and are able to concentrate on your task entirely. It does not include time spent on going for a smoke. The fact that you had too much beer the night before and now feel a bit dizzy is not factored into your ideal man day either. Luckily, this happens rarely in our team.

According to XP, each user story must be given an average value of all team members' estimates. So when a sub-team leader estimates a task himself, he tries to guess the average value of estimates of all his sub-team members. Again, we violate the theory. I would not suggest that you go this way unless your team has worked together for years like ours. In the beginning, it is very wise to stick to the rules, and then later adapt the rules to fit your project and needs better.

We do follow a simple rule to split a user story into smaller tasks. If a single task is above two story points, then it could be a sign that the developer does not fully understand the task and just gives a high number to be on the safe side. If the task is being estimated by all sub-team members and we get very different estimates, we discuss until the difference between estimates becomes reasonable.

The factor between a story point and a real day is called *velocity*. If we look up the definition in the XP books, velocity should keep more or less constant as long as we do not change the team size or exchange members. Unfortunately for us, it turns out that the velocity changes quite often, so we can't use it for iteration planning. When we realized this, we were a bit puzzled and tried to identify the reasons:

➤ The tasks that are not finished are moved into the next iteration. This distorts the measurement of the velocity. A possible solution could be to split the tasks into smaller pieces.

➤ It might be that not every activity is tracked. We could address this by reviewing the current iteration plan more frequently and improving the tracking of the actual work done.

➤ It is quite tricky to trust velocity if some team members go on holiday or are absent for some other reason.

But we are satisfied with the output of the team, so we've decided that we will leave the theory behind and not worry about this too much. Maybe someday we will address this issue. Our sub-team leaders know how many story points they can assign to every single team member per iteration, so we do not suffer from the missing constant velocity.

Based on the estimates and priorities given by management, tasks are assigned to the next iteration. Iteration planning is done by the sub-team leaders after a short talk about priorities with the CTO. Each iteration runs for two weeks, and with rare exceptions, it results in a deployment on the production servers.

Usually, we deploy even more frequently, as often as several times in a week. Some swoodoo applications, like agents, need to be modified and deployed several times a day!

Even though the team gets many interruptions through the insertion of ASAP tasks by management, we handle them without chaos. We leave some time buffer in each iteration for such tasks. If there are fewer ASAP tasks, then on the second part of the iteration, we just add more tasks to the iteration from the release backlog. Most often such interruptions are absorbed by the sub-team leaders, avoiding disturbing other team members. The sub-team leaders analyze these ASAP requirements. If these tasks take little time, they do them themselves. By doing so, we make sure the rest of the team is not disturbed and can focus on continuously adding new features and improving our system. If ASAP tasks take longer, then the sub-team leaders assign such tasks to other team members. We accept this as a normal real-life situation, and we often change the plan even for the current iteration that is in progress.

We organize new features and tasks into milestones. These milestones are major releases with a brand new functionality and tools for our users. Often they come along with some press releases that put pressure on us, because the marketing department creates a fixed plan regarding when and how to release the information to the public.

Working on complex tasks leads directly to pair programming. This key XP technique most likely sounds weird to many programmers. The idea of sitting together with one keyboard and developing is often rejected, as it was on the swoodoo team. In theory, pair programming should always be done to make sure that every team member knows all about other areas. If you regularly rotate developers between all areas of your code base, they should become versatile and should be able to work in any area. Furthermore, the number of bugs should decrease also because four eyes see more than two eyes. In swoodoo, pairing is used only on complex tasks and difficult bug fixing, for a few hours up to a maximum of one or two days. But because we do often get difficult tasks, we pair frequently. Our approach helps developers to find solutions for complex problems and, on the other hand, does not reduce the development speed too much.

To show how pair programming can be applied in real-life situations, let's see how we used pair programming in the past. Let's say we get a new team member who is not familiar with test-driven development. Therefore, an experienced developer teams up with him and explains the essence of TDD, the usage of mocks and why we need them. Together, they implement a few tasks. After a while, the new member can continue on his own.

Another example, which is not fully pair programming, is the development of new GUI functionality. Two developers sit together and discuss the functionality they need to implement, and then they split up. The first one is developing the needed functionality, and the other one is simultaneously writing Selenium tests. It is quite interesting that such paired work improves the mood of the team, as the one who is creating tests really loves to gently bash the developer working on the code if he fails to implement it correctly.

All you XP fans out there, hold your horses. We are aware of the theory that says development speed does not suffer because of pair programming. However, pairing for the whole day is really exhausting. It is lots of hard work and requires constant communication, and not all developers are extroverts. Too much communication is also tiresome, at least for some of them. After six hours of pairing up, you are brain dead. You miss usual short breaks that help your brain to recover, like going for a smoke, calling your family to make sure they don't forget you, or catching up with the latest blogs. Avoiding the ineffective work when One Guy Is Behind the Wheel and Another Guy Is Sleeping on the Back Seat is also quite hard.

Therefore, having discussed all pros and cons of pair programming, we decided not to use pair developing all the time.

In the swoodoo team, we take the term *collective code ownership* seriously. Every developer has to feel responsible for each part of the system. Any developer is welcome to refactor and improve modules written by other developers. If a developer, while adding a new feature, encounters some stinky code, he is encouraged to take time to make it clean, even if an initial feature estimation must be increased. We do not hear phrases like "Why did you change my code?! It might not have been perfect, but it worked!" or "Don't touch this module! Only I can do changes here!" It is not unusual for a Java expert to implement a feature in the PHP part of the code, or for the PHP guy to write deployment scripts in Ruby. If there is any need for help, any team member can be assigned to any part of the system. We have succeeded in making them feel responsible for the success of the overall project, not just the code part they are working in. We do not have only DBAs or only Java developers. Our developers have broad skills, but they also are experts in narrow fields, be it Java or PHP, and can play many roles. Finally, many of the swoodoo team members have evolved into all-arounders, who can work in all parts of our distributed system. It has taken us a long time to reach this point. In most teams, developers tend to keep their fingers in "their" source code; Java developers especially are often a bit proud about their skills and definitely hesitate before switching over to PHP. If you want your team to share their experience and to be curious about other areas, you need to make sure that everybody in the team is feeling comfortable and safe. The key factors are trust and courage. If you achieve that, every team member trusts their co-workers, management has the courage to jump into new unknown areas, and your team is definitely moving in the right direction.

We have created an environment where people are encouraged to share code and become generalizing specialists. We deliberately do not hire people who want to work only in a narrow niche, be it database or EJB. We have pushed collective code ownership by giving the same developer tasks in different modules, by encouraging him to refactor the stinky code parts, and not blaming him for making mistakes in areas that are new for him. Periodic rotation of the support phone, to which our Nagios monitoring system sends alarm e-mails, also has pushed people to dig into all parts of the system.

I once asked one of our Java developers why he didn't have any problems developing in PHP. His answer was quite funny, but it had lots of truth in it. He said, "Well, I do not know PHP well enough, so I can only help other PHP guys. But even if I don't know much about PHP internals, there are so many tests and CruiseControl, so I simply change and add my code and see what happens. It makes my life quite easy. And I can always ask my PHP colleagues for help if I need it."

Extreme Programming has a term called *embracing change*. All developers should happily welcome any new wish or changes coming from management. In reality, it is often difficult to maintain high morale if the work you did last week needs to be changed over and over again. In our case, the customer is in-house; we maintain our own platform and product. Therefore, we are responsible for the success ourselves. The management responds to market changes quite fast, which leads to frequent feature changes, some of them quite heavy.

It is usually a nasty situation when management has to change or remove the functionality that was developed recently. Developers might get the feeling that their work is being wasted. Such situations occur in every company, but in swoodoo we have them more often due to our fast response to market changes.

The key to avoiding bad feelings and misunderstandings is communication. Our management communicates the reasons for such changes and takes care that the team understands why these changes happen or why they cannot be avoided.

I asked my team why they do not freak out about all these constant changes. They told me they do not care so much about changes for the following reasons:

➤   Resisting improving a feature makes no sense because that isn't good for the users of our service. So if management tells us to change it due to user demand, why shouldn't we like it?

➤   We usually do not work overtime due to such changes, and management gives us additional time for implementing them. This helps us stay cool.

➤   Life is full of changes, so why should we care about small changes in our project?

This might sound a bit funny, but again, there is lots of truth in it. The team is dedicated to the overall success and is not stuck on a specific technology or functionality.

By the way, we do release all the metrics about our site to the developers, including sales figures, so they get instant feedback if their system runs smoothly and is successful or not. This helps even if the management has to deal with inquiries about bonuses or salary increases, based on the argument of our constant success and the increasing number of sales.

Let's get back to the changes. After a change has been done, the developers expect to get fast feedback on whether the feature has been implemented correctly. They get the first feedback from the integration server, which builds the whole application after each commit, runs tests, and informs whether the change has ruined anything. This first feedback should as fast as possible, so we try to keep our integration time at an acceptable level. The second feedback is given by the sub-team leaders. And finally, the feedback comes from the customer. As I said earlier, the swoodoo customer is our CTO, who works as a proxy between the developer team and the rest of management. For getting fast feedback from the customer, we strive to deploy as frequently as possible. The more frequently we deploy on the staging server, the earlier we can get feedback from management. All changes are visible on the staging system, which can be accessed from the outside world, but it is password-protected. Usually, after really testing the feature it requested, management asks for some improvements or even totally changes feature requirements.

Until now we have been more or less keeping to the rules of Extreme Programming. But there is one rule that we violate quite often—sustainable pace. Usually we work 40 to 45 hours a week on average, like most developers around the world. But sometimes it gets a bit stressful and things change. It sometimes happened that we had a few releases with absolutely fixed release dates. We got important feedback from management, and they insisted on adding new feature changes into those releases. And guess what happens if the release date and team size are fixed, but the scope increases? Correct, working overtime. We try hard to avoid this, because it sucks the motivation out of the team, but sometimes it is simply impossible.

THE ART OF EVOLUTION

As I mentioned in the introduction to this chapter, since its birth, swoodoo has been under constant refactoring. We have done at least four major refactorings during which we completely changed our technology and software architecture. This is a real case of a software evolution—a software project evolves because of the changes in requirements and market environment.

Before we look deeper into the techniques we used to make our refactorings successful, you might be interested in why we did not rewrite swoodoo from scratch, but insisted on the refactoring approach. There are a few very good reasons why refactoring should be used instead of rewriting, even though developers love to rewrite from scratch, because writing new code is more fun and easier than reading the old one.

First, your old code base most probably has been tested and bug-fixed, either by you or at least by your customers. During rewriting, you introduce new bugs and again you have to deal with the problems you have already solved. Second, and most important, rewriting takes longer than refactoring. There are a few good examples from history that prove these statements. Remember

Netscape 6, dBase for Windows, and Quattro Pro? These applications went for rewriting whereas their competitors (such as Excel) went for refactoring. The competitors were faster, so the market decision was clear.

Let's look what rules helped us to survive this evolution madness. First, the key to success is simplicity. Keep it simple, stupid, or KISS. Every developer should have a tattoo with this mantra on his fingers. It should help to write better code and might also assist in the pub after the day's work has been done and committed. Sound funny? It isn't. Obeying the KISS mantra is really important and, believe me, it's not easy. It is much easier to invent a complex framework, a nested class hierarchy, and some all-in-one base class than implement a straightforward, simple, and robust piece of code that's exactly what you need. Besides, following these very basic rules, we have benefited from our continuous integration server. There is a direct correlation between using continuous integration and a simple architecture. If developers commit frequently (at least once a day) and your build is "green" most of the time, this is a good sign that your architecture is simple and clean enough.

How does it work? Well, imagine yourself as a developer who wants to commit code that does not break the build. So your code must conform to the defined coding standards and your tests must run and not kill any functionality from others. Couple this with frequent commits, and you can understand that it is simply impossible to create heavyweight, complex architectures in a few hours. It forces your team to write small functions, which is fundamental for having good tests.

While introducing frequent commits, you might experience many discussions. Developers may argue that they can't work like this, or they may keep silent and simply not commit every few days, because they believe this frequent commit requirement is stupid. It is not. It works and definitely leads to better and shorter code, which does what it should do and not more. You need to keep an eye on the commit frequency in the beginning, because you may detect some guys who commit too seldom and most probably build something too complex. Talk to them, help them to think simpler and next time they will commit more frequently.

Doesn't this sound logical and promising? It does. But why do we still find developers who are arguing with you about this? Well, various reasons can explain creating a complex code where it is not needed, and we discuss these reasons for such over-engineering in the following sections.

Lack of Experience

Inexperienced developers tend to create much more complex solutions than needed. They may want to establish themselves as smart developers and tend to use all design patterns or language features available. Or they might copy some idea from another framework, but miss the context of their current problem. You need experience to start appreciating the value of the KISS principle.

The following example illustrates the use of class constants where they are not necessary at all:

```
class Currency_Converter
{
    const CURRENCY_FROM_SQL_PARAMETER = 'currencyfrom';
    const CURRENCY_TO_SQL_PARAMETER = 'currencyto';
    const XRATES_FIELD_NAME = 'xrate';
    const XRATES_SELECT_STATEMENT =
        'SELECT xrate
        FROM xrates
```

```
    WHERE currencyfrom = :currencyfrom
    AND currencyto = :currencyto';
// ...
/**
* Get conversion rate. Take from db or from private property
* if $fromCurrency-$toCurrency was already requested before
*
* @param string $fromCurrency three-letter currency code to
* convert from
* @param string $toCurrency three-letter currency code to
* convert to
*
* @return string
* @throws Swoodoo_Exception if conversion xrate not found
* in database
*/
private function
    _getConversionRate($fromCurrency, $toCurrency)
{
    if ($fromCurrency == $toCurrency) {
        return 1;
    }
    $result = $this->_db->select(
        self::XRATES_SELECT_STATEMENT,
            array(
                self::CURRENCY_FROM_SQL_PARAMETER => $fromCurrency,
                self::CURRENCY_TO_SQL_PARAMETER => $toCurrency
            )
    );
    if (!$result) {
        throw new Swoodoo_Exception(
            "Unable convert to {$toCurrency}",
            Swoodoo_IException::VALIDATOR_PARAMETERS_INVALID
        );
    }
    $conversionRate = $result[0][self::XRATES_FIELD_NAME];
    return $conversionRate;
}
}
```

As you can see, our developer added the database table field names and even a full SQL statement into class constants. He probably thought about how to make renaming the table fields easier. You know, just change the constants and that's it. But he broke two principles at once: YAGNI and KISS. He broke YAGNI (You Ain't Gonna Need It) by doing the preparations for some future changes that may never be needed. He violated KISS by making the code more complicated than needed. Because these table fields were used only in that particular class, throwing out those constants would have made the code simpler and shorter, even without making future renaming of table fields more difficult.

The Java-developer-coding-in-PHP Phenomenon

If you ask a Java developer to code in PHP, you most likely get a quite complex class structure, with each class having a minimum of two abstract classes, a few interfaces, and at least one factory.

A year ago, we decided to set up automatic monitoring of the swoodoo servers. We chose Nagios as a monitoring tool. Nagios has plenty of ready-to-use plugins, but we also needed some custom plugins, which can be written in PHP. At that time, our PHP developers were overloaded with work, so our Java developers volunteered to write Nagios plugins in PHP. And they did it successfully. Custom Nagios plugins worked correctly and had good unit test coverage. But after poking my nose into the source, I found interesting stuff up there. They needed some global configuration settings, and they implemented it, as shown in the following code:

```php
class Lib_Config
{
    /**
     * a single config data member
     * @var Config
     */
    private static $_instance;
    /**
     * static getter of single object instance
     *
     * @return Config itself single object
     */
    public static function getInstance()
    {
        if (self::$_instance == null) {
            self::$_instance = new Lib_Config();
        }
        return self::$_instance;
    }
    /**
     * Get configuration parameter value
     *
     * @param string $parameterName name of the parameter
     * @return mixed a config parameter
     */
    public function getConfigParameter($parameterName)
    {
        $config = Zend_Registry::get('config');
        return isset($config[$parameterName]) ?
        $config[$parameterName] :
        null;
    }
    /**
     * Set configuration parameter value
     *
     * @param string $parameterName name of parameter
     * @param mixed $paramValue value to set
     * @return null
     */
    public function
    setConfigParameter($parameterName, $paramValue)
    {
        $config = Zend_Registry::get('config');
        $config[$parameterName] = $paramValue;
        Zend_Registry::set('config', $config);
```

```
        }
    }
    class Lib_ConfigFactory
    {
        /**
        * configuration object
        * @var Config
        */
        private static $_config;
        /**
        * getter of Configuration singleton object.
        *
        * @return Config a config single object
        */
        public static function getConfiguration()
        {
            if (self::$_config == null) {
                self::$_config = Lib_Config::getInstance();
            }
            return self::$_config;
        }
    }
```

As you can see, they wrapped `Zend_Registry` into `Lib_Config` class, which is also a singleton. `Lib_Config` class did not add any new functionality compared with `Zend_Registry`; it simply delegated calls to `Zend_Registry`. Don't ask me where the win is, because I can't help here. So what else is missing for a solid solution? Ah, we need a factory! And here it was: `Lib_ConfigFactory` class. `Lib_ConfigFactory` was also a singleton with a static getter method to access the `Lib_Config` instance.

Configuration worked perfectly and looked solid, but it was heavily over-engineered. I laughed for two days after I found that. It was a good lesson for us. If you need to switch from a static programming language such as Java to a dynamic language such as PHP, you need to switch your way of thinking and habits as well. Stop thinking in Java when you code in PHP! Why not simply use `Zend_Registry` without any wrappers or factories? Life can be much simpler: You throw out `Lib_Config`, get rid of that factory, and end up with still the same functionality, but with fewer lines of code and less complexity. That was what we finally did.

The Nobody-but-me-understands-my-code Developer

The description says it all—a very basic and brutal method to save your working place. But it never works. Fortunately, we do not have such developers in swoodoo. Well, not anymore....

Keeping your code simple is one side of the medal. On the other side, "Never Add Functionality Early" is written. Do not implement what you do not need now. This is more or less coupled with KISS. An average developer tends to solve problems that haven't yet been identified.

If the implementation of your features takes longer than estimated, you may find that your developers are trying to implement some flexible and optimized structure, which should help them later when management asks for further changes. You need to train your team and co-workers to stop preparing for the far future. The far future is uncertain and guesses may be wrong, and then your precious, carefully designed extensibility is nothing but an over-engineered monument to your wasted time.

Here's an example of how this helps in evolving your software. In the beginning, we had only a few Selenium acceptance tests, and it took only a few minutes to run them all. The number of Selenium tests kept growing, so the whole build time kept increasing as well. But we did not start to optimize our tests until one day we ended up with the tests running almost one hour. We could not call this one-hour build "instant feedback" anymore, and it started to irritate us. So we investigated a bit and found that the loading of the database fixtures in the test cases' `setup()` and `teardown()` methods took a huge amount of time. At that time, PHPUnit still did not have suite-level setup/teardown methods. But JUnit already had. So we just patched our PHPUnit: We added suite-level setup and teardown methods and immediately reduced build time by half. Sound simple? It was! We could have implemented this feature earlier, but we didn't care about optimization until performance became a problem.

We turn a blind eye toward future requirements and extra flexibility, and we leave optimization for the last moment. Working through this has helped us in the last years, and we now focus on the real needs. Leaving optimization for the last step is okay in most cases. Premature optimization is considered to be an anti-pattern in terms of performance. (For a list of performance anti-patterns, visit http://highscalability.com/blog/2009/4/5/performance-anti-pattern.html.) In rare cases, you need to think about performance in advance. There is a difference between developing a small website with 1,000 users per day and setting up a news portal with 10 million users per day. You probably would end up with a different architecture for each case. But optimization in the final step is not going to help you to scale a small website by 10,000 times. You need to know about your performance needs and then choose the right architecture from the outset. Otherwise, you may simply fail to optimize enough.

You might be wondering when we are going to talk about the evolution of swoodoo. Well, we have done it already. Keeping things simple, using spike solutions frequently, and launching small releases frequently is exactly what the evolution is about. Changes can be small and minor, but keep updating your live system often. The correct term could be *incremental changes*, which is much better than monster milestones, released once or twice a year.

Sometimes you can't avoid a larger milestone because you need to make changes in the core parts of your systems, but you need to finish everything on schedule and thus can't deploy frequently. These milestones are really hard to cope with. They suck lots of energy and time out of the team because some members are still working and finalizing the milestone while others who want to go on cannot because the functionality they need has not been deployed yet. We try hard to evolve our system step by step and avoid big upfront designs.

And evolving design? Here is an example. Recently, we deployed a new release of swoodoo on our live servers, which included a flight duration feature. This feature has been missing for a long time and our users were asking for it quite often. Unfortunately, this isn't as easy as it sounds because many of our partners do not give us the duration or (even worse) make lots of mistakes. Therefore, we decided to calculate the duration ourselves, which is quite nasty because you need to deal with many different time zones. This flight duration feature hits all our systems. Flight duration must be calculated, stored in the database, displayed in swoodoo website and Open API versions, and so on.

We started by adding the fields in our database system and the flight server and deployed this. Then we introduced a new version of our TCP/IP-based protocol between the flight server and the AI3. The flight server still did support the old protocol without flight duration. Our Open API, an interface to the AI3 and the flight server, did not change. Our website did not do as well. We deployed the flight server and the AI3 with a new protocol version. Then we started to adjust the agents to return correct flight arrival dates, because earlier we simply assumed that an arrival date equals a departure date. When flight data came from the agents to AI3, the latter calculated a duration for each flight and stored these durations in the flight server. After some time, all flights in the flight server had flight duration. Finally, we added the fetching of the flight duration into our Open API and adapted our website to show the flight duration. Again, we deployed new website and Open API versions on our live servers. As you can see, displaying the flight duration was the last and easiest step; everything else had already been there for weeks and was well tested. In the end, we simply removed the old and outdated protocol without duration and cleaned it up. A feature that influenced the whole system was introduced step by step in incremental changes, and the risk of failure was reduced to a minimum.

CONCLUSION

For a smooth, continuous evolution, you need the right architecture. In our case, we implemented a service-oriented architecture quite a while ago. This helps us so much when we need to update or exchange only some relevant parts without touching the rest of the system.

PART VI
Non-Functional Aspects

14

Usability

Jens Grochtdreis

More topics follow as needed. In this case study, we talk about the *usability*[1] of websites. Usability as a quality characteristic of an interactive system means that users can use the website efficiently, effectively, and satisfactorily. Usability looks at humans in regard to a website. Usability should be a natural concern for every provider of a website. If that is not the case, users do not stay and do not turn into customers.

---

[1]Wikipedia, "Gebrauchstauglichkeit," accessed February 9, 2010, `http://de.wikipedia.org/wiki/Gebrauchstauglichkeit`.

Practical experience shows that, quite often, the focus is not on the consumer.[2] A website can be viewed as a dialogue. A form is a kind of dialogue.[3] Cancellations in multi-page forms demonstrate that this dialogue can be disrupted. Navigation is a form of dialogue as well, because consumers are being shown their way. The goal of usability is to make this dialogue easy and usable for consumers. Only then, when forms are comprehensive and usable, can a consumer start a dialog.

With usability, the devil is in the detail. Texts with bad wording can scare away consumers and make a page unusable, because on the web, more people scan than read intensively. Usability cannot be generated with simple technical tricks or a PHP function. Usability is about planning the right approach, long before the first "click dummies" are created.

When developing a website, you should always question what you are doing with respect to usability. Much too often, website operators think only of their own experiences. They completely forget that they do not build the website for themselves, but for their potential customers. They are the ones who must be addressed, kept on the page, and serviced.

But what do consumers want and what can they manage? It is pointless to reason about what others will want based on what you want. People who work on and in the Internet use a website quite differently from regular users. Regular users, however, are the vast majority, and usually are the target group. This is why it makes sense to focus on humans when we explore usability. Technical tools are useful, but they should not replace contact with consumers.

When I talk about testing usability by humans, I am well aware of the fact that many web projects do not have big budgets. Obviously, you cannot test low-budget projects through a large usability lab. But still you should talk to real users. There are cheap ways of doing this, as I elaborate on later.

When creating a website with decent usability, many problems can be avoided by the right approach. First and foremost, all parties involved should be aware that every design decision is an idealized picture of how a page should look. However, a website does not always look like what we expect, and it does not have to. Besides different screen resolutions and various operating systems, we have to deal with different browsers in various versions, each supporting only a certain part of the existing standards (X)HTML, JavaScript, and CSS. They also render form elements differently. Internet Explorer, for example, uses the form elements provided by the operating system. Mozilla Firefox has its own system, and they look quite different. Depending on the theme a user has selected in the operating system or in Firefox, the look and feel of the form elements change. Knowing this, we can hardly expect an identical representation of a website in all available browsers.

All in all, this is not really necessary, because nobody will ever compare. Only the creator of a website tests it in different browsers; the consumer does not. Even if we put lots of effort into making a website look identical in all tested browsers, the user can still modify our suggestion. This is one of the Internet's strengths that we should acknowledge and not work against.

---

[2]For the purpose of this case study, I call the user of a website a "consumer." This term does not refer only to the e-commerce aspect, because we can also say that somebody "consumes" a website. I like that term because it differentiates between service providers and clients.

[3]Timo Wirth, "Nutzerbeteiligung & Kommunikation: Mitmachbarrieren im Web 2.0," 2009, accessed February 9, 2010, http://www.slideshare.net/aperto/mitmachbarrieren-im-web-20.

As opposed to every other medium, on the Internet I can adjust the output of a page to my own needs. I am not primarily thinking about user style sheets, which are targeted at experts. Blind people view the content of a page in Braille or have it read to them. People with heavily impacted sight enlarge the page in the browser by 400% or more. A page can be printed or viewed on monitors of different sizes. These different kinds and contexts of use should always be kept in mind when creating a website. In web design, there is hardly one truth or true design. The fact that almost all designs are created in some kind of imaging software does not change anything. On the contrary, it makes things even more difficult. The imaging software—usually Photoshop—not only leads people to believe that there is only one design, but it also shows a different font rendering than most computers.

The design does not allow interaction, and there are no indications as to how the page displays in a smaller or wider browser window. Unfortunately, Photoshop designs are usually put forward as "the" design and not as a recommendation for an ideal case.

ANYTHING GOES, BUT WHAT IS THE PRICE?

Front-end development takes place in a hostile environment (the browser), and it's hard to understand when taking a back-end developer's view. Server-side code is targeted at a certain script version (for example, PHP 5.3), thus the possibilities and limitations are well known. In the front-end, these kinds of perfect conditions are only known in part in intranets or in pure Flash or Silverlight pages.

The browser is a hostile environment because every version interprets a different set of HTML, CSS, and JavaScript, and sometimes interprets these in their own special ways. In addition, the operating system and additional features like pop-up blockers or plugins have an influence. What's more, we do not know how the user has configured his browser and system. We have already mentioned the different output formats and display sizes. The output of a website does not happen under certain and equal conditions, as I could achieve on servers of a server farm, and I cannot even control the conditions. We cannot use the full scope of HTML, CSS, and JavaScript, because not all browsers support them.

Still, many believe that a website could look equal in all browsers. With the exception of form elements, this might be possible for very simplistic pages, but for more complex pages, it is problematic and not in the spirit of the medium.

In general, we can assume that every design request can be fulfilled. These questions arise: What is the required effort? What are the limitations? And how hard is the solution to maintain? If some detail can be realized with CSS, the overall effort is small, while maintainability is optimal. But even here, limitations start to show. Microsoft Internet Explorer does not master the really interesting CSS techniques, not even the current IE8. Many design requests can be implemented with CSS3 in modern browsers, but IE is out of scope. To realize the desired layout also with IE, you can use JavaScript or choose a different solution that works in all browsers right away.

There are three ways of helping IE to implement a design:

➤ Additional or more complex markup and CSS

➤ Use of images

➤ Use of JavaScript

These solutions do not ease the project maintenance, but require additional time and effort, and usually decrease performance. You should ask your customers whether they are willing to live with these disadvantages.

Let's take the famous rounded corners (also known as round boxes) as an example. In CSS3, they are no problem and are realized very quickly. For IE, we need special markup, because we need to use multiple images. If the corners need to be transparent on a color gradient, the next problem turns up, because IE6 does not support real transparent alpha channels.

JavaScript is often used to circumvent this. But this script decreases performance. Every time JavaScript is used to help IE, this means modifying the DOM. This takes time and makes the page slower. Using images usually implies that for every change, imaging software is required. This again takes time.

Because most customers use IE on a professional basis, they have difficulty accepting that they see a visually downgraded version. Many developers do not know about the possibilities of modern web browsers. Thus, often complex, time-consuming solutions that are hard to maintain are created, instead of maybe using CSS3 and allowing a slightly different visual experience in IE.

In front-end development, it is important to strike a balance between cost and effort. You should always ask yourself and your customer whether the benefit of a design detail really justifies its cost.

DESIGN ASPECTS

Accessibility

When talking about usability of a website, we focus on making a website accessible. Quite often, this focus is rather limited, though. It does not take into account that one of the big strengths of the Internet is that content can be consumed in arbitrary ways. This way, people with disabilities can take part in society and economic life much more easily. We should not limit ourselves to thinking of blind people here. A website's well-thought-out usability should always focus on avoiding needless barriers for people with disabilities, because they might make the pages unusable and inaccessible for this target group. Accessibility has many facets, and you cannot reduce them to "websites for blind people." As a matter of fact, we all sooner or later suffer from limited motor skills, so that we can make only limited use of a website. We might suffer from an injured hand or arm, or the perception of the website changes with age. Imperfect vision might force us to enlarge the page, and precise use of the mouse can become increasingly difficult. Accessibility not only refers to disabled people, but to everybody who lives with restrictions when accessing a website. Strictly speaking, these are also people who use a notebook or cell phone.

Readability

It sounds mundane, but it is often ignored: Each website supplier should strive to provide content that is easy to read. Next to good contrast (light gray on white is definitely not good contrast, but used surprisingly often), a font size that is easy to read is as important as readable line spacing. If the lines are too close together, try to modify or add the CSS `line-height` attribute of the element in question. For regular continuous text, values between 1.2 and 1.5, depending on the font size, have proven themselves successful. The `line-height` property accepts unitless values, and it is recommended that you use those rather than define measurement units like, for example, em-based values.[4] Figure 14.1 shows examples of font sizes and line spacing.

Avoid long paragraphs, and do not hesitate to use enumerations. Many users feel that enumerations are easier to read. Define a margin for the texts to prevent multiple columns from sticking together, as shown in Figure 14.2.

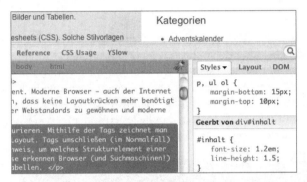

FIGURE 14-1: Font size and line spacing in CSS   **FIGURE 14-2:** Text with not enough margin

The page structure is also important. Consumers usually do not read, but they "scan" a page looking for keywords. It is advisable to place keywords in headings, at the beginning of short paragraphs, and in enumerations. The text should be written to maximize the use of keywords.

Labels for Form Elements

Each form element should have a label. This label should be linked to the unique ID of the form element using the `for` attribute:

```
<label for="email">eMail:*</label>
<input type="text" id="email" name="email" />
```

Thanks to this link, you can click the label to mark the element. Especially for radio buttons and check boxes, this is a noticeable improvement of the usability. Screen readers also benefit from this unambiguous relation.

Navigating by Keyboard

Not every user uses a mouse. We do not even have to think about disabled persons to find use cases without a mouse. Notebook users love to avoid using their track pad, because it makes the operation slow and cumbersome. Anyone using a cell phone or smartphone does not have a mouse either, and a mouse cannot be attached. Anyone who hurt his "click hand" or arm and was forced to wear a brace or a cast has noticed that a website navigable by keyboard can be a true blessing.

Drag-and-drop actions can be problematic when they are required for using a page, because those actions require a mouse. Suppressing the highlighting of active links, which is usually done by a dotted line, is a really bad idea. Developers cannot distinguish whether the mouse or the keyboard

---

[4]Eric S. Meyer, "Unitless line-heights," February 8, 2006, accessed February 9, 2010, http://meyerweb. com/eric/thoughts/2006/02/08/unitless-line-heights/.

activated the highlighting. Keyboard users, as opposed to mouse users, however, desperately need this marker to navigate the page, because it provides the required feedback that is otherwise missing in the form of a mouse pointer. Unfortunately, many developers suppress this orientation aid. TYPO3 does this by default with `onfocus='blurLink(this);'`, which is not turned off in most installations. You should search the CSS code for `outline: none`; and remove it.

Effective Contrast

Between 5% and 10% of all men have trouble seeing color contrasts. Light gray links on a white background are difficult for everybody. With backlight, sun rays from the side, or just bright artificial light, they become completely unreadable. The colors of a website should be rich in contrast. Avoid combining complementary colors. The frequently used combinations red on blue or red on green and vice versa are definitely bad choices. If you look at an area with these colors for a while, you can see the colors start to glow. Less obvious problems with the color contrasts can be tested and analyzed using the WCAG Contrast Checker[5] and the Juicy Studio Accessibility Toolbar,[6] as shown in Figure 14.3.

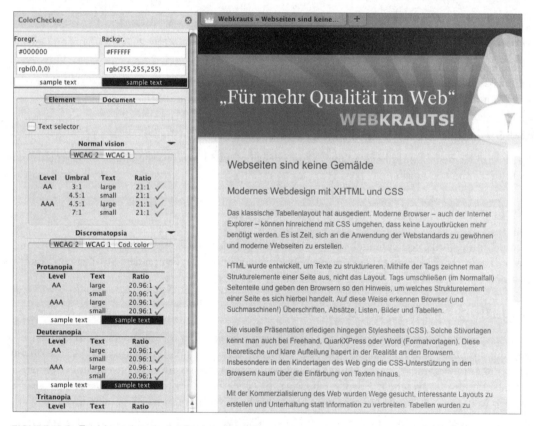

FIGURE 14-3: Tool-based analysis of color contrasts

---

[5]https://addons.mozilla.org/de/firefox/addon/7391

[6]https://addons.mozilla.org/de/firefox/addon/9108

Logo Links to Home Page

Over the years, it has become a convention to have the logo link back to the home page. It makes sense to follow this convention.

Alternative Texts for Images

There are many scenarios for images that do not get displayed. The consumer may have disabled images, the load time could be extremely long, or the consumer could be blind. These are only the common scenarios. If an image is meant to convey a message, instead of just being an accessory, a meaningful alternative text is an important detail that makes the page more usable. A screen reader reads this alternative text, the content is indexed by search engines, and while a large image loads, the user can already see some information about the content of the image.

Background Image in Background Color

Background images may not load or may take a long time to load. If there is text in front of the image, is a good idea to define a background color in addition to setting the image. This ensures readability.

Usable Print Version

I have already mentioned that you can never know in which way your website will be used. If the information is important or interesting enough, the page gets printed. Be sure to provide an appealing print version. Its design should be functional. Keep in mind that browsers do not print background colors and images, except if the user explicitly tells it to. When printing, hide all parts of the page that are unnecessary for the consumer, like the navigational elements or advertisements.

Visible Links

Links are the backbone of the Internet. Without links, it would not be possible to easily get from one page to another. So it is very important that the consumer can recognize links as such. Originally, links were highlighted as underlined text. If, as part of a design decision, this is changed, links should be identified by colors or possibly icons. Moving the mouse pointer across links (hovering) should trigger a change in design. Underlined text on a web page should only denote links and not be used for highlighting regular text. Visited links should be made discernible by using the CSS pseudo selector:visited. Links to the home page or imprint, however, should not be highlighted as "visited." The fact that the consumer has already visited these pages does not convey any information.

Good Bookmarks

The importance of the <title> tag is often underestimated. As long as the consumer visits a page, the browser's title bar is rather unimportant. The <title> tag, however, is also used to name bookmarks, as shown in Figure 14.4. You should put the company name at the end, not at the

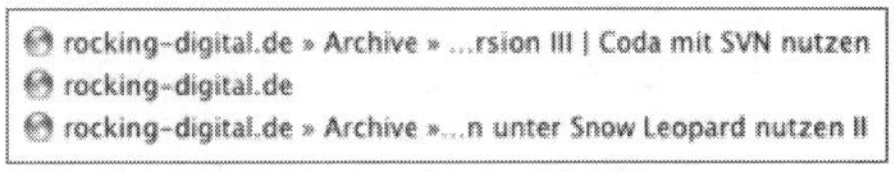

🌐 rocking-digital.de » Archive » ...rsion III | Coda mit SVN nutzen
🌐 rocking-digital.de
🌐 rocking-digital.de » Archive »...n unter Snow Leopard nutzen II

FIGURE 14-4: Page title in the browser's bookmark list

beginning, to avoid "Company XYZ and Sons Inc." appearing multiple times, instead of the actual title the consumer is looking for. A bookmark is part of the navigation, so a meaningful page title should be put at the beginning, followed by the name of the page operator.

No Frames

Early in their history, web frames, used properly, might have been useful, because the load time of important parts of the page could be reduced. These times, however, are long gone. Frames do not make sense anymore. On the contrary, they have only disadvantages. Frames prevent consumers from bookmarking subpages. Printing individual pages becomes more complicated, and refreshing a page using the browser button leads back to the home page. Do not use frames. They are obsolete.

Scalable Fonts

View your test page with IE6, and change the font size via the menu. If you have defined a font size in pixels, nothing happens. IE6 scales font sizes marked up in pixels only when explicitly told to. For the consumer, the only choices are to deal with a font size that he perceives as too small or to leave the page. Modern browsers do not scale the font, but rather the whole page. Still, as long as IE6 plays a considerable role in your site's access statistics, you should consider defining widths not in pixels, but by using a relative measure, preferably in em. As a general rule, 1em = 16px. Every user can modify this size, but only skillful users do this, and they can deal with any error this may cause.

TECHNICAL ASPECTS

Performance

The load time of a website is an important aspect of its usability, because longer page load times greatly increase the danger of termination. It thus makes much more sense to deal with a website's performance.

Steve Souders[7] has earned stripes in this area. He has investigated performance aspects in various places in production at Yahoo and later with Google. His findings are published in blog posts, presentations, videos, and books. Not long ago, everyone thought performance would mainly be determined by servers and server-side programming. Thanks to Steve Souders, we now know that the front-end plays a major role for the performance of a site.

Many of Souders's findings must be dealt with in detail, based on one of his books or articles. There are a few rules[8,9] to improve the performance, however, that you can follow without much research and discussion. You can use the Firebug extension YSlow[10] to examine a page and obtain the information you need to follow these rules.

---

[7] http://stevesouders.com/

[8] http://developer.yahoo.com/performance/rules.html

[9] http://stevesouders.com/examples/rules.php

[10] http://developer.yahoo.com/yslow/

Semantic Code

Clean, semantic, and valid HTML code prevents the browser from using its internal error correction, which wastes time and resources. In addition, it makes accessing the page by JavaScript and DOM scripting much easier.

Fewer Requests

Reducing the number of requests is at top of the list. This refers to the absolute number of requests and the number of requests to the same domain. Browsers limit the number of concurrent connections to one domain. This is why Steve Souders recommends loading JavaScript libraries from a Content Delivery Network (CDN).[11] All large libraries offer this service. Using multiple subdomains allows for additional parallel requests.

All JavaScript and CSS files should be concatenated and compressed. This saves on bandwidth and requests. I recently saw a website that included 24 CSS and 40 JavaScript files on the home page. They should have been condensed into one CSS and one JavaScript file and then compressed. Every additional file requires a request of its own, forcing the browser to wait until it is completed. Of course, you can split styles and scripts on development systems as far as you require, but in the live system, you should deliver as few as possible CSS and JavaScript files.

The creator of YAML, Dirk Jesse, recommends after lots of tests that you define the number of CSS files according to their size. According to his research, CSS files larger than 10 KB should be split, while having up to four CSS files does not impact the performance.[12]

CSS Sprites

We usually use many small images to design a website. They are placed on the page as icons or as decorative elements. If you embed all these little images as background graphics, you can create one or a few so-called Sprites,[13] and position the individual images correctly via CSS. To achieve this, the composite background image is assigned to all elements, IDs, and classes by just one rule. Then this image is positioned using the `background-position` attribute. This leads to just one request to load the large image, which can then quickly be aligned by CSS.

Creating such a large image can be tedious, and generating the appropriate CSS is even more tedious. Fortunately, there is a web service[14] that accepts a ZIP archive of all small images. The service generates and optionally compresses the sprite and the necessary CSS code. Alternatively, you can use the "bookmarklet" of another service.[15] It loads all images from the active page and outputs a sprite with the appropriate CSS.

---

[11]`http://developer.yahoo.com/performance/rules.html#cdn`

[12]David Maciejewski and Dirk Jesse, "Performance-Optimierung: Barrierefreiheit beginnt mit Ladezeiten," 2009, accessed February 9, 2010, `http://www.slideshare.net/dmacx/performance-optimierung-barrierefreiheit-beginnt-mit-ladezeiten`.

[13]Sven Lennartz, "CSS-Sprites Quellensammlung," 2009, accessed February 9, 2010, `http://www.drweb.de/magazin/css-sprites-quellensammlung/`.

[14] `http://de.spritegen.website-performance.org/`

[15] `http://spriteme.org/`

JavaScript on Bottom, CSS on Top

Put calls to external JavaScript files at the bottom of the page, right before the closing `</body>` tag. The reason is the progressive rendering of a page. While style sheets are loaded, rendering is suppressed. Rendering also is suppressed for everything after a script, until that script is loaded and interpreted. Thus, you should position scripts at the end of the page and put style sheets at the top so they load as early as possible.

Link CSS Instead of Importing

Steve Souders recommends that you not import style sheets, but use a `<link>` element[16] instead. He proved that IE loads imported style sheets after loading JavaScript files, even when they are loaded further down on the page. This has an impact on load time and appearance as well, should JavaScript and CSS interact.

JavaScript

Important areas of the website and all content should be available without JavaScript. JavaScript should enhance the page and support the use of the page, but do no more. This, of course, holds true only for normal, content-driven pages. A web application usually requires JavaScript.

JavaScript can be deactivated in the browser, as demonstrated in Figure 14.5. Some users do this because they are concerned with security and their browser's integrity. Mobile devices like the Blackberry do not support JavaScript at all. If JavaScript is used to create navigation or links, Blackberry users are locked out.

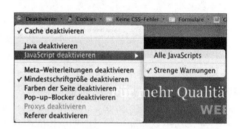

FIGURE 14-5 JavaScript can be deactivated in the browser

The popular and acclaimed e-commerce system Magento uses JavaScript in the checkout process. Without JavaScript, consumers cannot buy in a normal Magento-based shop. This is short-sighted and unnecessary.

JavaScript can be deactivated, but HTML and the server-side scripting language cannot be deactivated. Used properly, JavaScript can help to improve the usability of a website. A clever form validation, for example, uses JavaScript only in the first instance. Only the server-side validation is final, but validating with JavaScript provides quick feedback. Reloading the page is avoided, if the user is pointed to mistakes, and sending the form is prevented.

USER GUIDANCE

You should help the consumer to navigate your website by providing guidance. This starts with highlighting the current page in the navigation, usually by using a different color. In addition, you can use breadcrumbs navigation.[17] Pages that frequently change can use a timestamp.

---

[16]Steve Souders, "don't use @import," 9. April 2009, accessed February 9, 2010, `http://www.stevesouders.com/blog/2009/04/09/dont-use-import/`.

[17]Wikipedia, "Brotkrümelnavigation," accessed February 9, 2010, `http://de.wikipedia.org/wiki/Brotkrümelnavigation`.

A German newspaper, for example, clearly indicates when the page was modified. As shown in Figure 14.6, the developers used relative instead of absolute time, so instead of reading "Last updated at 02:14 pm," it says "Last updated 17 minutes ago." This makes it much easier for the consumer.

FIGURE 14-6: Relative instead of absolute time

The "Fold" Myth

Some customers, but also designers, think that the most important elements of a website must be above an imaginary fold. They think there is some kind of safe zone that must contain all important information and elements.

For many newspapers, the fold is very important. To sell papers at the newsstand, you have to sell via the title page. Because a newspaper is always folded, the most important headline must be above the fold, and it must attract readers. On the web, there is no such thing as a fold, because there is no fixed format. A newspaper or magazine always appears in the same fixed format. A web page, on the contrary, can be viewed in different sizes and with a varying color quality. A web page can be printed or read aloud. For a newspaper or magazine, only one form exists. A website has many different forms; thus the concept of a fold does not match the reality of a website.

If the customer cannot be convinced of this simple truth,[18] you can approach the non-existent fold by looking at the server usage statistics, which tell you what screen sizes are used. Take the least common denominator, and place the elements according to the maximum height of this resolution, while taking into account that the various operating systems and browsers require different amounts of space for themselves. A definition such as this, however, is just an expression of hope, but it does not make sense at all. If the content of the website is interesting, the user scrolls, just like they unfold and turn a newspaper around to read the rest of the page. A page that is not interesting does not turn into a banger by putting lots of buttons and prompts above the imaginary fold.

Feedback on Interaction

We usually expect a reaction following an action. When using a website, this is not different from real life. Interactive elements should take this expectation into account. After a consumer sends a form, success or failure should be communicated.

If an element has been changed by AJAX, this should be visualized. Applications like Basecamp[19] have made coloring an element for a short period of time quite popular. GoogleMail also uses this kind of effect. Showing a notification text is also possible.

---

[18]Rett Martin, "How to Discuss 'the Fold' with a Client," January 8, 2010, accessed February 9, 2010, `http://www.clockwork.net/blog/2010/01/08/372/how_to_discuss_the_fold_with_a_client`.

[19]37Signals (`http://37signals.com`)

Never leave the consumer disoriented and alone on a website. Content changes might be obvious to you, because you have conceived or programmed them. For the consumer, any changes are non-obvious, so you need to lead their way.

Navigation

Horizontal navigation is popular and frequently used. Keep in mind that, as opposed to vertical navigation, horizontal space is always limited. You should therefore start to test your design with real navigation entries as early as possible. Draft versions frequently use short placeholders or even "Lorem Ipsum" blind text. As soon as real navigation is tested, a rude awakening might be the consequence when entries do not fit next to each other.

This also can happen when translating into another language. The English language is short and precise; German and French, for instance, require more words and characters. Navigation entries thus require more space. An English "Home" requires fewer spaces than the German "Startseite." You might quickly find limitations in your design.

We want users of our websites to reach their goal quickly and without complications. Many drop-down navigation menus actually prevent this, especially when they have a submenu. The users have to move the mouse pointer precisely; otherwise, navigation does not work because the submenu disappears. These kinds of navigation elements usually are not usable by keyboard, because the developers do not think about keyboard navigation; they focus solely on the events the mouse triggers.

Sub-navigation is always triggered by a link. A link has limited height, for aesthetic and practical reasons. Figure 14.7 shows how the mouse must be moved along a small path to reach the sub-navigation.

FIGURE 14-7: Hard-to-use sub-navigation

It may sound obvious, but the navigation elements should be understandable for the user. This simple and logical rule is violated too often. Figure 14.8 shows an example. The organizational structure is being visualized by department numbers. This might work on an intranet, where people know what they are looking for, but on the Internet, where users know nothing about the organizational structure, they will be confused. They have to click all navigational items and read through the description until they can find the department they are looking for.

Das EBA
Organigramm
Der Präsident
Aufgaben und Struktur
Zentrale
Abteilung 1
Referat 10
Referat 11
Referat 12
Referat 13
Referat 14
Referat 15
Referat 16
Abteilung 2
Abteilung 3

› Startseite › Das EBA

Referat 10

Die Leitung des Re
Anerkennungsstelle ui

Mit Gründung der „Eu
die Realisierung ein
zahlreichen Arbeitsç
Eisenbahnbehörden
gesamteuropäische R

Zur Umsetzung des e
referatsübergreifend
Abstimmung und Hai
Aufsicht auf europäis
konventionellen Verl
Bahnsystems die so g
weitere werden folger

Pop-ups and Other Annoyances

You should deal carefully with everything that impacts the normal flow of reading. Pop-ups are annoying and,

FIGURE 14-8 Navigational elements that cannot be understood by users

what's more, they can be suppressed by the browser. Important content should never be presented in pop-ups, because it might not display. Light boxes cannot be suppressed by the browser, but you might run into trouble with the height of the viewport. Viewports with lesser height, as with iPhones or Netbooks, offer less space. A height of 600 pixels is much less than what you usually plan for. If a large light box is created, the viewport might not display the full content. Usually, light boxes are not scrolled with the page, so users cannot view the whole content. If an important button is out of reach, a part of the website cannot be used by the consumer.

Habits and Expectations

The placement of some elements is similar on most pages. These patterns make it easier for consumers to orient themselves. Commonly, the logo links back to the home page, while a search box is displayed in the upper-right corner. A link to the imprint or contact page is expected in the meta or footer navigation.

Consumers are not adventurers; they expect to get to what they want quickly and easily. Do not disappoint expectations; follow common usage schemes. If your design does not meet the expectations, you should make the design easy to understand.

Fault Tolerance and Feedback

When using a website or web application, faulty operations are always possible. It is important to deal with potential errors constructively, because you do not want to scare away the consumer. Faulty operations cannot end in a stalemate. A form with errors must be redisplayed. All content should be kept, because it is very frustrating to fill out the form again. All errors should be clearly marked, and hints on the correct input should be presented.

Before a form is sent, a first validation should be done with JavaScript to make sure wrong entries or empty required fields are not transmitted to the server application. Quite often, errors occur because the application expects a field in a certain format. Date formats are a good example. The different cultural circles have their own date formats, plus different textual descriptions of dates. You should think about whether you want to make the user responsible for correctly formatting a date or whether you can find a way of allowing free format. You can process the formats on the server and store the dates in any way you need. RememberTheMilk.com does this and also accepts input of the form "in three weeks." The application converts this text and stores a regular date. The additional effort for this pays off, because the result is much more user-friendly.

TESTING USABILITY

Creating a usable page does not mean that you have to conduct a test by potential users every time you change a page. Based on the experience of others, there are some rules to follow when designing and developing a website. You can test for usability details in the browser; after all, we are talking about front-end aspects. Because we usually deal with cross-browser aspects, one adaptable browser will suffice. Over the years, Firefox has proven itself for this job. Even if this browser becomes slow with too many add-ons, the extensibility makes Firefox the perfect tool for usability tests. The most frequently used tools are probably Firebug[20] and the Web Developer Toolbar.[21]

Websites are made for humans, even though some search engine optimizers paint a different picture. The most important insights are gained through humans. Keep in mind that you should not offer any help or make limiting statements to the testers. As a web professional, you deal with the web, browsers, and a website quite differently than a regular consumer. Remember: After the site is live, no instructions lead the consumer through the depths of the website, so you should not give any guidance during testing.

Try to look at the website from the consumer's point of view when creating it. Can users understand and work with the page without any background knowledge? At second glance, is any guidance missing? Keep in mind that you do not create the website for your customer, but for their (potential) customers. It cannot be stressed often enough, because this fact is often overlooked. It does usually not make sense, for example, to use internal descriptions and technical terms on a website.

Intensive tests of a website should be conducted in a usability lab. There are special service providers offering not only the technical equipment but also the know-how. Unfortunately, such tests do not always fit into the budget or the course of the project. There are also techniques and services that allow you to run tests on your own. Their significance is limited to a few aspects, but this also can be an advantage. You can record user tests with Silverback,[22] which is a Mac application. It uses a webcam (built into all Macs these days) to record the tester's reaction when using the page. Because the tester can be anywhere and the product is inexpensive, it is especially well suited for spontaneous user tests. You could use the tool to search for testers in a cafe. Buy people coffee and a piece of cake, and ask them to perform some short tasks based on a click dummy.

On live pages, scripts recording "heatmaps" are frequently used. Just like a thermal image, these JavaScripts record areas of high activity. They register where users click and the ways the mouse pointer moves on the page. Do the users find the buttons, links, and banners they are supposed to find? Which links and buttons are frequently clicked? Common providers of heatmaps are clickdensity[23] and Crazyegg.[24] Clickheat[25] is an open-source variant that you can run on your own.

The log files also can offer interesting answers, if you ask the right questions. For multi-page forms, for instance, it is very interesting to know whether your site is experiencing a significant number of terminations. They might indicate software bugs that should be explored with unit tests.

---

[20]http://getfirebug.com

[21]http://chrispederick.com/work/web-developer/

[22]http://silverbackapp.com/

[23]http://clickdensity.com/

[24]http://crazyegg.com/

[25]http://www.labsmedia.com/clickheat/index.html

CONCLUSION

When creating a website, being creative and putting some effort into programming is not sufficient. Although this is important, the focus should always be on the consumer. A website should be easy to use and comprehensive. Technical gadgets might enchant you or your customer, but for the consumer, they can quickly become obstacles.

Websites are very flexible constructs. We can adapt their output according to our desires and needs. Keep this strength in mind, and do not work against it. With the right approach, a page causes problems neither in the test browser, nor in the consumer's actual usage scenarios. Because you can never know all these usage scenarios and can only guess at some of them, websites should always be very flexible and adaptable.

Too often, we work with analogies to traditional media like newspapers and magazines. Websites offer more possibilities than these, but they do have limitations that some traditional media lacks. Thus, we should forget these analogies and find an approach that fits the web. If we do not put enough focus on flexibility, we might work against the consumer, which basically means working against our own website. This is definitely not our goal.

15

Performance Testing

Brian Shire

WHAT'S IN THIS CHAPTER?

➤ Overview of performance-testing tools

➤ Test environment considerations

➤ Load testing tools

➤ Resource usage monitoring tools

➤ System metrics tools

➤ Performance testing pitfalls

INTRODUCTION

Two primary questions must be answered when performance testing:

1. Is there a need for optimization?

    ➤ Is the application currently meeting performance requirements?

    ➤ Will users be satisfied with the responsiveness of the site?

    ➤ Is the site stable?

    ➤ Are the infrastructure costs reasonable or prohibitive?

➤ Will the above questions hold true if usage increases exponentially?

➤ How do the above factors weigh against other business priorities, such as delivering new features, fixing bugs, maintaining existing services, and so on?

2. What specifically should be optimized?

➤ Where should we begin looking for optimizations?

➤ What optimizations have the greatest gains for the least amount of work, time, and money?

➤ How can future limitations be identified as the application grows or changes?

Some of the items listed above are easy to execute, because a variety of tools can help developers to immediately answer these questions. Other questions require an understanding of the application or an insight that comes only with experience on a given project and optimizing PHP applications in particular.

In this chapter, we present common tools and the experiences from having used them for PHP performance testing. This should provide a foundation on which to build further experience for your specific application.

Tools

We discuss several popular tools categorized into load testing, profiling, and system metrics. Each tool has unique characteristics applicable to the test, environment, or just personal preference. Understanding the available tools and tests enables you to use them appropriately and to know the limitations or pitfalls.

Load testing tools such as Apache Bench (AB), Pylot, and HTTPLoad enable a full request cycle similar to what a user request executes. Load testing creates artificial loads to verify performance or scalability. These tools vary from performing simple HTTP requests to the server to making more complicated posts and result validation.

Profilers examine code execution to find bottlenecks and are often used as part of an optimization task to actively improve performance rather than just verification. These profilers typically hook into the code at a function or line level and measure at intervals the time the code spends in each function.

Profiling tools typically report on CPU metrics or similar information and match it to C or PHP level functions and even specific lines of code. This pinpoints specific areas that are estimated to consume the majority of CPU or other resources. They can then provide a report of what time is spent in which sections of code, making it easier to identify areas that need optimization. Profilers take much more time and effort, because they often require setup, collection, analysis, and sometimes recompilation. This increase in effort and time required makes profiling less ideal for regular testing, but the level of detail makes it an excellent source for highly granular information.

System metrics can be used in production to measure and compare performance, as well as with load testing to compare changes, verify results, or project scalability. `sar`, `top`, and `meminfo` system metrics can display disk, memory, CPU, and network information, identifying areas where the application is limited on system resources. During a load test or even in a production environment, these statistics can provide another mechanism for further feedback on total system resources and performance. On production systems that are actively performing more than one service, this can be more valuable than just the results from a single load test because it provides an overview of the entire system's health from an operating system (OS) level.

Finally, in very particular situations, the tools mentioned are too generic or high level to identify a specific aspect of performance. In these cases, it is sometimes necessary to implement custom metrics that can be gathered and analyzed from a development, test, or production environment. The important aspect here is to make sure that the additional effort required to instrument the code in this way is useful enough to put the effort into coding and accurate enough to be relied upon.

Environmental Considerations

Environmental considerations also need to be taken into account. Unlike functional tests, which often rely on each run of code to be started in a clean state, performance often has direct reliance on the CPU, network, disk, and possibly other components such as a remote database or Memcached[1] server. These all combine to make tests less reliable. If a test depends on a production database or Memcached server, the daily usage patterns could drastically affect the results. A run at 3:00 A.M. does not provide the same results during prime time at 7:00 P.M. (or whatever your daily user pattern is). The preferred choice here is to make a test environment completely isolated and independent from external sources. This is ideal and should be the setup you use, but in many cases, the amount of data stored in databases or caching servers makes it extremely difficult or impossible to reproduce a production scenario. This must be determined on a case-by-case basis and weighed with the cost of setup and necessity. In many cases, production can be used for testing, so it is not necessary to justify an expensive mirror environment. Good practices in this situation are to always run comparative tests in a close timeframe to reduce any temporal changes and to always reduce interference to a reasonable level. If caching is heavily used, all data should be in the cache before a test is conducted (unless cache misses are part of the test). It is necessary to "warm up" or "prime" a test with multiple requests before actually beginning a recorded test. For a heavily Memcached-reliant application, running a local instance of Memcached can help decrease any network latency or reliance on remote production servers. After the local Memcached instance is primed with data, most of the data should be able to retrieved locally. There should not be any chance of cache misses (because the requested data will likely be identical and therefore will not fall out of the cache). The downside of this method is making sure the Memcached instance does not affect your test because it is running on the same server and consumes more memory and resources. This is generally useful for a test or profile of PHP, but not for a full system test where you are monitoring all system activity, which Memcached is not normally a part of. This also excludes any code path that occurs when cache misses occur—something that should probably be investigated as part of an optimization for cache usage.

Before starting a test, you should be able to see a plateau for CPU, load, memory, or whatever metric you are tracking. Multiple samples should be taken to ensure that any outlying data can be either removed or averaged out to get reliable results. A database that has one slow response may not be relevant to the current test of a PHP application's CPU usage.

If you are doing your own builds from sources, be aware of the differences that may be present. PHP in particular has the ability to create "debug" builds (with the `--enable-debug` configure option), which adds a significant amount of overhead to lower-level components like the memory manager.

---

[1] `http://www.danga.com/memcached/`

Builds that have been built with CFLAGS=-O0 (for no optimizations) should be of concern as well. These builds are not representative of what is actually running in production (or at least we hope you are running with the most optimized version in production).

It is often the case that when working in a development environment, we forget to change our configuration to match production as closely as possible. Instead of testing for the production use case, it is easy to test the development environment and end up with drastically different results. This can be a source of frustration or—worse—complete ignorance if it is never realized. This is an excellent reason to always validate that the expected changes have taken effect once in a production environment.

LOAD TESTING

Load testing is probably one of the most reliable, easiest, and pertinent performance testing mechanisms. It allows full end-to-end requests and implicitly avoids many pitfalls of other profiling or testing procedures. However, to ensure accurate testing, the correct environment should replicate the client server relationship properly by using the load testing tools on one host and the server on a separate machine. This ensures that the overhead of creating and receiving requests by the client does not interfere with the normal operation of the server or any other statistics collection that may be performed on the host.

Load testing tools attempt to simulate multiple clients making requests simultaneously. This concurrency is an important consideration when using benchmark tools and profilers. Unforeseen issues such as file descriptor limits, cache locking, and memory exhaustion are aspects that can change when concurrency increases, and you should be testing these factors to ensure scalability and performance. Load testing above current capacity can give perspective on future thresholds that the application will exceed, such as memory usage or other resource limitations. Use load tests with both expected low loads and up to an excessive load to help make a road map for future research or areas of concern.

Getting a proper measurement can be difficult if the results are not significant. More specifically, a page that responds at 20 requests per second (RPS) can be difficult to measure if there is only a minor change in performance. To measure a 10% change in performance, you would need to have a 2 RPS change. Even if there is enough variance between requests to cause a 1 RPS difference, it would be a 5% margin of error! In these cases, it is important to note how much variance you see between multiple tests to know if the final results are of significance or possibly noise due to variance. Getting around this problem can sometimes be difficult, but options include reducing the number of iterations if it is a small synthesized benchmark or in general reducing the amount of work being done in the test. Sometimes, measuring smaller components can be useful, but it is critical to make sure important aspects of the application are not being excluded in the process.

If this cannot be worked around following the guideline of taking multiple samples, using a stable environment and recording system metrics to monitor resources can help ensure reliable results.

Apache Bench

Apache Bench (AB) is a performance benchmarking tool that is distributed with the Apache HTTP Server.[2] AB's advantages are its ease of use, simplicity, and availability with existing Apache installations. Running AB is a single simple command:

```
ab http://www.foobar.com/
```

This makes a single request to the given URL and reports back on various metrics. The -n option can be used to set the number of sequential requests, as in the following example to perform 10 sequential requests:

```
ab -n 10 http://www.foobar.com/
```

To increase the number of concurrent requests to 10, use the -c option. This creates 10 requests each from 10 individual threads running at the same time:

```
ab -n 10 -c 10 http://www.foobar.com/
```

AB is good for performing on-the-fly command line driven tests for both performance and scalability. The two most useful metrics are typically going to be Requests per second and Time per request. These should provide a quick comparison or validation, excellent for both permanent tests or during development.

```
Copyright (c) 1996 Adam Twiss, Zeus Technology Ltd, http://www.zeustech.net/
Copyright (c) 2006 The Apache Software Foundation, http://www.apache.org/
Benchmarking www.foobar.com (be patient).....done
Server Software: Apache/1.3.41
Server Hostname: www.foobar.com
Server Port: 80
Document Path: /status.php
Document Length: 19 bytes
Concurrency Level: 1
Time taken for tests: 0.081 seconds
Complete requests: 1
Failed requests: 0
Broken pipe errors: 0
Total transferred: 503 bytes
HTML transferred: 19 bytes
Requests per second: 12.35 [#/sec] (mean)
Time per request: 81.00 [ms] (mean)
Time per request: 81.00 [ms] (mean, across all concurrent requests)
Transfer rate: 6.21 [Kbytes/sec] received
```

More advanced requests also can be generated by passing cookies or additional header fields. The -C option accepts a key=value syntax for passing cookies and the -H option for passing header fields. Further information on these and other parameters can be found in the AB manual pages.

---

[2]http://httpd.apache.org/

If you are using Apache-1.3.x, the total request size as well as cookies and headers have compiled-in limitations. Specifically, the total request size is limited to 1024. This was changed in Apache-2.x, so it may be worth upgrading AB specifically if you require larger sizes. It is also relatively easy to modify the source to fit your needs:

```
diff --git a/src/support/ab.c b/src/support/ab.c
index 851d8d1..7050839 100644
--- a/src/support/ab.c
+++ b/src/support/ab.c
@@ -216,7 +216,7 @@ char fullurl[1024];
char colonport[1024];
int postlen = 0; /* length of data to be POSTed */
char content_type[1024]; /* content type to put in POST header */
-char cookie[1024], /* optional cookie line */
+char cookie[4096], /* optional cookie line */
auth[1024], /* optional (basic/uuencoded)
* authentification */
hdrs[4096]; /* optional arbitrary headers */
@@ -247,7 +247,7 @@ int err_response = 0;
struct timeval start, endtime;
/* global request (and its length) */
-char request[1024];
+char request[4096];
int reqlen;
/* one global throw-away buffer to read stuff into */
```

AB also measures the success of requests by measuring the content length. For dynamic pages that return different content, this can pose a serious problem because requests will appear to fail by AB's standards. AB's simplicity is also its weakness if formatted output, graphs, or configuration files are preferred.

Pylot

Pylot[3] is a relatively new tool similar to other load testing tools, but it's written in Python and attempts to create a much richer environment for generating graphs as output. It can be run as a graphical user interface (GUI) or from the command line.

In its simplest form, Pylot can be executed with a simple XML test case:

```
<testcases>
    <case>
        <url>http://localhost/</url>
    </case>
</testcases>
```

Executing Pylot with the command `python run.py ./test.xml` produces the following output:

```
-------------------------------------------------
Test parameters:
number of agents: 1
test duration in seconds: 60
rampup in seconds: 0
interval in milliseconds: 0
```

---

[3]http://www.pylot.org/

```
test case xml: testcases.xml
log messages : False
Started agent 1
All agents running...
[############ 31% ] 18s/60s
Requests: 28
Errors: 0
Avg Response Time: 0.448
Avg Throughput: 1.515
Current Throughput: 08
Bytes Received: 12264
------------------------------------------------
```

In addition, it outputs HTML reports with Response Time, shown in Figure 15.1, and Throughput charts, shown in Figure 15.2, in the `results` directory.

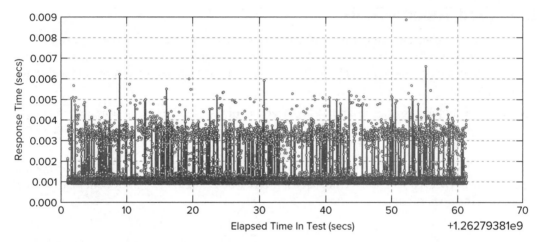

FIGURE 15-1: Response Time chart generated by Pylot

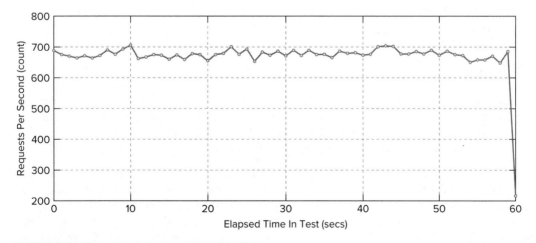

FIGURE 15-2: Throughput chart generated by Pylot

The default runtime is 60 seconds, which can be configured via command line arguments. Output directory, concurrency, and other options are also available. One feature of Pylot is its availability to run a GUI by launching Pylot with the -g command line argument.

Unlike AB, Pylot uses a duration option in seconds rather than total number of requests. It also has a ramp-up feature to spread out the startup of concurrent requests over a given period of time. It also provides an interval argument for a minimum time span between requests. Because Pylot is a heavier-weight application than something like AB, its ability to serve requests quickly is limited. AB may be able to serve many thousands of requests per second, but Pylot is limited to a few hundred (results vary by the abilities of the hardware and operating system). For larger web applications that have slower request rates, this is a good full-featured tool that provides full graphical and HTML-based reports. It is not well suited for extremely lightweight requests that rise above a few hundred requests per second, something most applications cannot attain anyway.

Other Load Testing Tools

We have only touched on a couple of load testing tools, but many more exist that may suit particular needs or preferences better than others. They all revolve around common features and trade-offs, such as ease of use, configuration, efficiency, types of tests that can be performed, and ability to play back requests.

JMeter, for example, provides a significantly larger set of tests that are not just limited to HTTPD. This could be valuable for someone looking to test a multitude of services without having to learn and configure a new tool for every test.

Other tools such as Siege, HTTPPerf, and Flood are mature projects and are similar to command line tools like AB, each with unique implementations. You can find more information about these projects at their websites:

➤ Siege (`http://www.joedog.org/index/siege-home`)

➤ HTTPerf (`http://www.hpl.hp.com/research/linux/httperf/`)

➤ Flood (`http://httpd.apache.org/test/flood/`)

➤ JMeter (`http://jakarta.apache.org/jmeter/`)

PROFILING

Profiling consists of running a process with instrumentation to monitor resource usage (often CPU usage or time). The output can then be analyzed by tools showing weights of sections of code, typically on a function level but sometimes line per line. More advanced profilers give the user the ability to view the generated assembly code, and the software suggests performance modifications.

Profilers can sometimes be a significant burden on the system, causing the application to run slowly, while others are designed to have minimum impact, allowing the possibility of quicker runs and therefore possibly capturing live metrics from production. Some profilers run as a separate process, some as kernel extensions, and others as instrumentation built directly into the code. We review and compare a few of these for both C and PHP, and we discuss how they relate specifically to testing for PHP applications.

A PHP stack has some special considerations and steps to obtain a proper profile. The following should apply to any PHP Server API (SAPI); however, we focus on Apache for simplicity. When Apache starts and loads a module such as PHP, it goes through an initialization stage, giving modules a chance to configure themselves and set up any long-standing structures or other states. Subsequently, as Apache accepts requests, PHP goes through per-request initialization phases to set up any state specific to the current request. A correctly optimized Apache module or PHP module attempts to do as much as possible in the first startup initialization stage, because we don't care how long it takes to start Apache, just how long it takes to serve requests. We want to exclude this costly initialization time from our profiling. As with load testing, we also should "warm up" our server with some requests before recording data. With profiling, we need a special command to exclude the startup and any warm-up time from our final data so it doesn't skew our results.

Another problem with profiling Apache is switching user IDs (UIDs). It typically is started with a root UID to gain access to privileged ports. But because it would be insecure if run it as a privileged user to serve requests, Apache switches to an unprivileged user, typically the user apache, and spawns sub-processes to accept requests. Some profilers, specifically Callgrind, described later, writes an initial file as root and then is unable to write subsequent data when it's running as another user. We demonstrate how to deal with this scenario in an example for Callgrind, our C-level profiler.

Profiling one or many processes also presents its own unique problem. Typically, it isn't necessary to profile more than one process at a time. Often, we can run Apache in standalone mode and not concern ourselves with even starting more than one process. However, it is always important when taking shortcuts such as this to be aware of what has been excluded from the test. In this case, we have removed any possibility of contention that could occur when serving more than one request. When multiple processes are competing for the same resource, a process can become serialized waiting for other processes to complete before it can obtain access. As an example, storing entries in the Alternative PHP Cache (APC) requires a lock on shared memory. Subsequently, delays may arise in the event that more than one process is attempting to access the cache. Perhaps other back-end services are a source of contention, such as file access, network services, Memcached, or databases. Although this is a more advanced issue, and probably not one that will be hit upon often, it is important to keep in mind what is being measured and what is not for any type of test.

We start our discussion of profilers with Callgrind, a C-level profiler, and move on to some more PHP-relevant tools like Xdebug, APD, and XHProf. Then we cover OProfile, a C-level tool that can capture a wider range of data for the system as a whole rather than just one process.

Callgrind

Callgrind is part of Valgrind,[4] a powerful toolset that is useful for profiling a number of different program aspects, such as memory bounds, cache profiles, heap profiles, and so on. We discuss only the Callgrind tool because it is likely the most useful for our purposes; however, readers should look at using the other tools available with Valgrind because they can be quite valuable. The downsides of Valgrind are its dependency on Linux and its significant impact on application speed. This makes the setup time considerable, and for a more complicated environment like PHP, a small mistake can cost you much more time and frustration than a simple AB load test that could take only a few minutes to set up.

---

[4]http://valgrind.org/

Callgrind is a CPU profiler that generates a call tree of C-level functions, giving you a good layout of how functions are structured and how much CPU time they consume relative to each other; see Figure 15.3 for an example. Even if you are not interested in optimizing the C components of your stack, this could provide an interesting insight into the lower levels of PHP. However, we recommended that you start with a PHP profile using APD or Xdebug because it often reflects larger opportunities for less effort. If you are already specifically interested in C-level optimizations, this tool is extremely valuable.

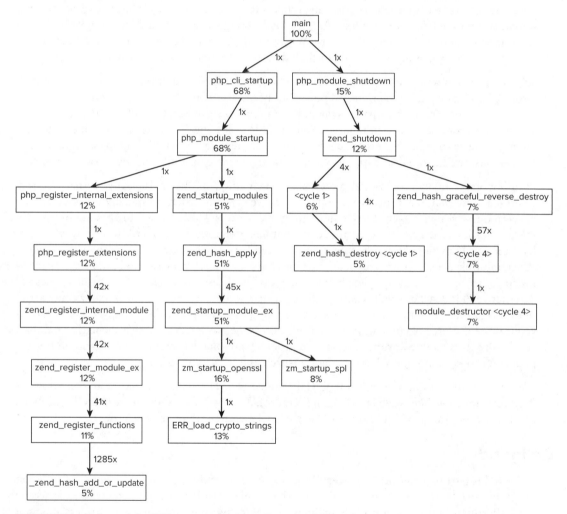

FIGURE 15-3: Call graph for PHP generated with Callgrind and KCachegrind

Using Callgrind on a single process is relatively straightforward. We simply run Valgrind, specifying our tool and a command to profile. An output file is generated that can be later analyzed. As an example, to get a profile of a simple PHP script, use this snippet:

```
valgrind --tool=callgrind php test.php
```

This outputs a `callgrind.<pid>.out` file, where `<pid>` is the process id of the profiled process. Be sure to include symbols in your binary files (the `-g` option with GCC); otherwise, profiler output cannot connect the function addresses with more convenient function names.

In the case of Apache, we run a process in standalone mode and start profiling only after we have warmed up the server. We start Apache using an `httpd -X` command to run a single process in the foreground. We also use the `--instr-atstart=no` option for Callgrind. This prevents gathering any statistics from the running process until we issue a secondary command to start profiling. This avoids gathering any data in the initialization phase or before the server is "warmed."

```
valgrind --tool=callgrind --instr-atstart=no httpd -X
```

We should now see some output and a hanging command waiting to serve HTTPD requests. If the Apache server configuration is set up to change UIDs from root to another user, we want to either fix the permissions on the newly generated Callgrind output file or change the Apache configuration to not switch users after startup. In the latter case, we likely have to listen for requests on a non-privileged port. Instead, we will change the permissions after starting Apache. Look for an output file in the current directory; it likely is owned by the privileged user with exclusive read and write permissions. You can change these permissions or ownership such that the new non-privileged user has access to write out data. You should also probably change the permissions accordingly for the current directory so files can be written by other tools like `calgrind_control`, described later. Do not forget to do this step; otherwise, at the end of your profile, you will end with a zero-byte file and have to start over. We can warm up the server for profiling by manually making requests via a web browser, or sometimes it is easier to use a load testing tool such as AB to handle this for us. Just be sure that whatever method is used replicates the same process that happens during profiling. Note that requests are likely to be significantly slower and that we have only one running process, so having any level of concurrent requests when using a load testing tool is pointless.

After we are satisfied that the server process is ready to be profiled, we can issue the `callgrind` command to enable collection of profile data. This can be accomplished with the `callgrind_control` utility. In this case, we use the `-i` option to start profiling instructions:

```
callgrind_control -i on
```

Sometimes you may notice that `callgrind_control` hangs. If this is the case, be sure it has permissions to write to the current directory (as it generates a file for the running process to check against). It sometimes is necessary to get some activity on the running process to trigger a read; issuing a simple request should do the trick. We can now issue some requests that you would like to have profiled, which should be the same as what the server was warmed up with prior to enabling data collection. After we are satisfied, we can again disable the gathering of profile data with the `callgrind_control` tool. This excludes any shutdown code from our test, which, like startup initialization, is not pertinent to our run-time performance.

```
callgrind_control -i off
```

Go ahead and shut down the Apache web server with either a simple Ctrl-C on the original `callgrind` command line or with a `apachectl stop` command. You should now have a Callgrind output file ready to be analyzed.

We recommend that profiler output be analyzed with a GUI interface like KCachegrind, described in the next section, but for those times when you want to take a quick look at the data, the command line tools for Callgrind can be useful. The `callgrind_annotate` command can be used to generate a quick listing of output data, and it supports different view options for a flat listing, trees, code annotation, and filters. The simplest form accepts the output file and displays a sorted list of functions:

```
$ callgrind_annotate callgrind.out.25184
--------------------------------------------------------------------
Profile data file 'callgrind.out.25184' (creator: callgrind-3.2.3)
--------------------------------------------------------------------
I1 cache:
D1 cache:
L2 cache:
Timerange: Basic block 0 - 7346912
Trigger: Program termination
Profiled target:  ./httpd -X (PID 25184, part 1)
Events recorded:  Ir
Events shown:  Ir
Event sort order:  Ir
Thresholds:  99
Include dirs:
User annotated:
Auto-annotation: off

--------------------------------------------------------------------
    Ir
--------------------------------------------------------------------
27,047,425 PROGRAM TOTALS
--------------------------------------------------------------------
    Ir file:function
--------------------------------------------------------------------
3,542,940 strncpy.c:strncpy [/lib64/libc-2.3.5.so]
3,369,517 ???:0x0000000000449D90 [/opt/httpd/bin/httpd]
3,111,078 ???:0x000000000044AEE0 [/opt/httpd/bin/httpd]
1,938,456 strcasecmp.c:strcasecmp [/lib64/libc-2.3.5.so]
1,759,914 zend_alloc.c:_zend_mm_alloc_int [/opt/httpd/libexec/libphp5.so]
1,321,174 ???:memcpy [/lib64/libc-2.3.5.so]
...
```

KCachegrind

KCachegrind is a GUI that can be used to visualize Callgrind output files. Xdebug and APD profiler output also can be converted a KCachegrind-compatible format. Although output on the command line can be useful, bringing complicated data into a visualization tool provides excellent analytic power. It gives you the ability to better understand what is happening in the code flow, see relative weights on resources, and easily navigate when drilling up and down into varying levels of details and code depth.

Because KCachegrind is a K Desktop Environment (KDE)[5] application, it requires some additional setup for systems not already running Linux with KDE. One option is to run an emulator and install Linux and KDE. Alternatively, if your operating system supports running an X Server, you

---

[5]http://www.kde.org/

can export the display of KCachegrind from another Linux desktop or server. MacOS X has the ability to install KDE and KCachegrind from its ports tool, although the compilation of this can be a lengthy process. Windows users may also want to try the KDE on Cygwin[6] project. Unfortunately, a detailed discussion of all the possible methods for different systems would be too detailed to cover here, so the above are left as suggested starting points.

After we have a working KCachegrind installation, loading profile data files is simple. Start KCachegrind, select the File ➪ Open menu, and select the output file. The Callgrind output files can be read directly into KCachegrind, but other profiler output may require a conversion to a format supported by KCachegrind. This is the case with APD and Xdebug, so we cover how to do that in the appropriate sections.

We cannot discuss every detail of KCachegrind, but we cover some of the highlights so users have a basic place to start exploring it further. When a profile data file is loaded into KCachegrind, it presents the data in a few different displays, with the main window split into panes. This should consist of a listing of all the functions in the leftmost pane, which can be sorted by weight, grouped by library, and searched. This provides a quick index to find a specific function of interest or to sort by the relative expense as measured by your profiler. The resource usage by each function is grouped by both Inclusive and Exclusive time (we use time here for simplicity, but it could be any resource measurement). Inclusive represents all the time spent within a given call and all its children. Alternatively, Exclusive is the time attributed to the single function call, but not any of the subsequent calls made within the function. The difference between the two can be used to isolate functions that are themselves expensive, versus functions whose time can be attributed to calling other functions. Initially finding a function with the highest exclusive time is the easiest way to find bottlenecks. Other panes are tabbed between callers and callees that display code, call tree graphs, and treemaps. Measurements can be displayed relative to their parent or to the entire profile, which is often useful if you are breaking down a specific function versus investigating the process as a whole. Values also can be displayed as an absolute value or a percentage. The best way to get acquainted with KCachegrind and your application is to start exploring. Try to determine what consumes time, and more importantly, why. Does it make sense? Is it necessary? Can it be improved? Is it a regression from previous versions?

APD

APD is a debugging and profiling extension for PHP. It shares many similarities with Xdebug, as discussed later. APD generates output dumps of time spent in PHP functions. Unlike C-level profilers, this provides valuable insight into major bottlenecks present at the PHP code level. This is one of the first places to look for performance problems because they are the simplest to correct—and likely the most significant. APD provides a command line tool `pprofp` to display its output in an easily readable format. However, it is probably better to harness the powerful GUI interactions of KCachegrind (described earlier). For this, APD provides another command line tool called `pprof-2calltree` to convert APD output into a KCachegrind compatible format.

Because APD is a Zend extension, we need to enable it in the INI configuration. It requires a specific format for loading the shared object file; refer to the APD documentation if you have any difficulties in configuration. Starting a profile is very simple: Add an `apd_set_pprof_trace($path)` line in the

---

[6]`http://kde-cygwin.sourceforge.net/`

code where the profiling should begin. The `$path` argument is a path to a directory where output files are created. As in our other profiling examples, we likely want to exclude previous runs used to warm the server before we start profiling. The simplest and most convenient method is to conditionally use the `apd_set_pprof_trace()` call with something like a GET variable. As requests are made, data is output to the given path, which can then be analyzed on the command line with the included `pprofp` tool (found in the compiled source directory of APD). Use the `-h` option to display all the options. Here is an example of sorting by memory usage:

```
$ ./pprofp -m /tmp/apd/pprof.77614.0
Trace for:
/Users/shire/www/wp/index.php
==
Total Elapsed Time = 0.21
Total System Time = 0.03
Total User Time = 0.12
Real User System secs/ cumm
%Time (excl/cumm) (excl/cumm) (excl/cumm) Calls call s/call Memory Usage Name
-------------------------------------------------------------------------------
7.7 0.01 0.01 0.01 0.01 0.00 0.00 562 0.0000 0.0000 1104018188 array_pop
2.8 0.00 0.05 0.00 0.04 0.00 0.01 537 0.0000 0.0000 1054468320 apply_filters
9.6 0.01 0.01 0.01 0.01 0.00 0.00 313 0.0000 0.0000 647343972 preg_replace
3.0 0.00 0.00 0.00 0.00 0.00 0.00 265 0.0000 0.0000 518972872 preg_match
3.6 0.01 0.01 0.00 0.00 0.00 0.00 249 0.0000 0.0000 493651992 is_object
1.8 0.00 0.01 0.00 0.01 0.00 0.00 215 0.0000 0.0000 422532956 WP_Object_Cache->get
0.9 0.00 0.01 0.00 0.01 0.00 0.00 201 0.0000 0.0000 394492852 wp_cache_get
5.7 0.01 0.01 0.01 0.01 0.00 0.00 347 0.0000 0.0000 381391436 is_string
1.5 0.00 0.00 0.00 0.00 0.00 0.00 182 0.0000 0.0000 367797120 array_slice
1.8 0.00 0.00 0.00 0.00 0.00 0.00 178 0.0000 0.0000 348199300 is_array
1.7 0.00 0.00 0.00 0.00 0.00 0.00 165 0.0000 0.0000 330145288 strlen
0.8 0.00 0.06 0.00 0.05 0.00 0.01 161 0.0000 0.0000 329237400 call_user_func_array
...
```

The `pprofp` command line tool has many sort and tree view options; however, we typically prefer to see data in a much more visually and interactive display. To import our files into KCachegrind, we use the `pprof2calltree` command:

```
$ ./pprof2calltree -f /tmp/apd/pprof.77614.0
Writing KCachegrind compatible output to cachegrind.out.pprof.77614.0
```

The subsequently generated file, `cachegrind.out.pprof.77614.0`, can then be loaded and viewed directly by KCachegrind. APD's approach to profiling your code is greatly simplified over other C-level tools, such as Callgrind, that require more setup time around the server process and permissions. APD also allows quick iterations over different sections of code, scripts, and modifications. Unfortunately, APD has much less active development than its close cousin Xdebug.

Xdebug

Xdebug is a full-featured profiler as well as a debugger for PHP. It is actively maintained and used by many developers.

```
xdebug.profiler_enable = 1
xdebug.profiler_output_dir = "/tmp/xdebug"
```

The above two configurations enable the output of profiler data by Xdebug into the specified path, similar to APD. A number of other configuration options like `xdebug.profiler_enable_trigger` enable a GET/POST trigger for profiling. As with the previously mentioned profilers, warming the server before profiling is recommended with either the GET/POST triggers or just ignoring the previously generated output files. Unlike APD, Xdebug generates files that are in Callgrind format and can be viewed directly by KCachegrind. Figure 15-4 shows a call graph visualization of Xdebug profiling data using KCacheGrind.

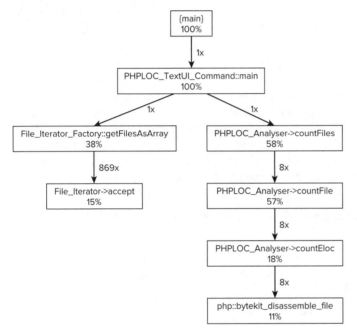

FIGURE 15-4: A call graph that has been generated using Xdebug and KCachegrind for an invocation of the `phploc` tool

A number of other tools have been developed to work with Xdebug:

➤ Carica CacheGrind (`http://ccg.wiki.sourceforge.net/`)

➤ Webgrind (`http://code.google.com/p/webgrind/`)

➤ MacCallGrind (`http://www.maccallgrind.com/`)

Because Xdebug and APD both include other debugging tools, use extra caution when using them on a production system. It is possible to display sensitive information about code or data to end users.

XHProf

XHProf is a profiler extension with a PHP-based front-end. It was initially written by Facebook and later provided under an open-source license. XHProf has the advantage of integrating well into an existing PHP application and displaying its output as part of a web-accessible interface. This makes integrating profile runs directly into PHP and displaying them as an integrated part of existing applications much simpler than most of the other profiler tools covered so far. The downsides are XHProf's relatively young age and its requirement to modify existing PHP source code.

The XHProf source contains three major directories to be aware of. The `extension` path contains the C-level extension code that can be compiled and installed like any other PHP extension. The `xhprof_html` and `xhprof_lib` directories contain PHP source code for generating and displaying the HTML viewable output of profiles. These must be included in the document root for the server you want to save and/or display reports on. A basic INI configuration would contain the extension line and a configuration option to specify an output directory for profile runs. This is very similar to the Xdebug and APD profilers we have covered already.

```
extension=xhprof.so
xhprof.output_dir="/tmp/xhpof/"
```

The XHProf web interface automatically looks for profiles in this directory, which you specify via a unique URL for each run. Profiling can be enabled using the `xhprof_enable()` function call, which also accepts various flags to enable different profile data such as memory resource tracking. Profiling is subsequently disabled and output captured via the `xhprof_disable()` function, which returns an array structure of the profiler output. This can be directly parsed by custom code, saved for later, or displayed directly within the page output for real-time feedback on the results of the request. Again, this is one of the powerful aspects of XHProf, at the expense of more code modifications.

To save output to the output directory, the following example code can be used (taken from the XHProf documentation):

```
include_once $XHPROF_ROOT . "/xhprof_lib/utils/xhprof_lib.php";
include_once $XHPROF_ROOT . "/xhprof_lib/utils/xhprof_runs.php";
$xhprof_runs = new XHProfRuns_Default();
$run_id = $xhprof_runs->save_run($xhprof_data, "xhprof_foo");
print
"--------------\n".
"Assuming you have set up the http based UI for \n".
"XHProf at some address, you can view run at \n".
"http://<xhprof-ui-address>/index.php?run=$run_id&".
"source=xhprof_foo\n".
"--------------\n";
```

This code requires files from the `xhprof_libs` path included in the source code and creates a class to save the generated output. In this example, a URL is displayed that can be used to directly reference the interface for this profile run.

Obviously, this code allows a fine-grained level of control over how you display and use the data in your particular code base. Any number of other actions could be taken at this point, including saving the URL in a database for later reference and using it as part of an automatic e-mail notification.

XHProf's documentation provides more details on its usage and walks through examples that can be used initially and expanded upon for a given use case. The ability to integrate directly into existing code is a powerful advantage, despite its initial extra effort and maintenance. This also should allow for quicker runs after it has been integrated as part of existing tools. XHProf also contains features that take into account production environments, such as decreasing the number of samples to minimize performance impact. Because XHProf handles its sampling via PHP function calls, keep in mind that this profiling is best used for measuring components of a larger system specific to the PHP code base. It is not a full profile from request start to finish and may exclude very low-level details. It is, however, an excellent tool for finding inefficient PHP code as part of performance testing or a regular development toolset.

OProfile

OProfile is an operating system (OS) level profiling tool that gathers CPU statistics for the entire system. Similar to application-level profiling with Valgrind or Gprof, OProfile gathers CPU usage and provides reports for later analysis. OProfile differs from other profilers, however, because it collects statistics for every running process as well as the kernel. This is a perspective on the health of the entire system that can allow users to get a better understanding of complete performance. This is especially helpful if other activity on the machine is suspected of a general slowdown. OProfile is also convenient to use on an ongoing basis because it does not have high overhead compared to other profilers. The downsides of OProfile are that it is currently described as alpha state and it requires compiling a Linux kernel module. Therefore, this particular tool is available only on Linux systems, although similar tools likely exist for other platforms you may be running.

Referencing the documentation for OProfile is a must to take advantage of specific features. A number of events can be tracked by the profiler, as well as other options specific to the OS and architecture. In the most basic scenario, after installing the OProfile tools and kernel module, the OProfile daemon, which collects statistics in the background, is started with the `opcontrol --start` command. Because OProfile takes regular samples of activity, the longer the daemon runs, the better the data collection is. To dump the latest data out, the `--dump` option can be passed to `opcontrol`; subsequently, the `opreport` command can be used to analyze the output. Simply running `opreport` as shown here lists the statistics on a library or binary basis:

```
samples| %|
------------------
2244 60.3064 no-vmlinux
1151 30.9325 libphp5.so
147 3.9506 libc-2.7.so
104 2.7949 httpd
103 99.0385 httpd
```

More detailed listings can be viewed, for example, with the -1 option to list by symbols.

```
samples  %        image name    app name      symbol name
2244     60.3064  no-vmlinux    no-vmlinux    (no symbols)
147      3.9506   libc-2.7.so   libc-2.7.so   (no symbols)
138      3.7087   libphp5.so    libphp5.so    _zend_mm_alloc_int
80       2.1500   libphp5.so    libphp5.so    _zend_mm_free_int
59       1.5856   libphp5.so    libphp5.so    zend_mm_add_to_free_list
48       1.2900   libphp5.so    libphp5.so    zend_mm_search_large_block
```

As with other profilers, OProfile output can be converted for use with KCachegrind via an `op2cg` command included with the KCachegrind source.

SYSTEM METRICS

strace

System calls can be of particular interest and may account for more time than what is obvious in a CPU profiler. Switching to kernel space, blocking, or otherwise can account for significant delays. System calls should be high on the list of items to check for obvious performance issues. strace is one tool commonly available on Linux operating systems, but counterparts exist on other operating systems. strace has a couple of specific features that can be useful when looking at performance testing. Particularly of interest are file system and network operations, because they have the tendency to have the most latency, which is not always apparent in a profiler. strace can filter these calls out for you with the -e trace= command line argument.

For example, to get a trace of all file-related activity for Apache in standalone mode, use this:

```
strace -e trace=file httpd -X
```

Likewise, to get a trace of all network activity, use this:

```
strace -e trace=network httpd -X
```

The other functionality of strace that is particularly useful is to get time estimations for each call. Without this feature, it could be difficult to quickly determine how relevant any given system call is. A file operation that is short lived is not as significant as an operation that hangs for 400ms while it reads megabytes of data from a disk. Several options for displaying time are available, both in specificity and how the time is calculated: timestamps, relative timestamps for the start of each call, or total time per system call. The -r argument for strace prints relative timestamps for every call, giving you a quick reference for the delays caused by each call.

In a multi-process server environment, such as Apache, it can be useful to connect to a single running process to capture requests. This can be especially useful on a production host where a restart or other actions would interfere with live requests. strace accepts the -p argument followed by a process ID to attach to a running process and trace its system calls.

```
$ strace -r -p 3397
Process 3397 attached - interrupt to quit
0.000000 accept(16,
...
```

When attached to an Apache process, it likely is blocked on an accept() call that waits for an incoming request from the client. In the following output, we can see that a request is accepted and we begin execution. Of significant importance are the lstat calls that occur for every directory level of the requested file. Individually, these lstat calls do not appear to consume a significant amount of time, but together they consume 0.001786s (0.000257s + 0.000255s + 0.000258s + 0.000713s + 0.000303s). In addition, the following is simply for one test file; this would have to be multiplied for every file included in the request. For a large code base, disk activity like this can cause significant and unpredictable delays in response time.

The specific problem shown below is typically resolved by using a full path with an opcode cache that has disk stats disabled, and via recent upgrades in PHP-5.3 to minimize file activity.

```
...  {sa_family=AF_INET, sin_port=htons(35435), sin_addr=inet_addr("127.0.0.1")},
     [2305843009213693968]) = 3
3.981991 rt_sigaction(SIGUSR1, {SIG_IGN}, {0x43f488, [], SA_RESTORER|SA_INTERRUPT,
     0x7f7f35647f60}, 8) = 0
0.000259 fcntl(3, F_SETFD, FD_CLOEXEC) = 0
0.000154 getsockname(3, {sa_family=AF_INET, sin_port=htons(80), sin_addr=
     inet_addr("127.0.0.1")}, [2305843009213693968]) = 0
0.000221 setsockopt(3, SOL_TCP, TCP_NODELAY, [1], 4) = 0
0.000418 read(3, "GET /test.php HTTP/1.0\r\nUser-Agen"..., 4096) = 86
0.010485 rt_sigaction(SIGUSR1, {SIG_IGN}, {SIG_IGN}, 8) = 0
0.000165 gettimeofday({1241644382, 643223}, NULL) = 0
0.000597 gettimeofday({1241644382, 643800}, NULL) = 0
0.000218 stat("/home/user/www/site/test.php", {st_mode=S_IFREG|0644,
     st_size=70, ...}) = 0
0.000489 umask(077) = 022
0.000144 umask(022) = 077
0.000236 setitimer(ITIMER_PROF, {it_interval={0, 0}, it_value={60, 0}}, NULL) = 0
0.000249 rt_sigaction(SIGPROF, {0x7f7f350a2a9b, [PROF], SA_RESTORER|SA_RESTART,
     0x7f7f35647f60}, {0x7f7f350a2a9b, [PROF],
SA_RESTORER|SA_RESTART, 0x7f7f35647f60}, 8) = 0
0.000139 rt_sigprocmask(SIG_UNBLOCK, [PROF], NULL, 8) = 0
0.001966 getcwd("/"..., 4095) = 2
0.000489 chdir("/home/user/www/site") = 0
0.000467 setitimer(ITIMER_PROF, {it_interval={0, 0}, it_value={120, 0}}, NULL) = 0
0.000278 rt_sigaction(SIGPROF, {0x7f7f350a2a9b, [PROF], SA_RESTORER|SA_RESTART,
     0x7f7f35647f60}, {0x7f7f350a2a9b, [PROF],
SA_RESTORER|SA_RESTART, 0x7f7f35647f60}, 8) = 0
0.000279 rt_sigprocmask(SIG_UNBLOCK, [PROF], NULL, 8) = 0
0.000310 gettimeofday({1241644382, 649124}, NULL) = 0
0.000257 lstat("/home", {st_mode=S_IFDIR|0755, st_size=4096, ...}) = 0
0.000255 lstat("/home/user", {st_mode=S_IFDIR|0755, st_size=4096, ...}) = 0
0.000258 lstat("/home/user/www", {st_mode=S_IFDIR|0755, st_size=4096, ...}) = 0
0.000713 lstat("/home/user/www/site", {st_mode=S_IFDIR|0755, st_size=4096, ...})
     = 0
0.000303 lstat("/home/user/www/site/test.php", {st_mode=S_IFREG|0644, st_size=70,
     ...}) = 0
0.000290 open("/home/user/www/site/test.php", O_RDONLY) = 4
0.000277 fstat(4, {st_mode=S_IFREG|0644, st_size=70, ...}) = 0
0.000718 read(4, "<?php\n\n\nfor ($i=0; $i < 100; $i++"..., 8192) = 70
0.000438 read(4, ""..., 8192) = 0
0.000345 read(4, ""..., 8192) = 0
0.000978 close(4) = 0
0.000480 chdir("/") = 0
```

Sysstat

Statistics collection over time can prove to be extremely valuable. When a performance or scalability problem arises, it can be immediately referenced for historical comparisons, to track trends as part of verification of a release, for ongoing system performance, or as proactive detection of possible upcoming issues. A number of tools and standards are available to collect, store, and display system metrics.

A full discussion of all the available options on this topic is out of the scope of this chapter, but it's definitely a must for any service. We briefly cover Sysstat, an excellent set of tools for collection of host statistics that can then be aggregated by various methods. We discuss details for single hosts only as it relates to performance testing. We recommend you include this tool or others as part of an aggregation for historical data across all your production hosts.

Sysstat is a collection of tools and may require some additional setup to collect statistics on a regular interval. We don't go into the details of installation, so refer to the online tutorials and documentation for further assistance. On many platforms with a modern package management system, most of these details can be handled automatically, allowing you to skip directly to the examples below.

The command line tool `sar` enables you to display various historical and current statistics for CPU, memory, and I/O. Running `sar -u` outputs a list of recently gathered statistics and an average at the very end:

```
Linux 2.6.26-2-amd64 (debian64) 05/07/2009 _x86_64_
02:05:01 AM CPU %user %nice %system %iowait %steal %idle
02:15:01 AM all 0.02 0.00 0.25 0.00 0.00 99.73
02:25:01 AM all 0.01 0.00 0.33 0.00 0.00 99.66
....
12:35:01 PM all 0.75 0.00 2.70 0.01 0.00 96.53
12:45:01 PM all 0.02 0.00 0.30 0.00 0.00 99.69
Average: all 0.11 0.00 0.59 0.00 0.00 99.30
```

Likewise, other statistics for the memory or I/O usage can be retrieved with the `-r` and `-d` options, respectively:

```
$ sar -r
Linux 2.6.26-2-amd64 (debian64) 05/07/2009 _x86_64_
02:05:01 AM kbmemfree kbmemused %memused kbbuffers kbcached kbswpfree kbswpused
        %swpused kbswpcad
02:15:01 AM 589516 415344 41.33 22712 207340 409616 0 0.00 0
02:25:01 AM 589396 415464 41.35 22772 207336 409616 0 0.00 0
...
12:35:01 PM 587340 417520 41.55 23288 209428 409616 0 0.00 0
12:45:01 PM 587452 417408 41.54 23340 209476 409616 0 0.00 0
Average: 588916 415944 41.39 22980 207816 409616 0 0.00 0
$ sar -d
Linux 2.6.26-2-amd64 (debian64) 05/07/2009 _x86_64_
02:05:01 AM DEV tps rd_sec/s wr_sec/s avgrq-sz avgqu-sz await svctm %util
02:15:01 AM dev3-0 0.15 0.00 2.38 16.37 0.00 1.01 0.32 0.00
02:15:01 AM dev3-1 0.15 0.00 2.38 16.37 0.00 1.01 0.32 0.00
02:15:01 AM dev3-2 0.00 0.00 0.00 0.00 0.00 0.00 0.00 0.00
...
Average: dev3-0 0.19 0.00 3.74 20.13 0.00 3.29 0.83 0.02
Average: dev3-1 0.19 0.00 3.74 20.13 0.00 3.29 0.83 0.02
Average: dev3-2 0.00 0.00 0.00 0.00 0.00 0.00 0.00 0.00
Average: dev3-5 0.00 0.00 0.00 0.00 0.00 0.00 0.00 0.00
```

Often, we are interested in gathering live statistics to record as we perform different configurations or load tests on the system. For this, sar accepts additional arguments specifying how often to display a line of data as well as how many lines. The first argument is how often in seconds, while the second argument specifies the number of lines. Some examples:

```
sar -u 2 10   # Display output every 2 seconds, 10 times (20 seconds)
sar -u 10 100 # display output every 10 seconds, 100 times (1,000 seconds)
sar -u 1 0    # Display output every second, indefinitely
```

Sysstat contains other useful tools for extracting and recording data. Pidstat, for example, can track these statistics and associate them with specific processes, greatly simplifying the hunt for a process consuming too many resources. Refer to the documentation and tutorials for other ways to use these tools; the discussion here is intended only as a taste for what output and data can be attained.

Custom Instrumentation

In some cases, profiling or testing tools does not provide the necessary information to test or analyze code. In these cases, custom instrumentation may be necessary. Use caution so you are not developing custom instrumentation simply for the sake of doing so. In most cases, the tools described here provide the necessary data. Sometimes, however, these tools either do not display enough particular information or cannot correlate it to application-specific details. Others may be too heavyweight for a simple or quick test or measurement. Any custom instrumentation must be regarded with skepticism because it is much more likely to contain faults due to its limited distribution and age. Regular sanity checks with other more well-tested tools is good practice and is worth the time, should it prove to contradict your custom results. It is often convenient in PHP to use microtime function calls, as well as the memory_get_usage functions. The microtime function call returns the time in seconds and microseconds. By default, it returns a string with seconds followed by a space and then the number of microseconds. If true is passed as the optional argument, the value returned is a float with the fractional part representing the microseconds. Microtime is most useful and applicable to active debugging or finding significantly inefficient sections of code. As an example, if an inefficiency is detected by some other means, the resolution may not be specific enough or it may be helpful to get a quick validation that a code change is in fact improving performance or accounting for the loss in CPU resources. This is the place where tests should be validated to ensure that such in-place timings have not misled the optimization process; it is easy to exclude code and changes that might affect the overall request time.

The memory_get_usage() call reports memory usage and accepts a Boolean argument to change its return value from the internal memory allocation to the actual real memory allocated from the OS. Memory allocations in PHP are optimized by allocating and managing larger chunks of memory from the native OS. PHP then manages these on a more fine-grained level to optimize performance and usage and to handle memory leaks and debugging specific to PHP. Because of this custom management layer, PHP can report both what the application is using from its system allocated pool and what it has allocated as a whole from the OS. Both are valuable and depend on what is being measured. For evaluating the general performance of a PHP script, the internal memory allocation is likely most valuable. This gives a good indication of how much memory the script utilizes. However, to get a better picture of what the PHP process as a whole is using from the OS, true should be passed to get the real memory allocation counts. An important catch exists here that illustrates possible faults with custom instrumentation, because PHP extensions may not always use the internal PHP memory manager, especially if they are linked into third-party libraries. This could result in memory use that goes unreported by PHP. In these cases, the only way to track down the errant memory usage is via higher-level operating system statistics or tools such as `sar` or Valgrind. Keep this and other possible misleading data in mind when developing any custom tests.

The function `memory_get_peak_usage()` is also of particular use, because it reports the highest memory usage for the duration of the script. You can quickly see the maximum amount of memory consumed at any given time or compare this with other memory get usage results.

COMMON PITFALLS

Development versus Production Environments

We have mentioned this before, but make sure your test environment matches as closely as possible the production environment. If at all possible, do some tests in the actual production environment. At the very least, production testing validates the results you saw in your test or development environment and ensures the gains are taking place. A good example of this is the `--enable-debug` option that can be passed to PHP's configure scripts during installation from source. This option enables very useful debug information like memory leak detection, but the downside is that it is an extremely costly option. PHP operates at significantly slower speeds when this is enabled, so it is sometimes enabled in development environments and disabled in production. Many performance changes have been fouled by tests on a development environment, which in reality represented nearly zero gains in the production environment simply because they optimized bottlenecks only present in development. Do not make this mistake; test in near production state and retest in production to ensure correct process and results.

CPU Time

Performance tools often measure two CPU metrics, either CPU time or real time. It is important to know the difference between the two and how to measure them. Typically, tools such as Callgrind and other profilers measure CPU time. This is the amount of time the task has been given execution time on the CPU, expressed in a cycles or ticks measurement. Other tools, say the PHP microtime function call, attempt to measure the actual passage of time as we know it. Unlike CPU time, this real-time measurement includes any time the process spends sleeping or waiting on I/O transfers—for example, MySQL or other remote service requests. CPU time is a great measurement for cutting down on actual CPU usage, but it doesn't account for delays seen in network activity or other latencies.

Micro-Optimizations

It is common for rumors of micro-optimizations to emerge in the discussion of optimizations and performance. Specific coding conventions are usually the subject, such as "I heard someone say that feature X is slow." Specifically in PHP, it is not uncommon to hear of avoiding or using double quoted strings, `ini_set()`, `define()`, objects, print, and variable references. Some of these have more weight than others, and some have historical applications that no longer apply. In all likelihood, these are not the things that will keep your application from scaling or performing well. It is important to be able to distinguish between what is an important issue and what is not. Discouraging developers from using double quoted strings doesn't keep a poorly written query from bogging down your site or keep a core framework function from becoming a new bottleneck for all requests. You should never leave it up to a rumor (or even a chapter on performance testing) to blindly determine the future direction of your code or your focus of attention. You must use good sense and strategy.

Micro-optimizations are more of a burden for developers and code maintainability than anything else. The only suggested use is for tight loops or often-called code that actually has a significant measurable speed improvement on the full request with limited development impact. Anything more is likely to be a burden on the code and developers, and in reality it's probably not that significant. Changes are also made to future PHP releases that nullify the effects of some historically slow language semantics. It is best to leave these changes to core optimizations of PHP where they can have a low impact on developers and high impact on performance.

PHP as the Glue

As part of the decision-making process of what to test for performance and how to make decisions based upon the results, you need to understand the designed limitations of PHP. Because PHP is developed as a simple web-centric scripting language for fast development and iteration, it does not have the same capabilities for performance that are present in C, for example. Specifically, network operations and byte handling tasks generally do not perform in PHP and many other high-level scripting languages. PHP is best used as "glue" for other larger, more optimized libraries that have been written and optimized for these tasks. This is not to say that these features should never be written in PHP; it is often very beneficial to implement initial business logic and framework code in PHP. This simplifies testing and development, especially when the code is expected to change. But after the code is solidified in its functionality and performance becomes a concern, these core components should be candidates for a move into the optimized world of PHP extensions or other libraries. Likewise, do not reinvent already existing extensions. PECL contains a plethora of extensions that link into existing libraries that are optimized for very specific tasks. If you find that some core functionality is limiting performance during tests, make sure it is not something that already exists in another form.

Priority of Optimization

The first determination that must be made about any optimization effort is whether it is worthwhile. Several factors come into play such as high-level priorities and the nature of the business. Startup web companies, for example, have a high level of interest in creating new features and making them available as soon as possible. Sometimes, these features are released well before they are really ready for users and fully tested. This may seem like a rash and unwise approach, but it can be advantageous to be first to market and often is a determining factor in the success of a business. In these situations, having the responsibility to test, perform, or otherwise is often reactive rather than proactive. This is especially true in viral growth applications where functionality, performance, and scalability can all break within hours of release. This becomes a point at which testing can become a critical skill in which time is key for determining the nature and source of a problem. Detecting regressions based upon previous data or simply experience can save time and money, not to mention having the correct tools and skills in place ready to execute at a moment's notice.

When business needs to move quickly, some features may not even be around long enough to be worth investing in. It should also become clear that the best gains for optimization work are in core functionality. This is the area most likely to be common across all activity, so it's the best investment for both optimizations and testing infrastructure. Conveniently, these also are likely the most heavily used and often-called portions of code.

As an application grows, performance can become a full-time concern. The operational cost of maintaining 10 regular users is vastly different than that of 10 million users, which is nowhere near supporting hundreds of millions of users. As growth and usage increase, new scalability problems emerge—sometimes slowly, sometimes immediately. It is very common to exceed an unknown threshold or limitation that can render a site useless. Proactive testing can help to bring to the surface potentially significant problems. You should create a road map, either literally or mentally, of what future thresholds are likely to be crossed and what development or testing should be done now or in the future. This helps everyone focus on building the product with less time spent fixing an unforeseen break in performance or functionality.

CONCLUSION

We have covered motivations, tools, and best practices for performance testing PHP and web-based applications. This outlines some of the core technologies and obstacles I've experienced optimizing high-demand, growth, and performance-driven web services. I hope that they can be a useful reference for you and the next generation of web services and that they encourage a realistic expectation of performance and usability. Above all, please keep the following in mind:

➤ Validate tests with different environments and different tools.

➤ Do what's reasonable for your business and technological goals and priorities.

➤ Take the time to make quality open-source contributions; a well-thought-out bug report makes the world a better place.

16

Security

Arne Blankerts

WHAT IS SECURITY?

When addressing the topic of security in the IT world, the first thing to do is define what the term "security" means and how customers as well as colleagues interpret it. If we were to ask politicians, security basically comes down to surveillance. And, of course, monitoring servers and infrastructure is a vital component, yet getting an alarm shows only one thing—that an attack has happened (and most likely was successful). Any type of surveillance or monitoring, by its very nature, triggers the alert but has no means to actually protect against it or the flaw in the application that made it possible. By this definition, monitoring is only one of many elements in a holistic security concept.

If we ask administrative IT staff what security means for them, the answer most probably goes in the direction of user accounting and permissions. It also covers the requirement to disable and remove unneeded services—so-called "hardening"—as well as applying strict firewall rules. Again, these answers are correct. But as already identified with surveillance, a secure infrastructure is not enough. Of course, it is of vital importance that the application, once developed, is executed in an environment that is trusted and relied upon. But even the best web application can't be secure if the database it connects to is reachable via unprotected public networks or the communication with external systems runs over unencrypted protocols.

Apparently, security requires various (small) aspects to be combined into complementing measures, which, by working together, make up a holistic concept and a secure environment.

The beauty of the measures mentioned so far is that they can easily be tested and thus not only the functionality of the applications and its components, but also the security can be verified and monitored using automated processes. Actually, yet another group could be polled on their opinion on security: users. Developers as well as designers with experience in dealing with customers may argue that users don't know what they want to begin with, and thus are not qualified to judge security. Even if that may technically be correct, their opinion and their sense of security should not be underestimated as factors in the success or failure of the application or website.

SECURE BY DESIGN

Analyzing the process by which most software projects get developed these days shows that there is hardly any time for security. Almost impossible deadlines are followed by ever-changing feature sets requested by clients as well as management. The usual short time to market does not allow for mistakes at development time, nor does it provide the option to add a security layer later on. This is an even greater reason to embed security into the process of planning and implementing right from the start, breaking up the "layer" into individual parts that take care of their respective fields.

This is exactly what the paradigm Secure by Design stands for: The application is designed from the ground up to be secure. Of course, nobody intentionally adds mistakes or security flaws to an application. But experience shows that a paranoid attitude helps block common attack vectors and avoids typical mistakes right from the start of the development.

Operations

Knowing that a secure environment is a pre-condition for a safe (web) application, planning the infrastructure for the production site should already start at development time. For many projects, this process starts with the question of what type of hosting it will have:

➤ A physical server

➤ A server farm

➤ A virtualized environment (a virtual root server)

➤ A simple shared hosting (often called "webspace")

Companies running a server farm most likely create dedicated systems per service, whether virtualized or not. For smaller projects, though, often the power of simple shared hosting is sufficient. The requirement to blindly trust the service provider is problematic from a security perspective here. Using a shared webspace, the customer is bound to the limitations and configurations of the OS— usually a Unix- or Linux-based environment—as made by the ISP. Not taking into account any possible technical limitations for development, this also affects the trustworthiness of session data and other content.

If newly discovered vulnerabilities within the software stack in use aren't closed promptly or published fixes don't get applied, the security for the whole application is, at best, undefined if not doomed. A vulnerable database server accepting connections only via local sockets, for instance, may be something you can live with for a short period of time on your own root server, but on shared hosting environments, this is automatically a fatal problem. It allows an attacker to gain control over any application or website by merely taking over its persistence layer.

Security holes in third-party applications are not the only source of potential trouble: A simple configuration mistake may very well disrupt the security of the server or "just" compromise all the websites hosted. A good and catchy example of a dangerous yet common mistake found in shared hosting environments is an identical and thus shared path for session storage for all websites hosted. It may look completely harmless at first glance—especially because PHP generates the session identifiers automatically and also handles the storage and retrieval on its own—but it has a fatal side effect. Because PHP logically needs to have read and write access to the shared folder, an attacker needs only to overwrite an existing session file with a version he needs to gain access to the application the session originally related to. This allows for hacking through the back door, without actually exploiting any mistake in the attacked application.

If there is no way to adjust the path for session storage by individual virtual hosts, the only way to gain protection from this type of attack is to not store clear text session data anymore. This can be achieved either by implementing a custom PHP Session Save Handler or by installing the Suhosin[1] extension and activating its transparent encryption of session data.[2]

All in all, using shared hosting requires dealing with quite some uncertainties that may disqualify it for many projects. The alternative—running a server infrastructure—also comes with a cost: It must be planned and maintained by qualified personnel.

The question whether the risks in shared hosting are actually a problem for a project or if the overhead and effort of administering custom servers is justified cannot be answered on a general level, but needs to get re-determined individually on a project-by-project basis.

Physical Access

Another interesting question to raise on the subject of hosting and housing is the question about physical access: Who has access, when do they have it, why and in what way do they have access to servers, data, and processes? It should be obvious that even the best security on the software level has no effect on physical theft of hard discs or even the full server.

This also includes accessing and handling backups, because the backup media must be stored somewhere. As important as it may be to recover from a crash by falling back to an existing backup, it can be about as dangerous to give out personal and potentially confidential data to a third party by relying on the ISP backup system. For an attacker, it may be much easier, and thus cheaper, to simply steal the backup media than to hack into a secured server infrastructure. It is thus obligatory to store all data given a defined level of sensitivity only on encrypted file systems and storage media.

[1] http://www.suhosin.org/

[2] http://www.hardened-php.net/suhosin/configuration.html#suhosin.session
.encrypt

All modern Linux distributions, for instance, ship with a powerful cryptographic solution called LUKS,[3] which allows for transparent disc encryption in the background. That approach makes it ideal to be integrated into an existing infrastructure.

Software Development

After getting all the server-side requirements for a secure and reliable infrastructure in place, we can finally start developing the actual software that is supposed to be run on it. To satisfy the needs of the Secure by Design paradigm, we have only a few rules to follow, which are covered in the following sections.

No Security by Obscurity

A secure software setup, exactly as a secure encryption algorithm, does not rely on a secret implementation. If it is foreseeable that the approach used becomes publicly known and the security is void, then the chosen concept is just plain wrong. For example, concepts behind the widely used software PGP or GnuPG respectively are completely open—for GnuPG, that is even true for the source code—and documented, but still secure. It is secure because the system does not rely on an arcane algorithm, but only on secret keys. This concept isn't actually new; it was formulated by Auguste Kerckhoffs in 1883 and is known by Kerckhoffs' Maxime or Kerckhoffs' Prinzip.[4]

It is a very bad idea to trust that a URL without any links pointing to it won't get "found" by accident. Believing that "nobody knowing the URL makes it secure," many developers are using the well-known database administration software phpMyAdmin[5] with an easy-to-guess path like /db or /phpmyadmin. Besides various security problems that have been discovered within this software, more often than not, this administration interface is protected only by means of simple .htaccess files—often using easy-to-guess usernames and passwords—allowing a root connection to the database from the Web. Not relying on more secure logins or accessing it by plain HTTP instead of an encrypted secure layer like HTTPS leaves it open for various attack vectors. Finding a generally available phpMyAdmin installation—for example, by means of scripts—equals a win from an attacker's point of view, requiring only some additional time to gain full access to the MySQL Server.

What holds true for phpMyAdmin, of course, also applies to other software. If need be, having access to bot networks, and by that bandwidth, allows for scripts to apply brute force[6] techniques to guess typical administrative URLs and check for their existence, passing on a hit to its respective owner.

Separation of Concerns

If you know object-oriented programming, you might wonder why one of its pillars—the Separation of Concerns principle—supposedly increases security. The reason is simple: Because the responsibilities are cleanly assigned to separate modules, each such module can take care of its specific security concerns.

---

[3]http://code.google.com/p/cryptsetup/

[4]Auguste Kerckhoffs, "La cryptographie militaire," *Journal des sciences militaires*, Volume 9, Pages 5–38 (January 1883), Pages 161–191 (February 1883).

[5]http://phpmyadmin.net

[6]http://en.wikipedia.org/wiki/Brute_force

Moreover, this simplifies the API for everyone else, because data can be passed to the persistence layer regardless of its potential danger to SQL. This is a fundamental principle of object-oriented programming: The calling code does not care where and how the data is persisted. This not only allows for easy switching of the storage backend, but also relieves the business logic of security concerns that it cannot and should not have to deal with.

Another advantage of a modular architecture that should not be neglected is that the loose coupling of the business logic allows for adding additional security measures in arbitrary places later on. One example of this could be adding checks that ensure that a user is authorized to perform a specific action.

A Matter of Rights

Rights are an important topic in the world of software. This is not limited to the rights that are assigned to a user within the applications, but also encompasses the rights given to areas of the source code that interact with the database or other external services. Often, a single login is used equivalently for all concerns of the application. The fact that this approach is less than optimal becomes apparent when the application's load increases and you want to spread it across multiple database servers. At this point, you want a clear separation between read and write access to the database.

With regard to security, such blanket logins become a problem even earlier: Parts of the code are granted more access rights than required. Why, for instance, does the database account used to perform a search query need write access? How nonsensical this is becomes obvious in a shared-hosting environment, where only a blanket login to the database can be used. This is the same database account that is used for the administration of the application. This means that the application has, from the database server's point of view, the right to create and delete arbitrary tables. If the application's code has security issues—for instance, in the form of SQL injections (as discussed later in this chapter)—they can be exploited to gain full access to the database. When separate logins for read and write access are used instead, the security issues are still in the code, but the possibilities of exploiting them are clearly reduced.

Error Handling

Especially important, not only when working with databases, is the clean handling of errors. What is an error, actually? Errors and problems can, both expectedly and unexpectedly, occur in various forms at different places in the application, and they all need to be handled individually. The application expects to deal with faulty inputs from a user; it is not for nothing that these inputs are validated before they are used. Not being able to write a file because no space is left on the drive, however, can already be counted in the category of unexpected errors. In both error cases, the user needs to be informed that something went wrong. The presented information, however, differs greatly.

In the case of a failed login attempt due to invalid credentials, it is important to report this to the user without providing too much information that could be exploited by an attacker. Often, too much information—for instance, that the username provided was valid but the password was not—is provided in such a situation because of misunderstood usability. With the knowledge that a particular user account exists, the attacker can now move on to trying passwords.

Unexpected error situations that are usually communicated by means of exceptions must be caught. Otherwise, they lead to a PHP fatal error, and having that displayed to the user is a really bad idea, because it exposes too many details about the inner workings of the application to a potential attacker. As well, it shows too much (and often confusing) information to a legitimate user of the website. This is similar to the "blue screen" of the Windows operating system that shows a hex dump of the memory, something that is of no use to the average user.

Displaying this level of information on a website allows an attacker to refine his methods. For the end user, it is enough to display a friendly error message stating that the request unfortunately could not be served correctly. Detailed error information should, however, be captured and made available to administrators and developers via logfiles, e-mail, or even SMS.

Basic Settings

It is interesting to see what kind of information a web server provides attackers by default: operating system, version, installed modules, and PHP extensions and their version. All this is data that should not interest anyone, yet they are reported in error messages as well as via HTTP headers. Fortunately, this talkativeness of the web server and other components can be turned off (or at least be limited) in most cases. This hiding of details about the used server software does not prevent attacks or fix security issues in the code, of course. But it makes it a little bit harder for the attacker because he cannot use the data to look up something to exploit in a database; he must try out several exploits. This costs time and increases the likelihood of discovering the attack in progress.

The general rule is that all information that is unnecessarily disclosed about a system plays into the hands of an attacker. It is, therefore, an advantage to avoid "marketing" such information in the form of additional headers, stack traces, and class and file names when an error occurs in a production environment. Just as the Miranda right states "anything you say can and will be used against you in a court of law," we can say here that "anything your application discloses will be used against you." A healthy level of paranoia helps when developing software that is exposed to attacks 24 hours a day on the Internet because it makes the daily work on the software more relaxed and prevents the closing of security holes later.

WHAT DOES SECURITY COST?

Project managers, customers, and management want to see numbers:

➤ How long does it take to implement the requested feature?

➤ How much does it cost me?

➤ When can I see it?

➤ When can I use or ship it?

These questions are hard to answer when it comes to security, especially because the question "When can I see it?" is fundamentally wrong. You do not see good security; it is just there. Selling something that you cannot see to a non-technical person can be a strenuous task.

The truth of the matter is that the question about the costs of security arises only when you start to think about security too late in the development process. If you think about security only in hindsight, then the findings of an audit, for instance, can lead to the rewriting of entire classes, the refactoring of parts of the architecture, and the scrutiny of core concepts of the application. The extent to which you attend to known security issues in an application depends on the problem itself and the associated business impact. A home page that has been modified by an attacker is always embarrassing, but when this happens to the home page of a security company, the financial harm is measurably higher than when this happens to a personal blog.

Even if there are no known acute security issues in the application, you must think about how far to go with regard to securing it. A beautiful example to illustrate this issue is the protection of a lamp. Imagine a room with a lamp on the ceiling. Now think about ten possibilities of turning off this lamp. The first thought is most likely the light switch. If this were an application, we would need authorization at this point. Removing the light bulb from its socket is another option to turn off the lamp that we need to protect against. Further possibilities include cutting off the power to the house, removing the fuse for the power circuit the lamp is connected to, and cutting the power cable that powers the lamp, as well as more far-fetched ideas such as demolishing the house or turning off the power plant that provides energy to the town where the house stands. Of course, you can protect yourself against all these attack vectors. But whether it's worth the effort and expense to protect yourself against the demolition of a house to secure a lamp is more than questionable. In addition, we must pose the question of how much money is required to prevent the lamp from being destroyed and to replace the lamp if it comes to the worst.

If you think this analogy through, you realize that at a certain point, the cost for preventing an attack outweighs the financial damage of the actual attack. At that point, it does not make good economic sense to invest time and money into security, as sad as this may be from the viewpoint of a paranoiac.

THE MOST COMMON PROBLEMS

Unfortunately, people can make many mistakes when developing software. As with other areas of software engineering, the root cause of security problems is basically faulty source code written by human developers. Astonishingly, most developers make the same mistakes over and over. As a result, the programming language and server technology used do not matter. In many cases, developers are saved by the strong typing of compiled languages. Others are protected from their own mistakes because they are forced to use APIs that are built with security in mind.

The Open Web Application Security Project (OWASP)[7] was founded so that dynamically typed and highly flexible programming languages such as PHP do not miss out on security. For a considerable time now, this project has published the "Top 10 Web Application Security Risks." Although it is hard to make a blanket statement about the riskiness of a security issue, the listed problems are found in many applications and again and again in open-source projects. It depends on the application and its audience to what extent a vulnerability that is caused by one of these (or other) security issues actually leads to measurable damage.

A10: Unvalidated Redirects and Forwards

Whether via JavaScript or using vintage HTTP headers and PHP, the automated forwarding of a visitor from one page to another is a common practice of many websites. Whether for control within

---

[7]http://owasp.org

the application or to track "exit pages," the 30X family of HTTP headers is used often. To make the forwarding scripts as generic as possible, many developers pass the target URL as a parameter, for instance, in the form of `?target=http://domain.tld`. Sadly, we often overlook that this type of link can easily be abused by a third party to perform a redirect. Although this does not harm the abused website from a technical viewpoint, it undermines its reputation nevertheless. Furthermore, the original referrers can be disguised using manipulatable redirectors to the effect that the original source of an attack cannot be determined without the help of an administrator or developer of the abused website.

Because the direct technical consequences of using an insecure redirect script are limited and the trust of a user in the redirecting website is commonly underestimated, the fixing of this security problem usually has a low priority. Securing the redirect script is actually quite simple: For redirects within the application, it is theoretically sufficient to enforce that only relative links are passed to the redirect script.

An approach that is not only cleaner but also more effective for later analysis is the usage of a map. By assigning identifiers that are used in a link and then replaced with the real URL that is looked up in an array or table, the redirector is protected from manipulation. The gained security and maintainability are well worth the little additional configuration and maintenance effort.

A9: Insufficient Transport Layer Protection

To work with an online service, you have to communicate with it. Naturally, this is also the case for web services and websites. The HTTP protocol used for this is text-based and readable in clear text. This makes it easy to debug but poses a problem from a security viewpoint. The protocol itself is not the problem, but rather the connection over which it is used is not encrypted by default. Without encryption, every system involved in the transport of the data can read the data without effort—similar to a vintage postcard in the offline world. This may pose no problem for reading the latest news or weather forecast, but when it comes to personal data, an encrypted transport layer is a must to ensure the privacy of the user. And sadly, it is here that most commonly the first mistakes are made: Instead of fundamentally and fully using HTTPS, some developers like to distinguish allegedly important and less important data and switch between HTTPS and HTTP all the time. The data transferred via HTTPS is, of course, still "secure," but some data (such as the Session ID) is transferred both over HTTPS and in clear text over HTTP. Because the possession of a valid Session ID is usually enough to gain access, the secure transmission sadly becomes worthless. The attacker must be on the same physical network or must have access to a system that is involved in the transport to exploit such a vulnerability. But this attack vector gets more relevant as more users use mobile devices to get on the Internet or log in to public WLAN hotspots.

If you cannot abandon HTTP completely for technical reasons, but still have the requirement to work with encryption, then you can at least ensure that the Session ID is only transmitted over a secure connection. This can be achieved using an option for (session) cookies that limits their transmission to HTTPS. A change in protocol usually coincides with a change to the rights of the user, which is why a new Session ID should be issued at this point. That way the "secure" ID is never transmitted over an insecure connection, and the problem can be worked around elegantly.

Another problem is posed by misconfigured web servers with invalid or expired certificates. Such certificates are not technically less secure and not an actual problem of the transport layer, but they train the user to ignore error messages with regard to the validity of certificates completely. This behavior makes attacks such as phishing easier because the user has no chance to distinguish between the different error messages and the reasons for them. In public projects, only valid certificates for which the Certification Authority[8] is accepted by browsers should be used.

A8: Failure to Restrict URL Access

A surprisingly common problem concerns the correct protection of pages against unauthorized access. This mistake is essentially based on the widespread mistaken belief that pages cannot be found or accessed when there is no link pointing to them. At the same time, the developers provide indirect clues that an alternate URL might exist that could provide additional rights or cheaper ways of using a service. The URL `wlan_login_pay.html` implies, for instance, that a variant with a different suffix than `pay` exists. Finding this alternate URL by trying out suffixes such as `free` or `guest` is just a question of determination and time.

It is dangerous to make assumptions about the clickpath of a visitor without validating them. Just because the workflow of the application logic does not intend for one page to be accessed before another does not mean that a visitor will not try to do so. This is especially a problem with AJAX-based websites where multiple requests are made in an arbitrary order and where the sequence of responses is not guaranteed.

Another popular mistake is the blind trust in external configuration that might not work in the same way (or not at all) when the web server is changed. For instance, many projects use `.htaccess` files for their security. This works only with the Apache HTTPD web server, and even then, the support for `.htaccess` files can be turned off. Because checking whether such a configuration file exists means an additional I/O operation for each part of the path, and given that parsing the configuration file costs CPU time, we cannot stress enough that `.htaccess` files should not be used for securing a site. The respective configuration directives should be set in the central configuration file of the web server instead.

The main reason why many projects use `.htaccess` files is nonsensical to begin with: They try to protect directories that contain library code from public access using the `Deny from all` configuration directive. Why these files are located in a place that is accessible from the outside is not well founded. It can only be explained by the fact that Shared Hosting providers did not allow customers to put files outside of the document root in the past. These times should be over, though. If your provider still restricts you to putting files only into the document root, you should consider switching to another provider.

A7: Insecure Cryptographic Storage

Encryption is also frequently used apart from data transport. Fortunately, it is widely known that storing passwords in clear text is a really bad idea. Unfortunately, however, many mistakes are made with regard to encryption. First and foremost, you need to figure out whether the data needs to be decryptable at all. With passwords, for instance, this is not required. If the data does not need to be decryptable, a hashing algorithm is used instead of encryption. Well-known hashing algorithms are

---

[8]A Certificate Authority (CA) is an entity that issues digital certificates that certify the ownership of a public key by the named subject of the certificate.

MD5 or SHA1. Although MD5 is no longer suited for securing large amounts of data because of computable collisions, it is still suited for securing passwords because the hash is usually longer than the password itself. If possible, however, you should favor newer algorithms such as SHA1 over MD5.

When hashes are used to "encrypt" a password, the hashes need to be "salted" in order to prevent attacks using so-called Rainbow Tables.[9] The "salt" can be a one-time generated string, for instance, that is suffixed to the inputted password. Only the modified password is used for the hash calculation. Even if the hash value and the string used for salting become known to an attacker, it is still impossible to compute the original password. Even the Rainbow Tables are useless in this case, because they have no notion of the salt and thus resolve the hash value to a wrong original string.

Naturally, there is also data that you want to be able to decrypt after you have encrypted it for secure storage. OpenSSL and GPG help with this because they are built on top of proven algorithms and implementations. The development and implementation of custom crypto-algorithms cannot be discouraged enough: The design of such an algorithm is hard and tedious work that includes, among other things, mathematical proofs. This is an effort that is usually not worthwhile, particularly because the implementation of a crypto-algorithm in PHP code is always slower than the C implementations provided by OpenSSL and GPG, for instance.

Data, and especially sensitive data, should be encrypted only for backup. Both OpenSSL and GPG provide the functionality to generate encrypted archives for storage, and the respective keys can be stored separately on a USB stick, for instance. This way, the backups are secure even when they are stolen.

A6: Security Misconfiguration

Misconfiguration is another common cause of security problems. Developers tend to blindly trust that the administrators "know what they are doing" and protect the application against attacks. Without conventions for what rights are required by which service, this is a hopeless endeavor.

Most operating systems and Linux distributions try to deliver a system that is as complete as possible so you can work productively with it out of the box. As useful as this may be for a desktop computer, for a server system, it's not only superfluous but can also be dangerous. After the installation, it is therefore important to disable and, ideally, remove services that are not required to run the application in order to harden the system. This includes the disabling of unused user accounts, the changing of default passwords, and the customization of default configurations that are too lax. Many UNIX and Linux systems allow the root user, by default, to log in remotely from any IP, for instance. This is not only unnecessary but also dangerous and one of the first things that should be turned off after creating one's own user accounts. These user accounts ideally use key-based authentication instead of passwords, by the way.

SSH is not the only possible gateway for an attacker: Services such as MySQL or the web server are also attackable. Access to the MySQL server via TCP/IP, for instance, should be disabled when PHP only connects to it locally. When multiple database servers are used, they should be put into their own local network to protect them from external access.

But all these measures cannot really help when security updates are not installed frequently and new configurations are not tested exhaustively. Especially small changes that are mistakenly categorized as harmless often have unexpected side effects on allegedly unrelated services and systems.

---

[9]A Rainbow Table is a large database of pre-calculated hash values.

A5: Cross-Site Request Forgery (CSRF/XSRF)

Cross-Site Request Forgery (CSRF/XSRF) is an attack that often works only because users do not cleanly log out of websites or because they are logged in to multiple websites that are open in separate tabs of their browser. Today, session-based logins are usually used where the Session ID is stored in a cookie and needs to be transferred for each request. This is a sufficiently secure method when only one website is used at a time. The problem only arises when the user leaves the website without logging off or when he is using multiple websites in parallel by means of tabbed browsing. Because the session is usually still valid (with PHP's default setting, it is valid for 24 minutes), subsequent requests to the web server still include the cookie with the Session ID and are authorized for actions that might not be in the interest of the user. To trigger such a request, it is sufficient, for instance, to include an image in a forum where the URL references said server. Although the response from the server most likely does not return an image, the request is still processed and—thanks to the Session ID cookie—can perform actions such as sending mail or placing an order in the name of the user. And because broken images are commonplace in a forum, visitors hardly entertain a suspicion about the image link.

The usage of a "kidnapped" URL in a forum cannot be prevented. What can be prevented, however, is the functionality of such an attack. First and foremost, one should use $_POST only to receive data and completely ignore the existence of the $_REQUEST super-global variable. By itself, this measure does not prevent Cross-Site Request Forgery, but it prevents the attack vector from using a simple image link. An additional request token is required to be completely safe from Cross-Site Request Forgery attacks. This token is added in the form of a hidden input field to each form that is sent to the server. Because this token is uniquely generated for each form and each request, an attacker would need to guess the value of the request token. To make this guessing impossible, it is vital that the values of the request token are not predictable. Using sequential numbers or timestamps as the request token, for instance, is a bad idea.

A4: Insecure Direct Object References

It is temptingly simple (and unfortunately showcased in myriad tutorials) to access an "object" in the database using an ID that is passed via the URL. This may be sufficient for many fields of application—for instance, for a news website—but it can be dangerous in the context of a social network, for instance. Who is responsible for checking whether the requesting user has the right to see a specific object? This authorization check is usually implemented in scripts that are conceptually accessible only by privileged users. A popular scenario for such a setup is a news portal that differentiates between publicly accessible information and content that is available only to paying customers. When the scripts involved in displaying a news piece do not explicitly check the authorization, then the "public" part of the website can be abused to view the content that is supposed to be restricted: Someone simply has to guess the appropriate object ID.

Security holes based on insecure direct object references are unfortunately much more common than you would assume. Often, the provider's configuration interface is also affected and inadvertently allows access to the data of other customers. It is fascinating to observe that more authorization checks for read access are implemented than for write access. This seems to be due to the popular misconception that an attacker first has to read the data before he can modify it.

In addition to explicit authorization checks—and especially for write access—it helps to not transmit the object identified in clear text, but rather using an alternate "Link-ID" that prevents inference of the actual ID. This concept is popular, for example, with photo and video portals that prevent the automated scraping and retrieval of their entire database using this approach. This is because the identifiers need to be guessed and tested, which is so slow that it is not worth the effort.

A3: Broken Authentication and Session Management

The safe storage, processing, and handover of session and login data are complex undertakings that many websites implement in an insecure way. Apart from the problems that were already discussed in sections "A9: Insufficient Transport Layer Protection" and "A7: Insecure Cryptographic Storage," the commonly found Forgotten Password functionality in particular has lots of potential for making mistakes.

A website that can send out the stored password constitutes a violation of "A7: Insecure Cryptographic Storage." Having the Forgotten Password functionality directly generate and send out a new password is only slightly better because it allows the change of passwords for arbitrary user accounts simply by guessing the respective e-mail addresses.

The right way, therefore, can only be to send mail to the user with a link that triggers the setting of a new password. To hamper the abuse of the functionality further, it should be triggered only once during a specified timeframe.

It is also important that the (new) password is strong enough. The best encryption is obviously worthless when the password is "12345." Upon input validation, the strength of the password should be checked. A good password is at least six characters long, must not contain only letters or only numbers, and contains at least one special character.

After a successful login, as well as after any change in access rights, the `session_regenerate_id()` function should be used to issue a new Session ID. In addition to the change from HTTP to HTTPS that was discussed in "A9: Insufficient Transport Layer Protection," this measure effectively prevents so-called Session Fixation attacks. Session Fixation means that an attacker can bring his victim to access the attacked website with a modified link that starts a session with a pre-defined Session ID. Because the security of a session is based on the fact that the Session ID is secret and unique to each visitor, the attacker can now access the website using the same rights of the victim.

PHP has the bad habit of using an ID that is passed to `session_start()` without validating it. This allows an attacker to specify the (first) Session ID no matter whether it has already been used on the server. Even if the original session with that ID is already expired, it is newly started. A flag should be created upon first usage that signals the flag that the Session ID was created by the application itself. If the flag is not found, a call of `session_regenerate_id(TRUE)` discards the current Session ID and all associated data. Now, the flag for the clean session can be set.

This is worth the effort only when the secured Session ID is transmitted using a cookie and not as part of the URL. The transmission of the Session ID within a link—this includes the context of a redirect using the `header()` function—makes the Session ID accessible to third parties such as ad servers or tracking software and, in general, to everyone who looks at HTTP referrers or logfiles.

A2: Cross-Site Scripting (XSS)

Cross-Site Scripting (XSS) is still by far the most common security issue for websites. An application is vulnerable to XSS when input data is not (or not appropriately) escaped and validated for output. Cross-Site Scripting in not limited to user input. Data from external sources or RSS feeds, for instance, can also contain unwanted HTML or scripts that are shown or executed when embedded into the website. Aside from the problematic nature of data import, the question of trustworthiness arises: By using Ad-Tags or Tracking Codes, for instance, you give third parties full access to the Document Object Model (DOM) of your page in the browser.

XSS does not differentiate between HTML and JavaScript. Most attacks use an HTML fragment to which JavaScript is attached. The purpose of the HTML fragment is to modify the original HTML in such a way that the attached JavaScript is executed by the browser. This commonly happens in such a way that the manipulation cannot be detected or is very hard to detect.

The most common varieties of XSS are called "non-persistent" and "persistent." Both require a communication with the server. The variant known as "DOM-level XSS," also called "local XSS," does not require a server and is not relevant to our discussion here.

A non-persistent XSS requires a link that is clicked by the victim to access the website to be modified by the attacker. A common misconception is that an XSS like this works only for GET requests. Any POST-based page can be manipulated using JavaScript. The commonplaceness of URL shorteners (which became popular due to Twitter and other microblogging services) plays into the hands of the attacker here: Using them, it is possible to hide the modified link as well as the intermediate page that is required to execute the JavaScript to send the POST request.

When the code that was infiltrated by the attacker is stored on the server and delivered to subsequent visitors of the website, we speak of a persistent XSS. Common targets of this type of XSS are forums and blogs with commenting functionality as well as vintage guestbooks.

The grave and often underestimated danger with XSS is that the user does not notice that data is tracked and transmitted to third parties. Another use case of XSS (from the perspective of the attacker) is the manipulation of content on the attacked website. When a news website is vulnerable to XSS, an attacker can publish faked news pieces that are allegedly reported by the news website's editorial team. If the attacker can manipulate other news websites in the same way and have the respective news pieces of different websites reference each other, he can make the faked news piece all the more believable, while at the same time making it harder for normal users to detect the manipulation.

From the perspective of PHP, XSS vulnerabilities are easy to prevent: Characters that have syntactic meaning in the context of (X)HTML need to be stripped from user-generated data before output. For HTML, these are the < and > characters that are used for tags as well as the " and ' characters that are used for attributes.

When XHTML is used, the & character needs to be taken care of, too, lest it be misinterpreted as the beginning of an entity reference. With the usage of vintage HTML, the & character triggers a warning in strict tools such as HTMLTidy, but this does not pose a security issue.

The `htmlspecialchars()` function that PHP provides for escaping replaces exactly these characters. This function accepts three arguments. The last two of these arguments are optional, but they should always be used. The second argument defines whether and how quotation marks should be escaped. It is recommended to pass `ENT_QUOTES` so both single and double quotation marks are escaped.

The third argument defines the character encoding to be used. Because the function does not perform a conversion between character encodings, the input data must already use the defined character encoding. An empty string is returned if that is not the case. It is, therefore, helpful to clean the string using `iconv()` and the `//TRANSLIT` switch before passing it to `htmlspecialchars()`.

A1: Injection

The term "injection" refers to all attacks where a value is passed unchecked to an interpreter and there, as part of the syntax, manipulates the original query. All systems that interpret queries can be attacked like this. These include the following:

➤ Execution of external processes and their arguments

➤ LDAP queries

➤ SQL queries

➤ XPath expressions

Because the consequences of an injection-based security hole depend on the attacked process or service, it is hard to estimate the possible damage. Security holes in the processing of external program execution, however, almost always lead to a complete takeover of the server or at least the user account involved. The possible damage caused by an injection-based security hole in the code responsible for authorization is obvious as well: An attacker very likely gains unauthorized access.

As with XSS, which is but a special variant of injection, the root cause of the issue is a deficiency in validation, or rather the absence of escaping appropriate for the involved interpreter. With SQL, the concept of Prepared Statements can help. These provide a templating mechanism for queries where values are assigned to placeholders through an API. But prepared statements are limited as placeholders and cannot be used for sorting or limiting the result rows. Values like these still need to be checked against a white list by the application before they are passed to the database and its SQL interpreter.

It is important to know that a generic `make_safe()` function does not and cannot exist because the individual interpreters are too different. Luckily, such a function is completely unnecessary when the application has a clean architecture.

The injection vulnerabilities that sadly can be found abundantly in real-world websites are extremely dangerous because they almost always allow the manipulation of content or even user account and server configuration. A system that has been hacked like this usually is a total loss from an economical perspective: Finding all manipulations, installed back doors, and other changes to the server requires more effort than making a fresh installation and restoring a backup.

CONCLUSION

The development of fundamentally secure applications is actually quite easy, because only a few rules need to be followed for the processing of input and output data. This can be achieved using little effort and in a generic way when you use an object-oriented architecture that cleanly separates concerns from each other. The appropriate filters can, for instance, be implemented in the logic of the view, because it is the view that knows which escaping is required for the requested output format. Likewise, the database layer is responsible for escaping the characters that are relevant to the database server that is used.

People who approach the development of software under the premise that "each access is first an attack" are safe from the mistakes and problems discussed in this chapter. Notwithstanding the above, it must be clear that security, especially with the fast-moving Internet, is not a one-time thing; it is a constant and permanent task for developers and administrators alike. The analysis of log files, the reading of security mailing lists, and the continuous installation of (security) updates for all software components used and the continuous review of security functionality and output filters are absolutely required.

What remains are conceptual security holes and novel security problems that are discovered during production. Modular architectures and paranoid system configurations allow for an effective and efficient response in a worst-case scenario.

One thing sadly is clear: When someone really wants to break into a server, he likely will be successful. It is merely a question of time, cost, and the ability of the attacker. But the more effort an attacker has to make, the more likely it is that one of the different systems involved will trigger an alarm or that the attacker will move on to the next possible victim. In both cases, the operator of a website can win.

Be that as it may, 100% security can be achieved only by turning off the server—and making sure it cannot be stolen.

17

Conclusion

In this book, we have showed you different approaches and techniques for assuring software quality. Testing plays an important part in this, although the tests themselves can neither increase the quality of the software nor prove that it is free of bugs. Tests can only prove the existence of bugs, never their absence. The vast space of possible inputs makes it impossible, even for a trivial web application, to prove that the software works correctly for all inputs.

The development and operations of web applications should be processes, not projects. In a project, you are prone to think only about the costs for the duration of the project and not about the costs for the entire lifespan of the software developed during the project. This can lead to abandoning internal quality, especially when the development of the software is outsourced to a third party. On the one hand, this is because a typical project has no financial scope to invest in internal quality up front and must amortize these costs later. On the other hand, there is no real motivation for a development agency to minimize the maintenance costs of the software because this is what they make their money from in the long run.

The value of software quality, especially the value of internal quality, is hard to express in a way that the management or the customer can understand. Only in the long run, when the maintenance costs explode and the software has become economically unreasonable to maintain, do the negative effects of low internal quality become obvious to the management or the customer.

Software usually lives longer than originally anticipated. Web applications especially have a high change frequency, which makes a high internal quality vital. Iterative development and agile methods help with producing high-quality software. It seems to play a secondary role which of the plethora of agile methods is used, as long as the developers produce software in small enough increments. Software is often developed using a bizarre mix of agile methods that must be presented to the customer as non-iterative development using the classic waterfall approach. Particularly big companies, as well as government agencies, have, in some cases, very strict and restrictive regulations as to how a software development project is to be executed. These regulations are more often than not originally intended for the development of hardware and are unsuited for the development of web applications of high quality.

Frequent changes are an integral part of software development efforts. Changing requirements make continual changes of the code necessary. The architecture of the software and the development processes should, therefore, encourage these changes and make them as easy as possible. Continuous refactoring of the software is indispensable to keep the software maintainable in the long run. Refactoring without automated unit tests is risky. Test automation is of the essence, if only to prevent regressions due to the high frequency of code changes. Readability and maintainability of the code are more important than the highest possible performance.

You should test your software as early as possible and in units as small as possible. There is a direct relationship between high internal quality and testability. Therefore, it is prudent to write the tests as close in time as possible to when the code that they exercise is written. Code that is hard to test is not good code, but testable code is good code because it has few dependencies, few execution branches, short code blocks, and clearly defined responsibilities. The fact that some tests, such as the ones for usability, are hard or impossible to automate should not discourage you from automating tests and build processes as much as possible and as early as possible. The project directly benefits from the repeatability that the automation ensures and indirectly benefits from the fact that the automation is a prerequisite for continuous integration and inspection of the code. This allows for impartial assessments of the state of the code and the project as a whole.

System tests are not always easy to implement, especially for complex software systems. Whenever possible, you should avoid writing system tests instead of writing unit tests. When writing unit tests is hard, this usually indicates too much coupling between the individual components of the software—for instance, due to the usage of a global state. This makes it needlessly hard to replace the dependencies with test doubles, thus increasing the required effort for testing. System tests should complement unit tests and test the software in its breadth and not in depth. Congruously, system tests are not a replacement for unit tests.

The individual architecture layers should be cleanly separated from each other. Insufficient separation of architecture layers—for instance, by interleaving business logic and data access (persistence logic) using an Object-Relational Mapper that is based on Active Record—leads to unit tests so complex that they should be called system tests. The interaction with the database as well as the rendering of output needs to be tested, of course. You should focus, however, on a proper separation of these concerns and first and foremost test their individual implementation in isolation. The more complex tests then play the role of integration tests that ensure that the components that have been tested in isolation by their respective unit tests also work correctly when used together. As long as the individual components interact only with each other based on clear and explicit programming interfaces (APIs), the writing of those integration tests should not be problematic.

We recommend that you practice intensive quality assurance in every project as early as possible, ideally right from the beginning. Although this seemingly slows the development (and thus increases the costs), the project will benefit from the investment in quality in the long run. The sustainable reduction of maintenance costs compensates the costs for quality assurance in most cases. The know-how that is built up with regard to quality, processes, and automation can easily be used in future projects. High-quality software, especially software with high internal quality, is an investment in the future.

BIBLIOGRAPHY

Ambler, Scott W. *Agile Modeling: Effective Practices for Extreme Programming and the Unified Process*. Wiley & Sons, 2002. ISBN 0-4712-0282-7.

Balzert, Helmut. *Lehrbuch der Softwaretechnik. Bd. 1. Software-Entwicklung*. Spektrum Akademischer Verlag, 2005. ISBN 3-8274-0480-0.

Basili, Victor R., Gianluigi Caldiera, and H. Dieter Rombach. "Goal Question Metric Paradigm." In *Encyclopedia of Software Engineering*, 2 Volume Set. John Wiley & Sons, 1994. ISBN 1-54004-8.

Beck, Kent. *Test-Driven Development: By Example*. Addison-Wesley, 2003. ISBN 0-3211-4653-0.

Bergmann, Sebastian. "Isolated (and Parallel) Test Execution in PHPUnit 4," December 19, 2007, accessed April 8, 2010, http://sebastian-bergmann.de/archives/730-Isolated-and-Parallel-Test-Execution-in-PHPUnit-4.html.

————. "PHPUnit Manual," 2010, accessed May 3, 2010, http://www.phpunit.de/manual/current/en/index.html.

————. *Professionelle Softwareentwicklung mit PHP 5: Objektorientierung, Entwurfsmuster, Modellierung und fortgeschrittene Datenbankprogrammierung*. dpunkt.verlag, 2005. ISBN 978-3-89864-229-3.

————. "Testing Your Privates," February 9, 2010, accessed April 8, 2010, http://sebastian-bergmann.de/archives/881-Testing-Your-Privates.html.

Bevan, Nigel. "Quality in use: Meeting user needs for quality," *Journal of Systems and Software*, Volume 49, Issue 1 (December 1999), Pages 89–96. ISSN 0164-1212.

Blair, Neate. "Code Rank: A New Family of Software Metrics," IEEE Software Engineering Conference, 2006. Warwick Irwin, Neville Churcher, Australia, 2006.

Boehm, Barry, Ricardo Valerdi, and Eric Honour. "The ROI of Systems Engineering: Some Quantitative Results for Software-Intensive Systems," *Systems Engineering*, Volume 11, Issue 3 (August 2008), Pages 221–234. ISSN 1098-1241.

Bruntink, Magiel and Arie van Deursen. "Predicting Class Testability using Object-Oriented Metrics," *SCAM '04: Proceedings of the Source Code Analysis and Manipulation, Fourth IEEE International Workshop*, 2004, Pages 136–145. ISBN 0-7695-2144-4.

Carr, James. "TDD Anti-Patterns," November 3, 2006, accessed February 9, 2010, http://blog .james-carr.org/2006/11/03/tdd-anti-patterns/.

Cunningham, Ward. "The WyCash Portfolio Management System," March 26, 1992, accessed April 17, 2010, http://c2.com/doc/oopsla92.html.

Dijkstra, Edsger W. "The humble programmer," *Communications of the ACM*, Volume 45, Issue 10 (October 1972), Pages 859–866. ISSN 0001-0782.

Duvall, Paul M. *Continuous Integration–Improving Software Quality and Reducing Risks.* Addison-Wesley, 2007. ISBN 978-0-321-33638-5.

Ellis, Tim. "Digg Database Architecture," September 12, 2008, accessed February 9, 2010, http://about.digg.com/blog/digg-database-architecture.

Evans, Cal. "Fluent Interfaces in PHP," December 20, 2006, accessed February 9, 2010, http://devzone.zend.com/article/1362.

Fleischer, André. "Metriken im Praktischen Einsatz," *ObjektSpektrum*, Issue 03/2007. ISSN 0945-0491.

Foegen, Malte, Mareike Solbach, and Claudia Raak. *Der Weg zur professionellen IT: Eine praktische Anleitung für das Management von Veränderungen mit CMMI, ITIL oder SPICE.* Springer, 2007. ISBN 978-3-540-72471-1.

Fowler, Martin. "Fluent Interface," December 20, 2005, accessed February 9, 2010, http:// martinfowler.com/bliki/FluentInterface.html.

———. *Patterns für Enterprise Application-Architekturen.* MITP-Verlag, 2003. ISBN 978-3-8-266-1378-4.

———. *Patterns of Enterprise Application Architecture.* Addison-Wesley, 2002. ISBN 0-3211-2742-0.

———. *Refactoring: Improving the Design of Existing Code.* Addison-Wesley, 1999. ISBN 978-0-2014-8567-7.

Franz, Klaus. *Handbuch zum Testen von Web-Applikationen.* Springer, 2007. ISBN 978-3-540-24539-1.

Freeman, Steve and Nat Pryce. *Growing Object-Oriented Software, Guided by Tests.* Addison-Wesley, 2009. ISBN 978-0-321-50362-6.

Gartner Inc. "Dynamic Programming Languages Will Be Critical to the Success of Many Next-Generation AD Efforts," 2008, accessed April 10, 2010, http://www.gartner.com/ DisplayDocument?ref=g_search&id=832417.

Goldberg, David. "What Every Computer Scientist Should Know About Floating-Point Arithmetic," *ACM Computing Surveys (CSUR)*, Volume 23, Issue 1 (March 1991), Pages 5–48. ISSN 0360-0300.

Grady, Robert and Deborah Caswell. *Software Metrics: Establishing a Company-Wide Program.* Englewood Cliffs, Prentice Hall, 1987. ISBN 978-0138218447.

Grochtdreis, Jens. "Schöner Navigationstitel," October 18, 2009, accessed February 9, 2010, `http://grochtdreis.de/weblog/2009/10/18/schoener-navigationstitel/`.

High Scalability. "Performance Anti-Pattern," April 4, 2009, accessed February 9, 2010, `http://highscalability.com/blog/2009/4/5/performance-anti-pattern.html` address.

Huggins, Jason. Twitter post, August 22, 2009, accessed April 15, 2010, `http://twitter.com/hugs/status/3462632802`.

Huggins, Jason and Jen Bevan. "Extending Selenium Into the Browser and Out to the Grid," Vortrag auf der Google Testing Automatic Conference, New York, 2007, accessed April 9, 2009, `http://www.youtube.com/watch?v=qxBatJ1N_Og`.

International Organization for Standardization. "ISO/IEC12207: 2008 Systems and Software Engineering–Software Life Cycle Processes," 2008-03-18, Geneva, Switzerland, 2008.

———. "ISO/IEC15504-5: 2006 Information Technology–Process Assessment–Part 5: An Exemplar Process Assessment Model," 2006-03-07, Geneva, Switzerland, 2006.

———. "ISO/IEC 9126-1: Software Engineering–Product Quality–Part 1: Quality Model," 2008-07-29, Geneva, Switzerland, 2008.

Janzen, David S. "Software Architecture Improvement through Test-Driven Development," *Companion to the 20th annual ACM SIGPLAN conference on Object-oriented programming, systems, languages, and applications.* Association for Computing Machinery, 2005. ISBN 1-59593-193-7.

Jeffries, Ron. "Quality vs Speed? I Don't Think So!," April 29, 2010, accessed May 1, 2010, `http://xprogramming.com/articles/quality/`.

Kerckhoffs, Auguste. "La cryptographie militaire," *Journal des sciences militaires*, Volume 9, Pages 5–38 (January 1883), Pages 161–191 (February 1883).

Khan, R. A. and K. Mustafa. "Metric Based Testability Model for Object Oriented Design (MTMOOD)," *SIGSOFT Software Engineering Notes*, Volume 34, Issue 2 (March 2009), Pages 1–6. ISSN 0163-5948.

Kniberg, Henrik. "Version Control for Multiple Agile Teams," *InfoQ*, March 31, 2008, accessed April 25, 2010, `http://www.infoq.com/articles/agile-version-control`.

Kunz, Christopher and Stefan Esser. *PHP-Sicherheit*. dpunkt.verlag, 2008. ISBN 978-3-89864-535-5.

Lanza, Michele and Radu Marinescu. *Object-Oriented Metrics in Practice: Using Software Metrics to Characterize, Evaluate, and Improve the Design of Object-Oriented Systems.* Springer, 2006. ISBN 978-3-540-24429-5.

Lennartz, Sven. "CSS-Sprites Quellensammlung," 2009, accessed February 9, 2010, `http://www.drweb.de/magazin/css-sprites-quellensammlung/`.

Lienberherr, K. J. "Formulations and Benefits of the Law of Demeter," *ACM SIGPLAN Notices*, Volume 24, Issue 3 (March 1989), Pages 67–78. ISSN 0362-1340.

Liggesmeyer, Peter. *Software-Qualität: Testen, Analysieren, und Verifizieren von Software.* Spektrum Akademischer Verlag, 2009. ISBN 978-38274-2056-5.

Maciejewski, David and Dirk Jesse. "Performance-Optimierung: Barrierefreiheit beginnt mit Ladezeiten," 2009, accessed February 9, 2010, http://www.slideshare.net/dmacx/performance-optimierung-barrierefreiheit-beginnt-mit-ladezeiten.

Marr, Stefan. "Horizontal Reuse for PHP," 2010, accessed April 18, 2010, http://wiki.php.net/rfc/horizontalreuse.

Martin, Robert C. *Agile Software Development: Principles, Patterns, and Practices.* Prentice Hall International, 2002. ISBN 978-0-135-97444-5.

——. *Clean Code: A Handbook of Agile Software Craftsmanship.* Prentice Hall International, 2008. ISBN 978-0-132-35088-4.

Martin, Rett. "How to Discuss 'the Fold' with a Client," January 8, 2010, accessed February 9, 2010, http://www.clockwork.net/blog/2010/01/08/372/how_to_discuss_the_fold_with_a_client.

McCabe, Thomas J. "A Complexity Measure," *IEEE Transactions on Software Engineering* Volume 2, No. 4. IEEE Computer Society Press, Los Alamitos, CA, USA, 1976.

Meszaros, Gerard. *xUnit Test Patterns: Refactoring Test Code.* Addison-Wesley, 2007. ISBN 978-0-131-49505-0.

Meyer, Eric S. "Unitless line-heights," February 8, 2006, accessed February 9, 2010, http://meyerweb.com/eric/thoughts/2006/02/08/unitless-line-heights/.

Nejmeh, Brian A. "NPATH: A Measure of Execution Path Complexity and its Applications," *Communications of the ACM*, Volume 31, Issue 2 (February 1988), Pages 188–200. ISSN 0001-0782.

Nohn, Sebastian. "Continuous Builds with CruiseControl, Ant, and PHPUnit," March 7, 2006, accessed April 28, 2010, http://nohn.net/blog/view/id/cruisecontrol_ant_and_phpunit.

OpenQA FAQ. "OpenQA FAQ–Selenium File Upload with Internet Explorer," http://wiki.openqa.org/display/SEL/Selenium+Core+FAQ\#SeleniumCoreFAQ-Ican\%27tseemtouseSeleniumCoretouploadafile\%3BwhenItrytotypeinthefileuploadtextfield\%2Cnothinghappens\%21.

Pahl, Dirk. "Automated acceptance tests using Selenium Grid without parallelization," August 17, 2009, accessed February 9, 2010, http://developer.studivz.net/2009/08/17/automated-acceptance-tests-using-selenium-grid-without-parallelization/.

PEAR. "PEAR Manual," PHP Group, 2009, accessed April 15, 2010, http://pear.php.net/manual/.

Potencier, Fabien. "What Is Dependency Injection?," March 26, 2009, accessed February 9, 2010, http://fabien.potencier.org/article/11/what-is-dependency-injection.

Priebsch, Stefan. *PHP migrieren: Konzepte und Lösungen zur Migration von PHP-Anwendungen und -Umgebungen.* Carl Hanser Verlag, 2008. ISBN 978-3-446-41394-8.

Schneider, Kurt. *Abenteuer Softwarequalität–Grundlagen und Verfahren für Qualitätssicherung und Qualitätsmanagement.* dpunkt.verlag, 2007. ISBN 978-3-89864-472-3.

Selenium Grid. "Selenium Grid," *OpenQA* 2008, `http://selenium-grid.seleniumhq.org/`.

Souders, Steve. "don't use @import," April 9, 2009, accessed February 9, 2010, `http://www.stevesouders.com/blog/2009/04/09/dont-use-import/`.

TIOBE Software BV. "TIOBE Programming Community Index for December 2010," 2010, accessed December, 2010, `http://www.tiobe.com/index.php/content/paperinfo/tpci/index.html`.

Whitgift, David. *Methods and Tools for Software Configuration Management.* John Wiley & Sons, 1991. ISBN 0-4719-2940-6.

Wikipedia. "Big Ball of Mud," 2010, accessed February 9, 2010, `http://en.wikipedia.org/wiki/Big_ball_of_mud`.

———. "Big Design Up Front," 2010, accessed February 9, 2010, `http://en.wikipedia.org/wiki/Big_Design_Up_Front`.

———. "Brotkrümelnavigation," 2010, accessed February 9, 2010, `http://de.wikipedia.org/wiki/Brotkrmelnavigation`.

———. "Gebrauchstauglichkeit," 2010, accessed February 9, 2010, `http://de.wikipedia.org/wiki/Gebrauchstauglichkeit`.

———. "K-factor (marketing)," 2010, accessed February 9, 2010, `http://en.wikipedia.org/wiki/K-factor_(marketing)`.

———. "Lint (Programmierwerkzeug)," 2009, accessed April 21, 2009, `http://de.wikipedia.org/wiki/Lint_(Programmierwerkzeug)`.

———. "Lock (computer science)," 2010, accessed February 9, 2010, `http://en.wikipedia.org/wiki/Lock_(computer_science)`.

———. "Model-View-Controller," 2010, accessed February 9, 2010, `http://en.wikipedia.org/wiki/Model-view-controller`.

———. "Multiton Pattern," 2010, accessed February 9, 2010, `http://en.wikipedia.org/wiki/Multiton_pattern`.

———. "Observer," 2010, accessed February 9, 2010, `http://de.wikipedia.org/wiki/Observer_(Entwurfsmuster)`.

———. "OSI Model," 2010, accessed February 9, 2010, `http://en.wikipedia.org/wiki/OSI_model`.

———. "PageRank," 2009, accessed April 18, 2009, `http://en.wikipedia.org/wiki/PageRank`.

————. "Partition (database)," 2010, accessed February 9, 2010, http://en.wikipedia.org/wiki/Partition_(database).

————. "Shard (database architecture)," 2010, accessed February 9, 2010, http://en.wikipedia.org/wiki/Sharding.

————. "Visitor," 2010, accessed February 9, 2010, http://de.wikipedia.org/wiki/Visitor.

————. "Zuständigkeitskette," 2010, accessed February 9, 2010, http://de.wikipedia.org/wiki/Chain_of_Responsibility.

Wirth, Timo. "Nutzerbeteiligung & Kommunikation: Mitmachbarrieren im Web 2.0," 2009, accessed February 9, 2010, http://www.slideshare.net/aperto/mitmachbarrieren-im-web-20.

Yourdon, Edward and Larry Constantine. *Structured Design: Fundamentals of a Discipline of Computer Program and Systems Design.* Prentice Hall, 1979. ISBN 978-0138544713.

INDEX